100448

History of the great mountaineering adventures

THE
MOUNTAINEERS

History of the great mountaineering adventures

Text
Stefano Ardito

Editorial coordination
Laura Accomazzo
Livio Bourbon

Graphic design
Patrizia Balocco Lovisetti

Translation
A.B.A., Milan

© 2000 White Star S.r.l.
Via Candido Sassone, 24
Vercelli, Italy.

 Published in North America by
The Mountaineers Books
1001 SW Klickitat Way, Suite 201
Seattle, WA 98134

Library of Congress Cataloging-in-Publication Data
A catalog record for this book is available at the
Library of Congress

ISBN 0-89886-722-3 (North America)
1 2 3 4 5 6 05 04 03 02 01 00

Printed in Italy by
Editoriale Johnson Spa

1 Mountaineering in the
Alps and the other
European ranges resembles
climbing in the high
mountains of the Himalaya
because it involves scaling
steep, snow-covered slopes.
In this photo, a climber is
tackling the North Face of
Grande Casse (3852 metres),
the highest peak in the
Vanoise massif.

Contents

2-3 Makalu (8463 metres), first climbed by a French expedition in 1955, is the fifth-highest mountain in the world. Its name, which means "the Great Black One" in Nepali, is inspired by the dark rock of the summit pyramid.

4-5 Although it has now been climbed by over a thousand people, the 8848-metre summit of Mount Everest still remains one of the most coveted destinations of mountaineers from all over the world. In this photo, sherpas Lhakpa Tsering and Pemba Dorje celebrate the successful ascent by the 1992 Canadian expedition.

6-7 Dougal Haston (1940-1977) was one of the greatest Himalayan climbers of all time. This photo shows him on the Hillary Step on Mount Everest at the end of the ascent of the South-West Face.

7 Italian Emilio Comici (1901) was one of the greatest climbers between the wars. This photo shows him tackling an overhang in Val Rosandra, near Trieste.

Introduction

"*Because it's there.*" These were simple words used by George Leigh Mallory to explain why men climb mountains, spoken before he set off for Everest, never to return. Since time immemorial, as well as exploring oceans and deserts, great rivers and the abysses of the sea, mankind has endeavoured to conquer the highest, most beautiful and most prominent peaks.

George Mallory, who began his journey to Tibet over three-quarters of a century ago, belonged to the first generation of climbers who had a real chance of setting foot on the highest summit on earth.

Other brave men long before him had travelled to different destinations. From 1775 onwards the men of Chamonix and Saint-Gervais tackled the glaciers of Mont Blanc in an attempt to scale the highest peak in the Alps.

Ninety years after them, on the summit of "the noblest crag in Europe," Englishman Edward Whymper won the race to make the first ascent of the Matterhorn. His adversaries in that contest, apart from the difficulties posed by the mountain itself, were fellow countrymen who were just as skilled but perhaps less determined than he was, and a team of guides from Valtournenche, led by Jean-Antoine Carrel. During the descent, just a few hours after their triumphant arrival on the summit, the death of four of the seven men in the party turned the victory into tragedy.

According to the "official" histories, mountaineering began at dusk on 8th July 1786, when Michel-Gabriel Paccard and Jacques Balmat, both from Chamonix and therefore subjects of the King of Sardinia, reached the 4807-metre summit of Mont Blanc.

This was not only a geographical conquest but a cultural victory. For centuries, throughout the Alps, the great icy peaks had until then been viewed as enemies of man, and high valleys which gave no access to mountain passes were ignored by travellers.

During the Age of Enlightenment, the glaciers of Mont Blanc (and the Bernese Oberland, Monte Rose, Ortler, and so on) began to attract the curious and the cultured. Not long after Balmat and Paccard's adventure, great names in European culture like Lord Byron, Chateaubriand and Goethe began to visit Mont Blanc.

A year after the ascent by the two Chamonix men, their pygmalion Horace-Bénédict de Saussure also reached the snow-capped summit.

After Napoleon's defeat at Waterloo, numerous English travellers once more embarked on the Grand Tour, and Chamonix and Mont Blanc were often included in their itineraries.

8-9 *The Barre des Ecrins, climbed for the first time in 1864 by a party consisting of British climbers Edward Whymper, Adolphus W. Moore and Horace Walker, Swiss guide Christian Almer and Chamonix guide Michel Croz, is the highest peak in the Oisans massif in the French Alps. The ordinary route, which is demanding but not especially difficult, is very popular nowadays.*

9 top *Although they were crossed by Jean-Nicolas Couteran, François Paccard, Michel-Gabriel Paccard and Victor Tissai "le Chamois" as early as 1775, the crevasses of the Jonction still offer a serious obstacle to teams climbing Mont Blanc by the ordinary route. This 1852 lithograph by British artist T.D.H. Browne shows a team crossing a great crevasse.*

9 centre *The Matterhorn, one of the best-known symbols in mountaineering, reaches an altitude of 4474 metres. The Liongrat, the present-day ordinary route from the Italian side, which was first climbed by Jean-Antoine Carrel and Jean-Baptiste Bich in 1865, can be seen on the left of this photo. On the right is the South Face, conquered in 1931, and the last part of the Furggen ridge, climbed in 1911 by Mario Piacenza with guides J. Gaspard and J. Carrel.*

9 bottom *The Monte Rosa range is the most suitable massif in the Eastern Alps for those wishing to climb a 4000-metre peak without particular difficulty. This 1893 picture shows Margherita of Savoy, Queen of Italy, crossing Col de Lys during the ascent to the refuge hut named after her, which had just been inaugurated on the 4554-metre Punta Gnifetti (on the right in the photo).*

10 top The ordinary route to the summit of Broad Peak, first climbed in 1957 by Austrians Kurt Diemberger, Fritz Wintersteller, Marcus Schmuck and Hermann Buhl, presents no particular difficulties, and is now repeated quite frequently.

10-11 All the ascent routes of the "eight-thousanders" in the Himalaya offer some magnificent scenery. This photo shows the first camp of a French expedition climbing the ordinary route on Annapurna.

In a book published to commemorate the 200th anniversary of the first ascent, historian Pierre Joutard rightly spoke of the "invention" rather than the "conquest" of Mont Blanc. It was Leslie Stephen, in the mid-19th century, who described the Alps as "the playground of Europe," a definition that still holds good today.

Of course, man's relationship with mountains goes back for longer than 200 years. In his *Life of Hadrian*, Spartian recounts the ascent by the Emperor Hadrian to the 3323-metre summit of Etna in about 126 A.D. When describing the mountain, Spartian seems to suggest that the route to the crater was frequently climbed by the curious as early as 19 centuries ago.

The ancients were by no means unfamiliar with the mountains, as demonstrated by the discovery in summer 1991 of the mummified body of Otzi, a Bronze Age traveller who died while crossing an Alpine pass at an altitude of over 3000 metres. Dressed in hides, wearing shoes stuffed with dried grass and armed with a bow, 14 arrows, a flint dagger and a copper axe, Otzi carried a bark rucksack containing ibex meat, a handful of coal and a stone amulet.

We do not know whether he was an outlaw or a trader, a stock breeder or a witch doctor; still less do we know the final destination of his journey. However, the discovery of his body demonstrates that man had settled permanently in the Alpine valleys by the end of the Ice Age. In addition to Otzi and the few remains of villages identified by archaeologists, human presence in the mountains is demonstrated by graffiti on the rocks of Val Camonica, Monte Bego and other "open-air museums" in the Alpine chain.

In both classical and Biblical culture, the mountains simply did not exist as a physical location. High peaks like Olympus, Parnassus, Ararat and Sinai were considered the residence of the gods. They were believe to constitute the meeting point between heaven and earth, a similar role to that now played by Mount Kailas for Buddhists and Hindus, Mount Demavend for Zoroastrians and Mount Fuji for Japanese Shintoists.

Later, from the Meteore to Mount Athos, from Ethiopia to Mount Maiella, crags and ravines provided a refuge for monks and hermits wishing to escape the temptations of the world. Saint Francis of Assisi chose the woods and rocks of Alpe della Luna and Subasio for his prayers and his encounters with "Brother Wind" and "Sister Water." In 1294, hermit Pietro da Morrone came down from the rocks of Abruzzo to become Pope with the name of Celestine V, and challenge the Church's immorality and appetite for power.

These stories, however, have little to do with climbing and the reasons for it. The first known ascent for contemplative purposes was that of Mont Ventoux in Provence, made by Francesco Petrarch in 1336. On the summit, the poet was "ecstatic" at the sight of a view that included "the snow-covered ridge of the Alps," and "the sea of Marseilles and Aigues-Mortes many days' walk away."

11 bottom This famous photo, taken by Doug Scott in 1975, shows Dougal Haston about to reach the summit of Everest after scaling the South-West Face. The route put up by the British expedition led by Chris Bonington remains one of the most demanding in the Himalaya. The tripod on the top persuaded sceptical Western climbers that the Chinese expeditions of 1960 and 1975 had reached the summit too.

by an attempted ascent, which terminated at an altitude of 4750 metres. Violent eruptions of Vesuvius, the volcano near Naples, in 1760 and 1794, attracted famous visitors from all over Europe. In 1841, the first volcano observatory in the world was built at the foot of Vesuvius by order of Ferdinando II of Bourbon. In 1770, ten years after Horace-Bénédict de Saussure's first visit to Chamonix, two more Geneva men, brothers Jean-André and Guillaume-Antoine Deluc, climbed the 3094-metre Buet, the magnificent viewpoint over Mont Blanc that separates the Chamonix and Giffre valleys. Another Swiss gentleman, Placidus à Spescha,

12 left The ice-axe traction technique is not used just on ephemeral icefalls, as demonstrated by this photo, taken during a winter ascent of the North Face of the Aiguille du Midi in the heart of the Mont Blanc massif.

A far more difficult ascent was made over a century and a half later by Antoine de Ville and his companions, who climbed Mont Aiguille, the most awesome peak in the Vercors range in the French Pre-Alps. The party fixed ropes and ladders in cracks in the mountain in order to reach the summit. The ascent was performed in 1492, a year which was to become famous for the ocean crossing made by Christopher Columbus. The order to climb the mountain was issued by King Charles VIII in person, for unknown reasons. Reinhold Messner, who 500 years later repeated the route inaugurated by Antoine de Ville, hailed the protagonist of that feat as "the man who opened the door to the vertical world for the human race."

In the 16th century, the relationship between cultured Europeans and the mountains became less sporadic. Leonardo da Vinci visited the Grigne, and in 1511 climbed the "Monboso," now called Cima di Bo, near Monte Rosa. In 1520, *conquistador* Hernàn Cortèz sent a patrol led by Diego de Ordaz to climb the 5452-metre Popocatèpetl in Mexico.

Between 1518 and 1555, Vadianus (Joachim de Watt), Johann Rhellicanus (Johann Muller) and Conrad Gesner from Switzerland climbed the Gnepfstein, the Stockhorn and the Niesen. "I declare that anyone who fails to judge the high mountains more than worthy of long contemplation is an enemy of nature..." wrote Gesner in 1541. In 1574, his fellow-countryman Josias Simler listed all the passes and populations of the Alps with typical Swiss precision in *De Alpibus Commentarius*.

The mountains of southern Europe also witnessed some interesting episodes in the 16th century. Before 1555, Mr. de Candale attempted the Pic du Midi d'Ossau, one of the loveliest peaks in the Pyrenees. Eighteen years later, Francesco de Marchi climbed the 2912-metre Corno Grande, the highest peak in the Gran Sasso range.

However, it was the 18th century that really paved the way for mountaineering as we know it today. In 1726, Venetian botanists Pietro Stefanelli and Giovanni Zanichelli climbed Cimon del Cavallo in the Oltre Piave Dolomites, which thus became the first peak in the "Pale Mountains" to be climbed by man.

In 1744, an expedition organised by the French Academy of Science and led by Charles-Marie de la Condamine measured the height of Chimborazo in the Ecuadorean Andes as 6310 metres, making it the highest mountain then known in the world. This was followed

left Disentis Abbey in 1788 to climb the Stochkhorn, the Oberalp and the Urlaun. In 1779, accompanied by hunters Genoud and Moret, Canon Laurent-Joseph Murit of Grand Saint Bernard climbed Mont Vélan (3734 metres).

The best-known symbol of scientific mountaineering in those years was represented by the expeditions of Alexander von Humboldt, the German naturalist who interrupted a crossing to the Americas to climb Pico de Teide (3718 metres), the highest point in the Canaries. Three years later, after exploring the Llanos of Venezuela and the Orinoco basin, von Humboldt made a new attempted ascent of Chimborazo with Frenchman Aimé Bonpland and Carlos Montùfar from Ecuador. The three climbers, who were subject to violent attacks of nausea and in poor condition because of their "bleeding lips and gums" and sun-scorched skin, were eventually defeated by "a cleft over 400 feet deep and 60 feet wide," flanked "on the left by a snow-covered precipice and on the right by a horrifying abyss." Although they failed to summit, the party had reached a height of 5875 metres.

Sixteen years before von Humboldt's last ascent in the Andes, back in the heart of the Old World, two more brave men had reached the summit of Mont Blanc. Jacques Balmat and Michel-Gabriel Paccard, both born in Chamonix, reached the highest point in Europe at 6:23 p.m. on 8th August 1786. That was the day when mountaineering history began.

12 above The southern exposure of the South Faces of the Aiguille du Midi and the outriders of Mont Blanc du Tacul means that they can be climbed by mountaineers wearing the same sort of clothing as they would use for cragging. They leave their rucksacks, climbing boots, crampons and ice-axe at the bottom of the wall ready for use after abseiling down.

12-13 Thanks to their training on the crags in the valley bottom, their smooth-soled climbing shoes and the nuts, friends and bolts they use to belay themselves, present-day climbers can now scale very tough pitches even at high altitude. The crack shown in this photo, which cuts through a tower near the Aiguille du Midi (Mont Blanc), is rated 8a on the French scale; according to the Welzenbach scale this pitch is between the 9th and 10th grades.

13 below Ice climbing was revolutionised in the Seventies by the introduction of the ice-axe traction technique, which uses ice axes and crampons for frontal progression. In this photo, French climber Catherine Destivelle is tackling an icefall near Col des Grands Montets (Mont Blanc).

14-15 On the great ridges of Mont Blanc, climbing has not changed in a century. In this photo, a team is about to reach the 4465-metre summit of Mont Maudit. The Aiguilles du Diable, Mont Dolent and the Aiguille de Leschaux can be seen on the left of the peak, and the Grandes Jorasses on the right.

The invention of Mont Blanc

8th August 1786 was an epoch-making date in the history of human adventure. It was just after 6 p.m. when the German Baron Adolf von Gersdorf in Chamonix raised his binoculars towards the summit of Mont Blanc. The icefields on the massif had already taken on the warm shades of evening, and farther down, the shadows were lengthening on the pastures, forests and villages of the valley.

Suddenly, two tiny dots appeared before the Baron's eyes on the snow slopes leading to the highest summit in Europe. They were two men born at the foot of the mountain, situated in the Arve Valley, which was to be part of the Kingdom of Sardinia for another 73 years. Jacques Balmat, 24, made his living by farming and

prevent Paccard and Balmat from planting a stick with a red cloth attached to it on the summit. Adolf von Gersdorf and the other observers in the valley bottom watched as that modest but proud sign of victory appeared.

At 6:47 p.m. the two climbers left the "roof of Europe." They covered the wide slopes between the summit and Mur de la Côte with a rapid slide controlled with the iron tip of the alpenstocks they both carried. Then they turned off to the left, retracing the steps of their ascent, and continued cautiously down the steep ice slope now known as the Ancien Passage, a pitch that no one would dream of tackling nowadays without ice-axe and crampons.

16 top Of the many viewpoints for Mont Blanc, the most popular are those on the slopes of the Aiguilles Rouges, from which the whole range can be seen. All the peaks in the range appear in this 1860 painting, from the Aiguille du Tour to the Aiguille du Goûter. Mont Blanc naturally dominates the scene in the centre.

16 bottom The cave where the waters of the River Arveyron gush out from the bowels of the Mer de Glace, which can be reached by a more convenient trail from Chamonix than the one that climbs to Montenvers, has inspired generations of travellers and artists.

prospecting for crystals on the slopes of the massif, and Michel-Gabriel Paccard, 29, was a doctor.

When the Baron sighted them, the pair were making slow progress just a short distance from the Rochers Rouges, boulders which protrude from the steep snow-covered slope at an altitude of around 4500 metres. At 6:12 p.m., von Gersdorf noted, the pair left behind the Petits Mulets, the last outcrop of granite rock before the rounded snowcap.

Eleven minutes later, the men were finally at an altitude of 4807 metres, standing on the summit of Mont Blanc, which is also the highest point in Europe. According to the Baron's diary, Jacques Balmat and Michel-Gabriel Paccard covered the last few metres on two slightly different routes, charging forward as if racing one another.

The late hour and the bitterly cold north wind left the first two real mountaineers in history little time to enjoy the limitless view that stretched before their eyes, but they would have plenty of time to enjoy the satisfaction of being the first to conquer the peak when they were back in the safety of the valley.

On the summit of Mont Blanc, the thermometer read 7.5°C below zero, and the barometer indicated an altitude of just over 5000 metres. The sky was clear and the snow was wind-hardened, but not so hard as to

At the end of the steepest section they reached the Grand Plateau, an icy hollow at the foot of the summit pyramid. They had to descend another 1600 metres to reach the moraines of Montagne de la Côte. There was no time to lose. The doctor and the guide ran down the treacherous ice slopes threatened by the seracs of Dôme du Goûter, and left the granite towers of the Grands Mulets to their right. In the last glimmerings of twilight they crossed the chaos of crevasses and seracs at the Jonction, where the Bossons and Taconnaz glaciers separate before

17 top The Talèfre Glacier (on the left), the Leschaux Glacier and Vallée Blanche all flow into the Mer de Glace, forming one of the most Himalayan landscapes in Europe. The Grandes Jorasses (left), the Dent du Géant and Mont Blanc stand out in the background.

16-17 In winter, when it is encrusted with ice, the range that comprises the Dru (left), the Aiguille Verte and the Aiguilles Droites is one of the most spectacular in the Mont Blanc massif. Points Croz, Whymper and Walker in the Grandes Jorasses glisten in the sunset in the foreground.

17 bottom A closer view of Point Walker (4206 metres), the highest peak in the Grandes Jorasses, clearly shows the exposed snow ridge that connects Point Whymper to the icy terrace of the summit. On the left, in the shadow, is the end of the Walker Spur on the North face.

plunging down to the Arve Valley.

It was nearly midnight when the two Chamonix men finally left the glacier and reached the rocky ridge where they had made their rudimentary bivouac the night before. They were both showing symptoms of frostbite on the hands, and Paccard suffered from slight snow-blindness, but despite these problems, it only took them four hours to return to Chamonix the next day, 9th August.

Michel-Gabriel Paccard's attempts on the summit of Mont Blanc had begun on 2nd September 1775, when he climbed to Montagne de la Côte and the Taconnaz Glacier with Scottish botanist Thomas Blaikie. They had climbed fast, and with a definite instinct for the mountain, but the attempt concluded at the foot of the steep slopes of the Dôme and Aiguille du Goûter.

Jacques Balmat had only recently become involved in attempts to climb the highest mountain in Europe. However, it was he who had discovered the key route from the Grand Plateau to the easy ridge leading to the summit. Two months before the victorious first ascent, during a solo attempt, he had been overtaken by darkness and forced to bivouac at an altitude of nearly 4000 metres in a hole dug in the snow with his alpenstock, with only his knapsack to cover him. Though dramatic, this experience helped him to overcome the ancestral fear of spending a night on the ice which had so far inhibited attempts by the mountain men of Saint-Gervais and Chamonix.

However, if we look even further back in history, the process that was to lead Paccard and Balmat to the 4807-metre summit of Mont Blanc began 16 years before Paccard's birth, and 22 years before Balmat's. It all started on the afternoon of 21st June 1741, when an odd party arrived in the Chamonix valley.

The expedition, organised by William Windham and Richard Pococke, two young English gentlemen who lived in Geneva, included six more British climbers and five servants. After a three-day journey with stops at Bonneville and Servoz, the group left Sallanches and Passy behind them, tackled the steep slopes of the Montées Pélissier, and arrived at the Chamonix valley, nestling at the foot of the spectacular glaciers that run down from Mont Blanc.

The Englishmen and their servants were so afraid of being attacked that they were wary, self-sufficient and armed to the teeth. However, the parish priest's

invitation to supper fortunately convinced the travellers that the people of Le Prieuré and the neighbouring villages were extremely hospitable to strangers.

Although this episode took place in the heart of Europe, nearly halfway through the Age of Enlightenment, the journey "into the wild regions of Chamonix," which bore more resemblance to a full-scale expedition into darkest Africa than to the normal travels of a party on the Grand Tour, clearly demonstrates that the awe-inspiring glaciers were still a mystery to cultured European travellers. Various writers of the period had described the spectacle seen from the ice peaks of the Oberland, which can conveniently be admired from Berne. Similar descriptions of Monte Rosa, which dominates the rivers, towns and paddy-fields of Italy's Po Valley on clear days, had been given at the time of Leonardo da Vinci.

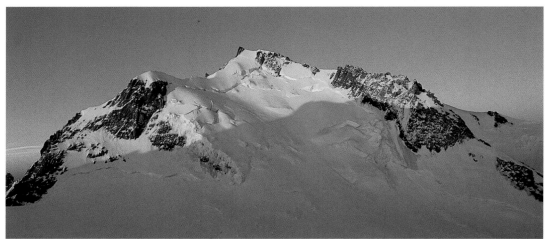

18-19 Anyone observing Mont Blanc from Chamonix can see much of the route followed by Paccard and Balmat in 1786. This photo shows the seracs of the Jonction (bottom), the steep ice slopes between the Grands Mulets and the Dôme du Goûter, and the last slope (on the left, against the sky) scaled by the two men before reaching the summit.

18 bottom Mont Maudit (4465 metres) is one of the highest and most spectacular peaks in the Mont Blanc range. This photo shows it from Mont Blanc du Tacul, illuminated by the first light of dawn. The highest peak can be glimpsed on the left.

Yet Mont Blanc had remained a mystery. Hard to see from Valle d'Aosta (it only appears to visitors halfway between Aosta and Courmayeur), the massif, with its great peaks and glaciers, towers over the lower mountains and green hills of Savoy. On clear days it can easily be seen from Geneva or Lyons.

"The *Glaciale Maudite*, the highest mountain in the country, is so awesome that it can be seen when leaving Lyons by S. Sebastian's Gate, despite the fact that it lies 40 leagues from the city," wrote Pierre d'Avity of Lyons in 1626. However, so far as the greater part of European culture was concerned, Mont Blanc simply didn't exist.

The English expedition of 1741, with its paradoxical and picturesque aspects, was not just a geographical exploration. As Philippe Joutard has written, it was a real "invention": the discovery by the élite of Europe of a landscape of exceptional beauty,

worthy of a visit for study or leisure purposes alike.

William Windham and his friends were the first to approach the mysterious glaciers. They asked the people of the Chamonix valley for information, and were directed towards the nearby Bossons glacier, which at that time ran down to a point not far from the houses and fields. However, the locals advised the strangers not to follow the steep path that led to the Mer de Glace, the most spectacular glacier of all.

But Pococke, Windham and his companions were not to be discouraged. The day after their arrival in the valley, they climbed for four hours through the woods towards Montenvers, an amazing viewpoint over the most spectacular glacier in the Alpine arc. Then, after a rest to get their breath back, the party finally walked onto the glacier.

"I'd never seen anything like it before," said Windham on his return to Geneva. "The best comparison is with travellers' descriptions of Greenland. You would have to image Lake Geneva stirred by a strong wind and suddenly frozen. And even that image may not suffice."

In fact, as later archive research was to show, Windham and his companions were not the first strangers to visit Chamonix. In our view, his dramatic tone was somewhat exaggerated to add excitement to the tale. But it was his account (which was never published in book form but circulated in manuscript form, in a few dozen copies) which aroused interest all over Europe.

In the years that followed, visitors to Chamonix were still few and far between. They included Pierre Martel, a botanist and geographer who visited the valley in 1742 with a party from Geneva and described the peaks surrounding the Mer de Glace for the first time. In addition to Mont Blanc, his report mentions the Dent du Géant (which Martel called *Mont Mallay*) and the rocky obelisk of the Dru.

19 top right William Windham, who was 22 or 23 at the time of his journey to Chamonix and Montenvers, was a typical young Englishman of the age of the Grand Tour. He became interested in the glaciers of Mont Blanc after reading books about the Alps by Swiss naturalist Jakob Scheuchzer.

19 bottom left Unlike Windham, Dr. Richard Pococke was a highly experienced traveller. He arrived in Geneva after a four-year journey through the Middle East. In this

portrait, painted before the celebrated journey from Geneva to the foot of Mont Blanc, he is dressed Turkish-style.

19 bottom right Horace-Bénédict de Saussure was fascinated by the ice cave from which the Arveyron gushes forth. "Imagine a deep cave, the entrance of which is a vault of ice over 1000 feet high… a river white with foam rushes impetuously out from the bottom of the great cavern… looking up, an immense glacier can be seen," wrote the scientist from Geneva.

The man who was to pave the way for the conquest of Mont Blanc arrived in Chamonix in 1760. Horace-Bénédict de Saussure, born just outside Geneva, was to become Professor of Natural Philosophy at the city's Academy a few years later, and married heiress Amelia Boissier, the best catch in Geneva at the time. But de Saussure was just as much in love with the Alps as he was with Amelia. Between 1760 and 1790 he performed "14 crossings of the Alps by eight different passes, and over 13 great expeditions," which he recounted in detail in *Voyages dans les Alpes*, published in 1804.

As soon as he arrived in Chamonix, de Saussure was awestruck by the sight of Mont Blanc. Accompanied by guide Pierre Simond, he climbed a steep footpath to the 2525-metre summit of Mont Brévent, still famous as one of the best viewpoints over the massif. "The majestic glaciers, separated by great forests and crowned by granite rocks which rise to incredible heights, offer one of the most magnificent and impressive sights imaginable," wrote de Saussure.

Then he did something that was to revolutionise life in Chamonix. In a proclamation posted in the parishes of Les Houches, Le Prieuré and Argentière, he offered a "very considerable" reward for the discovery of an access route to the summit of Mont Blanc. However, the people of Chamonix did not seem anxious to take him up on his offer.

In 1762 Pierre Simond, de Saussure's first guide, performed a reconnaissance trip along the Mer de Glace, known to the people of Chamonix because it led to the Talèfre glacier where crystals were plentiful. However, he soon discovered that the longest glacier on the massif did not lead to its highest peak.

A few weeks later, Simond identified the correct route. He climbed the ridge of Montagne de la Côte by an interminable zigzag trail, reached the ice plateau of the Jonction, and ventured onto its treacherous surface. However, it was to be the next generation of climbers who made real progress towards the summit. Simond continued to work for Horace-Bénédict de Saussure, guiding him on the first circuit of Mont Blanc and to the

20 top Engraver Jean-Antoine Linck from Geneva (1770-1843) depicted the details of the landscape of Mont Blanc with considerable realism in the early 19th century. Here, the Dent du Géant, the Aiguilles de Chamonix and the glaciers of Mont Blanc are seen from the Chapeau cave, on the orographic right of the Mer de Glace.

panoramic peaks of Crammont and Buet.

The first real attempt at an ascent was made in the summer of 1775. It was performed by Jean-Nicolas Couteran; Victor Tissay, nicknamed *le Chamois*, and the brothers François and Michel Paccard. The four climbed to Montagne de la Côte by night, set out onto "the ice plain at the foot of Mont Blanc which feeds the glaciers of Taconnaz and the Bossons" at the first light of dawn, then continued along "a very steep snow-covered slope surmounted by ice walls of a prodigious height."

On the edge of the Grand Plateau, at an altitude of nearly 4000 metres, the party was forced to turn back. However, they soon discovered that the snow,

warmed by the sun, made the descent far more dangerous than the ascent. Only an alpenstock which became wedged on the edges of a crevasse saved Couteran from certain death when a snow bridge collapsed beneath him. The following September Michel-Gabriel Paccard, then a medical student at Turin University, made his first attempted ascent. After that, the glaciers were left in peace for 8 years.

Attempts on the summit recommenced in 1783, when Joseph Carrier, known as *Bouquet*, Jean-Marie Couttet, and Jean-Baptiste Lombard, known as *Jorasse*, returned to the Grand Plateau and continued towards Col du Dôme, the large snow-covered saddle that separates Mont Blanc from Dôme du Gôuter. The next

20 bottom Now easily reached by cable car, the Aiguille du Midi is one of the best view-points on Mont Blanc. In this photo, the highest peak and Mont Maudit appear behind the icy slopes of Mont Blanc du Tacul. On the right, half-hidden by cloud, are the Bosses ridge and the Aiguille du Goûter.

20-21 Nowadays, the ordinary routes on Mont Blanc are indicated for much of the summer by deep tracks, along which viewers can observe climbers with binoculars or a telephoto lens without leaving the valley bottom. Here, the shoulder of Mont Blanc du Tacul, on the route from Col du Midi to Mont Blanc, is seen from the terraces of the Aiguille du Midi.

21 below Mont Maudit is not steep on the icy north side, but slopes sheer down to the Brenva with a severe wall of mixed terrain, climbed in 1929 by Lino Binel, Renato Chabod and Amilcare Crétier.

year, Michel-Gabriel Paccard explored for the first time what was to become the ordinary ascent route from Saint-Gervais, climbing rocks and snowfields as far as the Tête Rousse terrace, at the foot of the steep wall of Aiguille du Goûter.

This route appeared very promising to the climbers of the day, who were not equipped with ropes, ice-axes or crampons, as it allowed them to climb much higher without having to venture onto the glaciers. It was at about this time that rivalry began between the men of Chamonix and those of the Montjoie Valley, both seeking a route to the summit which began in their valley.

21 left The experienced, sure-footed crystal prospectors and chamois deer hunters of Mont Blanc began to accompany visitors up the mountain in the 18th century. The fact that the massif belonged to the Kingdom of Sardinia meant that the other famous Alpine activity (smuggling) was unknown in Chamonix and Courmayeur.

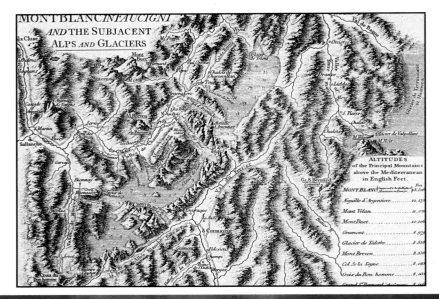

22 top A look at a 1789 map shows that by the outbreak of the French Revolution, topographers were able to represent the course of the Dora Baltea and the Arve rivers correctly. However, the heart of the Mont Blanc massif was still unexplored.

22-23 For those observing Mont Blanc from the Arve Valley, the Aiguilles de Chamonix seem to present an insuperable barrier. The Dent du Caiman and the Dent du Crocodile appear at the top of this winter view. The Aiguille des Pèlerins, the Aiguille du Peigne and their numerous grim outriders can be seen in the foreground.

In September 1784, artist and author Marc-Théodore Bourrit from Geneva organised a new attempt along the Saint-Gervais route. Accompanied by four guides, de Saussure's rival climbed from the village of Bionnassay to Tête Rousse. Jean-Marie Couttet and François Cuidet continued as far as the Aiguille du Goûter, where one of the busiest refuge huts on the massif now stands. A wide glacial ridge took them without difficulty to Col du Dôme, the highest point reached in attempts from the Chamonix side, and the rocks where the Vallot Hut was to be built a century later.

In 1785, Jean-Marie Couttet returned to the Aiguille du Goûter. Then, a party including de Saussure and Bourrit was forced to turn back by fresh snow that had accumulated on the rocks of the Aiguille du Goûter.

The safest route to the summit of Mont Blanc was eventually found by climbers from Chamonix in June 1786. François Paccard and Joseph Carrier, who climbed by way of the Jonction and the Grand Plateau, reached the 4360-metre Col du Dôme long before Jean-Marie Couttet and Pierre Balmat, who climbed the Aiguille du Goûter. From the pass, the four guides embarked on the steep, snow-covered Bosses ridge, where no one had ever set foot before. This route presents no problem for present-day climbers equipped with ice-axes and crampons, but proved impossible for those sturdy mountain men, equipped only with hobnailed boots and alpenstocks. The four men continued climbing on foot for a while, then sitting astride the icy ridge. Eventually, they were forced to turn back. But by this time there was no doubt in their minds; the route to the summit led from the steep icy slopes above the Grand Plateau.

The last piece of the puzzle was identified by Jacques Balmat, who had followed Joseph Carrier and François Paccard as far as the bivouac on Montagne de la Côte. When the four guides returned to Chamonix, Balmat climbed beyond the highest point they had reached on the Bosses ridge. Then he too gave up, and returned to the Grand Plateau, where a look above him

23 top Marc-Théodore Bourrit from Geneva (1739-1819) was the real loser in the race to conquer Mont Blanc. A musician and enthusiastic walker, he never came really close to the highest summit in Europe.

23 below Now reached by cable car, the Aiguille du Midi (shown here in midwinter), was the second peak in the Mont Blanc massif to be climbed by man. The lower North Peak was first climbed in 1818, and the higher South Peak was scaled in 1856 by three guides from Chamonix.

convinced him that a practicable ascent route existed.

Despite the late hour, Balmat left the trail that would have taken him back to Chamonix and began to climb one of the steep slopes of the glacier that appeared to connect the Grand Plateau with the Rochers Rouges. Before dusk, the ambitious crystal prospector had reached the end of the steepest section. In front of him, the mountains of Valle d'Aosta appeared beyond the icy precipices of the Brenva. It was getting late, and it looked as though the weather was about to break, so he was forced to turn back, but the 24-year-old Chamonix man knew that he had found the route to the summit. The icy bivouac he was forced to make on the way down did nothing to dampen his enthusiasm for another attempt.

23 right There was still a long time to go before the invention of the fisheye lens. However, this original engraving by Marc-Théodore Bourrit condenses the extraordinary view of Mont Blanc enjoyed from the 3099-metre summit of Mont Buet (also known as Mont Blanc des Dames), which lies beyond the Aiguilles Rouges. The highest peak in Europe is at the top right.

Balmat was unpopular with the other valley guides, but found an enthusiastic companion in Michel-Gabriel Paccard, who was back in Chamonix and still bewitched by Mont Blanc. However, their partnership was a marriage of convenience. Each young man knew that the other was his most dangerous rival in the race to the summit, and they preferred to join forces rather than tackle the venture as adversaries.

The pair set off from the Arve Valley on 7th August, following the long trail that leads to Montagne de la Côte, carrying a blanket, a thermometer, a barometer and their alpenstocks. At 4 a.m., when the first glimmerings of daylight began to appear behind Mont Blanc du Tacul, the pair picked their way between the crevasses of the Jonction, and reached the Grand Plateau.

Paccard was full of enthusiasm, but Balmat seemed to be flagging; he knew that his son was ill, and in fact, by the time Balmat returned, he had died. Nevertheless, he kept climbing. When they reached the Rochers Rouges, a gust of wind tore off Paccard's hat, and it disappeared in the direction of Courmayeur. It was just after that incident that Baron von Gersdorf spotted the pair through his binoculars on the slope leading to the summit. Less than half an hour later, they were on the summit.

Jacques Balmat and Michel-Gabriel Paccard were by no means the first men in history to climb mountains. Four-and-a-half centuries earlier, Francesco Petrarca (Petrarch) had described his excitement on reaching the summit of Mont Ventoux. Then Antoine de Ville and his companions had scaled the vertical walls of Mont Aiguille, Francesco de Marchi had climbed the crumbling rocks of the Gran Sasso, and other brave men had tackled the peaks of the Pyrenees and the Mexican volcanoes.

But there is no doubt that the birth of mountaineering really dates from the conquest of Mont Blanc. Apart from the fact that they had reached the highest point on the continent (a great feat in itself), the two young men from Chamonix had solved the environmental and technical problems posed by the great mountains of the Alps. The first ascent of Mont Blanc was not only a geographical conquest (as the ascents of Kilimanjaro, Everest, Mount McKinley and Mount Vinson were also to be), but also demonstrated that men could climb the snow slopes, avoid the crevasses and menacing seracs, and actually enjoy themselves in the process.

But when the pair returned from the summit, the celebration that should have united them was marred by lies and envy. Marc-Théodore Bourrit, the lover of Mont Blanc who never was to reach the summit, stirred up trouble by giving Balmat all the credit for the ascent.

His envy caused him to attack Paccard. On 22nd September the *Journal Historique et Politique de Genève* published an account of the ascent, sent in by Bourrit, which described Paccard as "breathless, tired and frightened," and almost dragged bodily to the summit by Balmat, who was "braver and fitter." A few days later it was Bourrit again who sent King Vittorio Amedeo III of Sardinia the account on the basis of which the Royal family

awarded to Balmat alone a cash prize and the letters patent which authorised him to change his name to "Balmat *dit* Mont Blanc."

Paccard reacted with inevitable firmness. He had Balmat sign an affidavit before witnesses which admitted that it was Paccard who had organised the climb, decided on the route, led the party for much of the ascent, and reached the summit first. But by now the damage was done, and of its two sons who had conquered Mont Blanc, Chamonix chose to love Balmat, the tough mountain man.

After a truce lasting several years, Balmat's bragging began again. In 1830 Alexandre Dumas *père* interviewed the elderly guide and wrote another disparaging portrait of Paccard, who had been dead for several years by then. For over a century, authors of every kind continued to adulate Balmat, totally ignoring his climbing companion.

The famous bronze monument erected in Chamonix in 1887 (in which Balmat alone shows de Saussure the route to the summit) was part of this ignoble "rewriting of history." It was not until 1986, when the second centenary of the ascent was celebrated, that a bronze monument commemorating Paccard was inaugurated on the banks of the River Arve.

The invention of Mont Blanc

Before Mont Blanc could really be said to have been conquered, however, something was still lacking – the ascent by Horace-Bénédict de Saussure. He travelled to the valley 10 days after the ascent by Paccard and Balmat, and organised an attempt on 20th and 21st August, but was forced to give up by bad weather conditions.

He succeeded the following year. On 4th July, in preparation for the attempt, Balmat returned to the peak with Jean-Michel Cachat and Alexis Tournier, who were just back from the first crossing of the Col du Géant. De Saussure set off from Chamonix on 1st

Then the party descended by the ascent route, and spent a last night at high altitude on the granite boulder which de Saussure named *Rocher de l'Heureux Retour*. The next day, de Saussure's party was welcomed with great rejoicing back in Chamonix.

Two years later, de Saussure spent 16 days in a stone shelter built at an altitude of 3350 metres on Col du Géant to complete the scientific exploration of the massif. Only six more days were to pass before the fourth ascent took place. It was made by Mark Beaufoy, the first of many Englishmen whose names were to go down in the history of the Alps.

August, accompanied by his manservant and 18 guides, and spent the first night in a stone shelter specially built on the edge of the glacier.

The next day the party climbed to the edge of the Grand Plateau, where they camped for the night. De Saussure slept on a folding bed carried by a strong porter, while the guides used straw and blankets. The next day, in the early morning cold, the snow on the slope leading to the Rochers Rouges was very hard, but the guides cut safe steps with their axes. Ropes were not yet used. The only "belay" available to de Saussure was a stick held by the guides climbing in front of and behind him, which he could use to hold on to.

At 11 a.m. on 3rd August, Horace-Bénédict de Saussure's most cherished dream finally came true: he was standing on the highest peak in Europe. The weather was fine, and although fog hid the plains of Savoy and Piedmont, all the major peaks of the Western Alps could clearly be seen.

The scientific experiments conducted by the party were made laborious by fatigue and the altitude, but they completed all their tasks. The "official" height of Mont Blanc was thus fixed at 2450 *toises* (4775 metres).

26 top Viewed from the Aiguille du Midi, the ridge that leads to Mont Blanc across Mont Blanc du Tacul and Mont Maudit resembles a gigantic staircase of ice. The route to the summit across the great slopes of Mont Blanc du Tacul and the shoulder of Mont Maudit was explored starting in 1853 by the Courmayeur guides, who reached it by crossing Col du Géant.

26 bottom The ascent of Mont Blanc by Horace-Bénédict de Saussure, performed in 1787 with the aid of a servant and no less than 18 guides, marked the end of the years devoted to the conquest of the great mountain. In this famous aquatint, the long party winds its way across the deep crevasses of the Jonction.

26-27 The last light of a magnificent winter sunset sets fire to the granite walls and edges of the Aiguilles de Chamonix. Very attractive is the ridge climbing from the Aiguille du Peigne (right) to the Aiguille du Plan across the Aiguille des Pèlerins and the Aiguille des Deux Aigles.

27 top This picture shows one of the decisive moments in the ascent of Mont Blanc by Horace-Bénédict de Saussure. It is dawn on 2nd August, and the guides and their famous client are leaving the rocks of Montagne de la Côte to venture onto the treacherous surface of the glacier.

27 bottom left Horace-Bénédict de Saussure, who was born in 1740 and reached the highest point in Europe at the age of 47, definitely deserves the title of "inventor" of Mont Blanc. This portrait, painted by Jean-Pierre Saint-Ours, shows a pause for thought during his examination of a number of crystals. His gaze inevitably seems to turn to Mont Blanc.

27 bottom right Though less tiring than the ascent, the descent of Mont Blanc should not be underestimated even today, because fatigue and soft snow can play unpleasant tricks on climbers. This picture shows de Saussure enjoying the experience of sliding down on the seat of his pants. Guides only used ropes under exceptional circumstances at this period.

Little men and great glaciers

28-29 top The East face of Monte Rosa, which can be seen from as far away as the Po Valley on clear days, is the highest and most awesome in the Alps. From the left, it is crowned by Points Gnifetti (known as the Signalkuppe by German-speaking climbers), Zumstein, Dufour and Nordend.

29 top right The North-East face of Mount Lyskamm, between 800 and 1000 metres high, dominates the Grenzgletscher and appears in all its splendour to climbers heading for the highest peaks of Monte Rosa. The seven young men from Gressoney who arrived at Colle del Lys in 1778 suddenly saw it looming in front of them.

28 bottom and 28-29 bottom Johann Jakob Scheuzcher, a doctor from Zurich who made nine journeys through the mountainous regions of Switzerland between 1702 and 1711, was one of the most famous protagonists of the renewed interest by the Swiss in the Alpine world. The four volumes of his Itinera per Helvetiae Alpinas Regiones, published in Leiden in 1723, contained detailed coloured maps like these, which represent the Pennine and Lepontine Alps. However, the representation of the peaks is still conventional.

29 bottom left When the valley bottom is shrouded in cloud, the peaks of Monte Rosa look like islands in a stormy sea. In this photo, Punta Tre Amici is seen from Punta Gnifetti. The undulating snow and rock of Signal ridge, crossed by one of the most classic routes in the Pennine Alps, can be seen between the two.

At 4 p.m. on 23rd July 1801, a doctor from Piedmont picked up his pen, dipped it in the inkwell, and began to write a letter to a friend. It is not the gesture in itself that makes this episode interesting, but the place where it happened. Pietro Giordani was sitting on a boulder at an altitude of 4046 metres, surrounded by the walls and glaciers of Monte Rosa.

His letter was also something out of the ordinary. "I'm writing to you from the top of the Alps; I'm above the summits of all the highest mountains apart from Monte Rosa, whose peaks are several hundred *toises* higher. A sloping slab of granite that projects from the snow just enough to rest my notepaper on serves as a desk for scribbling this note, and a piece of blue ice serves as my chair," he wrote to his friend Michele Cusa, a notary public in the nearby town of Varallo.

Having set off on foot from Alagna, Giordani climbed over 3000 metres, and reached the modest peak now named after him after many hours of effort. "I am inexpressibly disappointed to find myself in this natural sanctuary without the right instruments to measure heights and conduct the numerous physics experiments that I would have had the rare opportunity to perform here," he said in his letter to Cusa.

However, on reading his letter two centuries later, the impression is received that he felt obliged to make this statement, which did not reflect his true thoughts. Like many cultured men who lived at the foot of the Alps, Giordani knew all about the adventures of de Saussure, Bourrit and the other protagonists of the first ascents of Mont Blanc.

What inspired him to tackle the peaks and glaciers of Monte Rosa seems to have been curiosity and desire

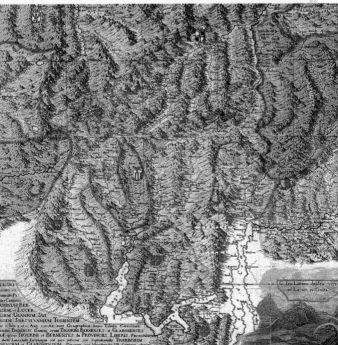

for adventure, the two main ingredients of mountaineering, as demonstrated by the enthusiasm that emanates from his letter before and after his excuses for not taking a barometer with him. "Just imagine the sight, my friend. It has to be seen to be believed!" continues his letter.

"To the north are the tall white peaks of Monte Rosa, to the north-west I can see the whole range of the great Alps as far as Mont Blanc, beyond them I can see the whole chain of the Graian, Cottian and Maritime Alps as far as the Ligurian Apennines, to the north-east the countless mountain ranges that divide Helvetia, S. Gothard, the Rhaetian Alps, and as far as the mountains of the Tyrol.

"Within this circle I can see the Cisalpine Republic, the whole of Piedmont, and countless towns and cities, now white in the reflected rays of the sun. I am thoroughly satisfied with my labours, with what I have seen, and with the consolation of having discovered a way of ascending the great colossus of Monte Rosa," concludes Giordani.

Monte Rosa, the second-highest mountain in Europe after Mont Blanc (Punta Dufour, the highest point on the massif, stands at 4633 metres, as against the 4807 metres of the "Roof of Europe"), is just as spectacular as its older brother, located some 80 km to the west. Lacking the compact granite walls of Mont Blanc, Monte Rosa surpasses the latter in terms of the truly Himalayan size of its glaciers and the number of peaks over 4000 metres high.

For those observing the Alps from the Po Valley, Monte Rosa is the symbol of high mountains. Tall and impressive, its East face dominates the paddy-fields and poplar groves of Lomellina and Piedmont. In winter, on a clear day, this enchanting sight can be seen from Milan city centre.

The first to observe Monte Rosa from close to, as we saw in an earlier chapter, was Leonardo da Vinci, who climbed the modest but panoramic

Cima di Bo in 1511. But the first mountaineer (or forerunner of mountaineering) to reach the foot of the massif where Valle d'Aosta, Piedmont and Valais meet was once again Horace-Bénédict de Saussure.

In 1787, after climbing Mont Blanc, de Saussure was "awestruck" on seeing the mountain from the top of Vercelli's bell-tower. During the same journey, in Turin, he met Count Morozzo della Rocca, who was shortly afterwards to make a courageous attempt on no less than the East face of Monte Rosa, the highest and one of the most dangerous in the Alps. After reaching an altitude of "1500 *toises*" (approx. 2900 metres), namely the area where the Marinelli refuge hut now stands, the nobleman from Turin decided to turn back.

Two years later, on 31st July 1789, de Saussure climbed with a large party towards Pizzo Bianco, a rocky peak on the divide between Valle Anzasca and Valsesia. A "deep ravine" prevented the climbers from reaching the 3215-metre peak, but the scientist from Geneva had achieved his aim.

Very popular with hikers even today, the Pizzo offers an exceptional view over Monte Rosa, which can be seen even by those who, like de Saussure and his party, stop at the northern fore-summit of the mountain.

If Monte Rosa is observed from there, it is evident that the steep and difficult East face did not offer an ascent route which was feasible with the techniques and materials of the 18th century. Conversely, although Punta Grober and Punta Tre Amici partly conceal it from view, it is obvious that the south side of the massif that descends towards Gressoney and Alagna offers a much better chance of ascent.

For unknown reasons, however, de Saussure never attempted that route. He returned to the area in 1792, on his seventh visit to the Alps, and climbed with seven guides and porters to the

Small Matterhorn (3883 m) which, despite its name, is a modest peak between Plateau Rosà and the Breithorn, now reached by a cable car very popular with climbers and skiers.

The ascent from Zermatt to the summit is long but easy, and the view of Monte Rosa, the Mischabel and the Matterhorn is magnificent. However, after that climb, de Saussure never returned to the second-highest mountain in Europe. In the meantime, a group of mountain men from Gressoney who had had no contact with him had already identified and partly climbed the correct route to the summit.

The valleys of Macugnaga, Gressoney and Alagna, colonised in the late Middle Ages by the Walsers (German-speaking mountain people from central Switzerland), have maintained commercial and cultural links with the world north of the Alpine divide for centuries. These include the legend of the *Verlorne Tal*, a Lost Valley surrounded by glaciers which, as in the rest of the Alps, began to expand rapidly in the 14th century, wiping out meadows, Alpine pastures and the ancient mule tracks that climbed up to the Alpine passes.

The legend of the Lost Valley, which had remained more vivid in Gressoney than anywhere else, fascinated numerous young people from the valley. On 15th August 1778, eight years before the triumph of Balmat and Paccard on Mont Blanc, seven young men from the valley set off confidently towards Monte Rosa. They were Valentin and Josef Beck, Étienne Lisgie, Josef Zumstein, François Castel de Perlatol, Niklaus Vincent and Sebastiano Linty. After crossing moraines and pastures, they ventured onto the Lys Glacier near the rocks where the Gnifetti hut now stands.

Roped together and wearing rudimentary crampons,

30 top This aerial photo shows one of the most spectacular views of the Monte Rosa massif. From Nordend, the second-highest peak in the massif, the Santa Caterina ridge slopes down towards the photographer. This rocky staircase that separates the East face, illuminated by the morning sun, from the shadows of the Monte Rosa Glacier, was not climbed until 1906, by British mountaineer Valentine J.E. Ryan, accompanied by the great Swiss guides Franz and Josef Lochmatter.

30-31 Although they pale by comparison with the other peaks of Monte Rosa, Pyramide Vincent (on the left) and Punta Giordani dominate the Gressoney valley and Valsesia. It therefore comes as no surprise that they were the first to be climbed by explorers of the massif.

30 bottom left A rocky tower flanks the Garstelet ridge, where the Gnifetti refuge hut has stood since 1876.

30 bottom right Zumstein reached the summit of the third-highest peak in the Monte Rosa Massif in 1820.

they skirted the rock and ice slopes of Pyramide Vincent and eventually arrived in sight of Colle del Lys (4248 m), situated on the main divide of the range. Instead of making straight for it they turned off to the right, and climbed a rocky escarpment which they named *Entdeckungfels* ("Discovery Rock").

From its summit, a few metres higher than the col, they found that the *Verlorne Tal* was very different from what they had imagined. The pastures and forests of Zermatt could be seen in the distance, and the colossal Grenz Glacier wound towards Valais, at the foot of the awesome ice walls of Punta Dufour and Mount Lyskamm.

It is not known whether their disappointment at not having found the Alpine equivalent of Shangri-La was to some extent mitigated by the outstanding beauty of the places they reached. However, by some means the news reached the *Journal de Paris* which announced it to its readers (who, it should be remembered, were Parisians on the eve of the French Revolution), suggesting that the *Verlorne Tal* was "the valley of the Golden Age, a Happy Valley forgotten by civilisation and lost to the modern world."

One of the seven young men involved in the 1778 ascent did not forget the glaciers of Monte Rosa. He was born Josef Zumstein, but under the Kingdom of Savoy his name was changed to Joseph Delapierre. In 1821, Zumstein/Delapierre became an expert forestry inspector and inspired the *Regie Patenti*, the law that prohibited "in every part of the royal dominions" the hunting of "the Ibex, called by the French *bouquetin des Alpes* and by naturalists *Capra ibex* and known by the vernacular name of *bouc-castagn* by the inhabitants of Aosta."

This document, which stated that only sovereigns of the Savoy dynasty could hunt the animal, paved the way for an increase in the numbers of ibex and its saving from extinction in the Gran Paradiso National Park. Apart from Pietro Giordani, whom we have already mentioned, Zumstein's new ascent to the higher peaks of Monte Rosa was preceded by an ascent by Johann Niklaus Vincent, son of the Niklaus Vincent who had climbed with him in 1778.

Accompanied by German doctor Friedrich Parrot, known for his explorations in the Pyrenees, on Mount Ararat and in the Caucasus, Vincent climbed the peak now named after him in September 1816 or 1817. Thick fog forced him to stop a few hundred metres from the highest point. However, on 5th August 1819, Vincent finally reached the 4215-metre summit of "his" mountain. But the surface of Monte Rosa had barely been scratched.

A week later, Josef Zumstein accompanied Vincent on the most important ascent performed on the massif to date. After a long walk-in from the valley bottom, the pair reached the Lys glacier together with "two porters, a workman from the nearby mine and a hunter highly skilled in climbing mountains."

Their knapsacks contained food, spare clothing, a barometer and other scientific instruments. "A six-foot long alpenstock with an iron tip and a hook" aided their progression, and the climbers wore crampons on their feet. "Vincent and the two porters covered their eyes with a veil. To protect mine, I used a pair of blue-tinted spectacles," recounted Zumstein in his *Le Voyage sur le Mont-Rose*, presented to the Turin Academy in 1820.

Many hours' walking "on stretches of ice that looked like the waves of the sea" took the party to Colle del Lys, which they were the first to cross. A traverse along the Swiss side of the massif led the six climbers to the base of a steeper slope, the access to which was barred by a huge crevasse. The workman, who according to Zumstein was "the bravest of the party," set off first, axe in hand, cutting steps in the ice. He was followed by the huntsman,

equipped with "a shovel to clear the path of ice splinters." The ascent continued with a difficult snow-covered ridge, a halt to finish off the generous supply of provisions ("bread, cheese, cold meat, a few onions and wine") and another steep, interminable slope. When they reached the summit, Zumstein worked with a barometer and a theodolite for three hours.

Finally satisfied, he concluded that "the highest peak of Monte Rosa must have an altitude of 15,600 feet above sea level. I may have made some surveying errors, but it is certainly true that the highest peak of Monte Rosa considerably exceeds that of Mont Blanc, and no other mountain can now challenge Monte Rosa for the honour of being the highest mountain in our continent."

31 right Johann Niklaus Vincent made the first ascent of Pyramide Vincent with Friedrich Parrot in 1819. A year later he summitted Point Zumstein with Josef Zumstein and four more companions.

31 far right Reached by a short detour from the trail leading up to Colle del Lys and Capanna Margherita, the sharp Corno Nero (on the left) and the rounded Ludwigshohe are often climbed by mountaineers collecting 4000-metre peaks in the Alps.

Now, almost two centuries later, it is impossible to know whether the mistake made by the forestry inspector from Gressoney was caused by tiredness, the altitude, lack of skill in the use of the instruments or, perhaps more touchingly, excessive love for his native valley. Instead of the 5067 metres measured by Zumstein, the peak now named after him stands at 4563 metres, and is therefore 70 metres lower than the nearby Punta Dufour, the true culminating point of the massif. However, it is separated from Punta Dufour by an elevated rocky ridge that was only to be entirely crossed 53 years later, when mountaineering techniques had made colossal strides forward.

The last of the great pioneers of Monte Rosa came onto the scene 13 years after the victorious ascent by Zumstein. Like his predecessors, he lived in the valleys at the foot of the Italian side of the massif, from which Monte Rosa looks quite awesome. Giovanni Gnifetti, the parish priest of Alagna Valsesia, made his first attempted ascent in 1834. His destination was the lowest and farthest west of the four main peaks of the massif, known as the *Signalkuppe* ("Signal Point") because of a sharp rock turret.

32 top Abbot Giovanni Gnifetti, parish priest of Alagna, led the first ascent (in 1842) of the fourth-highest peak in the Monte Rosa range, now named after him.

32 bottom A map of Monte Rosa published in 1862 shows the main routes on the glaciers of the massif.

32-33 The ice ridge that leads from Colle del Lys (4153 metres) to Point Parrot (4436 metres) offers a spectacular alternative to the walk on the glacier towards Capanna Margherita. It was first climbed in 1863 by a party guided by Melchior Anderegg.

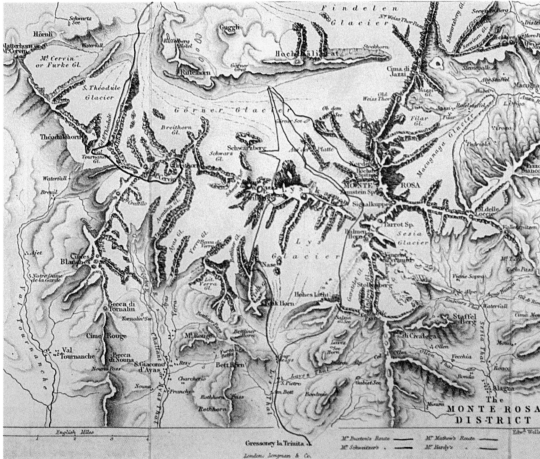

Though lower than Point Dufour, Nordend and Point Zumstein, that peak was very important from the geographical standpoint, as the ridge that separates Valsesia from Valle Anzasca starts there. For those viewing the mountain from Alagna, the Signalkuppe is the most spectacular peak of all, and for Gnifetti, this was more than enough reason to set off.

After a first failed attempt, Gnifetti tried again in 1836 and 1839. Success came in the summer of 1842. On 8th August, Gnifetti set off from peaceful Alagna with much of the town's *intellighenzia*: surveyor Cristoforo Grober, doctor Giovanni Giordani, notary

Giacomo Giordani, architecture student Cristoforo Ferraris and theologian Giuseppe Farinetti. There were also two porters in the party.

After a bivouac on the usual knoll at the base of the glacier, the party set off at 4:30 a.m., tormented by a "vehement, icy wind," amid "endless crevasses of an unparalleled depth." Around midday, having turned off to the right of the Zumstein route and crossed a last steep slope, the eight climbers finally reached the 4554-metre summit, surmounted by "a tip of antediluvian rock resembling a sharp tooth" which stuck out over the awesome abysses of the East face.

Here, Farinetti demonstrated great courage. "Using Giovanni Giordani's back as a stool," he climbed up to the summit of the tower, where a providential cleft allowed him to plant a red flag which was clearly visible from the houses of Alagna. Three years after the ascent, Giovanni Gnifetti published an interesting account called *Nozioni topografiche del Monte Rosa ed ascensioni su di esso di Giovanni Gnifetti Paroco* (instead of "parroco"!) *di Alagna* (Topographical Details of Monte Rosa and Ascents by Giovanni Gnifetti Parish Priest of Alagna) in Turin.

At the end of the account, without false modesty,

Gnifetti made a rather rambling but comprehensible proposal.

"Now this pyramid, already called the Signal, I hope to be allowed to call it in future Red Signal Point and, if it does not seem to show an excessive love of glory on my part (which indeed I do not want), the summit by my surname." There was nothing wrong with this, as Zumstein, Vincent and Pietro Giordani had already named the peaks they had conquered with their own names. But the Alagna priest's wish came only half true.

The summit he reached is called Punta Gnifetti on Italian maps, but German-speaking cartographers and climbers still call it the Signalkuppe.

33 bottom Pyramide Vincent is named after Johann Niklaus Vincent, the first to reach the summit on 5th August 1819, accompanied by chamois hunter Jacques Castel and two miners from Gressoney.

While Monte Rosa attracted climbers from Piedmont and Valle d'Aosta, and those from Geneva and France flocked to Mont Blanc, German-speaking Swiss climbers headed for another great Alpine massif. This was the Bernese Oberland, the extraordinary chain of peaks and glaciers that rivals Monte Rosa for the title of the most Himalayan massif in the Alps. Its peaks, though of exceptional elegance, are a little lower than those in the great mountains of Valais; the highest, Finsteraarhorn, measures 4274 metres, the Aletschhorn 4195 metres, and the Jungfrau 4158 metres. Its glaciers, starting with the Aletsch, are the longest in Europe, however, and it was on them that the scientists of the early decades of the 19th century focused their attention.

Before recounting their exploits, a word of praise

is due to the ascents made by brothers Hieronymous and Johann Rudolf Meyer of Aarau, accompanied as guides by chamois hunters Alois Volker and Josef Bortis. Now within easy reach for those who arrive at the convenient altitude of 3475 metres on the rack railway that climbs into the bowels of the Eiger, it took the four climbers four days to climb from the alpine pastures of the Lotschental to the summit of the Jungfrau and back.

Even more remarkable were the difficulties of the climb, which includes a long route on glaciers, the crossing of the 3235-metre Lotschenlucke, and finally a steep climb on the ice and rocks of the summit pyramid in the direction of the summit. A few days later, the same party tackled the higher Finsteraarhorn, but they were forced to stop just below the summit.

Eighteen years went by before guides Jakob Leuthold and Hans Wahren reached the highest peak in the Oberland (4724 m) on 10th August 1829, crossing a steep and difficult rock ridge covered with a sprinkling of snow at the end of a long section on ice. Part of the credit for this ascent must go to their client, geologist Franz Josef Hugi, a professor at Soleure university who devoted a great

deal of time to the geographical and glaciological exploration of the massif.

Hugi had a rudimentary stone shelter built on the Aar glacier during his 1829 trip, and another Swiss geologist who loved the Alps, Louis Agassiz from Neuchâtel in French-speaking Switzerland, arrived there in the summer of 1841 with Charles Vogt, Célestin Nicolet, Henri Coulon, François de Pourtalès and Edouard Desor.

Twelve years at that height is a long time, and Hugi's shelter was by now little more than a ruin. The group took up residence a few hundred metres higher up, in a shelter built at the foot of a huge boulder

which was immediately nicknamed the *Hotel de Neuchâtel*. The shelter, which was enlarged and improved over the years, is also mentioned in visitors' accounts by the names of "Noah's Ark" and the "Aar Pavilion," and became an increasingly popular destination for scientists and hikers venturing into the eastern sector of the Oberland. As well as collecting rock samples and conducting meticulous measurements of glacier movements, Agassiz and his companions performed a detailed geographical exploration of the area.

Together with guides Jakob Leuthold, Hans Wahren, Hans Jaun, Melchior Bannholzer, Johannes Aplanalp and Johannes Jaun, they climbed to the 4158-metre peak of the Jungfrau along the route followed by the Meyer brothers. The crux of the ascent was the crossing of the last crevasse, over which the guides placed a wooden ladder eight metres long.

The heroes of the day descended, elated, but for Agassiz the most exciting moment had yet to come. Wearing a marmot-skin cap and a chamois hide, he was lowered with a winch into the bottom of a 30-metre-deep crevasse.

In the bottom of the abyss the brave explorer found himself in an icy stream whose violent current threatened to sweep him away. Above him his companions, who could not hear his shouts, kept paying out the rope instead of pulling him up. "I would not advise anyone to repeat the exploit unless they have a very sound scientific reason for doing so," commented Louis Agassiz when he returned to the surface.

*35 bottom
right Seen from the
Jungfraujoch, where the
rack railway that climbs up
from Interlaken arrives, the
Jungfrau presents a
treacherous rocky face
interrupted by splashes of
snow and furrowed by ice-
filled gullies. The ordinary
ascent route runs farther to
the left, along the upper
slopes of the Jungfraufirn, the
Rottalsattel and the steep
slopes of snow and ice above it.*

In the nearly 50 years that separated Paccard and Balmat's ascent from the adventures of Gnifetti and Agassiz, climbing on Mont Blanc had undergone great changes. Ascents to the summit, which were rare at first, became more numerous after the Battle of Waterloo, when peace returned to Europe and increasing numbers of British travellers set off on the Grand Tour.

On 14th July 1808, during the ninth ascent, led by Jacques Balmat as usual, Marie Paradis became the first woman to reach the summit of the "Roof of Europe." In the summer of 1818, Jean-Michel Balmat and five other guides led Polish climber A. Malczewski to the north peak of the Aiguille du Midi (3795 m), the first of the minor peaks of the massif to be climbed.

Two years later, on 20th August 1820, the avalanche that engulfed Dr. Hamel's party, killing three guides, led to a two-year halt in ascents to the summit of Mont Blanc, and persuaded climbers and guides to seek a safer route than Paccard and Balmat's Ancien Passage. The problem was only solved seven years later, on 25th July 1827, when Joseph-Marie Couttet and eight more guides, climbing with Sir Charles Fellows and William Hawes, put up the safer Corridor route, which climbs from the Grand Plateau to Col de la Brenva along a wide, easy ice slope.

In 1821, the Compagnie des Guides was founded in Chamonix. In 1838, noblewoman Henriette d'Angeville became the second woman to reach the summit, and shortly afterwards wrote an interesting book which encountered great success all over Europe. In 1853, to make the ascent more convenient, Chamonix Town Council built the first rudimentary refuge hut at the Grands Mulets.

Finally, in 1855, both the Courmayeur guides and the Saint-Gervais guides inaugurated their own ascent routes to the summit of Mont Blanc in order to lead the increasingly numerous *touristes* to the 4807-metre summit. The first route, which was very long even for the robust walkers of the day, took in Col du Géant, Col du Midi, the shoulder of Mont Blanc du Tacul, Col du Mont Maudit and Col de la Brenva. The second, after the broken rocks of Aiguille du Goûter and the snow-cap of the Dôme, crossed the elegant elevated snow-covered ridge of the Bosses, and demonstrated definite technical progress over the past.

36-37 This photo shows the Aiguille Verte and the Dru (left) and the northernmost peaks of the Aiguilles de Chamonix. Mont Blanc du Tacul, Mont Maudit, Mont Blanc and the Dôme du Goûter are hidden by cloud.

36 bottom left In the summer of 1820, the avalanche that hit Dr. Hamel's party shot Mont Blanc into the headlines all over Europe. Three guides were killed.

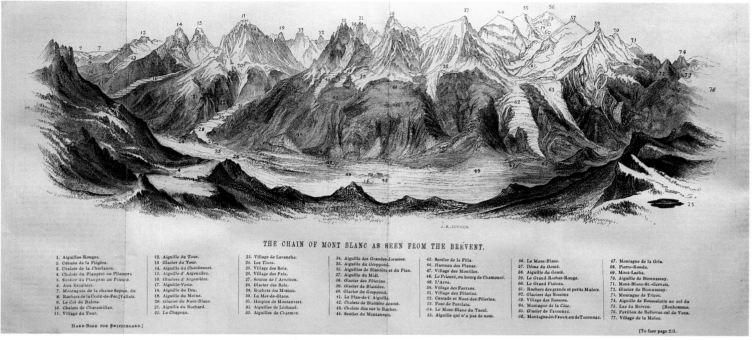

THE CHAIN OF MONT BLANC AS SEEN FROM THE BRÉVENT.

1. Aiguilles-Rouges.	12. Aiguille du Tour.	23. Village de Lavanche.	34. Aiguille des Grandes-Jorasses.	45. Sentier de la Filia.	56. Le Mont-Blanc.	67. Montagne de la Gria.
2. Cabane de la Flégère.	13. Les Tines.	24. Village des Bois.	35. Aiguilles de Stalitière et du Plan.	46. Hameau des Planaz.	57. Dôme du Goûté.	68. Pierre-Ronde.
3. Chalets de la Charlanon.	14. Aiguille du Chardonnet.	25. Village des Pris.	37. Aiguille du Midi.	47. Village des Mouilles.	58. Aiguille du Goûté.	69. Mont-Lachu.
4. Chalets du Planprat ou Pilampra.	15. Aiguille d' Argentière.	26. Village des Prés.	27. Source de l'Arveiron.	48. Le Prieuré, ou bourg de Chamouni.	59. Le Grand-Rocher-Rouge.	70. Aiguille de Bionnassay.
5. Sentier du Planprat au Prieuré.	16. Glaciers d'Argentière.	27. Source de l'Arveiron.	28. Glacier des Pélerins.	49. L'Arve.	60. Le Grand Plateau.	71. Mont-Blanc-St.-Gervais.
6. Aux Escaliers.	17. Aiguille-Verte.	28. Glacier des Bois.	29. Glacier de Blaitière.	50. Village des Pazrans.	61. Rochers des grands et petits Mulets.	72. Glacier de Bionnassay.
7. Montagnes de la chaine Septen, du	18. Aiguille du Dru.	29. Rochers des Mottets.	40. Glacier du Greppond.	51. Village des Pélerins.	62. Glaciers des Bossons.	73. Montagne de Tconnaz.
8. Rochers de la Croix-de-Fer,[Vallais.	19. Aiguille du Moine.	30. La Mer-de-Glace.	41. Le Plan-de-l' Aiguille.	52. Cascade et Nant-des-Pélerins.	63. Village des Bossons.	74. Aiguille de Boussalette au col du
9. Le Col de Balme.	20. Aiguille du Nant-Blanc.	31. Hospice de Montanvert.	42. Chalets de Blaitière dessus.	53. Pont de Pérulata.	64. Montagne de la Côte.	75. Lac du Brévent. [Bonhomme.
10. Chalets de Charamillan.	21. Aiguille du Rochard.	32. Aiguilles de Léchaud.	43. Chalets dits sur le Rocher.	54. Le Mont-Blanc du Tacul.	65. Glacier de Tconnaz.	76. Pavillon de Bellevue col des Voza.
11. Village du Tour.	22. Le Chapeau.	33. Aiguilles de Charmoz.	44. Sentier du Montanvert.	55. Aiguille qui n'a pas de nom.	66. Montagne des Fesaux, ou des Tconnaz.	77. Aiguille de la Mola.

HAND-BOOK FOR SWITZERLAND.] [To face page 231.

36 bottom right The first ascent of Mont Blanc by a woman was performed by a Chamonix girl called Marie Paradis, a waitress in a local inn. She was guided to the summit on 14th July 1808 by Jacques Balmat, whose not especially noble purpose seems to have been to turn Marie into a tourist attraction.

37 top Seventy years after the ascent by Paccard and Balmat, many travellers who visited Chamonix took a travel guide with them. This engraving, from the 1846 edition of "Travellers in Switzerland and the Alps of Savoy and Piedmont" shows newcomers the names of the peaks, glaciers and villages.

37 centre right The Chamonix Compagnie des Guides, founded in 1821, issued clients who attempted the climb or reached the summit of Mont Blanc a certificate commemorating the ascent. This one, designed by Charles Weibel in 1840, is a real work of art.

37 bottom right The social status of Henriette d'Angeville, the second woman to reach the summit of Mont Blanc, could not have been more different from that of Marie Paradis. According to a widespread rumour, the noblewoman who summitted the mountain in 1838 decided to make the ascent to annoy her friend and rival George Sand.

The crucial moment for the popularity of Mont Blanc came in the summer of 1851 when, after 13 years' dreaming, English draughtsman Albert Smith reached the summit. His climb was just one of many. But on his return to London, Smith gave evening lectures to a packed house at the Egyptian Hall in Piccadilly Circus, where the drawings he made during the ascent, copied on a large scale, were displayed by "a simple mechanism devised by a carpenter friend." Smith travelled the length and breadth of England with his brother in a gig nicknamed "The Sideshow," which carried "Mont Blanc on the back seat," carefully folded up.

The British public was fascinated, and the show, which ran for over 2000 performances, earned the author the huge sum of £30,000. The energetic Smith designed and sold all sorts of merchandise, including a curious "portable diorama" of Mont Blanc and *The New Game of the Ascent of Mont Blanc*, a board game which took players from Piccadilly Circus to the summit of Mont Blanc. Starting in the summer of 1852, the success of the show led to numerous ascents.

The ascents to the summit performed between 1852 and 1857 were as numerous as those made in the previous 60 years. Later, they multiplied even faster. In the meantime Chamonix had become a fashionable resort, and excursions to Mont Brévent, Montenvers and the Mer de Glace were among the favourite recreations of visitors.

It was against this backdrop that the climbers of the Golden Age came onto the scene; the age when all the highest peaks were finally conquered and, as a result of the tragic conquest of the Matterhorn, a huge number of people discovered the existence of mountaineering.

Little men and great glaciers

Conquest of the giants

14th July 1865 was both a glorious and a tragic day in the history of mountaineering. That day, at 1:40 p.m. on "one of those wonderful days of purity and calm that usually precede bad weather," seven men were the first to reach the 4478-metre summit of the Matterhorn, the most spectacular of the great mountains in the Alps.

The most difficult pitches were solved by lead climber Michel Croz, the best Chamonix guide of his generation. The organiser of the ascent, however, was Edward Whymper, who had taken part in no less than eight attempts on the summit in previous summers. Even today, the elevated summit ridge and the extraordinary isolation of the Matterhorn mean that reaching the summit for the first time is an emotional experience for even the most expert climber.

"Not one of the giants of the Alps was hidden from our gaze," recalled Whymper in his *Scrambles Amongst the Alps in the Years 1860-9*. "The foremost was the impressive Dent Blanche, then came the Gabelhorn, the Rothorn with its sharp pinnacle, the incomparable Weisshorn, then Monte Rosa with its numerous pinnacles, the Lyskamm and the Breithorn. Behind them rose the peaks of the Bernese Oberland, dominated by the Finsteraarhorn and the Simplon, S. Gothard, Disgrazia and Ortler groups.

"To the south our gaze ranged beyond Chivasso to the Po Valley. Monviso, over 90 miles away, seemed close. Over 100 miles away we could see the Alpes Maritimes… Then I recognised my first love, Mont Pelvoux, the Écrins and the Meije, the massifs of the Graian Alps and finally, majestic and sublime in the glory of the sun, the King of the Alps – Mont Blanc.

"I saw dark, mysterious forests, cool, pretty meadows, tumultuous waterfalls and calm pools, remote wildernesses, sunny plains and icefields… The most widely differing forms that the universe can combine, all the contrasts that the imagination could dream of."

Before that long moment of contemplation the ascent had been easy and almost lacking in incident, despite a minor mystery that had occurred a few days earlier. On arriving in Valtournenche by way of Colle di Valcornera, Whymper reached an agreement with Jean-Antoine Carrel, the best guide in the valley, that they should attempt the first ascent of the Matterhorn along the Hornli ridge on 11th July. Unbeknown to Whymper, however, Carrel had already agreed with Felice Giordano to make an all-Italian attempt along Lion Ridge. But Whymper did not give up. "The cunning plot of those bad men can be thwarted," he muttered to himself, while he prepared his revenge.

40 above Edward Whymper, born in London in 1840, organised the first ascent of the Matterhorn and was one of the most outstanding climbing personalities in the years when the highest peaks in the Alps were conquered. He made the first ascents of the Grandes Jorasses, the Aiguille Verte and the Barre des Ecrins, and wrote best-selling books like Scrambles Amongst the Alps, which tells the story of the tragic first ascent of the Matterhorn.

40 top right Michel Croz, born at Le Tour in 1830, was the best French guide of the mid-19th century, and the most famous victim of the tragedy that followed the first ascent of the Matterhorn. He climbed

with Edward Whymper on the Grandes Jorasses, the Barre des Ecrins and many other notable ascents, and is preceded by his inseparable client on the Aiguille Verte.

40 centre right Jean-Antoine Carrel, born in Valtournenche in 1829, was another victim of the "race to the Matterhorn." He climbed with Whymper and mountaineers like Francis F. Tyndall and Reginald J. MacDonald in the first attempted ascents, but discovered from the Italian ridge that the Anglo-Swiss party had reached the summit before him. It is unclear whether it was Whymper who "betrayed" Carrel or vice versa.

40 bottom right *Carrel (left) performed the first ascent of the Italian ridge (Liongrat) on the Matterhorn, and later climbed with Whymper in his successful 1879-1880 season in the Ecuadorian Andes.*

40-41 *This photo shows the upper part of the two Matterhorn ridges used in the first attempts and the first two ascents of the mountain. The Hornli ridge, climbed by Whymper, Croz and party on 14th July 1865, rises amid light and shade on the right; on the* left, *interrupted by the snow-covered ridge of the shoulder, is the Italian ridge, climbed three days later by Jean-Antoine Carrel and Jean-Baptiste Bich.*

41 top *A close look at the summit ridge of the Matterhorn enables the two peaks of the mountain to be distinguished. The "Swiss peak" on the right is the higher of the two, at 4478 m. The "Italian peak" on the left is two metres lower. In reality, both summits are on the frontier ridge.*

On 12th July, Whymper joined forces with the young Lord Francis Douglas, who was just back from the first ascent of the Obergabelhorn, to cross the Theodul Pass. Lord Douglas asked to take part in the subsequent attempt on the Matterhorn, and was accepted. The pair left 180 metres of rope in the meadows by the Schwarzsee, and rushed down at breakneck speed to Zermatt where they encountered Michel Croz, Whymper's companion in numerous ascents, and his current client, Rev. Charles Hudson. They were also heading for the Matterhorn.

A brief conference between the climbers led to the logical outcome – they would make the attempt together. Apart from the climbers already mentioned, the party included two more guides from Zermatt, Peter Taugwalder and his son of the same name, and a young climber whose inexperience was to lead to tragedy. His name was Hadow, and it was Hudson who insisted that he should join the party.

On the 13th, "a beautifully clear day," the party set off for the Matterhorn. After picking up the equipment they had left at the Schwarzsee, they continued along the easy ridge towards the summit pyramid. Before midday, they had pitched their tent on a ledge at an altitude of 3350 metres. Croz and Young Peter Taugwalder continued for quite a long way towards the summit. They returned happy, reporting that the rest of the climb was easy.

On the fateful day, they set off before dawn at a brisk pace. "We encountered no obstacles that forced us to turn back," recounted Edward Whymper. "Whenever we encountered an insurmountable difficulty we always found a way round it… Hudson and I took turns to lead."

It was just after 11 a.m. when the group reached the foot of the Head, the block of rock that forms the

42-43 The pyramid of the Matterhorn appears in all its beauty in this winter photo. The South face, which is between 1300 and 1400 metres high and overlooks the pastures of Breuil and the centre of Cervinia, can be seen in the middle. The entire Italian ridge can be seen on the left, amid sun and shade. The Wildhorn and Wildstrubel tower in the background, beyond the Dent Blanche.

42 bottom In the years of the "race to the Matterhorn," Hotel Monte Rosa in Zermatt was a meeting point for the British mountaineers who climbed in the Pennine Alps. This 1863 drawing by Edward Whymper shows (among others) Leslie Stephen, Adolphus W. Moore, John Ball, William Mathews, John Tyndall and guides Jean-Joseph Maquignaz and Peter Taugwalder senior.

43 top left Although the Matterhorn was his main objective in the Pennine Alps, Edward Whymper made many other ascents in the mountains that surround Zermatt. This drawing shows the crossing of a huge crevasse during an attempted ascent of the Dent Blanche, the icy pyramid on which the Mattertal, the Zinal Valley and Val d'Hérens converge.

43 bottom left The conquest of the Matterhorn attracted the attention of artists from all over Europe. This is how Gustave Doré portrayed the moment at which the party, organised by Edward Whymper and brilliantly led by Michel Croz, reached the summit. The first to reach the summit were Whymper and Croz.

summit of the Matterhorn. "Now things are going to change," announced Michel Croz, as he took the lead. In reality, however, the rocks that looked vertical when seen from below were not particularly steep.

The real problems were "the snow that filled the gaps in the rock" and above all "the thin layer of ice formed by the melted snow." Two long traverses, on which Hadow needed help several times, took the seven to the "easy snowfield" that precedes the summit.

On reaching the southernmost tip of the ridge that constitutes the summit, Whymper and Croz

caught sight of the Valtournenche guides, still down on Lion Ridge. They tried to attract their attention by shouting, then threw big stones down. "The Italians, terrified, beat a rapid retreat," noted Whymper, before praising Jean-Antoine Carrel, his climbing companion on three previous attempts. Then the time came to descend.

Croz went down first, and Whymper brought up the rear. On reaching the difficult section the climbers moved one at a time, with the maximum protection possible on such treacherous terrain. It was another 40 years before rock pitons were invented. Then, the

unthinkable happened. Croz, who was helping Hadow at every step, turned to face downhill to descend in his turn.

The young Englishman slipped and struck Croz on the back. Croz was hurled into the void, and the slack rope ripped Hudson and Douglas off the wall. It would have meant the end for the whole party, but the rope that secured Douglas to Peter Taugwalder Senior snapped. While the last three were left clinging to the rock, their companions plunged into the void, "their hands outstretched in desperation," disappeared into the abyss of the North face, and hit the glacier 1200 metres down.

Beside themselves with shock, sobbing and terrified, Whymper and the two surviving guides continued the descent in silence, with exasperating slowness. When they reached the end of the difficult section "an immense arc ... with two great crosses at the ends" appeared in the sky. "Stricken by superstitious terror," the trio watched the "terrible, wonderful, unique" spectacle.

Two days later it was a Sunday, and the Zermatt parish priest threatened to excommunicate any local guide who failed to attend the first mass of the

43 far right During the descent, the bright day of conquest of the Matterhorn was overcast by tragedy. Another famous lithograph by Gustave Doré shows the fall in which British climbers Hudson, Douglas and Hadow were killed together with Michel Croz. The other three climbers were saved because the rope snapped.

morning. However, Whymper was accompanied on his rescue expedition by three British climbers and five guides from Chamonix and the Oberland. By midday, the bodies of the victims were laid out on the glacier.

On the Monday morning, a grim procession of 21 guides carried the bodies to Zermatt cemetery by order of the local magistrate. Whymper's comment was as hard as an epitaph: "The Matterhorn had been a formidable adversary. Conquered with unexpected ease, like a ruthless enemy, bloodied but unbowed, it took the most terrible revenge for its defeat."

metres, is the highest peak in the inhospitable Oisans range. With him and fellow climber Adolphus W. Moore were two of the best guides of the day, Christian Almer of Grindelwald and Michel Croz of Chamonix.

Later, Whymper's interest turned to the Mont Blanc massif. Accompanied by topographer Anthony Adams Reilly, he first headed for the peaks which best enabled the structure and orography of the massif to be understood. On 9th July, guided by Michel Croz, Henry Charlet and Michel Payot, the two Englishmen reached Mont Dolent (3819 m), the lovely snowcapped peak where the borders of Italy, France and Switzerland meet.

"The summit was delightfully small; the prettiest and tiniest snowcap that has ever formed on the summit of a mountain. And this snow was so white, so immaculate that it seemed like sacrilege to tread on it. It was a miniature Jungfrau, a toy peak that you could cover with the palm of your hand," commented Whymper.

"The Dolent, at the point where three ranges meet, is a real look-out point over everything that surrounds it at a certain distance, with various breaks in the neighbouring chains which look as though they were opened on purpose to extend the horizon. From this point, Mont Blanc looks like a painting composed by a great master," added Adams Reilly. The expedition went on. On 12th July, after a comfortable bivouac, the party reached the Aiguille de Tré-la-Tête, another magnificent, solitary viewpoint overlooking the icy wastes of Tré-la-Tête, Lex Blanche and the Miage. On the 15th it was the turn of the Aiguille d'Argentière (3901 m), reached via the steep slopes of the Glacier du Milieu. Then came the year of the Matterhorn.

On 24th June 1865 Edward Whymper, accompanied by Michel Croz, Christian Almer and Franz Biner, reached

Edward Whymper, born in London in 1840, only shot to fame after the tragic ascent of the Matterhorn, but he was the key figure during the years in which climbing was revolutionised. Unlike most of the English gentlemen who frequented the Alps, he did not come from a particularly wealthy family. To pay for his climbing he had to sell his engravings (he was an excellent artist) and his books, the best of which, apart from *Scrambles Amongst the Alps*, were *Travels Among the Great Andes of the Equator* and the first travel and climbing guide to Chamonix and Mont Blanc, published in 1896. In 1880, after a successful season on the volcanoes of Ecuador, he offered samples of volcanic rock and lava for sale. In the mountains, Whymper was an exceptional walker (a very common gift at the period), and as sure-footed as a guide. Above all, he got straight down to business. He was interested in the highest peaks not yet conquered by other climbers, and bagged a dozen, one after another.

His career in the Alps began in 1861 with the first British ascent of Mont Pelvoux, and a first attempt on the Matterhorn. He devoted the summers of 1862 and 1863 to the Matterhorn again, and reached an altitude of over 4000 metres more than once, often with Jean-Antoine Carrel.

In 1864 he conquered his first unclimbed peak over 4000 metres high. It was the Barre des Écrins which, at 4101

44 top Whymper's tent remained pitched for a long time on the exposed snow-covered ridge of Colle del Leone in July 1862. The British climber made four attempted ascents that summer, and risked his life in a fall. On 28th July John Tyndall, guided by Jean-Antoine Carrel and Johann Bennen, reached the tower named after him at the start of the horizontal ridge of the shoulder.

44-45 The west face of Mont Blanc, which overlooks the Miage glacier, is one of the wildest in the massif and the whole of the Alps. The Brouillard ridge separates it from the glacier of the same name, shrouded in the evening shadows.

44 bottom Another famous drawing by E. Whymper shows a climber hesitating during the descent of the rocky West ridge of Barre des Ecrins in the Dauphiné.

the summit ridge of the Grandes Jorasses. As well as being an impressive mountaineering achievement, it was also an outstanding sporting feat. The party left Courmayeur at 1:30 a.m., walked up Val Ferret, then continued by what is now the ordinary route, reaching the summit in less than 12 hours from the time they left the hotel.

But for Whymper, the Jorasses were mainly a stepping stone to the Aiguille Verte, the next item on his programme. That is why (apart from the fact that it was getting late) the party stopped on the second peak of the mountain (now known as Point Whymper), leaving the higher peak (the difference is only 24 metres) to be conquered three years later by Horace Walker, Melchior Anderegg, Johann Jaun and Julien Grange.

Five days later, on 29th July, Whymper scaled the lovely Aiguille Verte (4122 m), the most beautiful of the peaks in the massif seen from Chamonix, with Almer and

Biner only. It was a difficult climb, which the party tackled via the steep and dangerous snow-filled gully streaked with rocky ribs (now known as Couloir Whymper) that overlooks the Talèfre glacier. The work with the ice-axe was exhausting and the descent was delicate, but the great Christian Almer had had no doubts ever since the start of the ascent. "Hey, Aiguille Verte, now you're dead and buried!" he shouted several times, as he cut footholds into the steep snowy slopes. Whymper particularly admired the view from the summit, which overlooks Chamonix and its valley from a great height. "You can see valleys, villages, tilled fields, endless chains of distant mountains which disappear in a pale blue haze. In the crystal-clear atmosphere you can hear the sweet nostalgic sound of bells and the dull thunder of avalanches," he recalled in his memoirs. The ascent of the Aiguille Verte led to a bitter dispute with the Chamonix guides, who were offended

because the loveliest mountain in the valley had been conquered by two foreign guides. Michel Croz, Whymper's usual climbing companion, who was engaged by another party at the time, was also bitterly disappointed. But Croz got even on 5th July, when he led another British party to the summit of the Verte along the South-West or Moine ridge. Whymper was not only interested in summits. On 26th June he crossed Col Dolent, and during his descent (cutting steps with an ice-axe, and without crampons!) crossed the 55° couloir which slopes down to the Argentière Glacier. "Few spots in the Mont Blanc range give better practice in the use of the ice-axe," was Whymper's laconic comment.

On 3rd July, Whymper and his guides scaled the easier Col de Talèfre, "one of the few passes in the range which might serve a practical purpose." Then he moved on to the Matterhorn, where the tragic victory of 14th July awaited him.

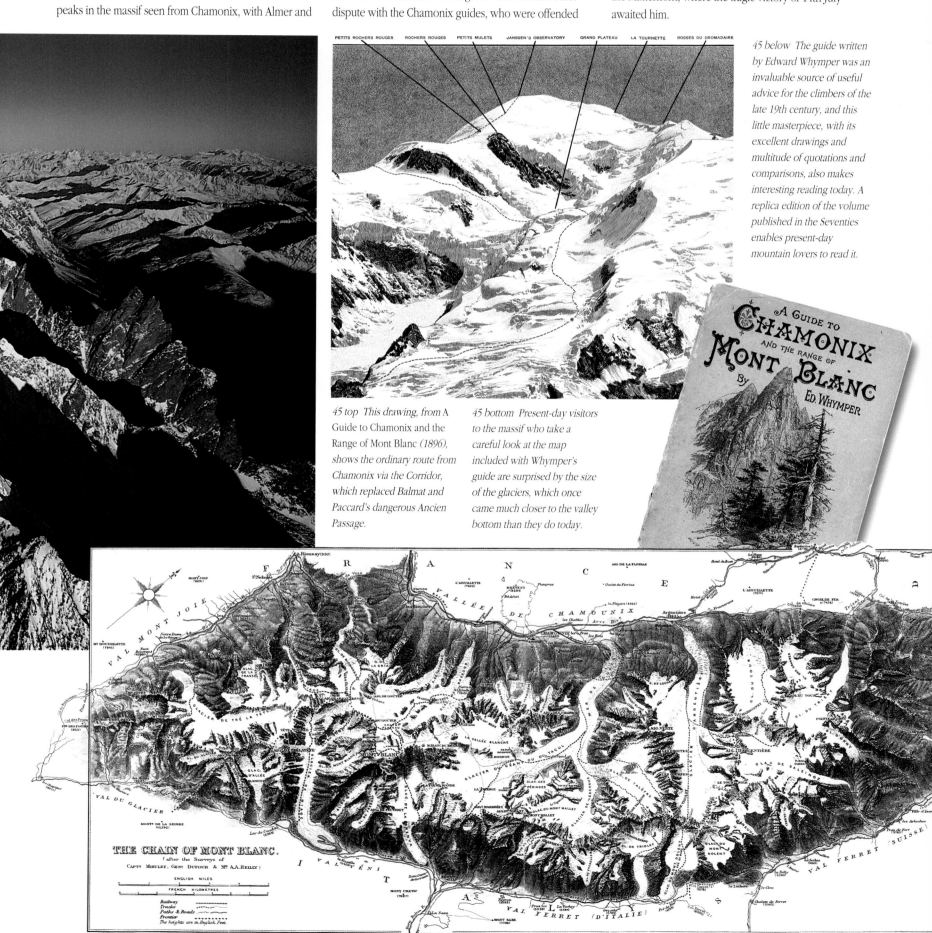

45 below The guide written by Edward Whymper was an invaluable source of useful advice for the climbers of the late 19th century, and this little masterpiece, with its excellent drawings and multitude of quotations and comparisons, also makes interesting reading today. A replica edition of the volume published in the Seventies enables present-day mountain lovers to read it.

45 top This drawing, from A Guide to Chamonix and the Range of Mont Blanc (1896), shows the ordinary route from Chamonix via the Corridor, which replaced Balmat and Paccard's dangerous Ancien Passage.

45 bottom Present-day visitors to the massif who take a careful look at the map included with Whymper's guide are surprised by the size of the glaciers, which once came much closer to the valley bottom than they do today.

46 far left An important place among the climbers of the "Golden Age" is held by Leslie Stephen (1832-1904), one of the founding fathers of the Alpine Club. He made the first ascents of the Zinalrothorn and the Weissmies and the first crossing of the Lyskamm ridge, and was the first to climb the Bosses ridge on Mont Blanc.

46 left Other great climbers of the day were Rev. Charles Hudson and Edward S. Kennedy. Hudson, who was killed on the Matterhorn in 1865, also climbed Point Dufour on Monte Rosa and the Moine ridge on the Aiguille Verte. Kennedy made many repeat ascents. Together, the two Englishmen made the first guideless ascent of Mont Blanc in 1855.

In reality, the systematic conquest of the great Alpine peaks had begun a few years before Edward Whymper came onto the scene. In the Pennine Alps and the Bernese Oberland, as we saw in the previous chapter, great peaks like the Jungfrau, the Finsteraarhorn, the Bernina and Points Gnifetti and Zumstein on Monte Rosa had been scaled by parties of climbers and topographers accompanied by local guides.

The great difference between them and the British did not lie in the latter's technical skills but in their systematic approach. Men born at the foot of the Alps aimed solely at the summit (or at most the summits) that dominated their native valley. The British, however, planned their summer campaigns with military precision, obtaining reports by their predecessors and rushing from

one massif to another. Their field of action was the entire Alpine range, which is why Leslie Stephen coined the famous definition of the Alps: "the playground of Europe."

The list of the feats accomplished in this "Golden Age" of exploratory mountaineering begins in 1855, when Rev. Charles Hudson (one of the first ascensionists who died on the Matterhorn) conquered Point Dufour which, at 4634 metres, is the highest peak in the Monte Rosa massif. With him were British climbers John Birkbeck, E.J. Stephenson, J.G. and C. Smythe, and guides J. and M. Zumtaugwald of Zermatt and Ulrich Lauener of Lauterbrunnen. Three years later, in September 1858, Johann Zumtaugwald, together with Johann Kronig and Hieronymous Brantschen, guided English climber J.K. Davis on the 4545-metre Dom, the highest peak situated entirely in Swiss territory.

In 1859 Francis Fox Tuckett, another of the best British climbers, scaled the solitary ice pyramid of the Aletschhorn (4195 m) in the heart of the Bernese Oberland. He was accompanied by local guides J.J. Bennen and P. Bohren, and by Victor Tairraz from Chamonix. The next year came the turn of Gran Paradiso (4061 m), which was scaled by British climbers J.J. Cowell and W. Dundas with Chamonix guides J. Payot and J. Tairraz. In 1861, John Tyndall made the first serious attempts on the Matterhorn, climbing with guides J.J. Bennen and U. Wenger to the Weisshorn (4505 m), considered by many climbers to be the most attractive rock and ice mountain in the Alps.

On 30th August the same year, the great Michel Croz went into action. With his brother and fellow-guide Jean-Baptiste, Michel led British climbers William Mathews and William Jacob to the summit of Monviso (3841 m), the highest point in the Cottian Alps, which can be clearly seen in all its beauty from the plains of Piedmont and from Turin. Two years later, during the third ascent to the summit, Quintino Sella from Biella and his climbing companions decided that it was time for Italian climbers to challenge

British supremacy, and founded the Club Alpino Italiano for this purpose.

For the time being, however, the British and their guides from Chamonix, Valais and the Bernese Oberland were way ahead of the field. 1864 was not only the year in which Edward Whymper made his first great climbs, but also brought the conquest of the Zinalrothorn (4221 m), the rock pyramid that stands between Zermatt and the lonely Zinal valley. The summit was reached by Leslie Stephen and Francis Craufurd Grove, accompanied by Jakob and Melchior Anderegg, two cousins from Meiringen who made one of the best teams of the day. For the first time in the Western Alps, various pitches verging on the fourth grade were conquered. The next year, in addition to the Aiguille Verte and the Matterhorn, another magnificent peak in the Mont Blanc massif, the Aiguille de Bionnassay (4052 m), was climbed. On 28th July that year British climbers E.N. Buxton, R.J.S. MacDonald and F.C. Grove, guided by Jean-Paul Cachat and Michel Payot, reached the summit by scaling the awesome icy slope of the North-West face, a marvellous ice route that is demanding even for present-day climbers.

48-49 The Aiguille Verte (on the left) and the rocky obelisk of the Dru became an extraordinary playground in the late 19th and early 20th century, when a new generation of climbers systematically tackled the highest and most difficult walls in the Alps. Mont Blanc can be seen in the background of this photo, taken from the Grands Montets.

48 below Melchior Anderegg (1828-1912), born in Meiringen at the foot of the Bernese Oberland, was one of the greatest guides of all time and a master of ice climbing. His most famous ascent was the Brenva Spur on Mont Blanc, which he climbed in 1865. Other important first ascents of his were Monte Disgrazia, the Dent d'Hérens, Point Parrot on Monte Rosa and the Bosses ridge on Mont Blanc.

48 left Adolphus W. Moore (1841-1887), a client of Melchior Anderegg on the Brenva Spur and many other ascents, made the first ascents of the Obergabelhorn, Piz Roseg and the Gross Fiescherhorn, and some of the first winter ascents performed in the Alps. He also took part in two of the first climbing expeditions in the Caucasus range.

49 The efficiency of present-day clothing and gear was still far in the future, but the equipment used by climbers in the late 19th century had made great progress since the time of de Saussure and his guides. Note the hobnailed boots, long ice-axes with wooden handles, thick hempen rope, and the metal lantern containing a candle.

breakfast of hot wine mixed with coffee ("a drink which disgusts me, but was approved by the majority of the party," wrote Moore), and witnessed a sunrise "of indescribable beauty" on the great wall. Next they scaled an awesome serac, and reached the snow-covered ridge (later named Col Moore) which precedes the actual face. Two hours of "assiduous labour" on the rocks brought them to a fearful, unexpected obstacle. In Moore's words, it was "the narrowest and most terrifying ice ridge I'd ever seen."

The leader of the party was Melchior Anderegg, the man from Meiringen of whom Whymper wrote "he is the prince, the Napoleon of guides. His kingdom is the eternal snows, his sceptre an ice-axe." However, it was his cousin Jakob who led the ridge at 8 a.m. Step after step, he opened a slippery path on the "ridge of blue ice, without a single particle of snow" which sloped sheer down to the glacier below. Farther on, the ridge narrowed, and the climbers had to sit astride it for a few dozen metres. Then Jakob got to his feet and started cutting steps again.

A few metres lower down, Moore could not help wondering, not entirely humorously, "what would have happened if someone had slipped down one side – what would the others have done? Would they have flung themselves the other way or not? And what would the outcome have been?".

The grim question was never answered. At 9:30 a.m. the party reached the foot of the next wall of snow, which was "terribly steep" but presented no particular obstacles. Two more hours of back-breaking toil for the guides brought them to the base of the seracs and the long crossing towards Col de la Brenva and the Corridor.

A delicate crossing of a crevasse and a final climb across the mountainside at the foot of "an enormous fringe of icicles" took the party to the ordinary route and Mur de la Côte. At 3 p.m. the group was on the summit, and by 10:30 p.m. they were back in Chamonix. "It was no joke," commented the great Melchior later. "A very interesting route," wrote Moore in the *Alpine Journal*.

1865 represented the culmination of the Golden Age of mountaineering, and was also a year of change.

But British climbers were not interested in conquering only summits. Around 1860, the great virgin slopes of mountains whose summits had already been reached became the next target. The first feat of this kind was the ascent of Mont Blanc starting from Saint-Gervais in 1859. After leaving their guides between the Aiguille and Dôme du Goûter, the climbers reached the 4810-metre summit following an inelegant roundabout route via the Grand Plateau, and the usual Chamonix route on the last section.

This feat was eclipsed two years later, on 18th July 1861, by Leslie Stephen and Francis Fox Tuckett. Accompanied by Oberland guides Melchior Anderegg, Johann-Josef Bennen and Peter Perren, who were more expert on ice than their counterparts from Savoy, they finally scaled the fearful elevated ridge of the Bosses (remember that crampons had not yet been invented!), now crossed by most parties heading for the summit.

In 1865, as already mentioned, three different routes were put up on the Aiguille Verte in just a few days. However, the most outstanding climb from the technical standpoint took place on Mont Blanc the day after the tragic first ascent of the Matterhorn. It was performed by Englishmen George S. Mathews, Adolphus W. Moore, Francis and Horace Walker, accompanied by the great Oberland guides Jakob and Melchior Anderegg.

The party set out from Courmayeur on the 14th July, following the narrow hunters' trails in the wilderness of the Brenva basin, and bivouacked on the edge of the most tortuous glacier in the entire massif. The wall awaiting them was equally awesome.

The climbers set off at 2:45 the next morning after a

After performing the ascent that he had desired more than any other, Edward Whymper gave up the race to the great summits of the Alps. And after a hundred or so first ascents, the men of the Alpine Club (London) began to make way for climbers of other nationalities. In 1866 a Swiss amateur, Edmund von Fellenberg, climbed the awesome North face of the Monch (4099 m), the great peak of the Oberland between the Eiger and the Jungfrau, with guides Christian Michel and Peter Egger. The crux of the ascent is the scaling of the Nollen (nose), a short but challenging ice slope that reaches a 60-degree gradient. This route is much quicker and easier than the Brenva, but the technical skills of the Andereggs were certainly equalled.

By now, only one great mountain in the western Alps had escaped the systematic campaigns of British climbers. It was Mont Meije, a magnificent, difficult rocky ridge in the

50 top This group includes some of the best climbers of the day. On the left is the brilliant guide Christian Almer (1826-1898) from Grindelwald. Next to him is American clergyman Rev. William Coolidge (1850-1926), who took part in 33 summer climbing campaigns in the Alps and made dozens of new ascents. Next are Meta Brevoort and Ulrich Almer, Christian's oldest son, far right.

50-51 The north faces of the Eiger (left) and the Monch (right) are one of the most magnificent sights in the Oberland. The famous grim North face of the Eiger was not to be climbed until 1938. However, Edmund von Fellenberg climbed the Nollen ("Nose"), the steep ice spur on the right of the North face of the Monch as early as 1866, with guides Christian Michel and Peter Egger.

heart of the Dauphiné. Its altitude is "only" 3984 metres, but the difficulty of its walls kept it tantalisingly out of reach of the best climbing teams of the day for years.

The ascent was attempted several times by Rev. William A.B. Coolidge, an American who had moved to Europe as a young man, and had taken part in no less than 33 summer climbing campaigns in the Alps and dozens of first ascents. In 1870, together with a friend, female climber Meta Brevoort, Coolidge reached the Doigt de Dieu, the central peak of Mont Meije, a few metres lower than the Grand Pic.

There, for the first time in 20 years, an all-French team achieved a first-ascent victory. The French team was composed of some very different personalities. The guides were Pierre Gaspard and his son of the same name, who had taken part in numerous great ascents in the Oisans

massif, and their client was young Henri Emmanuel Boileau de Castelnau. Boileau, who had reached the summits of Mont Blanc, the Matterhorn, the Dent Blanche and the Finsteraarhorn in his first summer in the Alps, was the guiding spirit behind the first ascent of the Aiguille de l'Olan and the first crossing of the Pelvoux ridge. During the ascent of the Meije, Boileau urged on the guides when they showed signs of flagging and led some of the toughest pitches himself, including the last, terribly exposed slab that leads to the 3984-metre summit. "Always a wonderfully elevated pitch," as Gaston Rébuffat described it nearly a century later. When the three Frenchmen shook hands on the elevated pinnacle of the Grand Pic de la Meije it was 16th August 1877, and times were changing, partly thanks to them. The saga of conquest was over, and mountaineering was ready to become a sport.

51 top In mountaineering history, the name of Henri Emmanuel Boileau de Castelnau (1815-1923) is associated with the Oisans massif. After the first ascent of the Aiguille de l'Olan and the first crossing of Mont Pelvoux, the Frenchman performed the first ascent of the Meije, a difficult, exposed rock climb, with guides Pierre Gaspard senior and junior in 1877.

51 bottom The South face of the Meije is the most awesome and famous of the many lovely rock walls of the Oisans. Now crossed by dozens of very difficult routes, it was first climbed in 1912 by the team led by Angelo Dibona, inset, one of the greatest guides from Cortina d'Ampezzo. The first ascent to the 3983-metre summit was made in 1877 by way of the Promontoire and the Glacier Carré.

The discovery of the Pale Mountains

The Dolomites of Cadore, 19th September 1857. Accompanied by a chamois hunter from San Vito (probably Giovan Battista Giacin, nicknamed "Sgrinfa"), British climber John Ball approached the vertical walls of Mount Pelmo, one of the tallest and most elegant peaks in the entire chain. After rapidly scaling the scree surrounding the mountain, the pair headed straight for one of the ledges intersecting the huge buttress that slopes south-east from the summit.

"These ledges are so narrow that only chamois deer and their equally agile pursuers can cross them," wrote Ball in his account of the ascent. Sometimes level and sometimes upward sloping, the ledge provides a route that is increasingly exposed but devoid of real difficulties, and was perhaps already known to the braver huntsmen of the district. Almost at the end, however, just a few minutes away from the large hollow leading to the summit, the ledge is interrupted by an overhang that can only be passed by crawling under it or, more elegantly, climbing round it in a totally exposed position.

The guide led the party along the first easy section of the ledge. Then Ball took the lead and was the first to tackle this difficult pitch, now known as "Cat Pitch," which he described in his report as the *Pons Asinorum* ("asses' bridge"). After crossing the scree and snow in the great hollow, the two climbers followed a friable rocky ridge to the 3168-metre peak, which provides a wonderful view over much of the Dolomites.

Born in Ireland in 1818, Ball was on his twelfth summer climbing season in the Alps. The year after the ascent of Mount Pelmo, he became chairman of the Alpine Club, and in 1863 started publication of *Ball's Alpine Guides*, the first ever travel guides to be devoted specifically to walkers and climbers.

His ascent of Mount Pelmo marked the "official" start of mountaineering in the Dolomites, which were trailing far behind the Western Alps. Ball, who had performed ascents in all sectors of the Alpine range, had first travelled to the Dolomites quite by chance, when his interest in botany led him to visit the botanical gardens created by Alberto Parolini in Bassano.

Later, his visits became more frequent, and in 1865 Ball married Alberto's daughter Elisa. However, the Irishman not only had eyes for flowers and his wife, but also for the mountains. It was to be this combination of motives that made him not only the first true climber in the Dolomites but also the prophet of these magnificent mountains among the members of the Alpine Club.

The Dolomites lagged a long way behind Mont Blanc so far as climbing was concerned. As we have seen, the first ascent of the highest peak in the Alps took place in 1786, and was repeated with pomp and circumstance the next year by Horace-Bénédict de Saussure. After Napoleon's defeat at Waterloo, Chamonix and its glaciers soon became fashionable

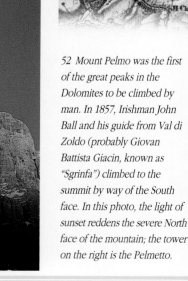

52 Mount Pelmo was the first of the great peaks in the Dolomites to be climbed by man. In 1857, Irishman John Ball and his guide from Val di Zoldo (probably Giovan Battista Giacin, known as "Sgrinfa") climbed to the summit by way of the South face. In this photo, the light of sunset reddens the severe North face of the mountain; the tower on the right is the Pelmetto.

52-53 The "Special Map of the Tyrol and Vorarlberg," published in Vienna in 1869, includes much of the Dolomites. However, a glance at the sector of the map reproduced on this page shows that the portrayal of the mountainous massifs is still rudimentary.

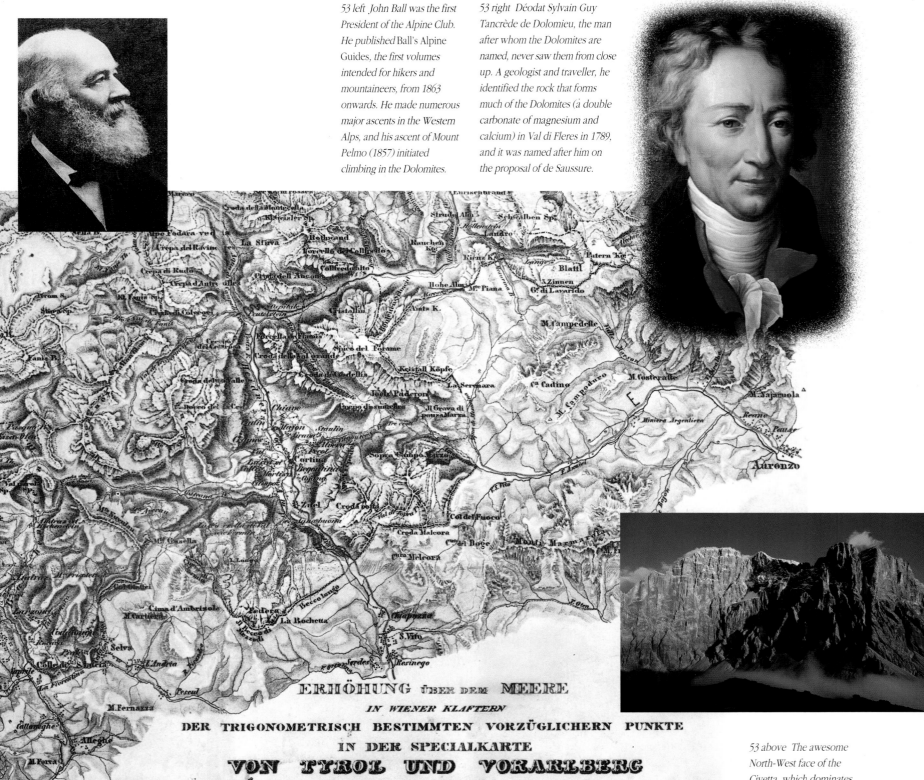

with British travellers. But in the early 19th century, nothing similar had happened in the Dolomites.

Used by armies, pilgrims and merchants but inconvenient of access from the Channel ports, the road leading from Munich and Innsbruck across the Brenner Pass to Bolzano, Trento and Verona was long excluded from the classic itineraries of the Grand Tour. It was Charles Joseph Latrobe, a curious, eccentric traveller with a little German blood in his veins, who finally discovered the wonderful rocks of Val Gardena and Val Badia. And it was only after the ascent by John Ball and his accounts of the climb that the first English-speaking

travellers began to visit the green valleys of the Italian Tyrol (Alto Adige), Trentino and Cadore, which had long remained practically unknown.

Some of them, like Englishmen Josiah Gilbert and George M. Churchill and American traveller Amelia B. Edwards, published enthusiastic accounts of their journeys, thus encouraging their fellow countrymen to visit the "Dolomite Mountains," which were just beginning to be known by the name we still use today.

In 1860, three years after his ascent of Mount Pelmo, Ball attempted the first ascent of Marmolada di Rocca with his friend Birkbeck and Chamonix guide Victor

Tairraz along the easy glacier on the north side, which offers one of the few "Western-style" routes in the Dolomites. However, the skilled party stopped short of the summit.

Next, Francis Fox Tuckett (accompanied by Melchior and Jakob Anderegg, the Swiss guides who had conquered the Brenva spur) made the first "official" ascent of the Civetta, the most impressive rocky peak in the Dolomites, in 1867. However, the mountain had probably already been climbed a few years earlier by Simeone De Silvestro, nicknamed "Piovanèl," one of the first guides in the Veneto Dolomites.

Starting in 1870, the very active Douglas Freshfield and Leslie Stephen (who had dubbed the Alps "the Playground of Europe"), accompanied by Charles Comyns Tucker and Edward Robson Whitwell, performed an intensive series of exploratory climbs, especially on the Pale di San Martino at the southernmost tip of the Dolomites.

"I hoped that at least some of the peaks would prove inaccessible," wrote Leslie Stephen a few years later. But his romantic hope did not come true. One by one, all the highest peaks in the Dolomites were scaled in the 1860s and 1870s. Unlike the situation on Mont Blanc, in the Bernese Oberland and in the Pennine Alps, however, British climbers played only a secondary part on the Dolomite stage.

The major ascents were performed by German-speaking climbers, whose supremacy became even more evident during the years around the first World War and declined only in the Thirties, with the emergence of Italian "sixth-graders" like Emilio Comici and Riccardo Cassin.

KARTE

DOLOMIT ALPEN

Sexten, Ampezzo, Cadore,
Buchenstein, Fassa, Groden,
Enneberg, Prags

Paul Grohmann
WIEN 1875.

The great protagonist of the exploration of the
Dolomites, who played a role comparable to that
performed by Edward Whymper in the Western Alps,
was Paul Grohmann. It was he, in the words of
mountaineering historian Antonio Berti, who "flung
open the doors of climbing history on these divine
mountains of ours with both hands."

Born in Vienna in 1838, Grohmann began to
climb in the Dolomites at about the age of 15. After his
first scrambles in Carinthia and the East Tyrol, he
scaled the Grossglockner, the highest peak of the
Tauern, in 1858. From there, he admired the
unmistakable, weird profiles of the Dolomites in the
distance, to the south.

"I looked at the crown of glaciers on the Tauern
Mountains to the north and the rocky marvels of the
Veneto world to the south... I decided to move to the
Dolomites and climb there. Rarely has a young man
devoted himself to his job with such enthusiasm," he
wrote in 1877 in his memoirs, *Wanderungen in den
Dolomiten*, still one of the most interesting German
climbing books.

Grohmann arrived in Cortina on a stifling afternoon in August 1862, at the end of a long journey by stage-coach. From Dobbiaco onwards, recounts a biographer, "he carefully observed the towering peaks at the sides of the hot, dusty road." Now at the foot of what were to become "his peaks," Paul Grohmann had to tackle a major problem – finding local men to accompany him on the ascents he was determined to make.

His first climb in the Dolomites took place a long way from the Ampezzo valley, on the Marmolada, the "queen" of the Dolomites. After leaving Cortina, the young man scaled Passo Giau and descended to Caprile where he stayed overnight at Osteria del Pezzé, a traditional stopover for the few travellers who crossed the Dolomites in those years.

The next day, accompanied by guide Pellegrino

However, this was his first approach, and it was an act of modesty and wisdom not to attempt the last elevated ridge leading to Punta Penìa. With his typically pioneering spirit, Grohmann considered the 1862 ascent and conquest of Marmolada di Rocca on a par with a mere failed attempt, and spoke little of it in his writings.

He succeeded in reaching the summit of Marmolada di Penìa two years later, on 28th September 1864, accompanied by Angelo and Fulgenzio Dimai, two of the Ampezzo guides who were to become Grohmann's favourite climbing companions between 1863 and 1869 (the others were Santo Siorpaes, Matteo Ossi and above all Francesco Lacedelli, better known as "Checo da Melères").

"They were either forest rangers, chamois hunters or farmers – none of them were guides. However,

when they acted as my guides in ascents that they were also performing for the first time… they exceeded every expectation. All good men, trusted guides, and excellent climbers in general," wrote Grohmann in his *Wanderungen*.

These ascents of the highest and most beautiful peaks turned some of the mountain men into professional, though not full-time guides. The most interesting character among them was "Checo da Melères." "He was the best guide you could hope to find," wrote Paul Grohmann. "I could not but be satisfied with his qualities, his strength, stamina, moderation and pride, and a courage that did not quail before any obstacle. This man did not climb mountains for the poor reward he received, because he was and is one of the wealthiest farmers in Ampezzo: he went out of ambition."

Pellegrini from Rocca Pietore (who had already made an unsuccessful attempt on the summit six years earlier) and a porter, Grohmann climbed the glacier, found the thermometer and note left on the rocks by John Ball, and then reached the summit of Marmolada di Rocca.

Punta Penìa, the highest peak in the Dolomites, was just a few hundred metres away and only 34 metres higher. But the ridge that separated the climbers from it looked too difficult. "It would be suicide to attempt it!" exclaimed Pellegrini.

Later, Grohmann was to tackle more difficult pitches with "his" guides from Cortina to reach Sorapìss, Cristallo and Cima Grande di Lavaredo.

56 top In this early 19th century print, Cortina d'Ampezzo looks very different from now. Some 2200 people lived in the provincial capital and the surrounding hamlets at the time. The main activities of the Ampezzo people were agriculture, sheep-farming and exploitation of the woods. Tourism had not yet arrived.

56 bottom The slopes of the glacier, now crossed by ski trails and lifts, reach the summit ridge of Marmolada di Rocca. The ordinary route on Marmolada di Penìa (on the right), used by Grohmann and his guides in 1864, crosses the right-hand branch of the glacier, a rocky face and the sinuous snow ridge of Schiena de Mul.

57 bottom left Pellegrino Pellegrini, a guide from Rocca Pietore, never became famous, unlike his fellow guides from Cortina and Sesto. However, it was he who guided Paul Grohmann in the first ascent of Marmolada di Rocca in 1862, along the easy but treacherous route that crosses the Marmolada Glacier.

57 This aerial photo clearly shows the contrast between the vertical South face of the Marmolada (left) and the gentle slopes of the glacier that covers the north side of the mountain. In the photo, Marmolada di Rocca almost entirely conceals the higher Marmolada di Penìa.

For Grohmann, 1862 merely gave a taste of what was to come. The next year, guided by the amazing "Checo" (who was then 67!), Grohmann scaled Tofana di Mezzo, the highest peak in the group. It was the first ever ascent of one of the great peaks that enclose the Ampezzo valley.

On the scree at the foot of Tofana di Rozes and Tofana di Mezzo, where the popular trail to the Giussani refuge hut now climbs, Lacedelli asked his client which of the two peaks he proposed to climb. The difference between them was only 19 metres, and was impossible to discern from a distance with the naked eye. Moreover, the survey being carried out for the Tyrol Land Registry was still under way, and the climbers did not have a reliable map.

After a short hesitation, Grohmann opted for the peak on his right, Tofana di Mezzo. "Checo da Melères" set off confidently, crossing a steep, difficult scree slope. Then he turned off to the left, scaled a rocky spur, traversed "a short stretch of highly exposed wall on a narrow ledge," and reached the small glacier that led to the summit ridge and the summit.

A few days later, Grohmann climbed Mount Pelmo

58 top "He was the best guide you could hope to find. He possessed a courage that did not quail before any obstacle. This man did not climb mountains for the poor reward he received, because he was and is one of the wealthiest farmers in Ampezzo: he went out of ambition." This is how Paul Grohmann described Francesco Lacedelli, nicknamed "Checo da Melères" (1796-1886), who accompanied him on the Antelao, Sorapiss and the Tofane.

58 below left Tofana di Rozes, clearly visible from the road that climbs from Cortina up to Passo Falzarego, is one of the most impressive peaks in the Dolomites. The top part of the South face, climbed in 1901 by the young Baronesses von Eotvos, guided by Antonio Dimai, Agostino Verzi and Giovanni Siorpaes from Cortina, can be seen in this photo. Tofana di Mezzo and Tofana di Dentro appear in the background.

with "Checo," accompanied by the latter's nephew Alessandro and the Zugliani brothers from Zoldo. The party ignored Ball's ledge and climbed by a different route, just as elevated but less difficult than the one followed by Ball six years earlier.

It was the first time on a great peak in the Dolomites that the first ascensionists' route had been ignored in favour of a new one. Perhaps this indicates that the huntsmen from Zoldo already knew a route to the great hollow. As always in 19th-century mountaineering, however, it is impossible to establish whether local pioneers had really reached the highest point.

No such doubts are possible with regard to the ascent of the Antelao, performed by Grohmann with the two Lacedellis 12 days after the ascent of Mount Pelmo. Matteo Ossi, the huntsman from Resìnego who went with them, was known in San Vito for having "already reached the summit."

However, at the end of the long but easy rock slabs of the Laste, where a short vertical precipice seems to bar

the way, Ossi stopped, hesitated, and was unable to identify the correct route. "Checo" took the lead, scaled a steep chimney, and led the party to the summit, where there was no trace that anyone had preceded them.

Summer of 1864 began with Tofana di Rozes, omitted the previous year, which Grohmann climbed with "Checo," Santo Siorpaes and Angelo Dimai. Next came Marmolada di Penìa, the highest peak in the Dolomites, which he scaled on 16th September with Angelo and Fulgenzio Dimai. Twelve days later came Sorapìss, where Grohmann, guided by "Checo" Lacedelli and Angelo Dimai, performed a courageous crossing.

The ascent took place from the north, via Passo Tre Croci, Tondi del Sorapìss, Fopa di Mattia and the spectacular summit ridge. During the descent, "elated and made somewhat imprudent by our victory," the three climbers made for the Forcella Grande scree slopes, until a precipice seemed to bar their way.

Lacedelli managed to get down unaided, but the pitch was too difficult for the others. Dimai let down Grohmann with the rope, and in order to get down himself was forced to "sling the rope" over "a small but strong spur of rock." Cited as a minor detail in the *Wanderungen*, this was probably the first example of abseiling in the history of mountaineering.

In 1865 Paul Grohmann completed his collection of the great peaks of Ampezzo with the ascent of Cristallo, which he scaled on 14th September with Antonio Dimai and Santo Siorpaes. His last great climbing season was in 1869, when Grohmann, now led by guides Franz Innerkofler and Peter Salcher from Sesto, successively climbed the lonely Punta dei Tre Scarperi, the imposing Sassolungo pyramid and the difficult, inhospitable Cima Grande di Lavaredo.

58 bottom Santo Sorpaes (1832-1900) was one of the best guides in Cortina in the late 19th century. Apart from Grohmann, he accompanied Edward Robson Whitwell and Francis Fox Tucket in their climbs. He made around 30 first ascents, including the first ever ascent of Cimon della Pala and Piz Popena, performed in 1870 with Whitwell and Swiss guide Christian Lauener.

All these were more difficult climbs than those of the preceding years, in which 3rd grade pitches were scaled.

Grohmann's years of adventures in the Dolomites were brought to an end by the depression of 1873, when his bank failed and he was ruined. At the age of only 35, the pioneer of mountaineering in the Dolomites, a wealthy young man accustomed to travel, suddenly found himself penniless. Forced to make a living, he published *Karte den Dolomit-Alpen* in 1875 and *Wanderungen in den Dolomiten* two years later (1877). In 1873 Cortina town council made him an honorary citizen, and in 1898 a monument bearing his portrait was unveiled in Val Gardena. For Grohmann, however, the carefree, adventurous climbing years were over. "The memory of those happy hours will go with me to the threshold of eternity," he wrote in his diary at the turn of the century. Grohmann's short climbing career paved the way for the birth of mountaineering and the associated infrastructures in the Dolomite valleys as well as the mountains.

58-59 This photo, taken around 1880 at the end of a hunting party organised by Baron Sommaruga, shows some of the first Alpine guides from Cortina acting as hunting guides. Pietro Siorpaes, Davide "Tadeo" Ghedina, Luigi "de Zinto" Menardi and Alessandro Lacedelli can be recognised, among others.

59 top right One of the leading guides associated with Paul Grohmann was Angelo Dimai (in the centre in this period photo), who accompanied the Viennese climber on

Sorapìss, Cristallo and Marmolada di Penìa.

59 centre right Almost the complete list of the major first ascents performed by Paul Grohmann in the Dolomites, written by Angelo Dimai, appears in the first pages of his guide's logbook.

59 bottom Tofana di Mezzo, less spectacular than the nearby Tofana di Ròzes, has become easily approachable since the installation of the cable car that leads from Cortina to the 3244-metre summit. However, it is still the highest peak in the

massif, and was the first great mountain in the Ampezzo area to be climbed by Paul Grohmann and his guides. The ascent took place in August 1863, when

Grohmann was accompanied for the first time by Francesco Lacedelli, nicknamed "Checo da Melères." It was to be the start of a long partnership.

60 top left This picture, dating from the late 19th century, shows some of the best guides to the Pale di San Martino. On the left is Bortolo Zagonel, and on his right are Michele Bettega, Virgilio Zecchini and Antonio Tavernaro.

60 top right Though less elegant than the nearby Campanile Basso, Campanile Alto di Brenta (on the right in this photo) is one of the most interesting and popular peaks in the Brenta Dolomites. The first ascent was made in 1887 by Gottfried Merzbacher and guide Bonifacio Nicolussi via the great chimney that cuts through the north side.

60 bottom left Among the guides to the Dolomites, an important place is held by Michele Bettega (1853-1937). Born at San Martino di Castrozza, he was one of the leading explorers of the Pale, where he made the first ascents of Pale di San Martino and Cima Canali. Elsewhere in the Dolomites, he made the first ascent of the South face of the Marmolada and the first winter ascents of Cima Grande and Cima Piccola di Lavaredo.

TARIFFA

fissata in conformità alle Ordinanze dell'Eccelsa I. R. Luogotenenza in Innsbruch 11 Maggio 1865 e 4 Settembre 1871 concernenti l'istituzione ed il Regolamento delle Guide di Montagna dall'I. R. Capitanato Distrettuale d'Ampezzo per le gite sia a piedi che con cavallo o veicoli, preso per punto di partenza Cortina.

La mancia non essendo calcolata sarà a piacere.

In 1865, the Lieutenant-Governor's District of Innsbruck issued an order for "the institution of Mountain Guides in the Captaincy of Ampezzo." One after another, professional climbers were given a *Bergfuhrer-buch* (mountain guide's licence) similar to those in use today, and in 1876 the first official fee scales were published, countersigned by the District Captain.

Cortina was not the only place where climbing was becoming popular. At Sesto in Val Pusteria, the Innerkofler family, which we shall be meeting in the next chapter, was beginning to make a name for itself. And outside the Adige valley, in the Brenta Dolomites, Bonifacio and Matteo Nicolussi, farmers and huntsmen from Molveno, came onto the scene. The two brothers, who were skilled bear hunters, demonstrated an equally sure aim in their first ascents of Brenta Alta, Crozzòn and other peaks on the massif.

It was not until a few years later that top-level professional guides started to operate farther south, between the Pale di San Marino and Mount Agnèr. The most outstanding among them was Michele Bettega of Primiero.

As throughout the Alps, the last quarter of the century saw the introduction and rapid multiplication of refuge huts in the Dolomites. The first hut was not actually a building, but an artificial cave excavated on the initiative of the Agordo section of the Italian Alpine Club, just below Marmolada di Rocca.

This rudimentary and by no means comfortable structure, inaugurated in 1876, was abandoned a few years later. In 1880, the first masonry refuge was built at Bocca di Brenta. Subsequently, this type of building rapidly multiplied all over the range, from the Tre Cime to the mountains around Cortina, from the Catinaccio to the Pale di San Martino.

60 bottom right In the last decades of the 19th century, excursions and ascents accompanied by guides were popular among holidaymakers. This is demonstrated by the first price list prepared by the Cortina guides, duly approved by the Imperial authorities in Innsbruck.

60-61 The winter snow, the aerial photo and the warm light of sunset make even the most modest peaks in the Brenta Dolomites beautiful, like these towers not far from the Sfùlmini range.

61 right This picture of the ordinary route on Cimon della Pala shows the elegant style and rudimentary gear used by climbers in the Dolomites in the late 19th century. The climber in this photo is tackling the exposed wall that follows the bus del gat pitch.

Cima Tosa in 1865, was a fervent Hapsburg loyalist, while the latter, one of the founders of the Trentino Mountaineers' Society, was a colonel in Garibaldi's army and acquitted himself with honour at the Battle of Bezzecca in 1866.

All the leading climbers from Veneto were nationalists, starting with Cesare Tomè, the most active Italian on the Dolomite scene in the 1860s and 1870s. Born in Agordo and fond of the southern massifs of the Dolomites, Tomè, who was soon nicknamed "Signor Cimone," performed the first ascent of Mount Agner in 1875 with Martino Gnech and Tomaso Del Col, a bricklayer from Voltago who was destined to become one of the best guides in the southern Dolomites.

The next year, together with Alberto de Falkner (who was Swiss by birth but so delighted by the new Italy that he enrolled as a volunteer in Garibaldi's army), Tomè

In the meantime, what had become of Italian climbers, who had taken a back seat during the first two decades of climbing in the Dolomites? The Club Alpino Italiano (CAI), founded at the foot of the Western Alps, rapidly grew in all the largest cities of Italy (including Rome, Naples and Palermo), but neglected the Dolomites until the early years of the 20th century.

In the *CAI Bulletin*, the mountains of the Abruzzo and Tuscan Apennines appear far more often than the Marmolada or the Tre Cime, which remained wholly foreign to Italian mountaineers and walkers at that period. In fact, although the Lacedellis, the Dimais and the other guides were Italian-speaking, Cadore became Italian only in 1866, while Trentino and Cortina were part of the Austro-Hungarian Empire until 1918. It is thus no accident that the history of the first Italian climbers on those peaks is closely linked to the political situation.

In the valleys of Trento, the Italian-speaking community was strongly divided between Irredentism and loyalism. In the mountains, the two groups coexisted without too many problems, as demonstrated by the friendship between Giuseppe Loss and Nepomuceno Bolognini. The former, who performed the first ascent of

62 centre The Sass Maor massif (left) and Cima della Madonna are clearly seen by those observing the Pale from San Martino di Castrozza. The former was climbed in 1875 by a party led by Battista della Santa and François Devouassoud. The Spigolo del Velo on Cima della Madonna, here in sun and shade, was conquered in 1921 by Gunther Langes and Erwin Merlet.

performed the first Italian ascents of Cimon della Pala and Marmolada. In 1877 he made the first ascent of Cima Immink, another of the loveliest peaks in the Pale di San Martino, with Santo Siorpaes and the loyal Tomaso Del Col.

Inspired by an undying passion for his home mountains, Tomè continued his explorations until the end of the century, tackling some extremely difficult walls such as the South face of the Marmolada and the North-West face of Civetta at an advanced age, using some rather unorthodox equipment such as large pegs which were the forerunners of modern bolts.

"Mister Cimone" was not a nationalist in the strict sense of the word, and one of his favourite climbing companions, apart from de Falkner, was German Count Heinrich Welsperg. However, ensuring a high-profile Italian presence in the Dolomites became one of the most important aims of the excursions, publications and "congresses" (really climbing rallies) organised by the Agordo section of the CAI. The same applied to Società degli Alpinisti Tridentini (Trento Mountaineers' Society) which, in addition to climbing and scientific activities, indulged in pro-Italian propaganda. The society was closed down by the Austrian authorities in 1876, but reconstituted the next year.

There were still 40 years to go before the outbreak of the Great War, but fire was smouldering under the ashes.

63 bottom left
Cesare Tomè, born at Agordo and a regular climber in the southernmost massifs of the Dolomites, was one of the promoters of Italian climbing in the "Pale Mountains." He made the first ascents ever of Mount Agner and Cima Immink and the first Italian ascents of Cimon della Pala and the Marmolada.

63 bottom right
On 18th August 1875, Tomaso Del Col, Martino Gnech and Cesare Tomè made the first ascent of the Agner. On 4th September came the turn of the British.

62 bottom The first Tosa refuge hut at Bocca di Brenta, completed in 1882, was the first to be built on the massif by SAT. To prepare for its construction, artificial steps were built along the two trails leading to the pass; these were the first aid routes in the Dolomites. A few years later, the Bremen section of DOAV built a larger refuge hut next to it.

62-63 With its walls of solid dolomite, small glaciers and scree, the Brenta massif (shown here in winter) has been a favourite haunt with climbers from Trento since the mid-19th century. Cima Tosa, the highest peak in the group, was first climbed in 1865.

Heroes on granite

It was 9 a.m. on 15th July 1880. The theatre of action was the inhospitable South-West face of the Grands Charmoz, one of the loveliest granite towers overlooking the Mer de Glace. After 10 days of storms the sun was shining again on the Grépon, the Aiguille de Blaitière and the awesome obelisk of the Dru, but the cracks and ledges were still encrusted with glaze ice and snow. However, that was not enough to put off a team of three climbers.

The guiding spirit behind the attempt was the best British climber of the day, 35-year-old Albert Frederick Mummery, born not far from the White Cliffs of Dover. Today he climbed third, carrying a knapsack weighed down by "a spare rope, two wooden pegs, the food, an ice-axe, a bottle of champagne and a flask of brandy."

Like Edward Whymper before him, Mummery was the brains behind the expedition; the one who decided on the destination and the ascent route. However, unlike the conqueror of the Matterhorn, Mummery was perfectly capable of (and enjoyed) leading. After conquering the Grands Charmoz and the Grépon with guides, he repeated those routes as leader. On some other peaks, starting with the Dent du Requin, he later made the first ever ascent, again without guides.

Only 15 years had passed since the conquest of the Matterhorn, but Mummery's style of climbing was very different from that of Whymper and Moore. For him, conquest and discovery were still essential, but he was as interested in how an ascent was performed as where. Mountaineering, once a feat of exploration and conquest, had begun to turn into a sport.

"I'm afraid that in the pages which follow, the accounts of rocks and seracs, storms and clear skies will not be accompanied by any scientific or topographical contribution, nor any kind of lesson," wrote Mummery in the introduction to his memoirs. "The mere name of theodolites and topographical maps is an abomination to me. I dedicate these pages to all those who, like me, think that mountaineering is pure enjoyment."

This was not just talk. On the Matterhorn, which he had scaled by way of the difficult Z'mutt and Furggen ridges, Mummery's thoughts turned "to my beloved Aiguille des Charmoz." On Mont Blanc, he had turned back when only a few hours away from the Grands Mulets because he was bored by the interminable hike on snow, "an occupation which calls to mind the treadmill on which British convicts are made to work non-stop."

On the Grands Charmoz, the going soon got tough. "*Es muss gehen*" (we've got to get through), muttered

Alexander Burgener, one of the best guides from Valais, who had accompanied Mummery on numerous tricky climbs. Unlike many of his fellow guides, Burgener did not consider it demeaning to let his client lead if he so wished. But on the most difficult pitches on rock, Burgener gave the lead to Benedikt Venetz, known as *l'Indien*, a highly skilled climber who proved to be the party's secret weapon on several occasions.

The crux of the ascent was a gully around a dozen metres long, which the three men found to be entirely covered in glaze ice. Burgener tackled the pitch first. He cut numerous footholds in the ice and braced himself as firmly as possible. Then Venetz moved into the lead, pulling himself up with the help of his companion's

shoulders, head and ice-axe. When he took his foot off the ice-axe, Venetz looked to Mummery as if he was "clinging like a cat to the slippery projections on the great icicle." After a few dramatic moments, a hail of stones and a yodel announced that the gully had been conquered. Burgener and the Englishman scaled the overhang by relying on the "persuasive influence" of the rope. At 11:45 a.m. the party uncorked a bottle of champagne on the summit. In the valley bottom, hotelier Couttet set off fire-crackers to celebrate the occasion.

For Mummery and his companions, the Grands Charmoz ascent was merely the first in a long series of conquests. On 30th July 1881, accompanied only by

Mountaineering

64 top *Englishman Albert Frederick Mummery, who was born in Dover in 1855 and died in 1895 during an attempted ascent of Nanga Parbat, was the most outstanding climber on Mont Blanc in the last years of the 19th century. His greatest climbs include the first ascents of the Grands Charmoz, the Dent du Requin and the Grépon, and the Y-shaped couloir on the Aiguille Verte.*

64-65 *The impressive range which includes the icy Aiguille Verte and the rocky obelisk of the Dru was one of the favourite venues with the best teams climbing in the Mont Blanc massif in the late 19th century. This photo shows the range from Chamonix, in winter.*

65 top *The other favourite location of Albert F. Mummery, Alexander Burgener and their climbing companions was the Aiguilles de Chamonix chain. The first ascent of the Aiguille des Grands Charmoz, clearly visible on the left of the photo, was made by Mummery, Burgener and Venetz in 1880. The following year the same team made the first ascent of the Grépon.*

65 centre *"Mummery's crack" on the Grépon, some 15 metres high, is one of the most famous pitches on Mont Blanc, and is still a good test for those wishing to tackle the typical cracks of the Aiguilles. This photo shows Mummery leading the pitch in 1892. Eleven years earlier, during the first ascent, the pitch had been conquered by Benedikt Venetz.*

65 bottom *The manners and features of Valais guide A. Burgener might have seemed to clash with Mummery's culture and laconic British humour, but the partnership between the two produced some outstanding ascents. Burgener climbed the Kuffner ridge of Mont Maudit and the Z'mutt ridge of the Matterhorn with other clients.*

Burgener, Mummery scaled the dangerous Y-shaped couloir of the Aiguille Verte. Two days later, the party tackled the East face of the Grépon, which overlooks the Mer de Glace. This time, Venetz was climbing with them. But after scaling the first two-thirds of the route, the three men decided to turn back.

However, the conquest of the Grépon was only a matter of time. Mummery, Burgener and Venetz were back in action on 5th August, this time via the rocks on the side that overlooks the Nantillons Glacier. The start was the same as for the ascent to the Grands Charmoz. A number of uncomplicated pitches took the party to the foot of a smooth crack around 15 metres high, now famous as "Mummery's crack." However, it was Venetz who went up first, jamming his hands and left foot into the crack and smearing the smooth slab on the right.

The ridge was now only a few metres away. Then a series of elevated passages presenting little difficulty (the *Rateau de chèvre*, the *Vire à bicyclette* and the *Fissure en "Z"*) took Mummery, Burgener and Venetz to the summit of the Grépon, where the customary firecrackers let off by M. Couttet in the valley bottom were answered by the "far more exhilarating pop" of yet another champagne cork.

In 1885 the second ascent of the Grépon was made by Henri Dunod with guides François and Gaspard Simond and Auguste Tairraz. On the summit, Dunod picked up the ice-axe left behind by Mummery.

66 left The awesome slabs of the West face of the Dru were impossible to climb with 19th-century gear. However, the two peaks of the mountain were climbed from the side overlooking the Charpoua Glacier. In 1878 Clinton T. Dent and J.W. Hartley, guided by Alexander Burgener and Kaspar Maurer, conquered the Grand Dru. The following year, Jean Charlet-Straton and his party reached the summit of the Petit Dru.

67 below In this photo, taken in 1904, some outstanding professionals appear among the Courmayeur guides, such as Laurent Croux and Joseph Pétigax (fourth and sixth from the left respectively in the front row).

In 1892, Mummery was back; this time he took his friends John N. Collie, Norman Hastings and William C. Slingsby to the summit, leading the infamous crack himself. By now, however, other men were ready to tackle a new challenge offered by Mont Blanc: the three magnificent rock towers that encircled the great mountains conquered by the climbers of Whymper's generation. The most obvious challenge for those observing the massif from Chamonix was the Dru, the rocky obelisk that flanks the Aiguille Verte and dominates the Mer de Glace with its vertical West face. The ascent from this side was quite unthinkable for the mountaineers of the late 19th century.

However, the same did not apply to the south side of the mountain overlooking the harsh Charpoua

66 right One of the best Chamonix guides in the last years of the century was Jean Charlet-Straton, who made the first winter ascent of Mont Blanc (1876) and the first ascent of the Petit Dru (1879). The abseiling technique was used systematically for the first time during this latter climb, performed with Frédéric Folliguet and Prosper Payot.

67 above This photo, taken in 1900, shows that the ordinary route on the Grépon had already become a classic among mountaineers. While two climbers have already reached the 3482-metre summit and a companion is about to join them, a second team is tackling the Vire à bicyclette, the wide but exposed ledge between the Grand Gendarme and the summit.

glacier, which was conquered on 12th September 1878 by British climbers Clinton T. Dent and J.W. Hartley, accompanied by Kaspar Maurer and the ubiquitous Alexander Burgener.

The following year a climber from Chamonix, Jean Charlet-Straton, planned and made the ascent of the nearby but more difficult Petit Dru, which marks the culmination of the North and West walls and the South-West corner of the mountain, where Walter Bonatti achieved one of his greatest feats in 1955. During the ascent, in which Straton climbed with Frédéric Folliguet and Prosper Payot, the 400-metre route tested the three men to their limit. During the descent, the party used the abseiling technique systematically for the first time to deal with numerous vertical pitches.

66–67 At the end of the 19th century, the peaks surrounding the Talèfre glacial basin were among the most popular on Mont Blanc. Teams of climbers heading for the Aiguille Verte (in the centre of the photo) by way of the wide Whymper couloir joined those making for the Drus or crossing the glacier towards Aiguilles Mummery and Ravenel and the Aiguille du Triolet.

68 top Nowadays, the tourists who take the cable car that connects Courmayeur to Chamonix come very close to the Col du Géant. The trip over the glacier, which is still very interesting, was a must at the turn of the century. This photo of the period shows a team, still without crampons, crossing a great crevasse.

68 bottom Émile Rey, born in Courmayeur in 1846 and nicknamed "le prince des guides" by his clients and colleagues, was one of the best guides of all time from Valle d'Aosta. Among his

major ascents were the Péuterey ridge of Mont Blanc and the first ascent of the Aiguille Blanche de Peutérey. He died in 1896, probably due to illness, while descending the Dent du Géant.

68-69 Despite its height of 3774 metres, the Aiguille Noire is only the first step in the gigantic staircase represented by the ridge that continues towards the sky with the Aiguille Blanc (4108 metres, recognisable by the snowy triangle of the summit) and Mont Blanc (4810 metres).

69 top right The Dent du Géant, an unmistakable sight in the Courmayeur landscape, is one of the loveliest granite peaks in the Mont Blanc range. This photo, taken from the Dent du Géant, shows the sheer South face (to the right, in the sun) and the dark profile of the North face, which was used for the 1st ascent in 1882 and is now the route to the summit.

69 bottom right Jean-Joseph Maquignaz (1829-1890) took part in the attempted ascent of the Matterhorn in 1865, which ended when they found that Whymper was already on the summit. The climber from Valtournanche got even with the first crossing of the Matterhorn (1868) and the conquest of the Dent du Géant (1882).

However, great rocky pinnacles are to be found not only on the French side of Mont Blanc. The Aiguille Noire de Peutérey, which dominates Val Vény and the Brenva Glacier, was climbed on 5th August by Lord Wentworth, accompanied by Émile Rey and Jean-Baptiste Bich. This was the first great feat on the massif to be planned and carried out by men from Valle d'Aosta.

Next came the Dent du Géant, a peak of relatively modest height but exceptional elegance, which stands on the great divide of the massif and was described as "steep, sharp and fierce" by poet Giosuè Carducci.

In 1871, Edward R. Whitwell made the first attempt on the Dent du Géant with guides Christian and Ulrich Lauener of Lauterbrunnen. "This pinnacle can be classed among the impossible ones," wrote the Englishman. Subsequent attempts were made by Jean Charlet-Straton and an Italian party, which attempted to fire a rope onto the summit ridge of the Dent with the aid of a rocket.

In 1880, Mummery and Burgener attempted the ascent. From the Col du Géant the pair easily reached the snow ledge at the foot of the pinnacle known as the "Gum." From there they moved to the North-West face, then climbed for some 50 metres to the base of a slab that barred the way. Mummery left a famous note in a crack expressing his opinion: "Absolutely Inaccessible by Fair Means."

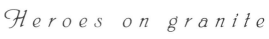 *Heroes on granite*

The first ascent was organised by Jean-Joseph Maquignaz, one of the best guides to the Matterhorn, aided by his cousins Baptiste and Daniel. Their clients on this occasion were Alessandro, Alfonso, Corradino and Gaudenzio Sella, sons and heirs of the family from Biella which had already given to mountaineering Quintino Sella (Prime Minister of the Kingdom of Italy and founder of the Club Alpino Italiano) and Vittorio Sella, famous mountain photographer and climbing companion of the Duca degli Abruzzi on many of the world's peaks.

It was Maquignaz who chose his clients. "I want the Italian flag to be planted up there for the first time... I contacted you because I knew you would understand and follow me," he wrote to Quintino Sella. On 18th July 1882, the guides and climbers reached the first spartan hut on the Col du Géant. Then the Maquignaz family began their coming and going on the Dent.

The men from Valle d'Aosta conquered the great slab by ignoring Mummery's "fair means" and cutting steps in the rock. Then they fixed spikes and ropes to facilitate their clients' ascent. On 28th July, the Maquignaz trio reached the summit for the first time. They returned the next day, leading the four Sella cousins. The day after that, great celebrations awaited the party back in Courmayeur.

A few years later, the ordinary route on the Dent was fully equipped with hempen ropes similar to those on the ordinary route on the Matterhorn. This facilitated the work of the guides, but was criticised by those climbers who remembered Mummery's message.

70 top and centre Alessandro, 25 (top) and Alfonso, 17 (bottom) were the oldest and youngest of the four Sella cousins who took part in the first historic ascent of the Dent du Géant.

70-71 bottom This photo, taken by Vittorio Sella in 1883, shows one of the classic views of Mont Blanc. In the background, the scene is dominated by Mont Blanc de Courmayeur, the highest peak, and Col de la Brenva. The Grand Flambeau and Tour Ronde can be seen in the foreground, and the dark Aiguilles Marbrées stand on the left.

71 top In this photo, the Dent du Géant is surrounded by some of the spectacular 4000-metre peaks in the Mont Blanc massif such as the Aiguille Verte (left), the Aiguille de Rochefort and the Grandes Jorasses, whose slopes overlook the Italian Val Ferret.

71 centre Vittorio Sella photographed the Dent du Géant from the "Gum." The route followed by the Maquignaz-Sella party crossed to the left as far as the North edge of the Dent and then just above it, as far as Punta Sella, the leftmost of the two summit towers.

71 bottom left and right Gaudenzio (left) and Corradino Sella (right) completed the family quartet led expertly by the Maquignaz family to the northern summit of the Dent.

72 top left *Although ropes were still made of hemp and hobnailed boots were still worn, climbing on granite in the Aiguilles de Chamonix reached an exceptional level in those years, as demonstrated by the team shown in this photo, tackling the smooth slabs of the Grands Charmoz.*

72 top right *Narrow or wide, rough or smooth, of all shapes and sizes, cracks are legion on the walls of the Aiguilles de Chamonix. Climbers in Mont Blanc at this period devised a sophisticated (though tiring) technique of scaling this sort of pitch.*

72 bottom *This group photo shows one of the best teams in the "Golden Age" of climbing in the Western Alps. The British clients (seated) are Thomas S. Kennedy and Marshall. The Swiss guides who accompanied them are Johann Fischer (left) and the great Ulrich Almer.*

72-73 *In the late 19th and early 20th century, Chamonix and the French side of Mont Blanc were the favourite playground of climbers from all over Europe. In this photo, the Aiguille Verte and the Dru (on the far left) and the Aiguilles de Chamonix range stand out in the sun. Mont Blanc and its glaciers are on the right, mostly in shadow.*

Some magnificent ascents on ice were performed in the last quarter of the century. The great Jakob Anderegg, who had climbed the Brenva Spur in 1865, scaled the steep side of the Aiguille Verte overlooking the Argentière glacier eleven years later. The Couloir Cordier, which exceeds a 55-degree gradient in some places, is commonly climbed nowadays by mountaineers equipped with modern ice-axe traction gear, but its ascent with nothing more than an old-fashioned ice-axe was an outstanding feat.

The great high-altitude ascents on the Italian side of Mont Blanc continued in 1872, when Thomas S. Kennedy and guides Jean-Antoine Carrel and Johann Fischer opened the Rochers de la Tournette route. Thirteen years later, Émile Rey, together with Swiss guides Ambros Supersaxo and Alois Anthamatten, guided the Englishman H. Seymour King on the Aiguille Blanche de Peutérey, the most difficult of the "over-4000" peaks in the Mont Blanc massif. In 1887 Alexander Burgener, Josef Furrer and a porter guided Viennese client Moritz von Kuffner in the first ascent of the South-East ridge of Mont Maudit. In 1888 Corradino, Erminio, Gaudenzio and Vittorio Sella, accompanied by Émile Rey and Jean-Joseph and Daniel

Maquignaz, performed the first winter crossing of Mont Blanc.

On 1st August 1890 Giovanni Bonin, Luigi Grasselli and Don Achille Ratti (who later became Pope Pius XI), guided by Joseph Gadin and Alexis Proment, descended what is now the ordinary Italian route to Mont Blanc via the Aiguilles Grises glacier. In 1893, Émile Rey, Christian Klucker and César Ollier guided Paul Gussfeldt along the Peutérey Ridge, one of the most spectacular routes in the Alps.

The early 20th century saw the entry of a new generation of climbers onto the scene. An outstanding feat was performed in the first summer of the century by Viennese climbers Heinrich Pfannl, Thomas Maischberger and Franz Zimmer, who climbed to the Dent du Géant by the North

ridge without using artificial aid of any kind. The action then moved to the Aiguilles de Chamonix.

In 1901 Émile Fontaine and the Ravanel brothers climbed the West face of the Aiguille de Blaitière. Next came the Dent du Crocodile, the Dent du Caiman, the Aiguille des Pèlerins and the Peigne, reached by climbing pitches verging on the fifth grade in hobnailed boots. Fontaine was particularly fond of the Aiguilles, where he scaled nearly all the peaks. Joseph "le Rouge" Ravanel was the first Chamonix guide to emulate the feats of the best Swiss and Italian professionals. Another French victory was won in 1904, when H.E. Beaujart and guide Joseph Simond reached the Aiguille de la République by throwing a rope.

73 top For many tourists who visited Chamonix in the late 19th century, one of the most exciting parts of the visit was a guided tour of the seracs and crevasses of the Bossons, the Jonction or the Mer de Glace.

73 bottom Joseph "le Rouge" Ravanel, one of the greatest guides from Chamonix, put up numerous new routes on

the granite of Mont Blanc. His most noteworthy ascents include the North-West ridge of the Aiguille de Blaitière, the North ridge of the Moine, the Z-shaped crack of the Drus, and the crossing from the Aiguille Sans Nom to the Aiguille Verte. This photo shows him on the summit of the Aiguille de l'M in the Aiguilles de Chamonix.

However, the best ascents in the early years of the 20th century were mainly performed by a new generation of Swiss guides and British climbers. Franz and Josef Lochmatter often climbed with Irishman Valentine J.E. Ryan. The team's masterpiece was the 1906 ascent of the magnificent East spur of the Aiguille du Plan in the wild *envers* of the Aiguilles de Chamonix. This is a very impressive route even nowadays. Access is difficult because of the huge bergschrund, which presents a series of difficult cracks that have to be climbed by jamming. The Lochmatters and Ryan scaled them in hobnailed boots, without pitons. A contemporary and often a rival of Ryan's was Englishman Geoffrey Winthrop Young, a confident, all-round climber who used to scale the walls of Trinity College, Cambridge for practice. He climbed with Josef Knubel, a guide from Sankt Niklaus, nicknamed *Le Petit J* by his robust colleagues from Valais because of his short stature. The best year for Knubel and Young was 1911. On 9th August the pair, together with H.O. Jones and Karl Blodig, scaled the Brouillard ridge on Mont Blanc in 7 hours. A few days later, accompanied by Laurent Croux, Young, Jones and Knubel descended the Hirondelles ridge of the Grandes Jorasses, which was considered impossible to ascend (and planted only one piton!). Two days later the party climbed to the summit by the West ridge, crossing Points Young, Margherita, Elena, Croz, Whymper and Walker.

On 10th August, the trio (who had been joined by Ralph Todhunter and Henri Brocherel) commenced their assault on the awe-inspiring East face of the Grépon which, with its 800 metres of slabs, spurs and cracks, dominates the Mer de Glace. This was where Mummery, Burgener and Venetz had had to give up 30 years earlier. The 1911 party, however, climbed at

top speed, got over the cracks and terraces on the lower part of the wall, and continued on a long and difficult spur.

A hundred metres below the summit, the party tackled an exceptionally difficult smooth chimney. While the guides sought a solution, the Britons were below, out of sight. "Our ears told us that Josef and Brocherel were grappling with something particularly ferocious," wrote Young. "The long chimney ended under an overhanging wall," added Todhunter. "The only way of climbing it was to stand on a companion's head to get across a smooth, steep slab, turn a corner to the right and scale a second equally exposed slab with no handholds. This pitch certainly approaches the limits of what is possible."

After scaling the chimney they came out onto the ridge, just a few metres from the summit. A deviation of just a few metres would have led to the ordinary route, but Young and Knubel were not interested in short cuts. The guide tackled the last smooth crack; where it closed he had to wedge in an ice-axe again, then stand on its shaft. This final crack was later classed as upper fifth grade (with rubber soles and some pitons already planted). In 1992 a rating of lower 7th grade was proposed for the bottom chimney, which was avoided by nearly all the repeaters of this route.

74 left One of the greatest Swiss guides of all time was Franz Lochmatter (1878-1933). Born into a family of guides at Sankt Niklaus, he climbed the South face of the Taschhorn, the East ridge of the Aiguille du Plan and the North-West ridge of the Aiguille de Blaitière with his brother Josef and Valentine J.E. Ryan.

74 right In summer 1911, the team formed by Englishmen G.W. Young (right) and H.O. Jones (left), accompanied by Swiss guide Josef Knubel (centre), took a week to climb the West ridge of the Grandes Jorasses and the East face of the Grépon. During the second ascent the trio were joined by Englishman Ralph Todhunter and Courmayeur guide Henri Brocherel.

75 left This photo shows the elegant snowy arabesques of the ridge that connects the Aiguille du Midi to the Aiguille du Plan. This route presents no great technical difficulty, but climbers who tackle it need to be very sure-footed.

75 top Karl Blodig (1859-1956), an ophthalmologist and skilled climber, became quite famous in the early 20th century when he was the first to climb all the Alpine peaks over 4000 metres high. His book The High Mountains of the Alps, published in German in 1923, is one of the best-selling mountaineering books of all time.

75 bottom This photo, taken from the summit of Mont Blanc, shows (from left) the Aiguille du Midi, Mont Maudit, Mont Blanc du Tacul and the Aiguilles du Diable. Col de la Brenva and the ordinary route to the summit of Mont Blanc from Col du Midi can be seen in the foreground. The Brenva wall is on the right of the climbers.

76 left The Brenva wall is crossed by some of the greatest routes on Mont Blanc and in the Alps. On the left is the Brenva Spur, conquered in 1865 by the team of G.S. Mathews, A.W. Moore, F. and H. Walker, guided by Jakob and Melchior Anderegg. Farther to the left are the three routes devised and climbed between the wars by Englishman Thomas Graham Brown: the Red Sentinel (1927), the Major route (1928) and Via della Pera (1933).

76 above Although it was climbed as early as 1865 by a party led by the great Michel Croz, the Arête du Moine on the Aiguille Verte is a great high-altitude ascent which leads to one of the most majestic 4000-metre peaks in the Alps. In this photo, a party is climbing the steep mixed terrain couloir that leads to the ridge; they still have another 700 metres to go before reaching the summit.

Then war broke out, and the great turn-of-the-century climbing generation was decimated. Many of Mont Blanc's leading climbers lost their lives in the trenches of the Somme and the Carso. After the war skiing became increasingly popular, and the Winter Olympics and more new hotels came to Chamonix. Increasingly large parties set off to the Grands Mulets and Mont Blanc, or the other refuge huts and the great peaks of the massif.

Two styles of climbing were practised on the most difficult ascents. On the one hand there were the great guides from Chamonix and Courmayeur, who continued to put up top-class routes with their best clients. On the other, there were the "guideless" amateurs belonging to the Club Alpino Accademico Italiano, the French Groupe de Haute Montagne and other similar associations, who no longer suffered from inferiority complexes.

On the Italian side of the mountain, one of the best guides of the period was Adolphe Rey, son of the great Émile. On 20th August 1919, together with his brother

the world), who was as active on the rock faces of the Aiguilles de Chamonix as on the ice walls of the Aiguille Verte. From 1923 onwards he concentrated on the Aiguilles du Diable, the elegant towers of rock on the South-East ridge of Mont Blanc du Tacul.

After climbing the Isolée, Pointe Mediane, Corne du Diable and Pointe Chaubert one after another, Charlet, climbing with guide Georges Cachat, Miriam O'Brien and Robert Underhill, scaled the entire ridge along a route of exceptional beauty in 1928. Here, as in all their ascents, Charlet and party climbed in hobnailed boots and carried neither karabiners nor pitons.

In the summer of 1926, Charlet conquered two of the great ridges of the Aiguille Verte, the Arête sans Nom and the Arête du Jardin. On 19th July 1929, together with fellow guide Jules Simond and client P. Dillemann, he opened a second route on the North face of the Aiguille du Plan.

The leading French guideless climbers in the early years of the century included Tom and Jacques de

Lépiney, whose feats were outstripped in the Twenties by those of Jacques Lagarde and Henri de Ségogne. It was the latter pair who conquered Trident du Tacul, the North face of the Aiguille d'Argentière and the Grands Montets ridge of the Aiguille Verte.

By far the most difficult and impressive route was traced by Lagarde and de Ségogne in July 1926, when they scaled the North face of the Aiguille du Plan by the couloir now named after them. This route includes gradients of up to 65 degrees, which the Frenchmen climbed wearing 10-point crampons, long before ice pitons were invented.

In the steepest 80 metres, as well as cutting hand- and foot-holds, Lagarde was forced to carve out niches that gave him room to move his knees. Almost as difficult, and much longer, was the route which Lagarde opened in July 1930 with Bobi Arsandeaux on the North-East side of the Droites. Neither route was repeated until 40 years later, when they were climbed by teams equipped for the new ice-axe traction technique.

77 bottom right Armand Charlet (1900-1975), known to the French as le grimpeur plus rapide du monde, *made numerous first ascents of the walls of the Aiguilles de Chamonix and the Aiguille Verte between the wars. In this photo, he demonstrates his elegant technique of progression on ice using crampons without front points.*

Henri and Swiss guide Adolf Aufdenblatten, he led British climbers S.L. Courtauld and E.G. Oliver along the Cresta dell'Innominata on Mont Blanc.

Courmayeur guides Laurent Grivel, Arturo and Osvaldo Ottoz and Albino Pennard used the same technique in 1927 to conquer the Père Éternel, a sharp monolith which is an outrider of the Aiguille de la Brenva. The four men from Valle d'Aosta aimed to repeat the same operation on the South ridge of the Aiguille Noire, but were halted several times there by bad weather.

The Hirondelles ridge leading to the Grandes Jorasses was scaled entirely by free climbing. This outstanding feat was accomplished by Adolphe Rey, who led a party consisting of G. Gaja, S. Matteoda, Francesco Ravelli and G.A. Rivetti in impeccable style with Alphonse Chenoz on 10th August 1927.

On the French side of Mont Blanc, the most famous guide of the period was Armand Charlet, known as *le grimpeur plus rapide du monde* (the fastest climber in

77 left Another moment in the ascent of the Arête du Moine on the Aiguille Verte, with Mont Blanc du Tacul and its granite outriders in the background. The climbers shown in this photo are crossing a snowy elevation on the ridge, not far from the summit.

77 centre On routes like the Arête du Moine on the Aiguille Verte, which presents no great difficulties but an interminable length, it is essential to move very fast on both snow and rock, a feat in which the Courmayeur and Chamonix guides still excel today.

In vertical world

Forcella Grande, situated amid the severe Marmarole and Sorapìss massifs, is one of the wildest spots in the Dolomites. Frequented by chamois hunters since time immemorial, it offers plenty of opportunities to see the graceful chamois, together with the ibex introduced onto the slopes of the Marmarole range a few years ago. No roads, ski lifts or refuge huts can be seen from Forcella Grande; here, the Dolomites still look just as they did long ago.

On 24th August 1877, a character destined to change the history of climbing in the Dolomites set off from Forcella Grande. Guide Luigi Cesaletti, who lived at San Vito di Cadore, was known to climbers for his skill and modesty, but the mountains never made him famous.

A few years later, Cesaletti left behind the forests and crags of Cadore, and emigrated to America with his wife and seven daughters. When he returned to live in San Vito he climbed Antelao again, in the summer of

1912, accompanying five clients who, as Severino Casara recounts, "were astounded by the ability of the old mountain man". A few days later, Cesaletti died peacefully at home.

However, in August 1877 Cesaletti was at the peak of fitness, and had thought up an original idea. On leaving Forcella Grande he turned off to the right of the ascent route to Sorapìss inaugurated by Paul Grohmann, crossed the plateau and headed for Torre dei Sabbioni, a small but elegant peak adjacent to the impressive Marmarole range.

Next, the climber from San Vito reached and scaled a chimney, turned left along a narrow ledge, then right, making a long, exposed traverse including a "cat pitch" similar to the one on Ball's ledge on Pelmo. An easy couloir took him to the scree of the summit. After resting on the summit, Cesaletti descended by the same route to the scree. There is no way of knowing whether Cesaletti realised it, but his ascent of Torre dei Sabbioni

78-79 The North faces of the Tre Cime di Lavaredo are one of the most famous sights in the Dolomites. While the sheer walls of Cima Grande and Cima Ovest were not climbed until the Thirties, the less steep wall of Cima Piccola (on the left, in the shadow) was conquered in 1890 by Viennese climber Hans Helversen with guides Sepp and Veit Innerkofler.

Mountaineering

marked the beginning of a new era. A couple of years later, climbers turned their attention to Cima Piccola, the magnificent tower flanking the Cima Grande di Lavaredo. Neglected ten years earlier by Grohmann, who was only interested in the highest peaks, the *Kleine Zinne* was observed attentively for the first time by Austrian brothers Otto and Emil Zsigmondy, who climbed the ordinary ascent route of the nearby Cima Grande with Michel Innerkofler in the summer of 1879.

The two climbers glimpsed an ascent route and discussed a possible ascent. "Sure, if we had wings," answered the guide. However, even great climbers can be wrong. Two years later, on 25th July 1881, Michel Innerkofler reached the summit of Cima Piccola with his brother Johann.

Three years after that, Otto and Emil Zsigmondy made the first guideless ascent with Ludwig Purtscheller, one of the first ascensionists of Kilimanjaro in 1889. Theodor Wundt, a young German officer and mountaineering enthusiast, wrote an exciting description of the route, which he repeated in 1887 with Michel Innerkofler.

"He climbed with an agility it is hard to describe, clinging to the rock like a cat," Wundt wrote. The cruxes of the ascent were a long traverse to the left and the subsequent chimney, "barred by a wedged boulder" and made of "particularly smooth rock". Now enamoured of Cima Piccola, Theodor Wundt returned at the end of 1892 to perform the first winter ascent with guides Michele Bettega and Johann Watschinger.

The next summer, with Dutchwoman Jeanne Immink and guides Mansueto Barbaria and Pietro Siorpaes, Wundt again climbed Cima Piccola, taking one of the bulky cameras of the period with him. His photographs of the ascent, with their magnificent resolution and composition, provide fascinating evidence of the style of climbers in the Dolomites at the turn of the century.

Jeanne Immink's description of the acrobatics of Wundt and his subjects when the photos were taken is delightful. When she posed, Jeanne put one foot on a boulder which broke away. She fell into the void, dangling from the rope held firm by Siorpaes. "You can be sure that I will never have my photograph taken again in my life!" she concludes.

80 left Bavarian Georg Winkler, born in Munich in 1869, made some outstanding ascents on the Torri del Vajolet, the Pale di San Martino and in the Wilder Kaiser. He was killed by an avalanche on the West face of the Weisshorn in the Pennine Alps in 1888 at the age of 19.

80-81 The Torri del Vajolet witnessed some exceptional solo ascents in the late 19th century. In 1887, Bavarian Georg Winkler climbed the tower now named after him (on the right in this photo) by way of a very difficult crack. In 1895, Hermann Delago from Alto Adige climbed the exposed edge of what is now Torre Delago, which can be seen in the centre of the photo.

81 left Attempted unsuccessfully by Paul Grohmann in 1869, Cimon della Pala was conquered in the summer of 1870 by Whitwell, Lauener and Siorpaes, and immediately became a classic. The crux of the ascent (shown in this photo) is a ramp with second and third grade pitches, now aided with a metal cable.

81 top right This photo shows the ordinary ascent route to Cimon della Pala. The team in the photo is climbing the summit ridge, just a few metres from the summit. The going is easy, but the exposure of the route is breathtaking.

81 bottom right This photo also shows the ordinary route on Cimon della Pala. The climber is scaling the exposed wall that follows the bus del gat, *a tunnel that avoids a third-grade pendulum. The Fiamme Gialle bivouac was inaugurated a little lower down, on a wide natural ledge, in 1968.*

Another page in the saga of Cima Piccola was written on 27th July 1890, when Viennese climber Hans Helversen, guided by Sepp and Veit Innerkofler, made the first ascent of the North face, along vertical chimneys with long sections of fourth-grade climbing. The team still climbed in heavy hobnailed boots; this was one of the last ascents to be made before the introduction of the rope- or felt-soled *Kletterschuhe* used by the sixth-grade heroes of the Thirties.

From Torre dei Sabbioni and Cima Piccola, the interest of the turn-of-the-century climbers turned to other massifs, considered "minor" by the pioneers, such as the Torri del Vajolet, not far from the Catinaccio range, the Torri del Sella and Cinque Dita, just a stone's throw from Passo Sella, and the Cadini di Misurina, which stand to the south of the famous Tre Cime.

In September 1887, a young Bavarian of outstanding courage tackled the most easterly of the three main Vajolet towers, the most elegant for those observing the massif from the trail that climbs from Gardeccia.

Georg Winkler was short, and sometimes used a metal hook fixed to a length of rope to reach a distant hold. With the aid of this device he scaled the Zsigmondy chimney on Cima Piccola, while on Punta Grohmann on the Cinque Dita, he actually used a rudimentary étrier.

It is not known whether young Winkler also used his home-made harpoon on the smooth, overhanging Winklerriss, the crack halfway up the Vajolet tower which has been named after him ever since, and offers present-day climbers (very differently equipped, and protected by a sound rope and three or four pitons) a pitch verging on the fifth grade.

The pitch, which is exposed, difficult and clearly visible from the trail, brought Winkler great fame among German-speaking climbers, and attracted some rather extravagant comments. "Alone with his rope and his legendary audacity!", exclaimed Arturo Tanesini in the first Italian guide to the Catinaccio range. "He inaugurated the period of art for art's sake," added Antonio Berti. "He was a meteor of mountaineering who soared through the sky leaving a luminous trail behind him," wrote Gian Piero Motti 90 years later.

In the summer of 1885, Georg Winkler, together with Alois Zott, put up a difficult route on Cima della Madonna in the Pale di San Martino, scaling a long fourth-grade chimney. A few weeks before the Torre Winkler, he soloed the awesome ice-filled couloir on the Croda Rossa d'Ampezzo.

In 1888 he moved to the Western Alps, where he climbed the Zinalrothorn and then attempted the Weisshorn, considered by many to be the most attractive peak in the Alps. Here, however, fortune deserted the meteor of Bavarian mountaineering. Winkler slipped, fell into a crevasse, and died. He was only 19. In that tragic summer for the great climbers in the Dolomites, Michel Innerkofler was also killed when a snow bridge collapsed on the Cristallo glacier. Despite a terrifying fall of some 15 metres, his two clients were unhurt.

guides in the Dolomites imitated their counterparts in the Western Alps, scaling the grim snow- and ice-filled couloirs that cut through the northern slopes of the highest peaks. In June 1887 Michel Innerkofler led C. Wydenbruck along the deep ice-filled couloir that intersects the North face of Cristallo.

The year before, a party of Italian soldiers had scaled the grim ice couloir on the North-East face of Antelao. An expert in this particular type of climbing was German mountaineer Oskar Schuster, who made numerous first ascents of this kind. The best-known of his routes is the icy couloir on the north-east side of Monte Popera, in the Sesto Dolomites, which the climber from Dresden scaled in 1893.

Other outstanding guides made their mark on the great Dolomite walls in those years, too. In 1897, Luigi and Simone Rizzi, guides from Campitello di Fassa, led Emil Munk on the awesome West face of Croda di Re Laurino. The same summer, Giovanni and Arcangelo Siorpaes guided the Witzenmann brothers on the

Apart from acrobatic climbs on the loveliest and sharpest peaks, the best climbers of the period in the Dolomites continued to climb the highest peaks. Among the best ascents of this kind were those led by Antonio Dimai from Cortina, the son of Angelo Dimai, who had been one of Grohmann's favourite guides.

The list begins in 1892 with the North face of Sorapiss, a grim wall almost 700 metres high, which Dimai scaled with clients F. Muller and S. von Waltershausen and fellow-guides Arcangelo Dibona and Zaccaria Pompanin. The next year, together with British climber Leon Treptow, he climbed the dangerous South Face of Cimon della Pala (550 metres, fourth grade) in the Pale di San Martino.

In 1895 two more British climbers, Arthur G. Raynor and John Phillimore, followed in the footsteps of Dimai and Giovanni Siorpaes on the North-West face of Civetta, the "wall of walls" 1000 metres tall that had already tempted Georg Winkler and Robert Hans Schmitt. The British route (devised and led by Dimai) was long and tortuous, with interminable traverses that tested the team's skills to the utmost.

"The ascent was continually difficult and also dangerous; the traverses needed the greatest attention almost everywhere. The two chimneys required tiring, even athletic work, which took place in a highly exposed position," wrote Phillimore and Raynor in their report on the ascent.

The first ascents performed by the great Antonio were not over yet. Between 1896 and 1901 he conquered the South face of the Pala di San Martino and the East face of Catinaccio, the South face of Punta Fiames and the South face of Antelao, the East face of Cima Grande and the North face of Cima Una.

In 1901, with fellow-guides Agostino Verzi and Giovanni Siorpaes, Dimai led young Hungarian noblewomen Ilona and Rolanda von Eotvos in the first ascent of his most famous route. This was the magnificent, often complicated route that climbs the impressive South face of Tofana di Rozes, the most spectacular of the Ampezzo Dolomites.

The crux, which leads from the heart of the wall to the exit cracks, is a third- and fourth-grade traverse on an exceptionally exposed wall, still a testing ground for those beginning to climb in the Dolomites.

On some occasions, the great turn-of-the-century

first ascent of the North face of Croda dei Toni.

The most attractive and spectacular route was opened on the South face of the Marmolada, now crossed by many of the most difficult routes in the Alps. The problem attracted the attention of British climber Beatrice Thomasson, who engaged Luigi Rizzi as guide. In a reconnaissance made in 1900, Rizzi climbed and descended the first and most difficult third of the great wall alone.

The next year, Rizzi asked for a higher fee, but Beatrice Thomasson was unwilling to pay it, and engaged Michele Bettega and Bortolo Zagonel, the two best guides on the Primiero, in his place. From the great ledge reached by Rizzi the team continued towards a tower of yellow rock, traversed towards a ravine and reached the second ledge that cuts across the wall. The last section was soaking wet and drenched by thundering waterfalls. The weather deteriorated too, but nothing could stop the team now.

82 top left German doctor Oskar Schuster (1873-1917) was one of the most active climbers in the Alps at the turn of the century. An excellent ice climber, he put up some 50 routes in the Dolomites (Popera, Catinaccio, Pale di San Martino and Cinque Dita) and in the Caucasus, where he made the first ascent of the South peak of Ushba. He died in a Russian prison camp.

82 top right As these climbers rest on the rocks of Becco di Mezzodi, the garments worn by mountaineers at the turn of the century can be seen. The guide is Arcangelo Siorpaes

from Cortina, who made the first ascent of the North-East face of Croda dei Toni. His client is Beatrice Thomasson, who made the first ascent of the South face of the Marmolada.

82-83 The North face of the Civetta is the most awesome and severe of the great North faces of the Dolomites. The first sixth-grade route in history was put up in its compact central part in 1925. However, a very long, indirect route had already been opened in 1895 by Englishmen Arthur G. Raynor and John Phillimore, guided by Antonio Dimai and Giovanni Siorpaes from Cortina.

In vertical world

They reached the summit, and toasted their success with the usual bottle of champagne in true British style. Some reports say that Bettega, Zagonel and Thomasson failed to meet up with the porter who was supposed to be bringing their boots, and were forced to descend the glacier in a blizzard wearing soaking wet climbing shoes. However, we have been unable to find any confirmation of this anecdote in contemporary accounts.

Other spires also hit the headlines in those years. The sharpest was Torre del Diavolo in the Cadini, which Antonio Dimai, Giovanni Siorpaes and Agostino Verzi scaled in 1903 together with the adventurous Baronesses von Eotvos with the aid of a rope launched from the nearby Cima del Gobbo and an acrobatic traverse over a total void. Friedrich Terschak, who was particularly fond of Cortina, described this ascent as "a feat that stunned the climbing world."

82 bottom In the early years of the 20th century, Italian climbers began to visit the Dolomites, which until then had been frequented only by Austrian and German climbers. Here is Ugo de Amicis between guides Michele Bettega and Bortolo Zagonel from S. Martino di Castrozza.

83 top The South face of the Marmolada is now crossed by some of the most difficult rock routes in the Alps. However, a series of cracks and chimneys enabled British climber Beatrice Thomasson, guided by Michele Bettega and Bortolo

Zagonel, to put up an excellent route with pitches up to the upper fourth grade in 1901.

83 bottom This group photo, taken at the end of the 19th century, shows all the Cortina guides of the day in

front of Osteria del Parco. The guides sitting in the second and third rows include Antonio Dimai, Agostino Verzi and Mansueto Barbaria. The owner of the Osteria, the District Captain and the local doctor also appear in the photo.

84-85 This winter photo of the Sfùlmini range shows Cima degli Armi (on the left), Torre di Brenta, the slender spires of the Sfùlmini and Campanile Alto di Brenta. On the right, silhouetted against the dark wall of Brenta Alta, is Campanile Basso.

84 bottom This photo immortalises a young climber with her guide during a brief stop to admire the severe, vertical dolomite walls. As can be seen from their clothing, this photo dates from the Thirties, when climbing in the Dolomites became very popular.

85 The Sfùlmini range, the heart of the Brenta Dolomites, includes some of the most elegant of the "Pale Mountains." This winter view shows Brenta Alta (left) and the elegant Campanile Basso di Brenta, first climbed in 1899 by Tyrolean mountaineers Otto Ampferer and Karl Berger.

85 bottom Austrian climber Gunther Freiherr von Saar made numerous first ascents of an exploratory nature in the loneliest parts of the Dolomites in the early 20th century. The best-known was the conquest of Campanile di Val Montanaia in the Oltrepiave Dolomites. Together with Viktor von Glanvell, von Saar completed the route attempted unsuccessfully a few days earlier by Napoleone Cozzi and Alberto Zanutti from Trieste.

In 1895, another great feat was performed on the Torri del Vajolet. On 22nd September, Hermann Delago from Bressanone made the first ascent of the westernmost tower of this miniature range which, like the nearby Torre Winkler, was named after the first ascensionist.

Not far away, in the summer of 1900, young guide Tita Piaz from Fassa soloed the vertical crack that cuts across the wall of Punta Emma. This was another great feat verging on the fifth grade, which the impecunious Piaz was able to perform only after Dr. Theodor Christomannos had given him 17 florins to replace his worn-out climbing shoes with a new pair. On the most difficult section, where the chimney becomes narrow and smooth, Piaz took a great risk. "For the first and only time in my climbing career I gambled with my life. It was do or die!", he recalled in his autobiography *Mezzo secolo d'alpinismo*.

The weirdest spire of all is Campanile di Val Montanaia, situated in the Spalti di Toro massif in the Oltrepiave Dolomites, which mark the border between the Veneto and Friuli regions.

This lonely, awesome tower, described by one of the first climbers to attempt it as "the petrified scream of a damned soul" and defended by horrific overhangs, was attempted on 7th September 1902 by Napoleone Cozzi and Alberto Zanutti from Trieste. The pair scaled the most difficult pitch, but were unable to find the traverse that would have

taken them out of the difficult sections.

The decisive pitch was discovered ten days later by Austrians Viktor Wolf von Glanvell and Gunther Saar. After climbing the crack already scaled by Cozzi, the pair moved to the left, traversed the overhangs, scaled a second crack and reached the easy rocks of the summit.

However, the most famous "belfry" in the Dolomites is Campanile Basso di Brenta, the extraordinary tower that symbolises the Trentino mountains. The first attempt was organised by Carlo Garbari, who hired guides Nino Pooli of Còvelo and Antonio Tavernaro of Primiero. The three scaled a first slab (now known as the Pooli Wall), then continued without any particular difficulties to the great ledge that they called the "*stradone provinciale*" (the Broad) and an elevated terrace at the foot of the terminal wall.

Here the rock is compact and vertical, exposure is total, and the lack of pitons meant that if the leader fell, all three could have been ripped off the mountainside. Garbari's account is dramatic. "The strong Nino made the last attempt (I still shudder to recall it)... the few poor holds meant that he progressed very slowly. It made your hair stand on end to see him seek out every asperity with uncertain, trembling hands, feeling for projections in the rock with his feet, pressing his whole body against the wall... he stayed there, immobile, for a few moments, then descended."

Two years later, two students from Innsbruck made another attempt. They knew nothing about the previous attempt, but unlike their predecessors they had a few pitons. On reaching the last terrace, Otto Ampferer and Karl Berger found the note left by Garbari, and now knew for certain that the peak was still unclimbed. However, the wall that towered above them was too much for them. They returned two days later, and this time it was Ampferer who found the solution. From the terrace he turned the corner of the Campanile, reached the base of a vertical but not excessively difficult wall, and climbed to the wide summit terrace. "Other men have conquered great islands with flat shores, but we have scaled a small one with superb tall sides," wrote the leader. The best eulogy of those years is to be found in the words of Angelo Brofferio, a climber from Turin, who wrote as follows in the *Bollettino* of the Club Alpino Italiano in 1906:

"A limestone, or rather dolomite peak can be compared to a dog: the smaller, the fiercer. In our valleys of Piedmont and Lombardy we have the inveterate habit of attacking giants. In the Tyrol, real climbers despise them and prefer pigmies, which have been sharpened to look taller. A climber who manifests this preference is consequently more sophisticated, because he prefers quality to quantity."

A new breakthrough in terms of technique was made in July 1911, when three people climbed the steep trail leading from Madonna di Campiglio to Bocca di Brenta and its refuge huts. The journey by train and coach across the Brenner Pass and Trento had been uncomfortable and tiring, their loads were heavy, and the only woman in the party was tired and miserable.

However, at the edge of the wood, a magnificent sight made the trio forget their fatigue. From the emerald meadows of Alpe di Brenta, Paul Preuss, his sister Mina and Paul Relly admired Crozzon di Brenta, "a scenario we had never seen the like of in the Alpine range," "which sent even the mundane Freshfield into ecstasies." Six years earlier, Fritz Schneider and Adolf Schulze had conquered its North ridge, a blade of dolomite 900 metres high that cuts through the Brenta skyline, but the East face was still unclimbed. "What a magnificent wall!", exclaimed Paul Preuss on seeing it. But there were still two days to go before their adventure on the Crozzón.

"We devoted the next day to Campanile Basso and to my sister, who was used to difficult but not excessively long routes," says the concise account written by Paul Preuss for the *Deutsche Alpenzeitung*. Behind those few words is one of the most amazing feats in the history of mountaineering. From the base of the Campanile, the trio climbed without difficulty along the ordinary route. Just before 10 o'clock, they reached the *stradone provinciale*. There, Paul's sister and friend sat down in the sun to have something to eat.

In the meantime Paul Preuss moved a little to the left and started climbing along the highly exposed, vertical East face of the Campanile. Alone and elegant, with the rope slung over his shoulder, he side-stepped some niches, scaled a roof and a dihedral, and stopped to leave a note with his signature and the date in a hole. Finally, he scaled a chimney of dark rock and came out onto the summit. It had taken him less than two hours to accomplish one of the greatest feats in the history of mountaineering.

Then he descended to the *stradone*, where he showed little sign of emotion when Paul Relly and Mina announced their engagement. "The ledge was awfully narrow," was his laconic comment. Finally, Paul Preuss

returned to the 2883-metre summit to show his sister and friend the exposure of the *Albergo al sole* (Sunshine Hotel), the subsequent traverse and the Ampferer wall. Three days later, after settling accounts with the Crozzon, Preuss downclimbed his new route, this time roped together with Relly.

For historians, the East face of Campanile Basso is one of the many top-class ascents performed by Preuss in 1911, the year when he astonished the climbing world with 93 ascents in the Dolomites, the Wilder Kaiser, the Totes Gebirge and the Silvretta. However, it was that ascent of only 120 metres that made him a legendary figure in the climbing world.

It was that route that made his friend and rival Tita Piaz describe Preuss as "Lord of the Abyss," and Severino Casara call him "the most audacious and aristocratic manifestation of rock climbing." Their opinion is shared by Reinhold Messner, who wrote about "the boldest route of all" in the Austrian climber's career in 1986.

Compared with the East face of the Campanile, the other ascents performed by Preuss during that magical summer fade into the background. The list includes the East face of Crozzon di Brenta (an "immense godforsaken wall in a grim, oppressive landscape"), the Chimney of San Giovanni on Punta Grohmann, the first solo ascent of the fearful West face of the Totenkirchl in the Wilder Kaiser, and the complete crossing of the Sassolungo massif, which Preuss performed on 17th August by climbing the main peak, the Spallone, Punta delle Cinque Dita and Punta Grohmann, which would be a noteworthy *enchaînement* even for modern climbing champions.

Two years later, on 3rd October 1913, Paul Preuss was killed when he fell from the North ridge of the Mandlkogel, not far from his home town of Alt Aussee.

86 bottom left Paul Preuss, known for his elegant climbing style, nonchalantly scales the taxing crack pitches common among the smooth slabs of the Wilder Kaiser. This photo was taken on Schiefe Riss, one of the most difficult pitches on the South-east corner of the Totenkirchl.

86 bottom right One of the few surviving photos of Paul Preuss shows the climber from Alt Aussee in mountaineering gear. A virtuoso climber on limestone and dolomite, Preuss also tackled the granite of Mont Blanc during his mountaineering career.

86-87 The cyclopic North edge of Crozzòn di Brenta (900 metres) is one of the loveliest climbs in the Dolomites. It was first climbed in 1905 by Germans Fritz Schneider and Adolf Schultze. The nearby West face, illuminated by the light of sunset, was climbed in 1933 by Italians Ettore Castiglioni and Bruno Detassis.

87 centre The Punta delle Cinque Dita (on the left, in sunlight, in this photo) witnessed two excellent feats by Paul Preuss in 1911. In August, he scaled the Camino di San Giovanni on Punta Grohmann with Walther Schmidkunz. Later, he crossed the entire range alone, climbing the Sassolungo, Spallone del Sassolungo, Punta delle Cinque Dita and Punta Grohmann.

In vertical world

87 bottom Especially when seen in winter, Sassolungo is one of the most imposing peaks in the Dolomites. It was first climbed in August 1869 by great Viennese mountaineer Paul Grohmann, accompanied by guides Franz Innerkofler and Peter Salcher from Val Pusteria.

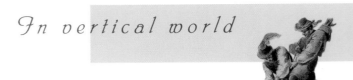

A virtuoso climber and advocate of climbing without pitons (more about that later), Paul Preuss was not the only star in action in the Dolomites in the years leading up to the Great War. From the Catinaccio range and the Tre Cime to the Brenta, valley guides and city climbers were competing to climb routes of ever-increasing difficulty.

The other outstanding amateur name was that of Hans Dulfer, the climber from Dortmund whose name is still associated with the layback method of climbing cracks and an abseiling method. The taciturn German was a tireless collector of peaks; he climbed 155 in 1912 and no less than 173 the next year, when he chalked up 23 first ascents.

Though a great free climber, Dulfer, unlike Preuss, occasionally used a piton, and was the first to use the karabiner systematically to clip the rope to the metal spike hammered into cracks in the rock. Dulfer entered the top-flight climbing world at the age of 19, in 1911, with the first ascent of the deep chimney that cuts into the grim West face of the Totenkirchl.

He made his début in the Dolomites the next year, climbing the short but vertical West face of the Cima Ovest di Lavaredo (which features fourth- and fifth-grade pitches) with Walther Schaarschmidt. In 1913 he put up three routes on the Dirupi di Larsèc, in the Catinaccio group. Then, with Willy von Bernuth, he opened an elegant fifth-grade route on the West face of Cima Grande.

Two days later, the same team free-climbed Torre del Diavolo in the Cadini di Misurina range, which Antonio Dimai had reached in 1903 by throwing a

88-89 Just a stone's throw from Val di Fassa and Bolzano, the Catinaccio range is still one of the most popular in the Dolomites and witnessed numerous great climbs in the early 20th century. This photo shows the walls of Catinaccio di Antermoia. The blue Lake Antermoia, near which the refuge hut of the same name now stands, can be seen on the right.

88 top Although it is only 2190 metres high, the Totenkirchl, one of the loveliest and most difficult peaks in the Wilder Kaiser, has played a leading role in the history of Austrian and German mountaineering. Great climbers like Georg Winkler, Tita Piaz, Hans Dulfer and Paul Preuss made their mark on its compact rock walls and corners between 1886 and 1913.

rope. A few days later, still among the weird spires of the Cadini, Dulfer and von Bernuth climbed a tower that was later named Campanile Dulfer.

However, the most difficult route put up by Hans Dulfer in the Dolomites dates from 1914. It was the yellow South face of Catinaccio di Antermoia, with a huge dihedral cutting across it. Dulfer climbed the first 50 metres roped to girlfriend Hanne Franz, then scaled a lower-sixth-grade overhang, but Hanne was unable to cope with this pitch. Hans lowered her to the first belay, had her untie, and continued alone to the summit on fifth-grade rocks. Then he abseiled down, picked up the girl, who had waited patiently for him, and reached the scree with a last abseil.

Next came an attempt on the menacing North face of the Furchetta, the most attractive and awesome peak in the Odle range, which Dulfer performed with Luis Trenker, destined to become one of the most famous directors of mountaineering films. However, after scaling the first two-thirds of the route, Dulfer gave up at the *Dulferkanzel*, a terrace at the foot of an overhanging zone. When the great Emil Solleder completed the ascent with Fritz Wiessner eleven years later, he had to scale various sixth-grade pitches. Hans Dulfer only survived his last ascent by a few weeks. He

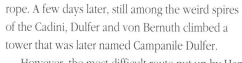

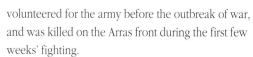

volunteered for the army before the outbreak of war, and was killed on the Arras front during the first few weeks' fighting.

The excellent level of the German climbers was confirmed by Rudolf Fehrmann, a climber from Dresden who learned his technique on the smooth sandstone towers of the Elbsandsteingebirge. As Fritz Wiessner told the author in a 1987 interview, "Climbers there, starting with Fehrmann, were scaling upper sixth-grade pitches, especially in cracks, as early as the beginning of the century."

In the Dolomites, Fehrmann made his name with two very elegant routes, both climbed with American mountaineer Oliver Perry-Smith. The first was the great dihedral of Campanile Basso di Brenta, a fourth-grade route with some fifth-grade pitches which the pair climbed in 1908, and is still one of the most classic and popular in the Dolomites. Next came the North face of Cima Piccola. In a Europe that was inexorably moving towards war, the international team of Fehrmann and Perry-Smith is deserving of praise.

89 above Though less famous than his contemporaries Dulfer and Preuss, German Rudolf Fehrmann was one of the best mountaineers of his day. He was among those responsible for developing climbing on the sandstone of the Elba, and climbed the great dihedral of Campanile Basso di Brenta (1908) and the North face of Cima Piccola di Lavaredo (1909) with American Oliver Perry-Smith.

89 left Luis Trenker from Alto Adige (1892-1990), famous for his numerous films devoted to climbing, mountain warfare and skiing, is one of the best-known personalities in the Alpine world. In the early years of the 20th century he made first ascents on the Tre Cime di Lavaredo and an attempt with Hans Dulfer on the North face of the Furchetta (Odle range).

89 below left German Hans Dulfer, who was born in Dortmund in 1893 and killed in the early days of the Great War, was one of the best climbers of all time. A crack climbing technique and an abseiling method are named after him. However, Dulfer also collected summits (he made 155 ascents in 1912 and 173 in 1913) and made some outstanding first ascents in the Dolomites and the Wilder Kaiser.

90

90 top Angelo Dibona from Cortina (1879-1956) was one of the best guides of all time. His greatest ascents in the Dolomites include the North face of Cima Una, the West face of Roda di Vaèl and the South-West face of Croz dell'Altissimo. In the rest of the Alpine range, Dibona put up some important routes on the Meije, the Dent du Requin and the Lalidererwand of the Karwendel.

90-91 The profession of mountain guide was well established by the end of the 19th century. Professional guides (this photo shows a group of Tyrolean guides) who pass an exam set by Alpine Clubs or local authorities are awarded a diploma. However, the majority also have another job.

What were the guides doing in the meantime? A new generation of professionals, capable of leading their clients on fifth-grade routes despite the fact that very few means of protection were then available, appeared in the Dolomites in the years leading up to the First World War. The best and most prolific of these guides was Angelo Dibona from Cortina.

During his "great years," from 1908 to 1914, he climbed on his home mountains and also in the Dauphiné, on Mont Blanc, and in the Gesause and Karwendel ranges. An excellent climber, Dibona particularly liked big walls, where he led his best clients, aided by top-class guides such as Agostino Verzi, also from Cortina, and Luigi Rizzi from Fassa.

The first important summer for Dibona was in 1908 when, with Verzi and British clients E.A. Broone and H.K. Corning, he climbed the West face of Roda di Vaèl and the friable North face of the East Tower of

91 top left A page of the guide's logbook signed by client Winifred Marples certifies that Angelo Dibona was an excellent guide in the ascents of Punta Fiames, Pomagagnon, Piz Popera, Cima Piccola and Torre Fanes.

91 centre top Angelo Dibona was famous among climbers and guides for his elegant style. His greatest ascents in the Dolomites include Cima Una, Roda di Vaèl and Croz dell'Altissimo, and he also made some great ascents in the Karwendel, the Dauphiné and the Mont Blanc massif.

91 top right In addition to the logbook containing clients' annotations, mountain guides also have a badge. The two on the right were issued to mountain guides by Club Alpino Italiano, and the one on the left is a ski instructor's badge issued by DOAV, the Austro-German Alpine Club.

Latemar (or Christomannos Tower), scaling various upper fifth-grade pitches in both cases.

As from the next summer, Dibona was accompanied in his major ascents by Austrian brothers Max and Guido Mayer. In 1909, the team of Dibona, Rizzi, Mayer and Mayer scaled the North ridge of Cima Grande di Lavaredo along a fourth-grade route that is still very frequently repeated.

However, the best year was 1910, when the practised team scaled the grim North face of Cima Una in the Sesto Dolomites, the sunny West face of Sass Pordoi, and the awesome South-West face of Croz dell'Altissimo in the Brenta Dolomites. Two-thirds of the way along the latter route, Angelo Dibona tackled a huge overhang with a horizontal crack cutting through it. It was a totally exposed pitch, which water and mud made even more difficult, and is now protected by numerous pitons.

On Croz dell'Altissimo, "that devil of an Angelo" probably went beyond the fifth grade of his other routes. Asked about the difficulty by *Rivista della Montagna* in 1990, the great Bruno Detassis called the route "a classic sixth grade," while Maurizio Giordani, who performed many modern ascents on the South face of the Marmolada, called it "a very tiring and dangerous pitch, a 6a according to the modern grading scale, which corresponds to the lower seventh on the classic scale."

91 bottom right Style, speed and confidence on easy ground are still among the characteristics of mountain guides today.

In this 1899 photo, Zaccaria Pompanin of Cortina belays Nelly Kirschten on the ordinary route on Cima Piccola.

Tita Piaz was quite a different kettle of fish. For a long time manager of the refuge hut at the foot of the Torri del Vajolet, he became famous in the climbing world in 1900 for soloing Punta Emma, as described earlier. However, what made "the Devil of the Dolomites" famous with the general public in the pre-war years was his Irredentist politics, as a result of which he was imprisoned by the Austrian authorities on several occasions. "He narrowly escaped the hangman under Franz Josef. He dreamed of Italy as the land of national freedom, but the 20-year period of Fascist rule wounded him to the quick," wrote Lidia Minervini in 1947, in the preface to *Mezzo secolo d'alpinismo*, this unusual character's autobiography. The same age as Angelo Dibona, Tita was born in Perra di Fassa, and had loved climbing since childhood. "I don't know when I learned to climb, because I feel as though I were born a monkey," he wrote in 1947. Piaz started work as a guide in 1898, and became famous the next summer as a result of his rapid solo

few places to drive in pitons. "I worked with protection for the first time," was his comment. The controversy over the use of pitons was about to break out with a vengeance. The first rock pitons, a tool unknown to the early explorers in the Dolomites, were employed in the late 19th century in the Wilder Kaiser and Karwendel ranges, and only came into use in the Dolomites later. The first climbers definitely known to have used them were Ampferer and Berger on Campanile Basso in the summer of 1899. A few years later, the use of pitons became more common. They were used fairly abundantly by Tita Piaz, and parsimoniously by Angelo Dibona. Hans Dulfer did not disdain them on a wall, and was one of the first to use a karabiner to clip the rope to a piton driven into a crack in the rock. Paul Preuss opposed what he considered a degeneration of climbing, and attacked all use of artificial aids, including abseiling, in his conferences and writings. At the end of a long debate in the pages of the *Deutsche Alpenzeitung*, the climber from Alt

Aussee stated his strict principles. The first fundamental principle laid down by Preuss was "it's not enough to be up to the difficulties you're tackling; you must be better." The second was that "the extent of the difficulties that a climber can tackle in the descent must represent the upper limit of the difficulties he tackled during the ascent." Preuss, a man of total moral honesty, took his reasoning to the extreme consequences. "In my opinion, the thought 'if I fall, I'll be left hanging from three metres of rope' has less moral value than 'one fall and you're dead!' If you merely want to do a bit of exercise without running any risk, you might as well stay at home and test your agility in the gym," he wrote in August 1911. In October 1913, the sworn enemy of all artificial aids, paid for his belief with his life, falling from the North ridge of the Mandlkogel. However, the controversy he started about the use and abuse of pitons has remained one of the key issues in mountaineering, and still flares up at intervals.

crossing of the Catinaccio massif and the Vajolet. "Seven peaks in eight hours" proclaimed the headlines in the local papers.

In 1906, together with German client Bernard Trier, Piaz discovered at the foot of Cristallo "such an improbably slender, elegant, tall peak that it looked more like a needle, a petrified dream… its four smooth walls made it seem a challenge to every rock climber in the universe." The next day, after spending four hours throwing "countless lead balls with metres of string wound round them," Piaz managed to construct "a barely perceptible overhead bridge, terrifyingly suspended over the abyss between the two peaks," along which he swung "just like a monkey." "If an inhabitant of Madagascar had witnessed the scene, he would have had difficulty in believing that a high level of civilisation had been reached in Europe," commented Piaz himself later, always ready to send up his ascents. From the summit, which he named Guglia De Amicis, the guide flew a red flag, a gesture which was not appreciated by the Imperial authorities. A few days later, with Trier and three more climbers, Piaz performed another acrobatic feat. He climbed to Campanile di Val Montanaia by the Glanvell and von Saar route, and descended on the other side with a 40-metre abseil, mainly over total emptiness. This would be a perfectly normal feat with today's ropes and solid belays, but seemed pure madness to many of his contemporaries. A few days later, again in the wild Oltrepiave Dolomites, Piaz and Trier climbed Campanile Toro, another spectacular obelisk very difficult of access. Sitting on the summit, Piaz commented that the ascent was "the most difficult climb in the Alps." The free climbing sections are indeed very difficult, with fifth- and upper-fifth-grade pitches and very

92 left The Catinaccio (2981 metres, known as the Rosengarten to German-speaking climbers) is one of the most elegant and popular peaks in the Dolomites. The first ascent was made in 1874 by British climbers Charles Comyns Tucker and J.H. Carson, accompanied by Chamonix guide François Devouassoud.

92-93 The Dolomites feature steep, severe rock walls that give climbers the chance to tackle some impressive granite pinnacles. In this spectacular aerial photo, the warm light of sunset highlights the severity of these awesome walls.

93 top left One of the best Dolomite climbers of all time was definitely Giovanni Battista (Tita) Piaz (1879-1948). Born in Val di Fassa, and for many years the manager of the Vajolet refuge hut, Piaz was a fervent Irredentist, and often arrested by the Austro-Hungarian

police for his political activities. His new routes include the chimney of Punta Emma, Guglia De Amicis (Cristallo) and the West face of the Totenkirchl in the Wilder Kaiser. Piaz performed the first enchaînement in the Dolomites on Mount Catinaccio.

93 right Climbed for the first time in 1869 by Paul Grohmann and Sesto guides Franz Innerkofler and Peter Salcher, the ordinary route on Cima Grande di Lavaredo became a classic in the late 19th century. The route, on the south side, is second grade, with two third-grade pitches.

93 bottom Croda da Lago overlooks the Cortina valley, and was one of the most popular peaks in the East Dolomites at the turn of the century. The ordinary route, climbed in 1884 by Hungarian noblewoman Rolanda von Eotvos with Michel Innerkofler, is an enjoyable second-grade climb.

Towards new horizons

On the evening of 17th May 1897, a small crowd gathered at the Porta Nuova railway station in Turin to see off an unusual party. Four of its members (Joseph Pétigax and Laurent Croux from Courmayeur, and Antoine Maquignaz and André Pellissier from Valtournenche) were mountain guides from Valle d'Aosta, while another member of the party, Vittorio Sella from Biella, was about to become the best mountain photographer in the world. Erminio Botta, Sella's inseparable assistant, also arrived from Biella, at the foot of the Piedmont Alps. Francesco Gonella, Chairman of the Turin section of the Club Alpino, had made numerous great ascents in the Western Alps. Surgeon Filippo de Filippi was to keep the official record of the expedition as well as providing medical care. "The day was warm, almost summery," was his first entry.

The organiser of the trip arrived at the last minute,

as was to be expected of a member of the Royal Family. Luigi Amedeo of Savoy, Duke of Abruzzi, accompanied by his orderly, naval lieutenant Umberto Cagni, climbed aboard at the last minute, just before the train pulled out of the station.

Two days after their departure, the ten Italians were in London, preparing their luggage. In addition to the 60 crates that had come on the train from Turin, they made up another 16 parcels in London containing the tents, ropes and waterproof jackets they needed for the trip. Then they set off again.

At noon on 22nd May the party left Liverpool on the Transatlantic liner *Lucania,* bound for New York, where they arrived six days later. Less than two days after their arrival they took a fast mail train to Chicago and San Francisco. From the windows of their compartment, the climbers looked out curiously at the

Rockies, which the train crossed at an altitude of 2512 metres. Then they crossed the Sierra Nevada, after which the train ran downhill, "skirting abysses hundreds of metres deep."

At 9 p.m. on 3rd June, after a short ferry trip from Oakland, the Duke and his men reached the Pacific coast, where they had to buy provisions. "The Prince's drawing room was soon filled with samples of hard tack, tinned meat, soup and vegetables, chocolate, and the like," recounts de Filippi. "Then, when we had accumulated everything we needed, we worked with the Prince for a whole day until late at night to form 50 rations, each of which had to contain everything needed by 10 men for one day."

On the evening of 9th June, another train took the Italian expedition north, towards Seattle.

95 bottom left The expedition to Mount St. Elias was not only a magnificent mountaineering achievement, but also a great feat in terms of stamina. The guides and climbers (including the Duke of Abruzzi) had to pull sledges containing the expedition's baggage across the interminable Hitchcock, Seward and Pinnacle Glaciers.

95 bottom right Any route in the St. Elias Mountains forces climbers to tackle an exceptionally harsh environment. This photo shows two skier-climbers descending at the foot of the awesome ice walls of Mount Logan. The highest peak in the chain was first climbed in 1925, by the expedition led by Albert MacCarthy.

94 left Luigi Amedeo di Savoia, Duke of Abruzzi (1873-1933), was one of the leading mountaineers to climb outside Europe in the late 19th and early 20th century. The expedition to the St. Elias Mountains (1897) was the first in a series of great adventures that continued with expeditions to the North Pole (1899), Ruwenzori (1906), Karakorum (1909) and the Webi Shebeli River (1928-1929).

94 right Although it presents no particular climbing difficulties, the high altitude, the crevasses and the great distances which have to be covered make the ascent route of Mount St. Elias particularly demanding. This photo by Vittorio Sella shows a member of the Duke of Abruzzi's expedition resting near a frozen lake that breaks up the vast expanses of Newton Glacier.

95 top Mount Logan is quite often climbed, especially by parties carrying skis. The climbers in this photo are tackling the King Trench Route.

95 centre Mount Vancouver is one of the highest and most difficult of the St. Elias Mountains. It was first climbed in 1949 by an expedition including British mountaineer Noel Odell, one of the members of the expeditions to Everest between the two World Wars.

Four days later, the party boarded the *City of Topeka,* bound for Sitka, the small capital of Alaska, in the company of "traders, a few young ladies who were going home after finishing their studies, and a number of miners heading for the mines of the interior".

After putting in at Juneau and skirting the spectacular front of the Muir Glacier, the ship reached Sitka. A final crossing on the *Bertha,* "a short, wide, very tall old boat" that "rolled in every direction in an disorderly way", took the Italians and ten American porters who had been recruited to the group to the Malaspina Glacier on the west bank of Yakutat Bay. Five weeks had gone by since the party left Turin.

The next stage of the Duke's journey bore rather more resemblance to an ordinary climbing expedition. After interminable journeys back and forth, carrying loads of up to 25 kg on their backs, the men reached the impressive glacier, which they crossed by loading their baggage onto four great sleighs. Next came a short stretch of scree and tundra, followed by the difficult ascent of the Hitchcock, Seward and Pinnacle Glaciers, beyond which their destination, Mount St. Elias (5514 m), finally appeared.

The final part of the journey, which involved the most actual climbing, began on 30th July with the ascent to the pass that separates Mount St. Elias from Mount Newton. The Duke named the pass after Israel C. Russel, who had ventured that far in 1891.

96 This aerial photo of the St. Elias Mountains shows just how impressive this great range is, with its huge expanse of glaciers that climbers can take days to cross.

97 top The St. Elias Mountain chain includes numerous lovely minor peaks of considerably difficulty, such as this unnamed peak near Mount Logan.

97 centre In a rare moment of relaxation, some members of the 1897 expedition rest by their tents, pitched on the endless snow-clad plateau of the Agassiz Glacier. The need to dry woollen jackets, trousers and sweaters in the sun was to remain one of the most serious problems for expeditions until pile fabric was invented.

97 bottom 31st July 1897 was an important date in the history of climbing in North America. This photo, taken by Vittorio Sella, shows all nine members of the expedition on the 5489-metre summit. The Duke of Abruzzi is the third from the right, sitting in the snow.

The next day, just before noon, Maquignaz and Pétigax, who were leading, stood aside to let His Highness go first.

The conquest of the first great mountain in Alaska was hailed with the shout "Three cheers for Italy and the House of Savoy!" Ten days later, at the end of the exhausting return trip to the coast, the Duke, so swollen with insect bites as to be unrecognisable, commented to an American climber who had come to congratulate him, "I got the better of Mount St. Elias, but your mosquitoes have got the better of me!"

The exploits of the Duke of Abruzzi made a vital contribution to the early years of mountaineering outside Europe. "He belonged to an almost vanished race of explorers who had the private means to organise their own adventures and, more important, the drive to carry them off," writes Chris Jones in *Climbing in North America,* the most comprehensive history of mountaineering in the USA and Canada.

Towards new horizons

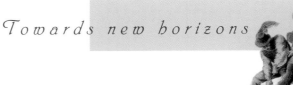

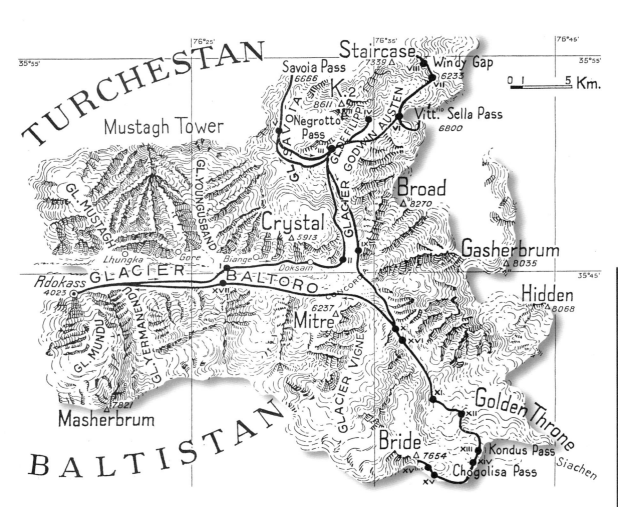

Luigi Amedeo of Savoy had gone to Mount St. Elias almost by chance; the expedition was originally supposed to climb Nanga Parbat, but the destination was changed because of a revolt in the Punjab. His exploits outside Europe continued with an attempt at the North Pole (1899) in which the latitude of 86°34' was reached, and the ascent of Mount Ruwenzori (1906), the most inhospitable and isolated mountain in Africa.

However, of all the Duke's expeditions, the one

98 top The Duke of Abruzzi's expeditions had both mountaineering and scientific aims, as demonstrated by the map of the locations visited by the 1909 expedition on the Baltoro Glacier. This expedition, well-known to climbers for the identification of the ascent route of K2 and the ascent to an altitude of 7500 metres on Bride Peak, explored all the glaciers that flow into the Concordia amphitheatre.

98 centre The long trek to the base of K2 and the Gasherbrums forces climbers to camp for several nights on the stony surface of the Baltoro Glacier. This photo, taken in 1909, shows Federico Negrotti Cambiaso, Filippo de Filippi and Vittorio Sella at the entrance of a tent pitched in the Concordia amphitheatre, overlooked by Gasherbrum IV, Mitre Peak, Masherbrum and K2.

best known by mountaineers all over the world is the 1909 Karakorum expedition, during which the easiest ascent route of K2 (the "Abruzzi Spur") was identified. This route was used by nearly all the later expeditions, including the Italian expedition that reached the summit in 1954. The members of the Duke of Abruzzi's team were mainly the same as in the previous expeditions; he was accompanied by Filippo De Filippi, Federico Negrotto, Vittorio Sella and Erminio Botta. The fact that a larger than usual number of guides from Courmayeur were included in the party (Joseph and Laurent Pétigax, Albert Savoye, Ernest Bareux, Alexis, Henri and Emile Brocherel) suggests that the Duke realised the ascent was going to be a tough nut to crack.

The expedition left Srinagar in early May, and reached the Concordia amphitheatre after a 25-day walk-in. De Filippi, the expedition's chronicler, enthusiastically described the appearance of the second-highest mountain on earth: "We could see the whole of the wide Godwin Austen gorge.

100 top Somewhat flattened when viewed from the Godwin-Austen and Savoia Glaciers, the second-highest mountain on earth appears slenderer when seen from further away, as demonstrated by this photo taken from the South-East ridge of Savoia III, an elegant 7018-metre peak. The snow-capped Angelus peak can be seen on the right of K2.

100-101 The awesome South-East face of K2, illuminated by the sunset in this photo, is one of the most difficult faces on the mountain, and can best be admired from the Savoia glacier in the afternoon sunlight. The first attempted ascent on this side of the mountain was made in 1978, by a strong British expedition led by Chris Bonington. Nick Estcourt was killed by an avalanche, and the route was later completed by a Japanese team.

101 top This picture, taken by Vittorio Sella, shows the south side of K2 near the confluence of the Savoia and Godwin-Austen Glaciers. The only possible access to the upper part of the mountain was identified by the guides as a spur of rock and snow not visible in this photo.

101 bottom The Duke of Abruzzi, together with other members of the 1909 expedition, climbs the Godwin-Austen Glacier towards the base of the Abruzzi Spur of K2. Expeditions heading for the ordinary route on the mountain still set up their base camp in this area.

"In the bottom, all alone, standing apart from every other mountain, towers K2, the true and rightful monarch of the region, in supreme grandeur…its shape is perfect, balanced and ideally proportioned, and its architectural design is exceptionally solid."

While the other members of the party explored the Godwin-Austen and Savoia Glaciers, reaching the 6233-metre Windy Gap and the 6666-metre Savoia Pass, a group of guides tackled the rocky spur that climbs towards the shoulder of K2. Despite the skill of the men from Courmayeur, they were able to get no farther than a height of 6550 metres, below the yellow rock steps that still constitute the crux of the route.

A few days later the group made an attempt on Skyang Kangri (the Staircase), but were halted at 6600 metres by two impassable crevasses. The Duke's attention then turned to Chogolisa which, at 7654 metres, is one of the most elegant seven-thousanders in Asia. His first attempt failed at 7150 metres, and the second was rebuffed by deep snow, cornices and fog only 150 metres below the summit. However, the altitude reached (7500 metres!) was a world record, not to be beaten until 30 years later.

The Duke of Abruzzi's small but brilliant expeditions astonished Italy and the rest of the world. However, many other climbers shared with him the

102 Dark outcrops of rock and "cauliflowers" of ice defend Margherita Peak which, with its altitude of 5119 metres, is the highest peak in the Ruwenzori Mountains. The Duke of Abruzzi named the three highest peaks in the range after the Queen of Italy, the Queen of England and the King of Belgium.

credit for being the first to explore the great mountains of the world.

"I saw something white on the summit of the mountain in the land of the Wa-Chagga. My guides did not know what it was called, but used the world *cold*. It was snow." This is the entry for 11th May 1848 in the diary of Johann Rebmann, a Swiss missionary who was crossing the savannah of what is now Tanzania on foot, and was the first European to glimpse the snows of Kilimanjaro from afar. A few weeks later, on reaching the lands of the Masai and the Kikuyu, Rebmann saw a second white summit— the rocks and perennial snow of Mount Kenya far off.

His observation was perfectly logical, and it would seem reasonable to assume that the Swiss recognise snow when they see it, even if it is at the equator. Yet when Rebmann's report reached London, famous geographer William D. Cooley called it "an unproven, imaginary,

ridiculous vision." The controversy was to continue for years.

Eventually, the dispute triggered by Rebmann's report was settled by a German nobleman, Karl Klaus von Decken, who made the first attempt on the 5875-metre summit of Mount Kilimanjaro in 1861. His expedition did not even reach 3000 metres, but he took back to Europe the first description of the forests at the foot of the mountain and the desert plateau that separates Kibo from the rocks of Mawenzi, the second-highest summit in the massif. Twenty-four years later, Scottish naturalist Joseph Thomson described Mount Kenya as "a gleaming peak that glitters with the superb beauty of a diamond." In 1886, Queen Victoria ceded Kilimanjaro to her grandson, the future Kaiser Wilhelm II, and Hungarian Count Samuel Teleki de Szek made a serious attempt to ascend both mountains.

Two years later, on 24th May 1888, Henry Morton Stanley was the protagonist of one of the most famous episodes in the exploration of Africa. While his expedition was camped on the banks of Lake Albert, one of his men cried out, "Look! A mountain of salt!".

"I saw a cloud with a very unusual shape, of the best silvery hue, which had the appearance and proportions of a summit crowned by snow. Then I realised that it was not a cloud at all but a solid body, a real snow-capped mountain," recounts the Anglo-American adventurer, who had just discovered Mount Ruwenzori, only the third-highest mountain in Africa, but certainly the most attractive.

The lonely, inhospitable "Mountains of the Moon," which mark the border between the Congo and Nile basins, comprise six different massifs and 24 summits over 4000 metres high.

103 top left This photo, taken from Albert Peak, clearly shows the rocks and ice scrolls of Margherita Peak (centre) and Alexandra Peak. All the highest peaks in the Ruwenzori range were climbed in 1906 by the Duke of Abruzzi and the Courmayeur guides who accompanied him.

103 bottom left Henry Morton Stanley, born in England but an American citizen, became famous when he crossed Black Africa from coast to coast and found Dr. Livingstone at Lake Tanganyika. In 1888, from the shores of Lake Albert, he was the first white man to see the Ruwenzori range, which separates the Congo from Uganda.

103 top right Hungarian Count Samuel Teleki de Szek, who loved Africa, was the first climber to reach fairly high altitudes on Kilimanjaro and Mount Kenya, the two highest peaks on the continent. The loveliest valley in Mount Kenya is named after him.

103 centre right The Ruwenzori range, which is steep on both the Ugandan side and the side facing the Congo, stretches from the highest peaks down to the snow-covered wastes of Stanley Plateau (4750 metres). The dark rock of Moebius Peak can be seen in the background.

103 bottom right A pretty stretch of groundsel provides the background for the best-known and most spectacular face of Mount Kenya, overlooking Teleki Valley, which was climbed in 1899 by Halford Mackinder and his party. On the right of the Nelion and Batian peaks stands the rocky Point Dutton.

104 left *The ordinary route on Kilimanjaro, climbed by Hans Meyer and Ludwig Purtscheller in 1889, follows an easy (though tiring) scree-filled couloir. The glaciers covering the sides of the volcano offer some fascinating, difficult climbs. This photo shows the ascent to Kibo along the slopes of Heim Glacier.*

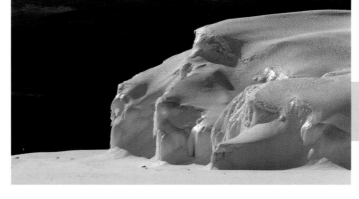

After a first attempted ascent by German naturalist Franz Stuhlmann in 1905, another serious attempt on Mount Ruwenzori was made from the Uganda side in 1905 by a skilled team consisting of British climbers Douglas Freshfield and Arnold L. Mumm, and guide Moritz Inderblatten from Zermatt. A year later, as already mentioned, the Duke of Abruzzi's expedition reached the 5119-metre summit of the highest peak in the group.

However, the age of conquest of the great African mountains had begun 17 years earlier, in 1889, when German topographer Hans Meyer and famous climber Ludwig Purtscheller from Salzburg reached the 5895-metre summit of Mount Kilimanjaro. "At 10:30 I set foot on the central point. I planted a small German flag with a 'hip, hip, hurrah!'… I named the summit of the Kibo, the highest point in African and German territory, 'Kaiser Wilhelm Spitze.'" The atmosphere of the "Scramble for Africa," the competition between the European powers to gain colonies on the continent, transpires very clearly from the expressions used by Meyer and many of his contemporaries.

On the more elegant and difficult Mount Kenya (5199 m), victory was won in 1899 by Scot Halford

Mackinder and Courmayeur guides César Ollier and Joseph Brocherel. The party travelled to the plateaus of the interior on the new railway line that connected Mombasa to Nairobi, then continued on foot towards the thick forest that surrounds the foot of the mountain.

On 12th and 13th September, the technique and intuition of the Mont Blanc guides enabled Mackinder to reach the 5199-metre summit. The route was difficult, with pitches up to the 4th grade on rock, and it took three hours' work with the ice-axe to cut steps into the short but tough slope which they named "Diamond Glacier."

Towards new horizons

104 above left *"As wide as all the world, great, high, and unbelievably white in the sun"; that is how Ernest Hemingway described the highest mountain in Africa in* The Snows of Kilimanjaro. *His description perfectly fits the volcano when viewed from the savannas of Amboseli National Park, famous for its herds of elephants.*

104 above right *Its "terraces" of ice make the crater of Kilimanjaro unmistakable. This photo shows Decken glacier, which runs along the west side of the easy snow-filled couloir used by trekkers climbing to the Kibo crater along the Machame route.*

104-105 Another photo of the Kibo ice terraces, surrounded by the dark slopes of volcanic rock forming the crater. This photo was taken from the ridge that joins Gillman's Point to Uhuru Point, which is followed by the thousands of hikers who visit Kilimanjaro every year.

105 right Hans Meyer, a teacher and topographer from Leipzig, reached the summit of Kilimanjaro with Austrian Ludwig Purtscheller in 1889. According to his report, "I gave three cheers and planted a small German flag. I named the summit of Kibo, the culminating point of African and German land, Kaiser Wilhelm Spitze."

105 above right Trekkers who look back from Uhuru Point can see the last part of the ordinary route to Kilimanjaro. On the bottom left is the caldera, and on the right is Stella Point. The rock towers of Gillman's Point, where the scree-filled couloir of the ordinary route joins the ridge, can be seen at the farthest point from the photographer. The rock towers of Mawenzi are visible in the background.

105 bottom right
The alternation of sun, ice and wind turns the snow that falls onto the crater of Kilimanjaro into a thin crust of ice moulded by atmospheric agents. This is the landscape crossed by the thousands of trekkers who reach the 5895-metre peak of Uhuru Point every year.

Towards new horizons

While the first expeditions to the great mountains of Africa were made by the leading names in European climbing, some entirely different characters made the first ascents of the peaks of the USA and Canada in the same period. The interior of the American continent, unknown until the late 18th century, was crossed between 1801 and 1803 by the expedition led by Meriwether Lewis and William Clark. They were followed by topographers, soldiers, gold prospectors and trappers, together with the first brave pioneers heading for Oregon and the Pacific coast.

In 1842, Lieutenant John Charles Frémont, ordered by the government in Washington to draw a detailed map of the Oregon Trail, climbed one of the highest peaks in the Rockies with his guide Kit Carson and German topographer Karl Preuss. They reached the summit after a three-day struggle. The report by Frémont, who was later a candidate for the American presidency, recounts the fatigues and difficulties of the ascent, but does not enable historians to identify the peak climbed with certainty.

"We had accomplished an object of laudable ambition. We had climbed the loftiest peak of the Rocky Mountains, and looked down upon the snow thousands of feet below, and, standing where never human foot had stood before, felt the exultation of first explorers," wrote Frémont in his *Report of Expedition to the Rocky Mountains*. The venue of his adventure has been identified variously as Fremont Peak, Mount Woodrow Wilson and other peaks of the spectacular Wind River Range in Wyoming.

By the middle of the century, the coasts and plains of Oregon and the then territory of Washington were being systematically colonised. On clear days, the inhabitants of Seattle, Portland and other cities of North-west America could easily see the impressive snow-capped silhouettes of the volcanoes in the Cascades chain: Mount Rainier, Mount Baker, Mount St. Helens and Mount Hood. There's no need to be a climber to see those peaks as a challenge.

In 1853, 11 years after Louis Charles Frémont's feat, Thomas Dryer, the owner and publisher of the *Weekly Oregonian*, reached the summit of Mount St. Helens, the 2950-metre volcano which was to become world-famous for the horrifying eruption that began on 18th May 1980. A year later he climbed Mount Hood, the elegant icy peak that forms the backdrop to the city of Portland, and now offers the most classic and popular ascent on glaciers in North America. Dryer and his climbing companions had to use ropes, hooks and rudimentary crampons to reach the 3421-metre summit.

An even tougher feat was planned in 1857, when Lieutenant August Kautz, an American of German descent who was stationed at Fort Steilacoom on the banks of Puget Sound, decided to attempt the ascent of Mount Rainier, the volcano covered with no less than 28 glaciers which can be seen from Seattle city centre on clear days.

107 top right Mount Rainier (4392 metres), which can be seen from downtown Seattle on clear days, is the best-known mountain in the State of Washington. It is scaled by thousands of climbers every year.

107 bottom right The ordinary route on Mount Rainier starts with a long walk-in to Camp Muir (at 3200 metres), and continues on the steep slopes of Nisqually Glacier.

106 top John Charles Frémont was not a climber, but the official responsible for escorting German topographer Karl Preuss to one of the highest peaks in the Rocky Mountains, together with guide Kit Carson. It is unclear which mountain the party climbed; some authors have identified it as Fremont Peak, and others as various peaks in Wyoming's Wind River Range.

106 bottom Treks to the foot of Mount Rainer became popular in the late 19th and early 20th century, as demonstrated by this photo, taken on Paradise Glacier.

106-107 With its rock walls, snowfields and deep, lonely valleys, the Wind River Range in Wyoming offers some of the most spectacular scenery in the Rocky Mountains. The highest peak is Gannett Peak (4207 metres).

After carefully studying accounts of the first ascents of Mont Blanc, Kautz set off for the mountain in early July, accompanied by doctor Robert Orr Craig and soldiers William Carroll and Nicholas Dogue. They were guided by an Indian called Wapowety. Even more than the difficulty of the ascent, Kautz and his party. underestimated the length of the walk-in, through thick forest where their horses were more of a hindrance than a help for long stretches.

It was not until the seventh day that the group, which had left Fort Steilacoom with only a six-day supply of food, reached the upper edge of the forest and began the actual ascent of Mount Rainier. During the day, fatigue forced Carroll and Craig to return to camp, while Kautz and Dogue continued towards the summit, amid "inaccessible pinnacles of ice and deep crevasses." Then Dogue turned back, while the Lieutenant reached the point above 4000 metres where "the mountains spread out comparatively flat", and it was much easier to make progress. However, the late hour, tiredness and the lack of food and drink forced him to descend, too.

Victory over the 4392-metre summit of Mount Rainier was won in 1870 by topographer Hazard Stevens and former gold prospector Philemon Van Trump, who reached the summit after scaling a long and difficult rocky ridge and a series of great crevasses, where daring manoeuvres with the rope were required.

At 5 p.m., on the rocks of Point Success, the pair found that the going was easy but the summit was still far off. Determination and courage persuaded them to continue to the summit, where they arrived as the sun was setting. Luckily, the fumaroles on the edge of the tiny crater of Mount Rainier offered the two climbers a rather warmer bivouac than they had expected. "Never was a discovery more welcome! We warmed our chilled and benumbed extremities over one of these Pluto's fires, and we passed the night, secure against freezing to death," wrote Stevens on his return from the ascent.

Englishman Edmund Coleman, who climbed with Stevens and Van Trump as far as the edge of the forest and was then forced to give up out of fatigue, made an interesting observation. "The absorbing pursuit of money, the strangely practical character of the American mind, are quite sufficient to account for the absence of that *passion des montagnes* which is so often to be met with in older communities. Those who come out to the Western States do so either to make money, or to build up a home for themselves and families. Consequently, they have neither the time nor the money to spend on what is generally considered to be a visionary, if not a foolhardy, pursuit."

The romantic adventures of John Muir, a nature lover of Scottish descent, now famous for his books, articles and his vital contribution to nature protection in the American West, at least partly gave the lie to these comments. Starting in 1869, Muir, the "father" of the Grand Canyon, Yosemite and Sequoia & Kings Canyon

108 right John Muir (on the left in the photo) was not a climber but a lover of nature in the American West. It was his books that made Yosemite, the Grand Canyon and the great sequoia forests popular with the American public.

108 inset The first ascent of the Grand Teton, like that of Mount McKinley, was claimed before it had actually been made. The 1870 ascent made by John James Stevenson (shown in this photo) and Nathaniel Langford is not recognised by historians.

108 right The upper part of Yosemite National Park offers far more Alpine landscapes than Yosemite Valley, the most popular area with climbers and tourists. In this photo, the twilight and the full moon illuminate Lyell Glacier, not far from the south-eastern boundary of the park.

108-109 "I reached the summit at noon, having loitered by the way to study the fine trees." These brief words were the only comment made by John Muir about his ascent of Cathedral Peak, the elegant rocky peak that dominates from the south Tuolomne Meadows and the road that climbs to Tioga Pass in Yosemite National Park.

109 inset The smooth granite walls that dominate Yosemite Valley provide one of the best-known and most spectacular images of nature in the USA. John Muir wrote about their beauty from 1869 onwards. However, these walls were not climbed until 1934.

National Parks, spent many years among the mountains and forests of the Sierra Nevada, where he made numerous ascents.

However, his writings, with their wealth of detail about nature, contain very few details of the routes followed or the difficulties overcome. "I made my way up to its topmost spire, which I reached at noon, having loitered by the way to study the fine trees," was Muir's only laconic comment on the first ascent of Cathedral Peak. "Well-seasoned limbs will enjoy the climb of 3000 feet required by this direct route. But soft, succulent people should go the mule way," he wrote after the first ascent of a difficult couloir (now known as the definitive Mountaineers' Route) to the summit of Mount Whitney.

While Muir openly boasted that he had "never left my name on any mountain, rock or tree," other climbers of the day, in particular topographers Clarence King and Josiah D. Whitney, devoted long, detailed reports to their feats and the difficulties involved.

In the Yosemite Valley, beloved by Muir and now frequented by climbers from all over the world, 1875 brought the first ascent of Half Dome, a spectacular granite peak whose smooth slabs forced Scot George Anderson to drive pegs into the rock. This method of ascent was similar to that used seven years later by the Maquignaz-Sella party to conquer the harsh walls of the Dent du Géant.

Climbing in North America came to resemble mountaineering in the Alps in the attempts on the summit of the Grand Teton, the magnificent granite mountain that stands in the heart of the chain of the same name, now protected by one of the most popular national parks in the States.

The ascent of the mountain was claimed by Nathaniel Langford and James Stevenson in 1872, but is only known with certainty to have been performed 26 years later, by William O. Owen and Rev. Franklin Spaulding. The mystery of who reached the summit first has never been solved. However, there is no doubt that its height (the Grand Teton stands at 4197 m), the Alpine setting and the difficulty involved make this ascent similar to those performed in the same years in Europe on the pinnacles of the Dolomites and the granite walls of Mont Blanc.

Towards new horizons

While climbing in North America was mainly developing thanks to local people, the best European mountaineers of the day were climbing the highest peaks in the Andes, the long and spectacular chain that forms the backbone of South America.

One of the first to make his appearance on the Andes scene was German climber Wilhelm Reiss who, with Angel M. Escobar of Colombia, made the first ascent of Cotopaxi (5897 m), the impressive Ecuadorian volcano whose lava has invaded the town of Latacunga on several occasions.

Seven years later, Englishman Edward Whymper, the most famous climber of the day as a result of the first ascent of the Matterhorn, landed at the port of Guayaquil. In six months' climbing on the volcanoes of Ecuador, Whymper, accompanied by guides Jean-Antoine Carrel (his climbing companion and later his rival on the Matterhorn) and Louis Carrel, made the first ascents of Chimborazo (6267 m), Cayambe (5789 m), Antisana (5705 m), Carihuairazo (5028 m), Sincholagua (4893 m), Cotacachi (4939 m) and Sara Urco (4676 m).

110 top In this engraving by Edward Whymper, the steep slopes of the upper part of Chimborazo are seen from a position (approx. 5800 m) slightly higher than the camp pitched by the Englishman and his guides. The ascent presented no particular problems, but the crossing of the summit plateau was far more difficult, as the thick layer of soft snow made the going very tiring.

The two Carrels made the first ascent of Illiniza Sur (5263 m) by themselves. Then the whole party, accompanied by two local porters, made the third ascent of Cotopaxi, which had been almost entirely stripped of its glaciers by the great eruption of two years earlier.

However, the key moment in the entire campaign was the first ascent of Chimborazo, which was considered the highest mountain on earth until the early decades of the 19th century. During the ascent, the three climbers scaled the cleft in the rock which had defeated Alexander von Humboldt 76 years earlier. "Anyone who is not a mountaineer can go this far and no farther," was

Whymper's comment on this difficult pitch.

On the upper part of the volcano, mountain sickness, soft snow and a raging blizzard tested the Englishman and the two Italians to the limit, while the snow made it difficult to tell the real summit from the many peaks surrounding the summit plateau. In the end, "reasonably firm" snow enabled the three to reach the summit "standing upright like men, instead of grovelling, as we had been doing for the previous five hours, like beasts of the field."

Despite a gale-force wind, Whymper and the Carrels managed to set up a mercury barometer and two

aneroids to measure the height of the mountain, and plant a flag. Then they set off across the plateau, descended as fast as possible, and just got back to their camp before darkness fell.

Before the century was out, British climbers and guides from the Western Alps returned to the Andes, where they reached some of the highest peaks ever climbed much farther south than Ecuador. In 1897, an expedition organised by Edward A. Fitzgerald attempted the ascent of Aconcagua which, at 6960 metres, is the highest peak in Argentina and on the entire American continent.

Easy but very tiring because of the high altitude, the

110 bottom The high passes of the Andes, frequented by the Indians of South America since time immemorial, still allow present-day travellers between Argentina and Chile to admire the lovely mountains from close up. This engraving by Alexander Coldclough shows a party travelling in the Andes around 1825.

110-111 Aconcagua, with its 6960-metre summit, is the highest peak in the Andes and the entire continent of America, and is the highest point on earth which can be reached without true mountaineering skills. Although it crosses some fairly easy stony ground and snowfields, the ascent is difficult because of the altitude and the wind, which is often particularly fierce.

111 top left The ordinary route on Cotopaxi is now climbed by mountaineers from all over the world. The route followed today is the same one used for the first ascent, made in 1872 by German climber Wilhelm Reiss, accompanied by Colombian Angel M. Escobar.

ordinary route on the mountain is now attempted by hundreds of climbers every year. Fitzgerald and the other members of the expedition stopped at an altitude of some 6500 metres, while Mathias Zurbriggen, one of the greatest guides on Monte Rosa, reached the highest point alone. A few days later this man of the mountains, born in Saas Fee but resident at Macugnaga, also reached the 6550-metre summit of Tupungato.

The next year two guides from Valtournenche, Antoine Maquignaz and Louis Pellissier, accompanied Martin Conway to the 6462-metre summit of Illimani, the highest and most famous peak in Bolivia.

111 top right Cotopaxi, the second-highest volcano in Ecuador, which dominates the town of Latacunga, has devastated the surrounding fields and villages with its lava flows on many occasions. For climbers who reach the summit, the appearance of the crater is the most exciting moment of the ascent.

111 bottom The very high altitude of the peaks, their isolation and their position between the Pacific Ocean and the Amazon basin mean that the weather on Ecuador's volcanoes is very changeable. This is demonstrated by the storm that took Whymper and the Carrels by surprise during the second ascent of Cotopaxi, not far from the summit.

In the same years, the first European expeditions began to visit the valleys of the Himalaya and the Karakorum range, where the triangulations performed by the Survey of India had just confirmed the presence of the highest peaks on earth. Everest, defended by the inviolable borders of Tibet and Nepal, was out of the question for the moment, so mountaineers turned their attention to mountains inside the borders of the British Empire.

The main one was K2, the second-highest mountain on earth, with a height of 8611 metres. The first to see the mountain from close to, in 1887, was English Captain Francis Younghusband, who made an adventurous

crossing from Peking to Rawalpindi, the crux of which was the crossing of the icy and difficult Muztagh Pass. "A mountain of awesome size. It seems to rise like a perfect cone, but an incredibly tall one," wrote Younghusband about K2, which he admired first from the Chinese side and then from the side situated in what is now Pakistan.

A year after the ascent of Illimani, Martin Conway led the first exploration of the Baltoro, Hispar and Biafo glacier basins. The expedition, which included some very different personalities, such as Mathias Zurbriggen, Major Charles Bruce (who later joined the first expeditions to Mount Everest) and Anglo-German climber Oskar Eckenstein, considered the inventor of

modern crampons, achieved some excellent geographical results. They were unable to make a serious attempt on K2, but fell back on the nearby Golden Throne (6890 m), the first major peak in the Karakorum range to be climbed.

A year later, Oskar Eckenstein led a new expedition to the Baltoro glacier. Differences between the members of the group and pulmonary oedema suffered by Austrian Hans Pfannl slowed the progress of the party, but they still managed to climb to 6250 metres, in the direction of the icy saddle that separates K2 from Skyang Kangri. The first serious attempt at an ascent of K2 was made 10 years later, by the Duke of Abruzzi.

112 top British topographers and their native assistants employed by the Survey of India identified the plain and the first spurs of the Himalaya, the highest peaks in Asia and on earth. This photo was taken in 1904. The discovery that Peak XV, with its 8848-metre summit, is the highest peak of all, was made in 1868.

112 bottom The British military expedition to Lhasa led by Sir Francis Younghusband in 1905 was sent to subjugate Tibet, and had no mountaineering objectives. However, two officers observed Everest from the Tibetan plateau, and suggested in a report that the North ridge might offer an ascent route to the summit.

112-113 The summit pyramid of Mount Everest, seen here from the Tibetan side, is illuminated by the warm light of sunset. The seven attempted ascents made between the wars took place on this north side.

113 top The Survey of India used some very powerful theodolites, which had to cover distances of 200-250 kilometres. The instrument shown in this photo was used by Colonel William Lambdon and Sir George Everest.

113 bottom Sir George Everest was not a climber, but Surveyor-General of India from 1830 to 1843. The highest mountain on earth, previously known as Peak XV, was officially named after him in 1865.

114 top It is so difficult to obtain a permit to climb Kangchenjunga from the Indian side that the mountain is mainly climbed from the Nepalese side. The awesome West face of "Kangch" can be seen in this photo. The main peak (8595 metres) is on the right, and the central peak (8482 metres) in the centre of the photo.

In the same year (1899), an entirely different feat was performed at the foot of Kangchenjunga which, at 8569 metres, is the third-highest mountain on earth. Organised by British mountaineer Douglas Freshfield, the party, which included climber Edmund J. Garwood, topographer Rinzin Namgyal and Italian photographer Vittorio Sella, took a month to make the circuit of the great mountain, crossing a series of passes at altitudes of between 5000 and 6000 metres. The weather was nearly always bad, which complicated things for climbers and porters alike, while the clandestine nature of the expedition (access to Nepal was strictly prohibited at the time!) added a spice of danger to this magnificent route, which anticipated the fashion for trekking by over half a century.

In the years before the circuit of Kangchenjunga, Douglas Freshfield, one of the most active climbers of all time, also played an important part in the British exploration of the Caucasus, whose icy peaks offered adventure in an exotic environment much closer to Europe than the great mountains of South America and Asia (remember that the aeroplane had not yet been invented!).

During his three climbing campaigns in the region (1868, 1888 and 1889), Freshfield climbed Kasbek (5047 m), Tetnuld (4853 m) and Skoda, and scaled the eastern peak of Elbrus.

114 centre British climber Douglas Freshfield (1845-1943) made numerous major ascents in the Alps and Pyrenees in the late 19th and early 20th century. His many non-European expeditions include three trips to the Caucasus, an attempted ascent of Ruwenzori, and the adventurous circuit of Kangchenjunga.

114-115 bottom This panoramic view of the Kangchenjunga chain, was obtained by skilfully combining a number of photos taken by Vittorio Sella during the 1899 expedition to the Himalaya.

114-115 top
Kangchenjunga, at 8595
metres the third-highest
mountain on earth, stands
on the border between
Nepal and Sikkim (India). In
this photo, taken from the

summit of Gocha La (nearly
5000 metres), the southern
peak of Kangchenjunga (8476
metres) appears on the far
right. The steep ice slopes of
Talung can be seen in the
foreground.

115 right Italian Vittorio Sella
(1859-1943), who made
numerous major ascents in
the Alps, is also one of the
best-known mountain
photographers of all time. A
climbing companion of the

Duke of Abruzzi in his
expeditions to Karakorum,
Ruwenzori and Mount St.
Elias, he also visited the
Caucasus and took part in the
circuit of Kangchenjunga led
by Douglas Freshfield.

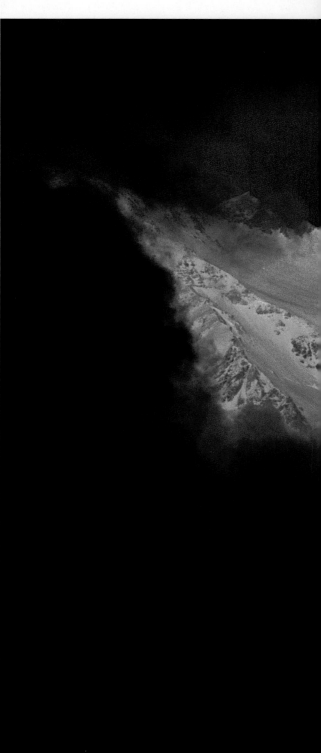

116 top "A rock and ice pillar 4500 metres tall, so awesome it's almost unearthly. For us, it was the quintessence of the insuperable." This is how Mathias Rebitsch, one of the best climbers of the day, described the Rupal face of Nanga Parbat in 1938. In order to admire this sight there's no need to be a mountaineer, as a convenient footpath connects Tap hollow at the foot of the wall to the village of Tarshing, from which a road leads to the Indus Valley.

116 bottom The ascent of the Rupal wall, over 4000 metres high, was another important moment in climbing history. It was scaled in 1970 by two teams from an expedition led by German Karl Herrligkoffer. Brothers Reinhold and Gunther Messner were the first to reach the summit. They were followed the next day by Felix Kuen and Peter Scholz. During the descent on the Diamir side, Gunther Messner was killed by an avalanche.

In the Caucasus he crossed paths with Albert F. Mummery, the leading turn-of-the-century climber on the Aiguilles de Chamonix and the Aiguille Verte, as he had done several times in the Alps.

After leaving his beloved Alps, Mummery ventured into the wild valleys of the Caucasus in 1888 to make the first ascent of Dych Tau (which, at 5203 metres, is the second-highest mountain in the range) with Swiss guide Hans Zurfluh. In 1890 Mummery returned to the mountains separating the Black Sea from the Dead Sea where he performed numerous ascents, many of them solo.

In 1895, after a series of brilliant summers in the Alps, Albert Frederick Mummery was again bitten by the exploration bug. Instead of the mountains of the Caucasus, he chose to tackle one of the highest and most difficult peaks on earth. Nanga Parbat, the 8125-metre mountain that marks the westernmost end of the Himalayan chain, overlooks the Indus Valley and the torrid plains of Taxila, Rawalpindi and Islamabad.

116-117 Nanga Parbat (8125 metres), now in Pakistan, is the peak closest to the plain. The Diamir side, attempted by Mummery in 1895, was climbed in 1961 by Germans Toni Kinshofer, Anderl Mannhardt and Sigi Low. This route later became the most popular with expeditions heading for the summit.

52 years after Mummery, another top-class climber of exceptional courage, Austrian Hermann Buhl, was to reach the summit of Nanga Parbat alone. Between 1934 and 1937, the catastrophic avalanches that hit two German expeditions, killing 26 climbers and sherpas, won this beautiful peak the evil name of "the Man-eater."

Mummery had no need of nicknames to realise that the mountain looming up in front of him was enormous, dangerous and awesome. Accompanied by two Ghurkas, he set off into the Diamir valley, dominated by one of the tallest and most inhospitable

walls of the Nanga, with the intention of making a solo ascent. But Mummery never came back.

His companions identified his tracks in the following days, but lost them around 6000 metres. One of the most brilliant, light-hearted, creative mountaineers of all time was probably killed by an avalanche. However, his courage and intelligence remain a magnificent example even today, when dozens of climbers, clothed and equipped a thousand times better than Mummery, climb towards the great peaks of the Himalaya without breathing apparatus.

117 bottom The 1895 attempt on Nanga Parbat was one of the greatest adventures in the history of mountaineering. Englishman Albert F. Mummery, together with porters Goman and Raghobir Singh, scaled

Diamir Peak, reached an altitude of 6400 metres on an unnamed peak, and then attempted the highest peak from the Diamir side. The three men were last sighted on 24th August. They were never seen again.

The advent
of the sixth grade

*118 bottom left The summit
of Mount Pelmo, known as
"Caregòn del Doge" in
Cadore tradition, entered the
history of climbing in the
Dolomites in 1857, when
John Ball and his guide made
the first ascent. Sixty-seven
years later, what was then
one of the most difficult
routes in the entire
Dolomites was put up on the
North face of the mountain.

118-119. The impressive
North-West face of the Pale
di San Martino offers one of
the most attractive spectacles
in the Dolomites. On the
right stands the sharp Cimon
della Pala. Next to it,
illuminated in the twilight,
are Cima della Vezzana, Cima
dei Bureloni, Campanile di
Valgrande and Cima del
Focobòn.*

In 1914, Europe was plunged into one of the
most horrifying tragedies in history. Triggered by the
assassination of Archduke Franz Ferdinand of
Austria, the war (the first in history to merit the
description of "World War") rapidly spread across
the continent.

The young men of France and Great Britain
confronted those of Germany in the trenches of the
Somme, Picardy and Artois, where place names like
Ypres and Verdun became synonymous with
massacres perpetrated by cannons, bayonets and
gas. A thousand kilometres farther south, bloody
battles were fought between the armies of Italy and
the Austro-Hungarian Empire on the plateaus of the
Carso and the banks of the River Isonzo. On the
Eastern front, the armies of the Kaiser and the Tsar
clashed on the plains of Poland and Byelorussia. The
collapse of the Russian army paved the way for a
revolution that was destined to change the face of
Eastern Europe for three-quarters of a century.

Many famous mountaineers lost their lives in the
carnage, as did millions of their peers. In the Central
Alps and the Dolomites, the conflict also changed
the landscape. Mountains like the Gran Zebrù,

Adamello, Marmolada, Pasubio, the Tofane and the
Tre Cime were perforated by emplacements and
trenches, brought closer to the plains by military roads
excavated in the rock, tamed by routes equipped with
steps, walkways and fixed ropes, and hideously
adorned with hundreds of kilometres of barbed wire.

When the war was over, climbing slowly began to
return to the Alps, scarred by cannon fire and mines.
In just a few years, many block-houses and barracks
were turned into refuge huts, thus contributing to the
development of tourism and mountaineering. In the
Dolomites, however, no particularly outstanding feats
took place in the immediate post-war years.

The first noteworthy routes were put up on the
Pale di San Martino, starting in 1919, by Gunther
Langes, a German-speaking climber born in Fiera di

Mountaineering

Primiero who had fought with the Austrian army. The most elegant of all is Spigolo del Velo (Veil Edge, known as *Schleierkante* to German-speaking climbers) on Cima della Madonna, which is clearly visible from San Martino di Castrozza.

Exposed and on solid rock, the route that Langes opened on 19th July 1920 with Erwin Merlet soon became one of the classics in the Dolomites. When Willo Welzenbach presented his proposal for a rating scale divided into six grades a few years later, he took this route as the pattern for the fifth grade.

In September 1921, an Italian team consisting of guide Francesco Jori from Canazei (brother-in-law of the great Tita Piaz), Arturo Andreoletti from Milan and Alberto Zanutti from Trieste conquered the impressive North face of the Agnèr which, with its height of 1500 metres, is one of the tallest and most awesome in the entire Alpine range.

"It rises with fearful swiftness; you have to twist

119 right Despite his Italian surname, Roland Rossi was a Bavarian climber. One of the leading representatives of the "Munich School," he took part in some excellent ascents in the Twenties. One

of the most outstanding, in terms of difficulty and length, was the North face of Pelmo (870 metres, upper fifth grade), which Rossi climbed in August 1924 with fellow-countryman Felix Simon.

119 above right The sharp Spigolo del Velo on Cima della Madonna (on the right in the photo), which overlooks the Cismòn Valley, features one of the most

interesting fourth- and fifth-grade routes in the Dolomites. It was inaugurated in the summer of 1920 by Gunther Langes and Erwin Merlet from Alto Adige.

your head upwards to look at it. It's the greatest architecture in all the Dolomites," wrote climber and author Dino Buzzati in *Il Corriere della Sera* in 1956. The route was described as "a magnificent climb on the tallest wall in the Dolomites, of the greatest mountaineering interest" by Ettore Castiglioni, who performed the first repeat in 1934 with Bruno Detassis and Vitale Bramani.

Then, in the Dolomites as in the Alps, the initiative passed to German-speaking mountaineers, especially the excellent rock climbers of the "Munich School," who had learned their skills on the rocks of the Karwendel, Wetterstein and Wilder Kaiser. The first great ascent by a Bavarian team was made on 11th and 12th August 1924, when Roland Rossi and Felix Simon scaled the gigantic North face of Pelmo along a 900-metre route still rated at the upper fifth grade.

The North face of Furchetta, the awesome wall in the Odle massif whose yellowish overhangs had defeated Hans Dulfer eleven years earlier, was climbed the next year. The crux of the ascent is a highly exposed traverse to the left at the foot of the yellow overhangs. It was identified and conquered by two outstanding characters, Emil Solleder and Fritz Wiessner.

Emil Solleder, born in Munich, was 26, and had led an adventurous life in America. He had worked as a labourer and bricklayer, and even prospected for gold in Alaska. He eventually became a mountain guide, and died on the Meije in 1931 to save his client. In the years of his great ascents in the Dolomites, his romantic view of mountaineering became famous among German climbers. "Bold climbers are often criticised for taking the game too far. But how can someone who isn't playing the game understand what it means to a climber?" he explained in one of his best-known articles.

Fritz Wiessner, born in Dresden in 1900, who had learned to climb on the sandstone of the

Elbsandsteingebirge, also emigrated in 1935 to the USA, where he made a great contribution to the development of American mountaineering. Climbing in the Karakorum in 1939, he just failed to reach the summit of K2.

Solleder and Wiessner left the Odle range behind them and went to Caprile to take a look at the Civetta. "I knew that there was a steep castle of rock called Civetta down to the south. I'd never seen it, but I'd often heard of it. People said that no one should climb that mountain – a gigantic wall with terrible hails of stones and a lot of ice." With those words, Emil Solleder introduced the mountain that was to make him famous.

The bad weather persuaded Wiessner to give up the attempt, but Solleder walked on to take a look at the wall. He followed a trail that "skirted half-demolished houses and climbed to the summit of a crater-shaped mountain that marks a bitterly-fought

border." After a long climb in the fog, the sun finally came out. Suddenly, to the south, "a superb mountain emerged from the fog," leaving the climber speechless.

"Can it be real? I've never seen a wall like that in the Alps before," he recounted when he was back in the valley. The next day, bent under the weight of a heavy knapsack, Emil Solleder climbed to the Coldai refuge hut. There he met up with two more Bavarian climbers, Gaberl and Gustav Lettenbauer, who had also been bewitched by the awesome wall, and they immediately decided to join forces.

Early next day, the trio made their assault on the

great wall, on the perpendicular of the summit. They scaled a loose base wall hit by frequent hails of stones, and the wall immediately became vertical. After passing a waterfall, the three found themselves at the base of "an extraordinarily exposed wall" which Lettenbauer climbed first in great style. Then Solleder took the lead.

He scaled a loose overhanging crack, reached a wet chimney, then moved to the left to skirt an 8-metre overhanging roof. He drove in a piton, left his cap in a hole, then traversed to the right, fighting against the friction of the rope, until he reached a second narrow chimney. While following on this pitch Gaberl fell, injuring his foot. After a bivouac 300 metres from the

scree, the rainy morning forced the team to descend.

Two days later, after leaving their friend down in the valley, Solleder and Lettenbauer were back in action. They reached the ledge where they had bivouacked, and continued for 250 metres on slanting slabs. This section is not too difficult, but it is "the most dangerous part of the whole ascent because of the stones that rain down nonstop." After a moment of uncertainty about the route to follow, a grey crack enabled them to set off upwards again.

The Bavarians scaled a "horrifyingly unstable edge," an overhang and an aid pitch, then reached the gorge that took them out of the difficult part of the

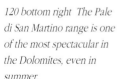

ascent. After an "icy shower" in a waterfall and a rest in the sun, the pair continued in the gathering darkness. "Suddenly, a crow flew by just above us, and a cold wind announced that the summit was close." In the starry night, the two German champions shook hands on the summit, then bivouacked a few metres below it. At 2 a.m., when the full moon finally appeared from the fog, they began their descent to the valley, and fame.

Thirteen months later, on 6th September 1926, Emil Solleder made another outstanding ascent, this time with Bavarian Franz Kummer. The venue was the East face of Sass Maòr, the highest and most awesome of the Pale. However, it was the route he put up on the Civetta that gave Emil Solleder a place in climbing history. Extremely long, dangerous and difficult, it was universally acknowledged to be a feat that surpassed anything previously achieved in the Dolomites. To define its difficulty, the advocates of a

rating scale had to create an entirely new standard: the sixth grade. These two words were to be of fundamental importance in the history of climbing in the next 50 years.

After Solleder's great achievements, Bavarian climber Walther Stosser made his name in the Dolomites, beginning with a direct route on the yellow summit wall of Tofana di Rozes in the summer of 1929. Next came Hans Steger, an Austrian climber who had moved to Italy in his youth.

Like Solleder, Steger roamed for years in different cities, trying his hand at various trades. He settled in Naples for several years, and put up a number of climbing routes on the limestone of Capri's Faraglioni. In the Dolomites, together with his girlfriend Paula Wiesinger, Steger scaled (among others) the severe Weg der Jugend (Youth Route) on the North face of Cima Una (1928) and a famous direct route on the East face of Catinaccio (1927).

122 top left This spectacular photo shows Emilio Comici stemming the wide, awesome chimney between Torre del Diavolo and Torre Leo in the Cadini di Misurina massif.

The advent of the sixth grade

Starting in 1929, a new generation of Italian climbers came onto the Dolomite scene. They included guides like Luigi Micheluzzi from Fassa, Bruno Detassis from Trento and Angelo and Giuseppe Dimai from Cortina. As in Germany and Austria, however, the new climbers were mainly city dwellers, and training grounds near towns, like Val Rosandra and the Grigne, became increasingly popular.

The most famous personality of the period was Emilio Comici who, apart from Riccardo Cassin, was the only Italian "sixth-grader" known to the general public. Born in Trieste of a humble family, he came to climbing by way of pot-holing. Between 1925 and 1940 he put up some 80 new routes in the Dolomites, the Julian Alps, the Greek Gàmila and Olympus ranges, and the granite mountains of the Sinai.

A free-climbing virtuoso but also an expert in climbing techniques using pitons, Comici had a complex and in many respects unknown personality. He left the city and a secure job and moved to Misurina in 1932 to earn his living as a guide, but made little progress because of strong opposition from local guides. He then moved to Selva Val Gardena where he became Prefectorial Commissioner and director of the local ski school, moving periodically to Aosta as an instructor at the Military Climbing School. He was definitely loyal to the Fascist regime ("Be bold. That's what *il Duce* (Mussolini) has taught us," he wrote in his only book). However, this loyalty did not make him a wealthy man; in fact, he was forced to perform in the "climbing stadiums" set up in many Italian cities for the occasion. He died in October 1940 while abseiling down the rocks of Vallunga, near Selva.

The list of his first ascents begins on the walls of the Julian Alps, and continues on the Dolomites. There, with Giordano Bruno Fabjan in August 1929, Comici scaled the awesome, friable North-West face of Sorella di Mezzo on the Sorapìss, a route that was to go down in history as "the first Italian sixth-grade." Two years later, roped to Giulio Benedetti, he was on the North-West face of Civetta, where he put up a highly demanding route to the left of the famous Solleder route.

In 1933 came the Tre Cime, where Comici scaled the North Face of Cima Grande and the Spigolo Giallo (Yellow Edge) of Cima Piccola one after another. The former, already attempted by Steger, was his toughest ascent, in which he had to call on all his stamina and piton placing technique. "The pitons went in scarcely an inch. I was no longer climbing on rock, but on four étriers," he wrote in *Alpinismo eroico.*

But it was the Spigolo Giallo, "resembling the prow of a Transatlantic liner marooned in that sea of scree" that really aroused his enthusiasm. "It was the most logical route to look at, though the most unlikely in practice… the most exposed climb you could possibly imagine," he wrote in his diary.

Then Comici, in his search for elegance, discovered solo climbing. His most outstanding ascent was performed solo, when he repeated his route on Cima Grande in 3.45 hours. Another short passage in his book gives a better insight into Comici's personality than any complex analysis. "At a certain moment, while I was bridging with my legs wide apart, I saw my ropes swinging free, and caught a glimpse of the scree at the bottom of the abyss. I was pervaded by a sensual pleasure I had never experienced before!"

The other outstanding personality in Italian climbing was Riccardo Cassin. He was short, thickset and exceptionally strong. In his youth he had been a boxer, then started work as a blacksmith. Born in Lecco, he first tried his hand at rock climbing in 1929 at the age of 20, when he climbed Guglia Angelina, one of the numerous pinnacles in the Grignetta, with Mario Dell'Oro, known as "Boga." This was followed by dozens of fifth- and sixth-grade routes in every corner of the range that dominates Lecco and its lake.

In 1933, a short spell in the Dolomites was devoted

124 left Among the various mountaineering venues, an important place is held by Campanile Alto and Campanile Basso di Brenta, flanked by Brenta Alta on the right.

124 right Giusto Gervasutti, nicknamed "Il Fortissimo," was well-known for his ascents of the rock walls of the Oisans and Mont Blanc. Having learned his climbing skills in the Dolomites, Gervasutti took to the Western Alps the elegant climbing style he had developed on the limestone walls of the Eastern Alps.

124-125 The sharp Vajolet Towers in the Catinaccio massif are one of the most famous sights in the Dolomites. They witnessed some outstanding climbs by Georg Winkler, Hermann Delago and Tita Piaz in the late 19th and early 20th century, but remained somewhat in the background in the Thirties, when the best climbers of the day preferred taller and more severe walls. This photo shows (from left) Punta Emma and the Central Towers (Winkler, Stabeler and Delago), with Gola delle Torri (Tower Ravine) and the less popular Northern Towers rising towards them.

to the classic routes: Campanile Basso, the Vajolet Towers and Punta Emma. The next year he began climbing seriously. The first day of his short holiday in 1934 was devoted to the Popena, where Cassin and his party repeated a route that had just been put up by another Lecco team.

The next day, Riccardo set off on virgin ground with Luigi Vitali and Luigi Pozzi, and put up a sixth-grade route on the short but vertical South face of Cima Piccolissima that is still a classic today. Before his week's holiday came to an end, he had time to repeat the Spigolo Giallo and North face of Cima Grande in record times, along the route opened the previous year by Emilio Comici with the Dimai brothers.

However, the great summer of the Lecco men was still to come. The group camped in the meadows around the Vazzolèr refuge hut at the foot of the extraordinary pinnacles (Busazza, Torre Venezia and Torre Trieste) where the ramparts of the Civetta terminate to the south.

On the first day, climbing with Mario Dell'Oro, Cassin made the first repeat of another masterpiece by Emilio Comici: the route opened in 1931 to the left of the fearful Solleder route. After a bivouac cheered up

by the lights of Alleghe, the team tackled a long traverse, followed by the most difficult pitch of the route. It was a marked overhang which Riccardo tackled with his usual vigour. He climbed from an étrier by grasping a thin plate of rock, stretched out towards a hold, grasped it, and tried to pull himself up. But the flake of dolomite suddenly broke off, and caused a terrifying fall.

"I was convinced that it was all up with me. I hit my head on a swelling in the rock and was knocked out. Then I came round to reality: I was dangling in the void, a fearful 700-metre drop below me, with a throbbing head. Bruised from head to foot and shaking with anger, I grasped the vertical rope and pulled myself up on top of the overhang, grasping the rock hand over hand."

After catching up with "Boga" at the belay station, Cassin set off decisively towards the summit, which he reached after putting up a direct variation on the route around a hundred metres long. The Lecco men were joined in the icy bivouac that followed by another of the best climbing teams of the day: Giusto Gervasutti from Friuli and French climber Lucien Devies, who were just back from one of the first repeats of the

already legendary Solleder route.

While talking things over with Gervasutti (known as *Il Fortissimo*), Cassin decided on his next climb. It was to be the gigantic South-East edge of Torre Trieste, which Cassin tackled on 15th August together with Vittorio Ratti. This was another exceptionally difficult route, which the team scaled with two bivouacs and 28 hours of actual climbing. In the long abseil down, the thirsty climbers continually stopped to lick the little water that trickled down the cracks in the rock. The Lecco men's short holiday was over, and Cassin and his party had to return to the lakeside. But a few days later, they made an exception to the rule that they only took one week's holiday a year.

News appeared in the press that Sepp Hintermeier and Josef Meindl, two excellent Bavarian climbers, had pitched their tent at the foot of the Tre Cime di Lavaredo. Their objective could only be the overhanging yellow North face of Cima Ovest, the only one of the great walls in the Dolomite that had not yet been climbed.

Cassin and Ratti hastily downed tools and headed for Misurina. They climbed to the Forcella Longères (now Lavaredo) refuge hut, laden like mules, and

125 top right In the Thirties, the walls of the Dolomites witnessed fierce competition between the best teams of the period. However, on 30th August 1935, Bavarians Sepp Hintermeier and Josef Meindl joined up with Riccardo Cassin and Vittorio Ratti to celebrate the Italians' victory over the North face of Cima Ovest di Lavaredo.

125 bottom right The crux of the North face of Cima Ovest is the exposed traverse that leads to the central part of the wall above the overhangs. In this photo, Riccardo Cassin is tackling this 40-metre long pitch, which took a 7-hour struggle.

enquired about the latest attempts (there had been twenty-seven in all!) made by the best teams of the day. The weather was terrible, but the Lecco men were not to be put off, and took advantage of the thick fog to hide from Hintermeier and Meindl, who were camped not far from the start.

They devoted 27th August to making a reconnaissance in the fog. The Germans heard suspicious noises and called out, but there was no reply. The next day, though the weather was still uncertain, the two Italians made a determined assault on the mountain. After three pitches, the fog suddenly lifted, revealing their presence to the Bavarians, who rushed into their tent to grab their gear, ran back to the start and climbed fast, in a desperate attempt to overtake the Italians.

At the beginning of the most difficult section, however, Meindl and Hintermeier abseiled back down. But for Cassin and Ratti, the race with the rival team was only a secondary concern. After leaving the initial cracks, they had to climb to the heart of the wall. The most awesome roofs were now below them, but here too, the wall "leans right outwards and has a smooth, hostile face with no holds," as Cassin recalled

in *Cinquant'anni di alpinismo.*

It took the great Riccardo 7 hours' struggle to cover those 40 metres, 4 hours of which were taken up by driving in a single piton. After two falls, one of which severed a rope, Ratti reached the leader on a ledge, where they spent the night. The next day the traverse continued, and another pitch took Cassin over 6 hours.

When the pair reached the base of the great crack that runs directly down from the summit, a storm turned it into a waterfall, forcing them to climb around it on safer but more difficult terrain. This was followed by another bivouac, a hailstorm that smothered the wall in ice, and a slip by Cassin which put both men's lives at risk. At 3 p.m. on the third day of their battle, the two climbers finally reached the summit.

They were welcomed by a friend from Lecco together with Hintermeier and Meindl, who had forgotten their rivalry on the second day and begun to cheer on the Italian team. The photo of Cassin and Ratti on the summit which later became famous was actually taken with Hintermeier's little camera. In the days that followed, the two Germans made the first repeat of the route.

126 top The North face of Civetta takes on a spectacular appearance at sunset. On the left is the compact wall of Punta Civetta, climbed by Solleder and Lettenbauer in 1925. Farther to the right, the horizontal light highlights the corners of Punta di Terranova and the great groove of Cima Su Alto, which was climbed in 1951 by a French team led by Georges Livanos.

The race on the West face demonstrated better than anything else how top-level climbing had changed. Between 1925 and 1926, Solleder's ascents on Furchetta, Civetta and Sass Maòr had taken place far from the limelight, and with only occasional use of pitons. A few years later, systematic use of pitons enabled the climbers of Cassin's generation to tackle even steeper and more difficult walls, performing moves or entire pitches with aid, ie. using pitons not only for protection in the event of falls, but also as a means of progression.

The second transformation was still more surprising for the mountaineers of the early years of the century, some of whom were still climbing in the Dolomites. Once a private challenge between man and mountain, top-level climbing was rapidly becoming a sport that interested both journalists and the public, in which the increasingly open competition attracted commercial attention from manufacturers of climbing gear and clothing.

Emilio Comici and Riccardo Cassin were only the best-known Italian climbers of the Thirties. Before them, a group of climbers from Veneto who mainly concentrated on the Civetta had made some outstanding climbs. Their organiser was Domenico Rudatis, who was born in Venice but began

126 bottom Attilio Tissi, seen here aid climbing, often scaled the big walls of the Civetta, the highest and most severe anywhere in the Dolomites.

126-127 A look at the rudimentary equipment carried by the best climbers of the Thirties demonstrates just how remarkable their ascents were. The hemp rope was tied directly round the waist, and was unable to withstand a fall by the leader of more than 6-7 metres. Climbers carried few pitons, that were not very different from each other.

climbing in the Turin area. He gave up climbing in 1934 after a motorcycle accident that left him with 60 stitches in the head and serious eyesight problems. After his retirement from active climbing he became famous for his articles in the specialist press, his theoretical studies of the history of climbing in the Dolomites and his essays, which combined climbing topics with the esoteric and transcendental aspects of oriental philosophies.

A highly erudite man, Rudatis was also a top-class climber. This was demonstrated in the summer of 1928 when he climbed the Torre di Babele with Renzo Videsott from Trento and German climber Leo Rittler. His masterpiece, performed with Rittler, was the Busazza edge, an extraordinary precipice 1200 metres tall that includes some pitches of extreme difficulty. It was Rittler, the first to repeat the route in 1925, who described the new route as being equivalent in terms of overall difficulty (and more difficult on some pitches) to those of Solleder and Lettenbauer.

After Rudatis, more climbers from Veneto performed some major first ascents on the Civetta. Brothers Giovanni and Alvise Andrich and Ernani Faè stood out for their class, intuition and stamina, but the real champion in the group was Attilio Tissi, a climber from Belluno who proved to have an exceptional feel for rock right from the outset.

127 right Left to right: Giovanni Andrich, Carlo Franchetti, King Leopold of Belgium and Domenico Rudatis.

127 bottom Raffaele Carlesso played an important part in climbing on the Civetta in the Thirties. In this photo, taken in the Little Dolomites near Vicenza, he can be seen on the left, with Maria Luisa Orsini and Carlo Baldi.

"Young Tissi is said to have preferred to spend his days in the Agordo café or running after the girls rather than slogging up the scree. He is also said to have started climbing for a bet," recounts Gian Piero Motti in his *Storia dell'alpinismo*.

A few years earlier, the great Dino Buzzati wrote in *Il Corriere d'Informazione*: "His genius immediately became apparent. He had hardly ever climbed, and was already over 30. But he instantly fell in love with the sport, and his most outstanding gifts were a will of iron and a moral soundness that are rarely encountered."

After a rapid repeat of the Solleder route (the first without a bivouac), together with Giovanni Andrich, Tissi scaled the North overhang of Campanile di Val Montanaia, then put up a very dangerous route on Tofana di Rozes. He continued with the North-West face of Pan di Zucchero (1932, with Giovanni Andrich and Rudatis) and the South face of Torre Venezia (1933, with Giovanni Andrich and Attilio Bortoli). In 1933 he also made the first ascent of Campanile di Brabante, a short route where Tissi free climbed an upper sixth-grade pitch on which many famous repeaters have used pitons and stirrups. Another motorbike accident in 1934 put an end to his extreme climbing career.

Raffaele Carlesso performed his greatest ascents on the Civetta in the Thirties. Born in Pordenone, he was one of the first to devise and perform systematic gymnastic exercises before climbing. Carlesso scaled the 700-metre South face of Torre Trieste, one of the first routes in the Alps rated at upper sixth grade, with Bortolo Sandri in 1934, taking turns to lead.

Carlesso opened an equally difficult route with Mario Menti two years later on the 600-metre North-West face of Torre di Valgrande. In 1937, both Sandri and Menti were killed during one of the first attempts to climb the North face of the Eiger.

The overhangs of the Tre Cime and the walls of the Civetta and its outriders were not the only field of action for the best climbers in the Dolomites in the Thirties. A group of climbers from Trentino, the most outstanding of whom were Bruno Detassis, Giorgio Graffer and Matteo Armani, made their name on the walls of the Brenta, known for their exceptionally solid rock.

However, it was the South face of the Marmolada that became one of the few "universities" of mountaineering in the Dolomites. Now criss-crossed by the most difficult free-climbing routes in the Dolomites, the wall that dominates Val d'Ombretta was conquered in 1901 by Beatrice Thomasson and her guides along a system of gullies and cracks. In the Thirties, however, improvements in climbing techniques and systematic use of pitons allowed climbers to venture onto open walls. The first major ascent was performed in 1929, when Luigi Micheluzzi scaled the South-West pillar of Punta Rocca with Demetrio Christomannos and Robert Perathoner. This outstanding feat, in which the guide from Val di Fassa used only five pitons, was long underestimated by climbers.

Seven years later, two more very elegant routes were put up in a single week. The first, on the South-West face of Punta Penìa, was opened between 28th and 30th August 1936 by Gino Soldà and Umberto Conforto, two Recoaro men who had learned to climb on the limestone pinnacles of the Piccole Dolomiti, a pre-Alpine range on the border between Trentino and Veneto. Even so, Soldà had a hard time on the Marmolada. Although he felt

inspired, the 550-metre route, on rock that was loose in sections, required him to spend an interminable amount of time placing protection in "smooth cracks where it was hard to drive in pitons," that came out very easily. "These little falls 300 metres from the ground on such insecure pitons are certainly no joke," he wrote in his report.

Two days later, another outstanding team reached the base of the wall. The leader, Hans Vinatzer, born in Val Gardena, was a rock-climbing virtuoso. Tough, good-natured and quiet, he had an extraordinary instinct for finding the route, and had already performed numerous climbs of outstanding difficulty. "When I made an ascent I didn't worry too much about what I ought to do: I mostly looked at the start and the exit. When I was in trouble or the rock was bad, I thought to myself 'The rock quite likes me.' And the rock let me through." These two excerpts from an interview in the early Eighties sum up the simplicity and talent of this outstanding climber.

On 8th August 1932, Vinatzer made his assault on the North face of Furchetta, the most difficult peak in the Odle range, together with Hans Riefesser. Their equipment was spartan: five pitons, three karabiners and a hammer between the two of them. Vinatzer, who was leading, climbed barefoot because he couldn't afford the rope-soled shoes used by the best climbers of the day. The pair soon reached the Dulferkanzel, the ledge where Hans Dulfer had abseiled down and Emil Solleder had had to traverse to the left. The two Gardena men continued upwards, free climbing, and successfully tackled a series of overhangs made of menacing, friable rock. Long unknown even to top climbers, the route was first repeated in 1957 by a team which, on its return, described the route as having been put up by "an irresponsible madman." Today, its rating includes some lower seventh-grade pitches.

Vinatzer also climbed barefoot on the Marmolada, where he used pitons in some places. Nevertheless, his is a very demanding, exceptionally attractive route, and is still the most often repeated of the classic routes on the South face. The taciturn Gardena man's climbing companion was a character who at first sight appears entirely different from him. Ettore Castiglioni, musician and author, erudite reader and profound thinker, was a real artist of the mountains, and one of the first city dwellers to earn his living in the mountains in a different way from

the traditional jobs of hotelier and guide.

Born in Trento of a Milanese family, Castiglioni worked for the Club Alpino Italiano and Touring Club Italiano for a long time, and wrote some outstanding climbing guides. Castiglioni was friendly with many of the best climbers of the period (Gabriele Boccalatte, Bruno Detassis and Celso Gilberti as well as Vinatzer) and performed hundreds of ascents in the Dolomites and the Central Alps.

He was strongly anti-Fascist, and after war broke out he put his mountaineering skills at the service of justice and peace. Although he continued to make first ascents, they alternated with a different task: guiding groups of Jewish refugees across the Alps.

In March 1944, he was arrested near Passo del Maloja by the Swiss frontier police, who confiscated his skis, boots and trousers. However, he insisted on returning home, and walked off half-dressed onto the Forno Glacier, where he died in a raging blizzard.

In his last summers in the mountains, Castiglioni climbed with his nephew Saverio Tutino, who was destined to achieve fame as a journalist for his reports on Cuba under Fidel Castro. This is how he remembered Castiglioni in his afterword to *Il giorno delle Mèsules*, the summary of Castiglioni's diaries published nearly 50 years after his death.

129 bottom Hans Vinatzer, born in Val Gardena, who was one of the best climbers of all time, put up some excellent routes on the Odle range, Mount Marmolada and the Sella massif. Here, he signs the summit book on the Terza Torre di Sella.

The conquest of the great walls

Three of the most famous mountains in the Alps overlook the heart of Switzerland. Just a stone's throw from Interlaken, clearly visible from Berne city centre, the wall of rock and ice that closes the Bernese Oberland to the north looks like a severe, glittering fortress. Behind it, invisible from this side of the range, stretch the largest and most Himalayan glaciers in Europe.

The highest peak, on the right for those looking towards it, is the 4158 metre Jungfrau (Virgin), whose

conquest in 1811 was one of the first major feats in European mountaineering. The 4099-metre summit of the Mönch (Monk), which stands in the middle of the trio, was reached in 1857 by a team led by the great Christian Almer. Their feat was not surpassed until nine years later, when Christian Michel and Peter Egger scaled the steep ice slope of the Nollen (Nose) with Edmund von Fellenberg.

The third mountain in the group is less attractive and spectacular than the others. Instead of the bright snow-covered ridges of the Jungfrau and the Mönch, it features a dark, grim, rock wall. Its 3970-metre summit just fails to reach 4000 metres, the magic altitude for the great mountains of the Alps. It is called the Eiger (Ogre), and has certainly lived up to its name in mountaineering history.

"The Eiger mountain forms a bare rocky mass which did not impress us in the slightest," somewhat presumptuously wrote the young Hegel, who travelled through these valleys in 1796. "It looms up above the meadows like a nasty surprise. It's a stone in a flower bed," added Gaston Rébuffat, one of the best-known authors of books and films about the Alps, 150 years later. "It's frightening, that's why it's famous," commented Heinrich Harrer, one of the first men to conquer the great wall.

Harrer, born at the foot of the Lienz Dolomites, became known to the general public in the Fifties when, having reached the forbidden city of Lhasa after an adventurous journey, he settled at the court of the Dalai Lama and witnessed the Chinese invasion of Tibet. On 20th July 1938, however, the great horizons

of upper Asia had not yet entered the life of this climber from the east Tyrol.

At the first light of dawn, together with the inseparable Fritz Kasparek, Heinrich Harrer was scaling the first easy slopes of the North face of the Eiger, one of the "last problems" in the Alps. Almost two kilometres high and frequently hit by lethal showers of stones, the North face features slabs and pillars of friable vertical limestone alternating with steep snow and ice slopes. It wasn't attractive, but it was large, difficult, awesome and unclimbed. The best mountaineers of the Thirties could not have asked for more. Barely grazed in 1932, when a team led by Hans Lauper scaled the icy North-East side, the wall was attempted for the first time in 1935 by German climbers Karl Mehringer and Max Sedlmayer.

130 left The easy snow-covered ridge of the ordinary route on the Mönch was climbed in 1866 by a party led by the great Christian Almer, and is still one of the most popular routes in the Bernese Oberland today.

130-131 The summit of the Jungfrau (on the right in this photo), which overlooks the heart of the Oberland with a glacial side that is not especially steep, looks particularly attractive in the first light of dawn.

131 top Swiss climber Hans Lauper, a dentist by profession, is mainly associated with the Bernese Oberland, where he put up numerous routes on ice and mixed terrain between 1915 and 1932. The most famous is the route named after him on the North-East face of the Eiger, inaugurated in 1932 with Alfred Zurcher and guides Josef Knubel and Alexander Graven.

The two climbers from Munich began their assault on the night of 20th July, and climbed rapidly along an elegant direct route. After two days, their rate of progress slowed on the First Icefield. On the fourth day, a Saturday, the weather suddenly broke. First a violent storm, then a blizzard hit the wall of the Eiger. The next day the wall could be seen again, and the crowd which had gathered at Kleine Scheidegg caught a glimpse of the two men, who kept on gallantly climbing.

Then the weather worsened again, and a thick curtain of cloud hid the Ogre from view. It was not until a week later that the pilot of a light aircraft flying close to the wall sighted the bodies of Mehringer and Sedlmayer on a rocky terrace, which has been known as "Death Bivouac" ever since.

131 bottom Austrian Heinrich Harrer became well-known among climbers all over the world when he made the first ascent of the North face of the Eiger with fellow-countryman Fritz Kasparek and German climbers Andreas Heckmair and Ludwig Vorg. However, he became famous with the public when he escaped from a British prisoner of war camp and fled to Tibet, where he lived at the court of the Dalai Lama.

The conquest of the great walls

The next year, Willy Angerer and Edi Rainer from Austria tackled the wall of the Eiger together with Bavarian climbers Andreas Hinterstoisser and Toni Kurz. In two days, they covered two-thirds of the wall. They followed a less direct and less difficult route than Mehringer and Sedlmeyer, identified and scaled the pitch (now known as the Hinterstoisser Traverse) which gives access to the heart of the wall. Half the wall was already below them when Angerer was seriously injured by a rockfall on the Second Icefield.

The four men decided to keep on climbing. But the next day, not far from "Death Bivouac," the injured man's condition forced them to descend. As always on the Eiger, drama came with a change of weather. A blizzard hit the climbers at the base of the icefields, in sight of the start of the Hinterstoisser Traverse; however, this pitch is impossible when wet. The only solution was to descend directly in the direction of the Stollenloch, the aeration duct that leads to the tunnel of the Jungfraubahn, the rack railway which climbs from Grindelwald and Wengen into the heart of the massif.

Four brave valley guides (Hans Schlunegger, Arnold Glatthard, Christian Rubi and Adolf Rubi) came out of the duct onto the wall to rescue the endangered climbers. But by the time they sighted Toni Kurz, disaster had already struck. Andreas Hinterstoisser had fallen from the wall, while Willy Angerer and Edi Rainer had died of cold and fatigue, and were still hanging from the ropes. Kurz was alive but exhausted, and an overhang prevented the guides from climbing up to him.

Summoning up his last reserves of strength, Kurz managed to fix a rope and abseil down towards the rescuers, who were shouting encouragement. But 20 metres from safety, the abseil krab got caught in a knot. Too weak to untie it, Toni Kurz died just a few metres from the outstretched arms of the men from Wengen.

In 1937, Austrian Mathias Rebitsch and Bavarian

Ludwig Vorg attempted the ascent. The pair climbed along the route followed by Hinterstoisser and party and covered two-thirds of the wall, but were forced to descend by the usual sudden deterioration in the weather. After a 100-hour battle they managed to escape the deadly embrace of the Ogre, and returned to the meadows of Alpiglen and the trail leading to Kleine Scheidegg.

The attempt by two leading Italian climbers, Bortolo Sandri and Mario Menti from Vicenza, ended in tragedy. In June 1935 the Italian team retraced the direct route followed by Mehringer and Sedlmayer, which they judged to be the more difficult but safer route. Again on the lower part of the wall, for reasons which will never be known, Menti and Sandri fell from the rocks of the Ogre. The morbid legend of the *Mordwand* (Wall of Death) began to circulate all over Europe.

132 bottom left The West face of the Eiger, seen here from the ordinary route on the Mönch, gives no hint that the severe, steep North face is concealed on the other side of the mountain.

132 top right This nineteenth-century view shows a team crossing an ice bridge on the Eigergletscher, on the East side of the mountain.

132 bottom right The ordinary route to the summit of the Eiger, climbed for the first time in 1938 by a team led by Christian Almer, follows the rocks and snowfields on the west side of the mountain. In this photo, a party is descending the snowfields at the foot of the West side.

132-133 The warm light of late afternoon makes the North face of the Eiger appear less severe. The 1938 route climbs it with marked zigzags, exploiting the weak points on the great wall. The slopes of the Lauper route can be seen on the left, and those of the ordinary route on the right. Some difficult routes have been put up on the compact rock walls on the right-hand side of the North face since 1979.

133 top left Bavarian climber Toni Kurz took part in the most famous of the unsuccessful attempts on the North face of the Eiger with Willy Angerer, Andreas Hinterstoisser and Edi Rainer. He died hanging from an abseil rope, just a few yards from the rescue team.

133 top right Andreas Hinterstoisser fell to his death in the tragic 1938 attempt on the Eiger. It was he who identified the difficult, exposed traverse that gives access to the central part of the wall.

134 top Fritz Kasparek led the Hinterstoisser Traverse during the victorious 1938 ascent. The snow that blocked the way did not cause much difficulty; what made the traverse particularly treacherous was a thin layer of glaze, which Kasparek had to smash with his ice-axe. Andreas Heckmair and Ludwig Vorg caught up with the Austrian team higher up, on the Second Icefield.

134 centre left Heinrich Harrer, climbing as second man, cautiously scales the Hinterstoisser Traverse, where his companion Fritz Kasparek had been forced to leave his rucksack hanging from the rope.

The twentieth of July was a sunny day, however. Harrer and Kasparek climbed fast, without using ropes until the Hinterstoisser Traverse, where the difficult pitches begin. They continued at a fast rate on the rocks and mixed terrain pitches that follow, but were then forced to slow down. The great icefields in the central part of the wall consist of bare ice, and the climbers had to cut an interminable series of steps with the ice-axe.

On the Second Icefield, halfway up the ascent, Harrer looked down, and was stunned by the sight that met his eyes. "I saw the New Era arriving at an incredible rate. Two men were running up the icefield towards us. It was Heckmair and Vorg, equipped with 12-point crampons. I suddenly felt old and outdated."

Vorg, a veteran of the North face, had reached that point before with Mathias Rebitsch. The strongest climber, however, was 32-year-old Anderl Heckmair, who led the group for much of the three days that followed. The teams scaled the rocky Flatiron pillar, passed close by Sedlmayer and Mehringer's "Death Bivouac," and continued along the Third Icefield and the glaze-covered rocks of the Ramp, where Harrer

managed to stop a fall by Kasparek.

Then Heckmair fell too, and a storm and an avalanche threatened to rip the four climbers off the wall. After an uncomfortable bivouac, Heckmair identified the elevated system of ledges known as the "Traverse of the Gods" that leads to the icy Spider hollow.

On the exit cracks all four men were roped together. A furious hailstorm nearly tore them off the rocks, but by now the worst was over. They came out onto the summit at 3 p.m. on the fourth day of their struggle. Harrer and Kasparek had been on the wall for 85 hours, and Heckmair and Vorg for 61 hours. The descent was tough and the men were silent, tormented by hunger, exhaustion and a raging blizzard, "We were tired and aching, our faces encrusted with ice. Joy was to come later," recounts Harrer today.

A vintage year for European climbing, 1938 marked the culmination of the race to solve the "last great problems," the hardest and most awesome walls in the Western and Central Alps. As in the Dolomites, the new challenges were devised and tackled by a new generation of climbers.

134-135 On the North face of the Eiger, like all the great walls of the Alps, bivouacs are uncomfortable, interminable and freezing cold. This photo shows Austrian Heinrich Harrer engaged in the tedious task of melting snow over a primus stove. The four victorious climbers had to spend no less than three nights on the big wall in this way.

135 bottom The North face of the Eiger is particularly beautiful in twilight. The Ramp, the Spider and the Exit Cracks can be seen towards the top of this photo, not far from the summit.

134 centre right In July 1938, much of the lower part of the North face of the Eiger was covered with snowfields, which did not present any particular difficulty to climbers.

134 bottom The four climbers who had just conquered the North face, and were plagued by bad weather on the last day of the ascent, were hailed as victors on their return to Kleine Scheidegg. From left: Heinrich Harrer, Fritz Kasparek, Andreas Heckmair and Ludwig Vorg.

136 bottom left This famous photo, taken in 1931, shows Bavarian brothers Franz and Toni Schmid, with the North face of the Matterhorn in the background. They had just made the first ascent. Franz made the first ascents of the North faces of the Ortler and Griubenkarspitze the same year. Toni died in 1932 during an attempted ascent of the North face of the Wiesbachhorn in the Upper Tauern.

136-137 The Matterhorn is one of the loveliest and most often photographed mountains in the Alps. This photo shows the structure of the North face: the initial part consists of a steep slope of snow and ice, the central part is rocky, and the part preceding the summit is again snow-covered. The overhanging Zmutt Nose, situated on the right of the route put up by the Schmid brothers, was first climbed in 1969 by Italians Alessandro Gogna and Leo Cerruti. The Hornli ridge, the East face and the Furggen ridge can be seen to the left of the North face.

The popularity of mountaineering had expanded incredibly since the Great War, before which it had been restricted to a wealthy élite who could afford the long and expensive summer seasons with guides. Since the war it had become a mass sport, a form of escapism which was affordable (with some inevitable sacrifices) by students, office workers and manual workers alike.

From Turin and Geneva, Paris and Vienna, Lombardy and Bavaria, thousands of young people flocked to the rocks of the Grigne and Fontainebleau, the Rax and Mont Salève, then went on to the higher ranges. The progress of climbing on those limestone massifs was due to the development of pitons and karabiners, which allowed climbers to ascend in relative safety.

In the Wilder Kaiser, Karwendel and Dolomite ranges, the fifth grade was rapidly superseded by the sixth. For the first time, the best climbers could travel with relative ease from one end of the Alps to another. As Gian Piero Motti writes, "The technical input of the Eastern school now enables us to look at the great Western walls with very different eyes." In fact, it was

climbers associated with limestone walls who solved the three major problems: the North face of the Matterhorn, the North face of the Grandes Jorasses and the North face of the Eiger.

While Austrian and German teams performed many of the major ascents of the day, Italian climbers also held their own thanks to champions like Giusto Gervasutti and Riccardo Cassin, while Pierre Allain from Paris and Armand Charlet from Chamonix flew the flag of French mountaineering.

For the first time in the history of Western mountaineering, British climbers played second fiddle. Some commentators (one of the most famous being Colonel E.L. Strutt, editor of the Alpine Club's bulletin) criticised what they described as "gladiatorial exhibitions" and Fascist and Nazi fanaticism. But it wasn't true. The Italian and German dictatorships were indeed preparing to fight another bloody European war, and official organisations encouraged mountaineering, but the young climbers of those countries were not interested in goose-stepping, and it was their training, experience and courage that enabled them to tackle the great walls.

The first to succumb was the shadowy, elusive North face of the Matterhorn, whose elegant silhouette dominates the Zermatt skyline. Magnificent when seen from the viewpoints of the Schwarzsee and the Gornergrat, the North face is actually a maze of unstable stones precariously attached by ice, preceded by a steep snow slope and separated by winding ice-filled couloirs, as climbers who scale the nearby Hornli and Zmutt ridges are well aware.

"Anyone who has climbed the North face hasn't brought back memories of an enjoyable, elegant climb, but remembers the urgent desire to get out of that chaos of piled-up boulders and gullies filled with transparent ice as soon as possible," recalls Gian Piero Motti.

"The rock is bad and the ice is glassy. There are no belays, and not the slightest protection if a storm blows up. Above all, avalanches of stones fall almost continuously," wrote Gaston Rébuffat.

For climbers of the old Western school, the risks of a wall like this one were too great. This was demonstrated by the outcome of the first attempt on the North face, performed by Swiss climber Émile Blanchet and his guides Kaspar Mooser and Viktor Imboden in the summer of 1930. They formed one of the best teams of the day, and the difficulties of the first part of the route are not excessive. However, the obvious danger led the three to turn back to the Hornli Hutte and Zermatt.

A year later, two very different characters pitched their tent in sight of the big wall. Brothers Franz and Toni Schmid had cycled all the way to Zermatt from Bavaria, their bikes heavily overloaded with climbing and camping gear. Conditions on the wall were good, and the two Germans were used to big ice walls. Franz, the older brother and more expert climber, had made the first ascent of the equally steep (and perhaps even more dangerous) North face of Mount Ortler at the end of June with Hans Ertl.

On 30th July 1931, just after midnight, the brothers left their tent in the meadows of the Schwarzsee. Two hours later, they asked the manager of the Hornli Hutte to tell climbers heading for the ordinary route on the Matterhorn to make sure no stones fell on the North face.

They began their assault at 4 a.m., and rapidly climbed the initial snow and ice slope without cutting steps. Then the terrain became mixed and treacherous, the first rockfall started to beat down on the wall, and their progress was inevitably slowed. At 8:30 p.m. they set up their bivouac on a tiny ledge at an altitude of 4150 metres.

They were very tired, but by now they had covered most of the route. At dawn the next day Franz and Toni set off again, confidently and cautiously climbed the last 300 metres of the route, and reached the snow-covered ridge and the great metal cross on the summit.

"The North face of the Matterhorn has been conquered!" The first, uncertain news items were received by expert climbers with an unbelieving smile, and attributed to ignorant, headline-seeking journalists. But it was true. "Whatever feats the future holds in store, none can ever equal this one. Fate has concentrated all the resources of its art on it," wrote great ice climber Jacques Lagarde in *Alpinisme*, the journal of the French Groupe de Haute Montagne. Even the sceptical editor of the *Alpine Journal* for once took the general view. "Faced with this kind of feat, criticisms, like praise, must be silenced once and for all."

137 bottom left At sunset, the clouds shrouding the unmistakable silhouette of the Matterhorn make it particularly attractive. This photo was taken from the Zermatt side.

137 bottom right Whatever ascent route is followed, the summit of the Matterhorn offers an exceptional view over the Pennine Alps and the glaciers of Monte Rosa.

The conquest of the great walls

However, the race to solve the "last great problems" in the Alps turned into a full-competition on the North face of the Grandes Jorasses. Tall, severe and streaked with ice, the wall that dominates the Leschaux Glacier is between 1000 and 1200 metres high, and over 2 kilometres wide. Two gigantic spurs resembling the prows of great ships cross the wall at Points Walker and Croz, offering two elegant, logical but exceptionally difficult ascent routes.

Unlike the North faces of the Matterhorn and the Eiger, the North face of the Jorasses had been attempted by the best climbers of the previous generation. In 1907, Geoffrey W. Young and Josef Knubel reached the terminal crevasse, but dared not climb any farther. The real attempts at ascent began in 1928, on the initiative of Chamonix guide Armand Charlet, who tackled the spur of Point Walker. In 1931, Amilcare Crétier and Lino Binel from Valle d'Aosta and Gabriele Boccalatte from Turin reached the foot of the North face. In 1933, Italians Giusto Gervasutti (known as "*Il Fortissimo*" in Turin climbing circles) and Piero Zanetti made a more decisive assault.

However, the real race began at dawn on 30th July 1934. When the sun reached the wall, continual hails of ice and stones rained down impartially on some of the best European climbing teams of the day on the steep rocks of the Croz Spur.

The German pair Haringer and Peters, who had begun their assault the previous day and were now a third of the way up the wall, were in the lead. They were followed by French guides Armand Charlet, known in Chamonix as *le grimpeur plus rapide du monde* (the fastest climber in the world) and Fernand Belin; next came Italians Renato Chabod and Giusto Gervasutti, followed in turn by a party of three Austrians.

At mid-morning, Charlet and Belin were the first to give up; they fixed the first of a long series of abseil ropes in a treacherous mixed couloir which cuts through the Croz Spur on the side facing the Périades. Gervasutti and Chabod caught up with the Germans,

but then the weather broke. They decided to turn back, and the Austrians abseiled down with them.

Peters and Haringer considered turning back too, but then resumed their ascent, despite the fact that conditions on the wall were rapidly becoming prohibitive. The blizzard trapped them for two nights when they were just over halfway up the Spur. As they abseiled down, the exhausted Haringer fell to his death. Rudolf Peters eventually reached the glacier after a five-day fight for survival.

The breakthrough came in 1935. The Swiss team of Robert Gréloz, Raymond Lambert and Loulou Boulaz made the assault in addition to the climbers who had made the previous attempts. But it was Rudolf Peters, climbing with Martin Meier, who made the first ascent, on 28th and 29th June. They were followed, three days later, by Gervasutti, Chabod, Lambert and Loulou Boulaz.

"When a man has spent five days on such a formidable wall, covered with snow because of an unexpected blizzard, has seen his companion plunge into the void and carried on the desperate battle alone for two days, and then has the courage to go back there, I say hats off to him, because he well deserves to be the first!" commented Renato Chabod fairly.

But there were still plenty of climbing problems left on the North face of the Grandes Jorasses. Now that the Croz Spur had been conquered, there still remained Point Walker, which offered an even more difficult route. On the left-hand spur, however, a race like the one on the Croz Spur never even got started,

138 top This photo, taken in front of Chamonix railway station, shows four of the competitors in the "race" to make the first ascent of the Croz Spur in the Grandes Jorasses. On the left are Rudolf Peters and Martin Meier, the first ascensionists. On the right are Loulou Boulaz and Raymond Lambert, who made the second ascent with Giusto Gervasutti and Renato Chabod.

138 bottom Raymond Lambert did not only climb in the Jorasses. He reached an altitude of 8595 metres on Everest with Tenzing Norgay in 1952, and on the North face of the Petit Dru he rectified the route inaugurated by Pierre Allain and Raymond Leininger in 1935 by scaling a difficult upper fifth-grade crack (shown in this photo).

138-139 The northern wall of the Grandes Jorasses is one of the most spectacular in the Alpine range. This photo shows Col des Hirondelles, the Hirondelles ridge and the Linceul. The heart of the wall is the two spurs that reach Point Walker (left) and Point Croz. Mont Blanc can be seen on the left.

139 bottom A moment during the first ascent of the Croz Spur. In this photo, Rudolf Peters can be seen scaling the granite slabs in the central part of the route.

because Riccardo Cassin, whom we have already encountered on the Tre Cime and Civetta, scaled the wall at his first attempt.

In the summer of 1937, Cassin had climbed the North-East face of Piz Badile, the most impressive granite wall in the Central Alps, with Vittorio Ratti and Luigi Esposito. Two men from Como, Molteni and Valsecchi, had joined up with them. This outstanding feat was made tragic but no less important by the death of Molteni and Valsecchi during the descent, exhausted by a climb that was probably beyond their ability.

In 1938 Cassin was aiming for the North face of the Eiger, but reached Kleine Scheidegg just after the victorious ascent by Heckmair, Harrer, Kasparek and Vorg. On his return to Lecco he found a postcard from journalist Vittorio Varale waiting for him. It showed the North face of the Jorasses, with a pen line marking the Walker Spur, and the message simply read, "This is the wall for you."

Cassin travelled to Courmayeur, accompanied by Ugo Tizzoni, rushed up to the Torino refuge hut, and asked the astonished manager how to get to the base

of the wall. He then sent a telegram to summon Luigi Esposito from Lecco. The party commenced its assault on the Spur at dawn on 4th August. When the three men reached the start of the rocks, traces left by other climbers made them wonder whether they had missed a first ascent again.

In the next two days Cassin, Esposito and Tizzoni scaled the 75-metre Groove, the Black Slabs and the Grey Slabs, then used pendulums to get round the awesome Red Tower. A storm hit the group just before the third bivouac. Finally, at 3 p.m. on 6th

August, Cassin came out onto the snow ridge of the summit.

After a last bivouac during the descent, they were met not far from the refuge hut by "an odd guy holding a camera in one hand and a bottle of spumante in the other." It was Guido Tonella, a Swiss journalist, who had watched the ascent from the Leschaux refuge hut and come out to meet the returning climbers. His photo of the three Lecco men, happy and still roped together, is one of the most famous in mountaineering history.

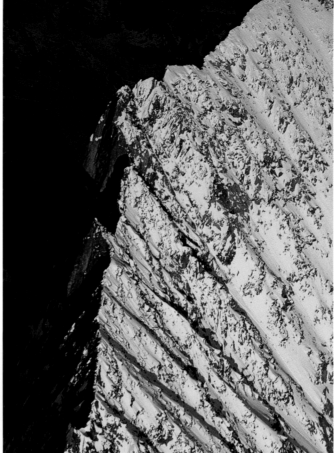

141 top This aerial photo of the summit ridge of the Jorasses clearly shows the contrast between the two sides of the mountain. The rarely climbed Point Margherita is in the centre of the photo.

140-141 The South side of the Grandes Jorasses, which overlooks the pastures and woods of the Italian Val Ferret, is less severe than the North face. However, some very difficult routes have been put up on it such as the

Tronchey Ridge (on the right, silhouetted against the sky). The ordinary route to the summit, which has to be descended by those who climb the North face, follows the tortured glacier on the left of the photo.

141 bottom This famous photo, taken by journalist Guido Tonella, shows Lecco men Riccardo Cassin (leading), Ugo Tizzoni and Luigi Esposito arriving back at the Jorasses hut, now the Boccalatte-Piolti refuge, after the first ascent of the Walker Spur on the Grandes Jorasses.

142-143 *The Aiguille Blanche de Peuterey, Mont Blanc, Mont Maudit and Mont Blanc du Tacul appear (from left to right) in this photo, taken from the summit of Tour Ronde. Of all the great routes put up on these walls in the Thirties, the North face of the Aiguille Blanche, the three great routes on Mont Blanc (Sentinel, Major and Pera) and the South-East face of Mont Maudit are particularly outstanding.*

The history of the Western and Central Alps in the Thirties was not only written on the Matterhorn, the Grandes Jorasses and the Eiger. Climbers from the limestone Alps made yet another excellent "away" ascent on the South ridge of the Aiguille Noire in the Mont Blanc massif on 26th and 27th August 1930. This time, it was German climbers Hermann Schaller and Karl Brendel who stole the magnificent route from under the noses of Courmayeur guides Arturo and Osvaldo Ottoz, Laurent Grivel and Albino Pennard. In 1935 two Austrians, Herbert Burgasser and Rudolf Leitz, scaled the overhanging South face of the Dent du Géant.

The ascents of Thomas Graham Brown, a professor from Edinburgh, were performed in a completely different style. Between 1927 and 1934 he identified and climbed three outstanding routes on the Brenva wall to the left of the Spur, which had been climbed in 1865 by the Anderegg, Moore, and Walker team.

On 1st September 1927, climbing with fellow-countryman Frank Smythe, Graham Brown crossed Col Moore and bivouacked at the foot of a great spur of rock; then they continued on steep mixed terrain to the summit of Mont Blanc. Their Red Sentinel route is named after the tower where they bivouacked.

The next year the same pair attacked the main spur of the wall. After another bivouac at the foot of the Sentinel, a dangerous gully and increasingly steep snow ridges led to the rocks and seracs which bar the way to the summit.

142 bottom left *The team formed by Frenchmen Pierre Allain and Raymond Leininger was one of the strongest and most united of those that climbed on Mont Blanc in the years leading up to the Second World War.*

142 bottom right *British climbers Thomas Graham Brown and Frank Smythe (in the centre and right respectively in this photo) won a place in the history of Mont Blanc in 1927 and 1928 when they inaugurated the Red Sentinel and Major routes on the Brenva Wall.*

They had opened the Major Route.

Later, the pair split up on bad terms. Graham Brown claimed his share of the credit for the two ascents, while Smythe described him as a "bad climber" who was "absolutely terrified" on the steep slopes of the Major Route. Smythe then turned his attention to Everest, where he reached 8500 metres in 1933. The professor returned to the Brenva to complete his hat trick with "Via della Pera," this time in the safe hands of Zermatt guides Alexander Graven and Alfred Aufdenblatten.

More outstanding ascents were performed on the ice and mixed terrain of Mont Blanc by local climbers during this period. In 1929, Renato Chabod, Lino Binel and Amilcare Crétier of Valle d'Aosta climbed the South-East face of Mont Maudit. The next year, French climbers Pierre Chevalier and Guy Labour scaled the north-east slope of the Courtes. In 1931, Swiss climbers Robert Gréloz and André Roch conquered the steep North face of the Aiguille de Triolet, which was destined to become one of the great classic ice climbs on the massif.

In 1934, Chabod scaled the most awesome couloir of Mont Blanc du Tacul with Giusto Gervasutti. The North (or Nant Blanc) face of the Aiguille Verte was conquered by Armand Charlet from Chamonix, who scaled it with Dimitri Platonov in 1935. Another great Chamonix guide, Fernand Tournier, ascended the North-East spur of the Droites with Ch. Authenac in 1937.

On rock, the brightest star in the Chamonix firmament was undoubtedly Parisian Pierre Allain. A frequent visitor to the sandstone towers and boulders of the Fontainebleau forest, this outstanding mountaineer became famous with climbers all over the world as a manufacturer of karabiners and climbing shoes, and with Parisians for the first ascent of the Eiffel Tower, in 1936. "It was strictly prohibited, but the cops didn't fancy coming up to get me," he wrote in his memoirs.

In the Mont Blanc massif, his best creations were the South-West ridge of the Aiguille du Fou (with Robert Latour, 1933), the East ridge of the Dent du Crocodile (with Jean and Raymond Leininger, 1937) and above all the North face of the Dru (with Raymond Leininger, 1935), where Allain scaled a series of extremely difficult cracks. This was a magnificent feat, somewhat overshadowed after the war by the great French, Italian and American ascents on the nearby West face of the same mountain.

143 bottom left Frank Smythe, who led Thomas Graham Brown in the two ascents of the Brenva, also made some outstanding ascents in the Himalaya. In 1931 he reached the 7756-metre summit of Mount Kamet, and in 1933 he almost reached an altitude of 8600 metres on the Tibetan side of Mount Everest.

143 top right The North face of the Aiguille de Triolet, which overlooks the Argentière Glacier, was climbed in 1931 by Swiss mountaineers Robert Greloz and André Roch, who thus inaugurated one of the classic ice routes in the Western Alps.

143 bottom right The team consisting of American H. Bradford Washburn (left) and Chamonix guides Alfred Couttet and André Devouassoud climbed the largest and most important couloir on the north side of the Aiguille Verte in the Mont Blanc massif in the summer of 1926.

144 top left One of the most
elegant Italian climbers of
the Thirties, Gabriele
Boccalatte from Turin, put
up many top-level routes on

Mont Blanc, often with his
wife Ninì Pietrasanta. He was
tragically killed by a rockfall
on the Aiguille de Triolet
in 1938.

144 bottom In this unusual
photo, taken from the
entrance to Val Vény, the
Aiguille Noire (on the left)
and the Aiguille Blanche de
Peuterey dominate the larch

woods, whitened by a
summer snowfall. The lack of
snow midway between the
two summits emphasises the
verticality of the South-West
face of Point Gugliermina.

144-145 *This aerial photo does full justice to the impressiveness of the archetypal "great ridge," which runs from the Aiguille Noire de Peuterey (on the right) to the Dames Anglaises, Point Gugliermina and the Aiguille Blanche. Col de Peuterey and Mont Blanc are farther to the left, out of sight. The Frêney Glacier can be seen in the foreground.*

145 right *Willo Welzembach, born in Munich and killed by an avalanche on Nanga Parbat, was one of the best ice climbers in mountaineering history and the inventor of the classic rock climbing scale of difficulty. One of the towers of the South ridge of the Aiguille Noire in the Mont Blanc massif is named after him.*

Noteworthy ascents on rock performed by Italian climbers included the West face of the Aiguille Noire (Gabriele Boccalatte and Ninì Pietrasanta, 1935), the South-South-West pillar of Picco Gugliermina (Boccalatte and Giusto Gervasutti, 1938), the North face of the Aiguille de Leschaux (Riccardo Cassin and Ugo Tizzoni, 1939) and the gigantic East face of the Grandes Jorasses (Giusto Gervasutti and Giuseppe Gagliardone, 1942), a wall over 1000 metres tall, standing in one of the wildest corners of the massif.

In 1946, Gervasutti climbed the right-hand Frêney Pillar with Paolo Bollini, opening up new mountaineering terrain which was to witness great ascents and dramas in the post-war period.

Although it was one of the favourite venues for top-level mountaineering on ice and mixed terrain, Mont Blanc was not the only location frequented by the best climbers of the day. This is demonstrated by the activities of the great Bavarian ice climber Willo Welzembach, who devised the rating scale for rock climbing and performed some excellent ascents all over the Alpine range. Some of his best ascents were the North faces of the Grosses Wiesbachhorn in the Upper Tauern (1923), the Dent d'Hérens in the Pennine Alps (1925), the Grands Charmoz in the Mont Blanc massif (1931) and the Gletscherhorn in the Bernese Oberland (1932).

Giusto Gervasutti, a climber from the Dolomites who had moved to the Western Alps, also made his mark on the most difficult rock and mixed walls of the Oisans, the wildest massif in the French Alps. Climbing with Lucien Devies from Paris, who was also to become known as an editor of climbing guides and promoter of the first French expeditions to the Himalaya, "Il Fortissimo" scaled the North-West face of Mount Olan in 1934, and the South-South-East ridge of Pic Gaspard, one of the most elegant peaks of the Meije, the next year.

The peaks and walls of the Bernese Oberland and the Pennine Alps, where Christian Almer, Melchior Anderegg and other great guides had made some magnificent ascents half a century earlier, remained further from the limelight in those years, with the exception of the inhospitable walls of the Matterhorn and the Eiger. There, apart from the most famous walls, top-level climbing remained the sole province of guides, with their European and British clients, who put up major routes on the Dent Blanche, the Zinalrothorn and the Taschhorn.

However, it was a famous team of French amateurs, formed by Lucien Devies and Jacques Lagarde, who in July 1931 put up an amazing route on the East face of Monte Rosa, the Alpine wall that closely resembles the Himalayan giants.

Here, where the Pennine Alps bear comparison with Lhotse and Annapurna, the ascents performed by the brave and innovatory mountaineers of the Thirties were little different from those of 19th-century climbers like Imseng and Zurbriggen.

Gentlemen in the Himalaya

On 19th July 1939, as the first evening shadows lengthened on K2, the history of mountaineering very nearly changed.

Two men were at an altitude of over 8400 metres on the difficult rocks to the left of the steep snow-filled couloir that constitutes the crux of the ascent route to the summit. Fritz Wiessner, a German from Dresden who had moved to the USA ten years earlier, was just 10 metres from the end of the rocks, belayed to a firmly placed piton. Above him, within arm's reach, glistened the snow of the long but easy slope leading to the summit. The voice of Pasang Dawa Lama brought him down to earth with a jolt. "No Sahib, tomorrow," exclaimed the sherpa, who had stopped a dozen metres lower down. Pasang was concerned by the late hour, the cold, and the spirits that lay in wait at night on the second-highest mountain on earth.

"The sherpa was adamant; I was even tempted to untie myself and climb to the summit alone. But I couldn't bring myself to do it; I've never abandoned a fellow-climber. The weather was perfect, and I was convinced that I'd be able to try again. I'd never climbed so well before; I was certain that I could

make it. I took a last look at that slope, so inviting and so close, then prepared the last double rope and abseiled down," Wiessner told the writer in an interview 38 years later.

But as often happens, Wiessner had missed his chance to climb K2 forever. As they abseiled down, Pasang Dawa Lama dropped both climbers' crampons, and it proved impossible to recover them. They spent the next day resting at camp nine, at an altitude of 7940 metres. The weather was so pleasant that Wiessner sunbathed bare-chested. But the sun and freezing cold turned the good snow in the couloir into a sheet of ice.

The next day, without crampons, the two men were again unable to climb. They decided to go back down to camp eight at 7712 metres to look for more crampons and stock up with provisions. But their problems had only just begun. There were neither crampons nor food in the tents, only Dudley Wolfe, who had been waiting for them to return. The only solution was to go down to the next camp, but on the way Wolfe slipped and Wiessner, still without crampons, had difficulty holding him.

After leaving Wolfe at camp seven, Wiessner and Pasang, who had left their sleeping bags up at camp

nine, continued down the mountain. But the descent brought a succession of unpleasant surprises. Believing that the three leading climbers were dead, *sirdar* Pasang Kikuli had ordered his men to dismantle all the camps. There was not a crumb of food or a sleeping bag anywhere on the Abruzzi Spur. After a terrible night spent at camp two, Fritz Wiessner and Pasang Dawa Lama arrived exhausted at the moraine, but Wolfe was still up on the Shoulder.

The next day, Jack Durrance and three sherpas set off up the mountain to rescue Wolfe. However, the

American and one of the sherpas were taken ill, and were soon forced to give up. It was not until 29th July that three sherpas (Pasang Kikuli, Pasang Kitar and Phinsoo) managed to reach camp seven. Dudley Wolfe was in a bad way, and unable to go down with them. The trio returned to camp six where another sherpa was waiting for them, but they were only able to climb again after a two-day blizzard ended. Then, silence and bad weather descended on K2. On 1st August, sherpa Tsering returned to the base camp with the news that his companions and Wolfe were all dead.

More bad weather prevented any further attempt at an ascent, and by the time Wiessner and his party

146 The south side of K2 is the best known and most photographed on the mountain. Since 1909, all attempted ascents have taken place along the Abruzzi Spur (on the right in

this photo), which offers a relatively easy route to the icy terrace of the Shoulder. The last part of the route becomes steep and difficult again. The base camp can be seen in the foreground.

146-147 After being sighted by Francis Younghusband in 1887, the north side of K2 was to remain a mystery to climbers until the Seventies, when the

Chinese government authorised first a Japanese and then an Italian expedition to attempt an ascent of the mountain from that side.

reached Srinagar at the end of the long homeward march, the Second World War had broken out. Thus the last pre-war expedition to K2, which might have opened new horizons in the history of mountaineering, ended in tragedy.

The Himalayan ascents performed between the wars, though somewhat overshadowed by the victories achieved in the Fifties, deserve to be better known. More than once, men dressed and equipped as if for a normal climb in the Alps nearly reached one or another of the fourteen highest peaks on earth.

147 bottom Fritz Wiessner, born in Dresden in 1900, is one of the most surprising personalities in the history of mountaineering. After learning to climb on the sandstone walls of the Elbsandsteingebirge, he put up some major routes in the

Dolomites and the Wilder Kaiser. He then moved to the USA, where he obtained American citizenship and took part in the exploration of the mountains of Wyoming and Alaska. In 1939, he reached an altitude of 8300 metres on K2.

Mountaineering in the Himalaya, which was initiated at the turn of the century by pioneers like Mummery, Freshfield and Conway (not to mention the Duke of Abruzzi), soon brought some interesting results, like the ascent by the Duke and his guides of the 6980-metre Golden Throne (1909) and Tom Longstaff's ascent of the 7120-metre Trisul, performed with two Courmayeur men in 1907. However, the expeditions performed in those years were mostly exploratory.

Himalayan mountaineering was changed at the end of the First World War by British climbers, many of whom were used to seeing the glistening snow of the high Himalayan peaks from the hills and plains of India on clear days. However, apart from the climbing difficulties and the altitude, their field of action was seriously restricted by political problems. The closure of Nepal to foreigners, which continued until after the Second World War, prevented them from reaching no less than six of the world's fourteen 8000-metre peaks, together with the south side of Everest and the west side of Kangchenjunga.

However, nothing prevented them from tackling Nanga Parbat and the great mountains that overlook the Baltoro Glacier in the heart of present-day Pakistan, apart from the length of the access route, which led from Srinagar across the Zoji-La Pass and the Indus valley. The peaks of the Garwhal region, which were a little lower but much easier to reach, were particularly popular with climbers heading for the Asian mountains in that period.

However, the British had an ace up their sleeves: their relations with Tibet enabled them to apply to the Dalai Lama for permission to attempt the ascent of Everest. Tibet had long been disputed between Great Britain, Russia and China in the difficult years of the "Great Game," in which the three most powerful empires on earth confronted one another on the steppes of upper Asia, and after Lhasa was occupied by British troops in 1910, the Tibetans were not inclined to oppose even the most outlandish requests made by the Viceroy of New Delhi.

On 20th December 1920, a telegram sent from the Indian capital to London informed the Royal

Geographical Society and the Alpine Club that the Dalai Lama's permission had finally arrived. By the end of April, the first exploratory expedition to Mount Everest was ready to leave for Asia. The expedition was led by Charles Kenneth Howard-Bury, responsible for the mountaineering side of operations, and Harold Raeburn, known for his difficult guideless ascents in Scotland and the Alps.

The climbers in the group included George L. Mallory, G.H. Bullock, A.F. Wollaston and Alexander M. Kellas. The group responsible for the topographical

survey left Darjeeling on 13th May 1921, crossed Sikkim, entered Tibet via Phari Dzong and waited near the Khampa Dzong fortress, where the team of climbers joined them a week later.

The death of Kellas from a heart attack was a hard blow to the group. Then Raeburn, who suffered from the altitude, had to return to Darjeeling. Though depleted, the expedition set off again, while topographers Henry T. Morshead and Oliver Wheeler and geologist A.M. Heron mapped valleys and plateaus never visited before by Western travellers.

148-149 top The North face of Everest, which overlooks the seracs of the main Rongbuk Glacier, was too steep to offer a practicable route for the climbers of the Twenties. The first British expeditions discovered that the eastern branch of the glacier enabled them to reach the foot of the slopes rising to the North Col without difficulty.

148-149 bottom To reach the foot of Everest, the 1921 expedition had to cross Lhakpa La and then descend the east Rongbuk Glacier. In this photo, Everest and the wide saddle of the North Col can be seen beyond the camp set up on this pass. The summit ridge of Lhotse appears to the left of the highest peak.

149 top right The climbers in the 1921 British expedition pose for a group photo. The expedition leader, Howard-Bury, is second from the left in the row of standing climbers, and George Mallory is the first on the left among the seated climbers. The first on the right in the second row is Scot Harold Raeburn, who made some major summer and winter ascents in the Highlands.

149 bottom right The equipment tried out by the British expedition of 1921 included snowshoes, which they systematically used in the flattest sections where the snow was fresh or softened by the sun. In this photo, Bullock (right) is accompanied by three sherpa porters.

While Morshead and his party camped below the fortress of Tingri, Mallory and Bullock finally reached the Rongbuk valley, at the end of which Everest rises in all its glory. "At the end of the valley, above the glacier, towers Everest, not like a mountain peak, but a prodigious pile. Nothing distracts the gaze from it," wrote Mallory, clearly fascinated by that pyramid of rock and ice.

On 1st July, the two climbers ventured onto the main Rongbuk Glacier. A few days later, observing the mountain from a secondary peak almost 7000 metres high, they wrongly decided that the only way to the ridge giving access to the summit led through the Kharta valley, east of the Rongbuk valley.

They had to go back down to the plateau, climb up another valley, and scale the almost 7000-metre Lhakpa La, from which they realised their mistake. Between the pass and Everest lay the easy east glacier of Rongbuk, which joins the one already crossed by the climbers at around 5500 metres. Nevertheless, on 24th September the first team finally reached the North Col, at the start of the most logical ascent route of the mountain. However, the icy winds of the Tibetan autumn forced them to return to India.

A few months later, a new expedition was ready to leave England. In addition to Mallory and Morshead, the team, led by General Charles G. Bruce, included climbers George I. Finch, Edward F. Norton, John Noel, Geoffrey Bruce and John Morris, and no less then three doctors with great experience in the mountains: Arthur W. Wakefield, Howard Somervell and Tom Longstaff, an energetic 47-year-old who had set the record for the highest peak ever climbed by man on Mount Trisul 15 years earlier. For the first time the expedition was accompanied by a number of sherpas, the Nepalese mountain men who had already become world-famous as high-altitude porters.

The expedition was equipped with breathing apparatus, but each unit weighed over 15 kg. However, the experience gained the previous year enabled the group to make rapid progress. On 22nd May 1922, Mallory, Morshead, Norton and Somervell set off from a camp pitched at 7600 metres, and made a first attempt on the summit without oxygen cylinders which

concluded at a height of 8170 metres. The second attempt, in which breathing equipment was used, was halted by a raging blizzard.

On 26th May, after a difficult night spent at 7900 metres, George Finch and Geoffrey Bruce climbed the easy but treacherous rocky slabs on the right-hand side of the ridge, unroped. Then they returned to the main ridge, but fatigue and the poor performance of their breathing apparatus forced them to turn back at 8320 metres. Ten days later, during a new attempt, nearly all the expedition's members were hit by an avalanche on the way to the North Col, and seven sherpas disappeared forever. It was time to go home.

Two years passed before British climbers returned to the Tibetan plateau. As a result of the high altitude reached in 1922, an atmosphere of calm confidence surrounded the new expedition. In addition to six veterans of Everest (Charles and Geoffrey Bruce, Norton, Mallory, Somervell and Noel), the group included Andrew Irvine, Noel Odell, John Hazard, Bentley Beetham, E.O. Shebbeare and R.W. Hingston.

Although an attack of malaria forced Bruce senior to return to Darjeeling, the expedition reached the Rongbuk monastery at the end of April. The breathing apparatus had been improved, as the experience of the 1922 expedition had demonstrated that climbers'

progress becomes much slower at around 8000 metres. For this reason, the expedition decided to install no less than three camps beyond the North Col.

The weather was nearly always bad that May, and little progress could be made, but eventually, the climbers and sherpas were able to set off up the mountain. On 1st June George Mallory, Geoffrey Bruce and four sherpas pitched camp five at an elevation of 7700 metres. Two days later Norton and Somervell pitched camp six at 8170 metres, and set off for the summit the next day. Keeping some 100 metres below the ridge, they climbed the treacherous limestone rocks of the Yellow Band, where Somervell

was forced to stop. Norton continued alone to a height of 8570 metres.

After that, it was Mallory and Irvine's turn. On 8th June, the pair left camp six equipped with breathing apparatus, heading for the summit. Noel Odell, who was climbing up from camp five, saw them several times from below, silhouetted against the snowy hillocks of the ridge. The last sighting was around midday, when the leading team was at a height of some 8450 metres, ie. between the first and second of the two steep rocky steps that interrupt the ridge. The weather deteriorated, but improved again in the afternoon. However, Odell could no longer see the pair. Mallory and Irvine had disappeared on Everest forever.

Noel Odell made a rescue attempt on 10th June, but found no trace of his friends. Mallory and Irvine may have reached the summit, although there is no evidence either way. After the expedition's sad return home, Everest was left in peace for another eight years.

150 top The view of Everest shows the summit from the Nepalese side. Yet this side of the highest peak on earth was seen for the first time by Western climbers in 1951, when Nepal was opened to foreigners.

150 bottom left The members of the 1924 British expedition pose for a group photo, a common practice. In this photo (taken by Noel), Irvine and Mallory are the first two standing on the left. Odell, who was to watch them climbing towards the summit, is the second from the right, standing.

150 bottom right The British expedition of 1922 was the first to use breathing apparatus systematically, beginning from their arrival on the Tibetan plateau. However, the apparatus was so heavy, bulky and fragile that it proved to be of little use on Everest.

150-151 From the advanced base camp which all expeditions set up at around 6400 metres on the east Rongbuk Glacier, Everest (on the left in the photo) and the wide snow-covered saddle of the North Col do not look in the least threatening.

151 top This photo, taken by Noel Odell at the 1924 expedition's camp four, shows George Mallory and Andrew Irvine who disappeared on 8th June on the summit ridge. No one knows whether they reached the summit.

151 bottom Layers of schist rock covered with fresh snow and glaze make the last part of the route to the summit of Everest particularly treacherous. This photo shows Norton and Mallory not far from the highest point reached during the first attempt in 1922.

The next expedition left London in early February 1933, and reached Rongbuk monastery on 16th April. In view of the time that had elapsed since the last expedition, most of the climbers were different. In addition to the expedition leader Hugh Ruttledge, the group included climbers Frank S. Smythe, Eric Shipton, Percy Wyn Harris, Lawrence Wager, Jack Longland, T.A. Brockleband, E. Birnie, Raymond Green, George Wood-Johnson and Hugh Boustead. The only veteran on the expedition was Shebbeare.

152 left On the slopes leading to the North Col, some steep pitches have to be protected with ladders and ropes to allow heavily laden porters to climb. The real problem in this area, however, is avalanches, which can be colossal. This photo was taken in 1933. Eleven years earlier, in 1922, an avalanche killed seven sherpas at this point. Reinhold Messner risked death here too during his 1980 ascent.

152 top right After they had crossed the great crevasse, easier slopes led the British climbers and their sherpas to the wide snow-covered saddle of the North Col, at an altitude of 7000 metres. This photo also dates from 1933.

152 bottom right The fresh snow, the icy climate of the high altitude and the rudimentary climbing boots of the Thirties meant that frostbite was a real risk for pre-war climbers. In this 1933 photo, a climber is having his numb feet massaged by his climbing companions.

Smythe, who had led the first ascents of the Red Sentinel and the Major route on Mont Blanc in 1927 and 1928, was the first to scale a difficult ice wall that blocked the access to the North Col on 12th May. After a few days of bad weather, Longland, Wager and Wyn Harris set up camp six at 8350 metres on 29th May. Wager and Wyn Harris set off for the summit at 5:30 a.m. the next day.

Keeping a little higher than their predecessors, the pair found one of Mallory and Irvine's ice-axes after an hour. Then they climbed towards the ridge, but a difficult rocky step forced them to descend in the direction of the Norton Couloir. At 12:30 p.m. they were close to the highest point reached in 1924.

The time and their physical condition would have allowed them to continue, but the large amount of fresh snow that had accumulated on the rocks persuaded them to turn back. An attempt by Frank Smythe, who had been forced to climb alone when Eric Shipton was taken ill not far above camp six, ended at the same point two days later.

Two more years went by, and the fifth British expedition arrived in the Rongbuk valley. However, the aims of this expedition, led by Eric Shipton, did not include the ascent of Everest. The climbers' objective was to increase geographical knowledge of the area and take home information that would be useful for a new attempt on the summit. Apart from Shipton, the group included Harold W. Tilman,

another great Himalayan explorer, Charles Warren, L.V. Bryant, Edwin Kempson, Edmund Wigram and topographer Michael Spencer. One of the sherpas was a 19-year-old destined to become world-famous – Tenzing Norgay.

The most interesting results of the expedition included the ascent of Lho La by Tilman and Wigram, and the ascent of three peaks in the Lingtren massif by Shipton and Bryant. From these magnificent viewpoints, they could see the forbidden Nepalese side of the mountain for the first time, as well as the North face and West ridge of Everest. However, 16 years were to pass before it could be established that a route from the south was feasible.

152-153 The route that climbs to the summit by way of the east Rongbuk Glacier, North Col and North Ridge, is now the ordinary route from the Tibetan side of Mount Everest. It does not present excessive difficulties, and is one of the most crowded routes in the Himalaya. This photo shows a line of climbers on the trail that climbs the ridge above the North Col, on which the tents of a camp can be seen.

153 top In case of accidents, the return to Sikkim became an interminable journey in the Twenties and Thirties. In this 1933 photo, Birnie is carried across the moraine of Rongbuk Glacier by a sherpa.

The Alpine Club and the Royal Geographical Society called on Hugh Ruttledge once again to lead the 1936 expedition, which finally aimed for the summit. The members of the team who had already set foot on Everest were Shipton, Smythe, Wyn Harris, Kempson, Warren, Wigram and Morris, while the newcomers were P.R. Oliver, J.M. Gravin and Dr. G.N. Humphreys. The team was strong, but the weather was even worse than on the other occasions. At the end of May, the monsoon had already reached the slopes of the Himalaya, and copious amounts of snow fell on Everest. The party was forced to turn back as soon as it reached the North Col.

The last pre-war expedition (though the participants did not know it at the time) left England in 1938. The budget was tighter than usual, but the climbers were skilled, and worked well together. The expedition was led by Harold Tilman, accompanied by veterans Shipton, Smythe, Wyn Harris, Odell and Warren. The only newcomer was Peter Lloyd. This time, when the party reached Rongbuk, the weather and conditions on the mountain were absolutely perfect.

After a period of acclimatisation the weather began to deteriorate, and the climbers set up camp four on the North Col immediately after a copious snowfall that made the ascent far more tiring than expected. Tenzing, now 22, demonstrated his stamina by trail-breaking much of the way in the deep snow, despite his load. On 8th June Shipton, Smythe and seven sherpas pitched camp six at 8270 metres. The next day, however, the cold and the snow that had fallen during the night forced the two Englishmen to give up after climbing only 50 metres.

Before returning to the UK, Tilman and Lloyd

154 top Unlike previous expeditions, the 1935 expedition gave climbers a view over a huge area, including summits, valleys and glaciers not yet shown on the maps. In this photo, the trail rises towards an unnamed peak overlooking the Kharta valley.

154 bottom In the Thirties, as now, much of the energy of climbers on Everest had to be used to beat tracks in the snow and cross the treacherous snow bridges.

returned to the North-East ridge, equipped with breathing apparatus, but got no farther than their companions. As on the six previous occasions, when the climbers took their leave of the Rongbuk valley, they expected to return in a year or two. In fact, it was to be 40 years before Western climbers were able to enter Tibet again. When Everest was finally climbed in 1953, the ascent took place from the Nepalese side, which had been opened to foreigners by the newly-crowned King Tribhuvan.

155 top Remote as it is, the wide basin of the east Rongbuk Glacier indicates the start of the difficulties for climbers who begin the ascent to the North Col, just as it did in the Thirties. The scene is dominated by the summit of Mount Everest.

155 centre With a powerful telephoto lens, the summit of Everest seems almost within reach of the photographer who took this photo from Rongbuk Glacier. In reality, the summit is several kilometres from the base camp and 3600 metres higher up.

155 bottom Another famous photo taken by the 1935 exploratory expedition shows Everest (left, shrouded in cloud) and Nuptse from a ridge almost 7000 metres high that overlooks the Rongbuk Glacier. From here, climbers can see the Nepalese side.

Although Mount Everest attracted the most attention from climbers, other great mountains were also tackled by determined expeditions between the wars. Britons Frank Smythe and Eric Shipton, with Holdsworth and sherpa Lewa, reached the 7756-metre summit of Mount Kamet in 1931. Five years later, Harold Tilman and Noel Odell made the first ascent of the elegant Nanda Devi (7816 metres).

The Americans took the initiative on K2 after the Italian expedition of 1929 turned into a scientific mission.

In 1939 an expedition led by Charles Houston had been the first to climb the whole Abruzzi Spur and reach the snow slopes of the Shoulder. The following year it was Fritz Wiessner's turn. In 1953, another team led by Charles Houston again reached the Shoulder, but was halted by a blizzard and a fall involving six climbers. Art Gilkey was killed during the descent.

Three different expeditions tackled the equally difficult Kangchenjunga, only accessible from the Indian side. In 1929, a German party led by Paul Bauer tackled the North-East spur of the mountain, reaching a height of 7400 metres. The next year, an international team led by Gunther O. Dyrenfurth had to stop 1000 metres lower, and the mountain claimed two victims. In 1931, the second Bauer expedition reached 7800 metres, but lost two climbers. In 1934, Dyrenfurth led another expedition to the Gasherbrum massif. However, the maximum altitude reached on both Hidden Peak and Gasherbrum II was just over 6000 metres. On the higher of the two peaks, a French team was forced to turn back after reaching 6900 metres in 1936.

Apart from Everest, the most coveted mountain in the Thirties was Nanga Parbat, which of all the fourteen 8000-metre peaks is the most easily accessible from the Indian plains. In 1932, the first of five Austro-German expeditions arrived at the foot of Nanga Parbat. The group was led by Willy Merkl, a Bavarian climber who made some excellent ascents in the Alps and the Caucasus. However, the climbers were forced back even before reaching 7000 metres, mainly through lack of Himalayan experience.

Two years later, Merkl was back in action, accompanied by Willo Welzembach, one of the best ice climbers of all time. More skilled and better organised than the 1932 expedition, the group reached the ice shelf they named the Silberplateau (Silver Plateau), then tackled the long ridge that leads to the summit. On the ridge, Peter Aschenbrenner and Erwin Schneider reached 7850 metres. Then, during the descent, a terrible blizzard killed four climbers, including Welzembach and Merkl, and six sherpas.

Things went even worse in 1937, when an expedition led by Karl Wien again attempted the ascent of Nanga

Parbat. When the climbers were at a height of just over 6000 metres, a colossal avalanche buried all the camps they had set up on the mountain, killing all seven climbers and all nine high-altitude sherpa porters.

In 1938, another German expedition attempted the north side of Nanga Parbat, but the results were mediocre. The next year, a small expedition led by Peter Aufschneiter attempted two ascents on the Diamir side. However, they found their return hampered by the outbreak of war. In just a few days, the climbers' excitement at the challenge of climbing on the snow of Nanga Parbat gave way to the depressing routine of an Indian internment camp. But this unpleasant situation led to one of the most fascinating adventures of the 20th century. Heinrich Harrer, one of the first ascensionists of the North face of the Eiger the year before, decided to make a break for freedom. He and Aufschneiter escaped from the camp and headed for the Himalayan valleys. The pair were soon caught and severely punished, but managed to escape again, and this time, the Sikhs and

Gurkhas were unable to catch them. After a horrific trek the two climbers, suffering from malnutrition and dressed in rags, finally managed to reach the Tibetan plateau and Lhasa, the capital of the forbidden country. They should have been expelled immediately, but the courtesy and curiosity of the Tibetans got the upper hand. The two men stayed in Tibet for seven years, during which Harrer became the friend and confidant of the young Dalai Lama. In that capacity he witnessed the Chinese invasion of the country, without being able to do anything to change the course of history. When Chinese troops marched into Lhasa, Harrer was forced to flee the country with many other refugees. A few years later Tenzing Gyatso, the 14th Dalai Lama, fearing for his life, took refuge in India. *Seven Years in Tibet*, the book written by Harrer about his adventure, became one of the best-selling books of all time. For the Tibetan population, the sympathy that it created all over the world still represents a formidable weapon that gives them a glimmer of hope for a better future.

156 top The ordinary route on Gasherbrum II is now one of the most popular routes on the "eight-thousanders." This photo, taken from camp three, shows the Duke of Abruzzi Glacier, the Golden Throne (or Baltoro Kangri, on the left) and the trapezoidal summit of Chogolisa.

156-157 This photo, taken from the ordinary route on Gasherbrum II, shows the spectacular snow-covered walls of Gasherbrum V (7321 metres, on the right) and Gasherbrum VI (7003 metres). The Golden Throne can be seen farther away on the left.

157 bottom left American doctor and mountaineer Charles Houston is mainly known for his two expeditions to K2, made in 1938 and 1953, which got no farther than the snow-covered slopes of the Shoulder. The 1936 expedition, which made the first ascent of Nanda Devi, and the 1950 exploratory journey into the Nepalese valleys of Khumbu also deserve to be remembered.

157 bottom right The impressive Gasherbrum massif acts as the background to the march of expeditions climbing the upper Baltoro and the Duke of Abruzzi Glacier. The snow-capped pyramid of Gasherbrum I (or Hidden Peak), at 8068 metres, is the highest peak in the entire range, can be seen on the right.

158 top *New Zealander Edmund Hillary was one of the protagonists of the conquest of Everest. In 1951, with Eric Shipton, he observed the mountain from the slopes of Pumori and climbed to the end of the serac band. On 29th May 1953, Hillary finally reached the 8848-metre summit together with sherpa Tenzing Norgay.*

8000 Metres and beyond

Of all the important dates in climbing history, 29th May 1953 is one of the few to be mentioned in all the history books. That day, at around 10 a.m., two men were climbing the highest snow ridge in the world: the ridge decorated with fairy-tale snow cornices that stretches from the 8750-metre South summit to the 8848-metre summit of Everest, the highest and most coveted mountain on earth. The weather was magnificent, the view was fantastic, and all the great surrounding peaks (Makalu and Kangchenjunga, Cho Oyu and Lhotse) were now below the two climbers.

The leader of the team was a lean 34-year-old New Zealander named Edmund Hillary. He climbed the ridge slowly but surely, cutting steps large enough for his

158-159 The warm light of sunset makes the summit pyramid of Everest, seen from the Nepalese side, particularly enchanting. This side of the mountain was observed and photographed for the first time in 1951 by a small expedition led by Eric Shipton.

158 bottom This photo, taken by Alfred Gregory shortly after the first ascent of Everest, shows the climbers, researchers and sherpas of the 1953 British expedition. Edmund Hillary, John Hunt and Tenzing Norgay are the fifth, sixth and seventh from the left respectively of the men standing.

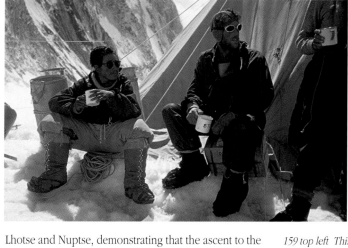

Lhotse and Nuptse, demonstrating that the ascent to the summit was really possible.

Hillary was roped to the best climber in Asia. Tenzing Norgay, a sherpa of Nepalese descent who lived in Darjeeling, India, was three years older than his companion, and had accompanied British expeditions on the Tibetan side of Everest before the war in 1935, 1936 and 1938. In 1951, with a French team, he had performed the second ascent of Nanda Devi, one of the most spectacular 7000-metre peaks in the Himalayan chain.

In 1952, Tenzing had climbed towards the summit

159 top left This photo, taken at the advanced base camp, shows Tenzing (left) and Hillary, exhausted but happy, on their return from the summit of Mount Everest. The bulky, heavy clothing used by the two men is worthy of note.

159 top right John Hunt, who was appointed the expedition's leader amid great controversy, deserves much of the credit for the British ascent of Everest. It was the work of this professional soldier, who had lived in Asia for many years and taken part in various expeditions in the Himalaya, that enabled the climbers and sherpas to work together without argument or difficulty.

159 bottom Between 1921 and 1937, no less then seven British expeditions tackled the Tibetan side of Everest. After the war, however, the Chinese invasion of Tibet and the opening of Nepal to foreigners sent climbers towards the valleys of the sherpas and the south side of the mountain, shown in this photo.

colossal high-altitude boots with the ice-axe. A beekeeper by profession, Hillary had spent much of the past few years exploring the valleys that form the heart of the Himalaya.

On 30th September 1951, Hillary and Eric Shipton had discovered from the buttresses of Mount Pumori that Everest could be attempted, and probably climbed, from the Nepalese side as well as the Tibetan side, where the British attempts of the Twenties and Thirties had been made. A few days later, with Shipton, Tom Bourdillon and H.E. Riddiford, Hillary climbed the dangerous serac band of the Khumbu until he overlooked the Western Cwm (also known as the Valley of Silence), the wide, easy glacial depression that extends between Everest,

of Mount Everest with Swiss mountaineer Raymond Lambert, reaching an altitude of 8595 metres. Then, fatigue and lack of oxygen had forced him to descend. Now the sherpa followed Hillary, who was more expert in cutting steps. However, on the dangerous slopes preceding the South Summit, he led for long stretches. Both men were there to achieve a long-standing ambition.

After numerous short pitches (the rope with which the climbers were tied together was no more than 9 metres long), Tenzing suddenly slowed down. Hillary realised that his breathing apparatus was clogged, dismantled it, removed a thick plug of condensation ice from the tube, and urged his companion on. After an hour's march from the snow-cap of the South Summit, a last obstacle seemed to bar the way.

It was a steep rocky step a dozen metres high which the climbers had seen on aerial photographs of Everest and with their binoculars from Tengboche. "The rock, which was smooth and almost devoid of holds, would have constituted an interesting problem for a party of expert climbers on a Sunday afternoon in the Lake District," commented Hillary ironically. "But here, in our weakened state, it was an insurmountable obstacle."

Fortunately, on the side facing Nepal, a narrow cleft separated the rock from the snow cornice that

jutted out over the South-West face. Hillary jammed the crack, digging his crampons into the snow and pushing against the rock with his hands and back. He inched upwards, "praying fervently that the cornice would remain attached to the rock." At the end of the pitch, a convenient snow-covered ledge allowed him to get his breath back, and help the sherpa climb up to join him.

The last section of the ridge was easier, but seemed endless. At exactly 11:30 a.m. the two men finally came out onto the narrow snowcap that constitutes the summit of Mount Everest. Hillary held out his hand to his companion, but Tenzing threw his arms around him and clapped him on the back. Next came the usual photographs, then Hillary descended a few metres towards the last rocks on the North-East ridge. He was looking for traces left by Mallory and Irvine, but found nothing.

Then came the long, dangerous, exhausting descent. After the vertical step and the narrow snow ridge, a ledge just below the South Summit provided a convenient belay station for the two climbers. A little lower, two oxygen cylinders left by Tom Bourdillon and Charles Evans enabled Hillary and Tenzing to fill up with oxygen. When they were in sight of the South Col, George Lowe, the other "Kiwi" on the expedition, climbed to meet them. He was the first to hear the news of the victorious ascent.

The other members of the expedition, who had gathered at the advanced base camp at 6400 metres, had to wait till the next day, when the tired party climbing down the wall of the Lhoptse betrayed evident signs of exultation.

A few days later, as Queen Elizabeth II's coronation procession wound its way through the streets of London, loudspeakers boomed out the news: "Mount Everest has been conquered!" However, Her Majesty's subjects were not the only ones to be thrilled by the ascent. In a world still licking its wounds after the bloodiest war in

the history of the human race, this great peacetime adventure aroused extraordinary enthusiasm. For years, the members of the victorious expedition, especially Hillary, Tenzing and Hunt, attended one conference, official lunch and gala evening after another. As Pete Boardman commented 20 years later, Tenzing thus became "the first Asian of humble birth in history to achieve international fame."

The only person to be upset, understandably enough, was Eric Shipton. He had taken part in many minor expeditions in Africa, Patagonia and the

Garwhal Himalaya, and had participated in some of the first British attempts on Everest in the Thirties. He discovered and explored the ascent route on the Nepalese side, but was then brutally pushed aside to make way for John Hunt, the leader of the victorious expedition. He did not get involved in any public controversy, but his comment on the feat was cutting: "When the race to conquer the mountain is over, real climbing can begin on Everest."

In reality, the age of victorious feats on the highest mountains on earth had begun three years earlier. As

160-161 Now, as in the Fifties, large (sometimes enormous) crevasses cut through the great serac band of the Khumbu Glacier. To cross this route in safety and carry loads up the mountain, expeditions are forced to construct rickety bridges made from metal ladders and ropes. In this photo, a sherpa belonging to the 1953 British expedition crosses one of these precarious bridges.

160 bottom In this photo, taken by John Hunt, Hillary and Tenzing are climbing the Everest ridge towards camp nine at 8500 metres, where they spent the night before their victory.

161 top left One of the secrets of the conquest of Everest in 1953 was the important role played by the breathing apparatus used, which was much lighter and more efficient than the type employed before the war. Much of the credit for this development is due to the research conducted by the RAF during the war.

161 top right The first ascent of Mount Everest galvanised the attention of the world's press, as demonstrated by this cover of La Domenica del Corriere, the most popular Italian weekly magazine of the period, which shows the climbers reaching the summit.

often happens in history, the war led to improvements in technologies used in peacetime. The climbers of the Fifties had no more courage or breath than Mallory, Wiessner, Welzembach, Merkl and party, but instead of heavy wool or tweed jackets and trousers they had light, comfortable, high-altitude suits based on those used by pilots; their ice-axes and crampons were better and lighter, and their double or triple boots, though bulky, were far warmer than before. Above all, thanks to aeronautical technology, their breathing apparatus was much lighter and more efficient than in the past.

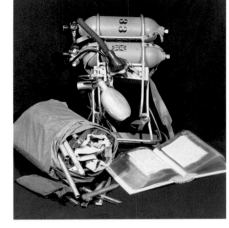

161 centre The light of sunset tints the upper part of the South-West face of Everest, which was climbed by a British expedition in 1975. The ordinary route runs diagonally from the Lhotse wall (from which this photo was taken) to the wide saddle of the South Col, and continues across snow and rock towards the South Peak and the summit.

161 bottom left Shortly before their departure for camp nine and the summit, Edmund Hillary (left) and Tenzing Norgay prepare their rucksacks and breathing apparatus. The snow and débris of the South Col stretches all round the two men, at an altitude of nearly 8000 metres.

161 bottom right This photo was published all over the world. Taken by Edmund Hillary, it shows Tenzing exulting after finally reaching the summit of Everest. It was midday on 29th May 1953, a date destined to go down in the annals of history.

It became clear that things had changed radically in the spring of 1950, when a French expedition finally obtained permission to venture into the lovely, unknown mountains of central Nepal. The expedition, led by Maurice Herzog, was hampered by maps full of mistakes and the numerous problems posed by unexplored territory. They were even able to choose their objective from between two magnificent mountains, Dhaulagiri (8167 m) and Annapurna (8091 m), which would be

unthinkable for the hurried, codified modern expeditions.

The party entered Nepal on 5th April, followed the Kali Gandaki valley that separates Annapurna from Dhaulagiri, camped near Tukucha, and started their explorations towards the two great nearby mountains. On the Dhaulagiri front, the news was not good. Apart from having a very inhospitable look, that peak was much farther from the Kali Gandaki valley than the maps indicated. An attempted ascent would be impossible, not so much because of the difficulty of the route but because of the huge walk-in.

Things were difficult on Annapurna too. The Tilicho Col, which according to the maps held by Herzog and his party seemed to give access to the north side of the mountain, actually connects the upper Kali Gandaki valley with the Marsyangdi Khola and Manang. However, on 27th April, Jean Couzy, Marcel Schatz and the expedition's doctor Jacques Oudot discovered a passage that gave access to the mountain via the wild gorges through which the Miristi Khola flows. This was the route to follow.

The party decided to concentrate their efforts on Annapurna just two weeks before the monsoon was expected. Despite the serious delay, the class and stamina of the French climbers enabled them to make rapid progress up the steep, icy slopes that form the north side of the mountain. On 23rd May, Louis

Lachenal and Gaston Rébuffat finally found the route to the upper part of the mountain. Four days later, Maurice Herzog, together with sherpas Dawa Thondup and Angawa, reached the unmistakable crescent-shaped hanging glacier that gives access to the easy slopes leading to the summit ridge.

On the evening of 1st June Herzog, this time with Lachenal, pitched the small tent of camp five at 7400 metres. Indian radio announced the arrival of the monsoon for the 5th, but neither of the two climbers had any intention of leaving before climbing to the summit. At 2 p.m. on 3rd June, after an exhausting, steep climb in deep snow, the two men, who carried no breathing apparatus, embraced on the 8091-metre summit of the tenth-highest mountain on earth. An 8000-metre peak had been climbed for the first time, but the price the climbers paid for their victory was heavy indeed.

Exhausted by their efforts and the altitude, the two men made mistakes that turned the descent into a nightmare. Herzog lost his gloves 200 metres below

the summit. It didn't occur to him to cover his hands with the spare pair of socks he had brought in his rucksack, and his hands were soon frostbitten. Lachenal, who could no longer feel his feet even on the way up, slipped on a steep slope and disappeared into the fog that enshrouded Annapurna.

Gaston Rébuffat and Lionel Terray came to the rescue of the two climbers who had reached the summit. After Herzog made it back to camp five, they found Lachenal and led him back to the relative safety of the tent. But the two men were suffering from serious frostbite of the hands and feet, and the weather had worsened considerably. On the morning of 4th June, the four climbers continued their descent despite the bad weather. The fog, and the snow that had covered their tracks, prevented them from finding camp four, and they were forced to make an unpleasant bivouac in a crevasse.

The next day, Marcel Schatz reached the four men and guided them down. Herzog and Lachenal had great difficulty moving because of their frostbitten feet, and Terray and Rébuffat were almost snow-blind. Near camp three, when the odyssey seemed to be

nearly over, an avalanche hit the group and catapulted them much of the way down the slope.

At camp two, Dr. Jacques Oudot hurriedly set up a field hospital, and saved Herzog's life with a makeshift transfusion. For the two frostbitten climbers, the return to Pokhara was a terrible ordeal. The porters who carried them on rudimentary litters kept slipping on the muddy ground; several times they risked dropping them in places where they would have met certain death. Amputations of Herzog and Lachenal's hands and feet began on the return journey, and were particularly extensive in Herzog's case.

Yet in his book *Annapurna, the First 8000-Metre Peak*, Maurice Herzog never expressed any recrimination or regret. "Swaying in the stretcher, I thought about the adventure that was coming to an end and the unexpected victory. We had gone to Annapurna penniless, and found a treasure on which we would live for the rest of our lives. That insight was a revelation to me. A new life was beginning. There were other Annapurnas in the life of men."

162-163 The South face of Annapurna, which is more impressive and wilder than the north side, is one of the most difficult in the Himalaya. Unthinkable for the climbers of the Fifties, it was finally climbed in 1970 by a small but skilled British team led by Chris Bonington.

163 bottom left Here, five members of the 1950 French expedition to Annapurna are gathered in a tent at the base camp. Left to right: Louis Lachenal, doctor Jacques Oudot, Gaston Rébuffat, Maurice Herzog, and photographer and film-maker Marcel Ichac.

163 bottom right The impressive bulk of Dhaulagiri is a common sight for trekkers following the trails of central Nepal. This peak was among the possible objectives of the 1950 expedition, but was ruled out because of the difficulties and the length of the walk-in.

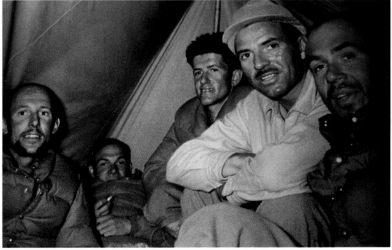

162 left On the north side of Annapurna, the main problem for the 1950 expedition was the thick layer of unstable snow, as a result the climbers' progress was fatiguing, and involved the risk of causing major avalanches.

162 right For the French expedition which conquered Annapurna in 1950, the descent proved harder than the ascent. This photo shows Marcel Schatz (left) helping Lionel Terray, who was suffering from snow-blindness, to cover the last few metres separating them from the base camp. Sherpa Ang Tharkey is behind them.

Between 1951 and 1952, various minor expeditions increased knowledge of the great mountains of Nepal and opened a route towards Mount Everest which was eventually conquered in the pre-monsoon season in 1953. While the world was beginning to celebrate the achievement of Hillary and Tenzing, however, an Austrian expedition was approaching the summit of Nanga Parbat, the "killer mountain" that took the lives of no less than 32 Austrian and German climbers and the sherpas engaged to help them between 1932 and 1939.

The expedition, led by Karl Herrigkofler, climbed methodically to an altitude of 6900 metres. Then the appalling weather conditions persuaded the expedition leader to order the upper camps to be evacuated. However, three men decided to continue the ascent at all costs. They included Tyrolese climber Hermann Buhl, who had made numerous great ascents in the mountains of the Tyrol and the Dolomites.

After leaving the last camp at dawn on 3rd July, Buhl slowly made his way up the interminable snow ridge that rose to the summit. His friend Kempter, who had left the tent with him, soon gave up the attempt. From the Silbersattel (Silver Saddle) which gives onto the summit ridge, they had to cross the fore-summit reached by Aschenbrenner and Schneider in 1934, then continue in switchback fashion.

At 6:45 p.m., after climbing an incredible 1230 metres in a day, Hermann Buhl finally reached the summit most coveted by German-speaking climbers. Pep pills helped him cope with the descent and a horrific bivouac on a slab of rock. The next day, his companions came to meet him and helped him down the rest of the descent. In the eyes of the Austrian and German press, Buhl had finally taken revenge for all their compatriots killed on Nanga Parbat.

164 The morning light seems to bring to life the east (or Rupal) side of Nanga Parbat, which Mathias Rebitsch described in 1938 as "a rock and ice pillar 4500 metres tall, so awesome it's almost unearthly." The first ascent to the summit from this side was made in 1970 by Reinhold Messner, Gunther Messner, Felix Kuen and Peter Scholz.

165 top This photo, taken at the Nanga Parbat base camp, shows the climbers and high altitude porters of the Austro-German expedition of 1953.

165 centre Hermann Buhl (right) rests at the base camp before setting off for the summit of Nanga Parbat.

165 bottom left The scheduled flights connecting Islamabad to Gilgit and Skardu offer an exceptional view of the north (or Rakhiot) side of Nanga Parbat, used by pre-war expeditions and the victorious 1953 team.

165 bottom right In addition to climbing, the first route to Nanga Parbat forced climbers to make a very long walk-in. In this photo, taken at camp four at an altitude of 7000 metres, the summit still seems very far away.

The next summer, in 1954, a skilled Italian expedition tackled the second-highest mountain on earth: K2. Only 237 metres lower than Mount Everest (and on the basis of recent measurements, the difference seems to be even less), K2 is far more difficult than its big brother. While the ascent of Everest, though dangerous, involves an easy walk on glaciers for long stretches, the ordinary route on K2 requires some serious climbing on rock and mixed terrain from an altitude of 5500 metres. Then the easy snow slopes of the Shoulder give way to the steep, exposed, avalanche-prone couloir giving access to the summit.

Seen at first hand for the first time in 1888 by Captain Francis Younghusband, the mountain known by the Balti as Chogori was first attempted at the beginning of the century. In 1909 the Duke of Abruzzi and his guides from Courmayeur identified the correct route to the top, then three American expeditions arrived within a few hundred metres of the summit.

The Italian expedition, led by Professor Ardito Desio, reached Pakistan around mid-April, took a heart-stopping flight to Skardu, and set off for the mountain on the 30th. They made the classic halts at Shigar, Askole, Liligo, Urdukas and Concordia. On 15th May, the base camp was finally set up on the desolate moraines at the foot of the South-West face of K2.

In Italy, great controversy had accompanied the formation of the team, from which leading climbers like Riccardo Cassin had been excluded. The climbers from the Dolomites and those from the Western Alps were used to a wide variety of mountain conditions, but the bad weather made their progress difficult.

On 21st June, Courmayeur guide Mario Puchoz died suddenly from edema. In early July, a series of raging blizzards began to make the climbers wonder whether they should give up the attempt. But on 20th July, the seventh camp was firmly established on the snow-covered Shoulder of K2. On the evening of 28th July, when the weather finally took a turn for the better, the first team, formed by Achille Compagnoni and Lino Lacedelli, started climbing.

On 30th July, after a tiring day, the two men set up camp nine on a small ledge at an altitude of 8050 metres, a little higher than their planned position.

166-167 The pyramid of K2, observed from the base camp set up on the moraine of the Godwin Austen Glacier, is a particularly attractive sight at the first light of dawn.

167 bottom Unlike Compagnoni, Lino Lacedelli was an excellent rock climber. Born in Cortina d'Ampezzo, he belonged to the Scoiattoli (Squirrels) group, and put up some exceptionally difficult routes on his home mountains. The first ascent of K2 in July 1954 brought together these two very different representatives of Italian climbing.

166 top In this photo, taken at Skardu before the start of the long trek to K2, the members of the 1954 Italian expedition are gathered around expedition leader Ardito Desio. Compagnoni is the first on the left at the top, and Lacedelli is sitting next to Desio. Walter Bonatti is seated on the right.

166 bottom Achille Compagnoni, born in Santa Caterina di Valfurva at the foot of the Gran Zebrù and the Cevedale, was not a virtuoso rock climber but a fighting-fit mountain man who stood up particularly well to the rigours of Himalayan climbing.

Walter Bonatti and Hunza porter Mahdi, who had the job of supplying the first team, were unable to find the tent and were forced to make a horrific bivouac in the freezing cold which cost them serious frostbite. The next day, unaware of the drama that had taken place not far from their camp, Compagnoni and Lacedelli completed their preparations and set off for the summit.

After a short descent to collect the breathing apparatus left by Mahdi and Bonatti, the pair began the hard climb. Wallowing in the snow up to their waists, they reached the base of the steepest section, where hard snow had allowed Wiessner to climb directly in the gully. Now, however, a deep layer of unstable snow prevented them from making any progress whatever. Compagnoni made a first attempt on the rock, fell, and landed on the snow. Lacedelli tried next, free climbing a 30-metre step rated between the third and fourth grades. A dangerous traverse at the foot of a wall of ice and a section where the snow came up to their shoulders took the climbers to the easier slopes that rose towards the summit. The rest was mere slog, and a hard slog it was!

Carrying their heavy oxygen cylinders, now empty (which they could not get rid of due to the steepness of the slope), Lino and Achille inched their way upwards, while the morning fog gave way to sun and icy wind.

At 6 p.m., as the report written by the two climbers recounts, "the snow became firm and the slope more gradual, almost flat, and finally flat! After months of effort, there was nothing more to be climbed. There was only sky above us. We embraced."

After photos and a short film had been taken, the dramatic and dangerous descent began. Despite the darkness and their tiredness, the unstable snow did

not give way under the feet of Compagnoni and Lacedelli during the traverse and the descent of the steep gully. On the plateau, however, walls of ice and crevasses created more serious problems. Achille fell some 15 metres, but landed in a snowdrift, and Lino somehow managed not to fall on top of him, crampons first. Eventually, at midnight, the pair reached the tents of camp eight, where Walter Bonatti, Erich Abram, Pino Gallotti and Hunza porters Isakhan and Mahdi embraced them joyfully. ·

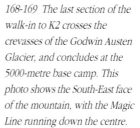

168-169 The last section of the walk-in to K2 crosses the crevasses of the Godwin Austen Glacier, and concludes at the 5000-metre base camp. This photo shows the South-East face of the mountain, with the Magic Line running down the centre.

8000 metres and beyond

168 bottom Like all the great mountains in the world, K2 rebuffs climbers with steep, tiring snow-covered slopes. The mountaineers in this photo are Guido Pagani and Ugo Angelino.

169 top left As in all climbing expeditions, the Italian base camp at the foot of K2 was a gear dump. Ropes, rock and snow pitons and breathing apparatus were piled up beside the collective tents.

169 top right The photomontage used to promote the film of the expedition shows Achille Compagnoni and Lino Lacedelli at an altitude of 8616 metres, on the summit of the second-highest mountain on earth.

169 centre Camp two of the Italian expedition to K2 was set up on a small ledge at an altitude of 6100 metres, flanked by a characteristic "finger" of rock.

169 bottom left A look at the base camp depot shows the footwear used by the climbers. Fur-covered boots are used at altitudes exceeding 8000 metres.

169 bottom right The most tragic moment for the Desio expedition came on 21st June, when Mario Puchoz of Val d'Aosta died of edema. This photo shows the other climbers carrying their companion's body to the place of burial.

170 centre left Hermann
Buhl, who was born in 1924
and died on Chogolisa in
1957, was one of the most
famous Austrian climbers of
all time. He made numerous
major ascents in the Alps,
and became world-famous
as a result of the first ascents
of Nanga Parbat (1951) and
Broad Peak (1957).

170 bottom left Nowadays,
Cho Oyu (8201 metres) is one
of the most frequently climbed
"eight-thousanders." The first
ascent was made in 1954 by
sherpa Pasang Dawa Lama
and Austrians Herbert Tichy
and Sepp Jochler (from left in
the photo). It is a difficult,
dangerous climb.

When the monsoon of 1954 left the mountains of
Nepal, another virgin 8000-metre peak was conquered.
Austrians Herbert Tichy and Sepp Jochler, together with
sherpa Pasang Dawa Lama, were the first to set foot on
the 8201-metre Cho Oyu at the end of a dramatic
expedition.

The golden years of Himalayan expeditions ended
in 1955, when two expeditions conquered the third-
and fifth-highest mountains on earth.

The French were back in action, this time on
Makalu, the massive pyramid of rock and ice that stands
just to the east of Mount Everest. The expedition, led by
Jean Franco, benefited from excellent weather (the

170 top The use of oxygen
dispensed by revolutionary
breathing apparatus, even at
night, as recommended by Jean
Franco, coordinator of the French
ascent of Mount Makalu in
summer 1955, enabled the
members of the expedition to
make the final assault on the
summit when rested. This photo
shows a high-altitude base camp.

170-171 The French expedition
that made the first ascent of
Makalu in 1955 was an
outstanding success, as all
members of the expedition
reached the 8463-metre summit.
In this photo, a climber stops to
get his breath back during the
ascent. The East face of Everest
(on the right in the photo) and
the turreted silhouette of Lhotse
can be clearly distinguished in
the background.

170 bottom right
Austrian climber Kurt
Diemberger entered the
history of the "eight-
thousanders" in 1957,
when he made the first
ascent of Broad Peak
with Fritz Wintersteller,

Marcus Schmuck and
Hermann Buhl. The
expedition concluded
tragically a few weeks
later, when a snow cornice
gave way on Chogolisa
and Hermann Buhl fell to
his death.

same weather that helped the British on nearby Kangchenjunga) and new lightweight breathing apparatus. On 15th May, Annapurna veterans Jean Couzy and Lionel Terray reached the 8463-metre summit with no particular problems. In the next two days, all the climbers and sherpa Gyaltzen Norbu summited in turn.

Kangchenjunga, the third-highest mountain in the world, was climbed by the British. Led by Charles Evans, one of the members of the expedition to Everest two years earlier, the team tackled the awesome ice wall separating India from Nepal in mid-April. On 25th May, after a night spent at an altitude of 8200 metres,

George Band, another veteran of Everest, and brilliant young climber Joe Brown, reached the 8596-metre summit. The next day, as in the case of the French expedition, two more climbers summited in their turn.

Compared with these feats, the ascent of the other 8000-metre peaks inevitably took second place. In May 1956 Japanese climber T. Imanishi made the first ascent of the 8163-metre Manaslu with sherpa Gyaltzen Norbu. The sherpa thus became the first man in history to climb two 8000-metre peaks.

A few days later, a Swiss expedition made the second ascent of Mount Everest, thus taking revenge for the Swiss defeat in 1952. On 18th May, two

members of the team, Luchsinger and Reiss, made the first ascent of the 8516-metre Lhotse, the fourth-highest peak on earth. The following 7th July three Austrians, Fritz Moravec, Hans Willenpart and Sepp Larch, summited the 8035-metre Gasherbrum II.

In 1957, an Austrian expedition organised in a particularly spartan manner appeared in the heart of the Karakorum range. Composed of Kurt Diemberger, Fritz Wintersteller, Marcus Schmuck and the already famous Hermann Buhl, the team climbed without installing fixed ropes for protection, thus inaugurating what is now described as the "Alpine style."

On 9th June, all four climbers reached the 8047-metre Broad Peak. Buhl, like Gyaltzen Norbu, had now climbed two 8000-metre peaks. A few days later, however, during an attempt on the nearby Chogolisa, a magnificent 7654-metre peak, Buhl left the beaten upward trail in the fog, stepped on a snow cornice and fell to his death.

The race to conquer the 8000-metre peaks continued. In 1958, American climbers Nick Clinch, Pete Schoening and Andy Kauffman scaled the 8068-metre Hidden Peak. Two years later, Austrian Kurt Diemberger scaled the 8167-metre Dhaulagiri, one of the most remote and hard to reach 8000-metre peaks, with Swiss climber Albin Schelbert and sherpa Nawang Dorje.

171 bottom left The last part of the ordinary route on Mount Makalu crosses easy but steep slopes of snow and rock, which are very tiring when the snow is deep.

171 right Two climbers are scaling the last part of the ordinary route on Broad Peak. The north summit of the mountain can be seen behind them.

The years of conquest concluded on 2nd May 1964 when six Chinese and four Tibetan climbers scaled the 8046-metre Shisha Pangma (long known by the Nepalese name of Gosainthan), the only 8000-metre peak situated to the north of the Himalayan divide.

Four years earlier, on 25th May 1960, Chinese climbers Wang Fu-Chou and Chu Yin-Hua and Tibetan climber Gonpa had reached the summit of Everest from the Tibetan side, scaling the ridge attempted by Mallory, Irvine and party as far as the summit. This ascent, initially disputed by Western climbers, was only universally accepted in 1975, when a second Chinese team again reached the summit, and left a highly visible tripod there.

However, not all the climbers who headed for the Himalaya in the Fifties were involved in the race to conquer the 8000-metre peaks. Some of the most

attractive 7000-metre peaks, like Nanda Devi (7816 m), Kamet (7756 m) and Kabru (7388 m), had already been climbed by pre-war expeditions. The new series of conquests began in 1950, when a Norwegian team led by Arne Naess reached the summit of Tirich Mir (7706 m), the highest and loveliest peak in Pakistan's Hindu Kush. In 1956 came the ascent of Muztagh Ata (7446 m) in the Pamir by a Soviet expedition, and the ascent of the elegant Muztagh Tower (7273 m) in the Karakorum range, scaled by a British and a French team a few days apart.

In 1958, the Russians scaled the difficult Pik Pobedy (7439 m) in Tien Shan, while the British reached the summit of Rakaposhi (7788 m), the impressive ice mountain that dominates the green Hunza valley. In the same year, an Italian expedition led by Fosco Maraini and Riccardo Cassin conquered Gasherbrum IV (7980 m), the spectacular mountain

that dominates the Concordia amphitheatre.

The sharp summit ridge, on which unstable snow ridges alternate with compact towers of rock, forced the first team, consisting of Walter Bonatti and Carlo Mauri, to tackle the toughest climbing pitches that had ever been scaled at high altitude. For Bonatti, one of the best-known and toughest mountaineers of all time, the victory made up for all the suffering, frostbite and controversy involved in the ascent of K2.

In 1958, back in the Karakorum, the Americans climbed Masherbrum (7821 m) while the Austrians summited Disteghil Sar (7885 m). Two years later, the British climbed Annapurna II (7937 m) and the Japanese scaled Himalchuli (7864 m). In 1961, another British team reached the summit of Nuptse (7855 m), one of the most elegant outriders of Mount Everest.

A young climber who was to hit the headlines in

172 bottom In this photo, taken by Carlo Mauri, Walter Bonatti rests on the summit of Gasherbrum IV, which consists of a huge, treacherous snow cornice attached to the rock. It was 12:30 p.m. on 6th August 1958.

172-173 In the late Fifties, when all the "eight-thousanders" had been conquered, climbers' attention turned to the most spectacular "seven-thousanders" in the Himalaya and Karakorum, many of which offer more difficult routes than their higher neighbours. This photo, taken near Lobuche, shows the exceptional beauty of Nuptse, which flanks Everest to the west. It was first climbed in 1961 by a British team.

173 bottom Among the peaks that come close to the magical height of 8000 metres, one of the most spectacular is Gasherbrum IV (7980 metres), first climbed in 1958 by a strong Italian expedition. Walter Bonatti and Carlo Mauri reached the summit. This photo shows the awesome West face of the spectacular mountain, which dominates the Concordia amphitheatre.

the years to come reached the summits of both Nuptse and Annapurna II. He was named Chris Bonington, and the expeditions he led tackled some of the most difficult walls in the Himalayan chain in the Seventies. The greatest ascents of the 7000-metre peaks ended with the conquest of Jannu (7710 m) in East Nepal by a French team in 1962.

Among the many expeditions of those years, one stood out for its carefree atmosphere, spartan equipment and outstanding results. Composed only of Kurt Diemberger and Dietmar Proske, the "1967 Austro-German Hindu Kush Exploratory Expedition" set off from Europe by car, reached the high valleys of Pakistan, spent a month and a half in the mountains climbing three 7000-metre and four 6000-metre peaks, and made the first complete circuit of Tirich Mir. The years of the feats performed by Reinhold Messner and others were about to arrive.

172 top left From the flat Gasherbrum valley, the difficult Italian Serac Band leads to the foot of the North-East ridge of Gasherbrum IV. The climbers in this photo are at an altitude of approximately 6500 metres.

172 top right The last part of the ordinary route on Gasherbrum IV crosses some particularly difficult, steep, mixed terrain. In this photo, Walter Bonatti is leading the ridge.

Beyond the vertical

The Second World War, unlike the First, left the Dolomites in peace. Clashes between partisans and Wehrmacht troops took place at the foot of the Brenta and in the Belluno Dolomites in 1944 and 1945, but in many areas, top-level climbing was able to continue during the war years.

In 1941, guides Mariano De Toni and Cesare Pollazòn from Alleghe climbed the compact crack that runs down the south side of Torre di Valgrande in the Civetta group, which includes a pitch now rated at the lower seventh grade. In 1942, Ettore Castiglioni and Gino Pisoni opened a difficult route on the South face of Piz Serauta in the Marmolada group.

But the oasis of tranquillity was Cortina, which was used first by the Italians and later by the Germans as a centre for the treatment and convalescence of wounded soldiers. There, on 1st July 1939, a group of young climbers founded the "Società Scoiattoli" (Squirrel Club). Some of them did their military service with the Alpine Troops, others worked in the valley's military hospitals, while others had to wear the German *Alpenjäger* uniform when Cortina was annexed to the Third Reich in late 1943.

Despite the problems, however, many Scoiattoli (Squirrels) were still able to climb. This is demonstrated by the difficult exit variation on the Comici-Dimai route put up by Carletto Alverà and Ettore Costantini in September 1941 on the North face of Cima Grande, and Via della Julia, opened on Tofana di Rozes by Romano Apollonio, Albino Alverà, Ettore Costantini and Luigi Ghedina in 1942.

174 left Ettore Costantini, known to his climbing companions by the nickname "Il Vecio" (old man), was one of the most active of the "Scoiattoli di Cortina" in their early years. The list of his ascents includes Pilastro di Rozes, the Direct Route on the South-East face of Col Rosà, and the Julia route on the South face of Tofana di Rozes.

174-175 The west side of the Pale di San Martino is one of the best-known and most attractive sights in the Dolomites. This photo shows Cima Bureloni (on the left) and Campanile di Val Strut.

175 left This rare group photo taken on the summit of Becco di Mezzodì in June 1942 shows some of the best climbers from the Ampezzo area in the Forties. On the

left are two unidentified climbers, followed by the Scoiattoli Luigi Ghedina, Luigi Menardi, Romano Apollonio, Ettore Costantini and Albino Alverà.

The great revelation of the period, however, was Pilastro di Rozes, the monolithic bastion that flanks the South face of Tofana di Rozes. The ascent was attempted by Ettore Costantini, the best climber in Cortina of the period, who made two attempts in the summer of 1943. A year later, *Il Vecio* or "old man" Ettore was back in action again with Romano Apollonio.

After taking a moment to "caress the rock as if to ingratiate himself with it," Costantini climbed the first 70 metres with no trouble. After that, the wall became tougher. A black crack and a series of roofs forced the leader to free climb and aid climb some extremely difficult pitches. After they dropped 12 of their 25 pitons, the pair were forced to climb very short pitches.

After a trouble-free bivouac, the overhanging yellow crack of the "Muleback," impossible to free climb but too wide for pitons, forced Costantini to hook the stirrups onto precarious chockstones. After the exit from the crux, the last rush of adrenaline was produced by a ledge where it was impossible to place pitons, and to belay his companion, Apollonio had to entwine his fingers in the grass.

But the most insidious enemy was the heat, which was really terrible on this south-facing wall. On the second day the climbers attempted to quench their thirst by sucking the grass and moss. At the end of the ascent, Costantini found he had lost 5 kilos. The result of all this exertion, however, was an exceptionally elegant route, now one of the most repeated in the Dolomites.

That tool was to cause great controversy in the future, but Eisenstecken never abused it.

In summer 1946, on the South face of the Gran Mugon, he only used two of his "special pitons" in the traverse on the last pitch. He did the same a few weeks later on the West face of Croda di Re Laurino, also in the Catinaccio group. The next year, on the awesome *Rotwand* (Red Wall) of Roda di Vaèl, a few other bolts appeared in the more compact stretches where placing ordinary pitons was impossible.

In the Fifties, life in Europe got back to normal. More and more of the small cars of the boom years wound their way up the roads of the Dolomites, bringing tourism and wealth back to the Italian- and German-speaking valleys. For many impecunious young climbers, however, the journey from Vienna, Munich or Milan to the coveted walls of the "Pale Mountains" was still an adventure, towards which they travelled by coach, train or bike.

One of these *Bergvagabunden* was Austrian Hermann Buhl. He made his début on the top-class climbing scene with a solo repeat of the Cassin route on Piz Badile after cycling all the way from the Tyrol, and became famous in 1953 for the first ascent of Nanga Parbat, which we described earlier.

In 1949, with Walther Streng, Buhl put up a magnificent route on Piz Ciavàzes, just a stone's throw from Passo Sella. The next year he soloed another magnificent new route on Cima Canali in the Pale di San Martino. However, his most important achievement came in March 1950, when he made the first winter ascent of the Soldà route on the South face of the Marmolada with Kuno Rainer.

That feat, though unknown to the general public, marked the birth of systematic winter climbing in the Dolomites. Three winters later, in 1953, two up-and-coming Italian climbers, Walter Bonatti and Carlo Mauri, performed the first winter ascent of the Cassin route on Cima Ovest di Lavaredo, encountering a section of extreme difficulty at the foot of the exit crack on rocks which are not difficult in summer, but which the pair found to be hazardously encrusted with glaze ice and unstable snow. We shall be coming back to the winter ascents performed in the Sixties shortly.

175 top right Many of the most outstanding ascents of the Scoiattoli, from the Forties to the present day, have taken place in the Tofane massif, just a stone's throw from Cortina d'Ampezzo.

Then the war ended, and climbing came into its own once more throughout the Dolomites. In 1946, Ettore Costantini returned to Pilastro di Rozes and climbed the South-West spur, another sixth-grade route with some aid sections, with Luigi Ghedina. A number of new faces were also beginning to appear in the Dolomites. They included Gabriele Franceschini, a guide on the Pale di San Martino, who performed the first solo ascent of the Solleder route on Sass Maòr, the first sixth-grade route on the massif, in 1948.

Then Otto Eisenstecken, a climber from Bolzano, came on the scene. He was to go down in history as the inventor of bolts, inserted not into natural cracks in the rock but into a hole made with a drill.

In the Fifties, in addition to Austrians, Italians and Germans, French climbers finally put in an appearance in the Dolomites. The most interesting among them was Georges Livanos. Of Greek descent (he was universally known in climbing circles as "Le Grec"), Livanos lived in Marseilles, a long way from the Alps. However, he was within easy reach of the Calanques, a rocky coastline where towers, walls and isolated pinnacles of solid limestone offer climbers routes of exceptional beauty which can be climbed all year round. Here, "the Greek" put up over 400 new routes over the years.

In the Dolomites, Livanos immediately headed for the toughest walls. He repeated two great pre-war classics, the Cassin route on Cima Ovest and the Carlesso route on Torre di Valgrande, in impeccable style, then opened an amazing new route. Between 10th and 12th September 1951, with Robert Gabriel, he climbed the huge groove of Cima Su Alto, on the north side of Civetta.

Free climbing, sometimes on crumbling rock, alternated with long aid pitches in which, as Gian Piero Motti wrote later, "the gear factor (namely better pitons, wooden wedges and stirrups) played an essential part." Fast and determined, the two Frenchmen, carrying nylon ropes and ultra-light krabs, opened the first route in the Dolomites that was far more difficult than the pre-war routes.

For Livanos, this ascent was just the start of a collection of new routes that continued with the West spur of Ciavàl delle Conturines and the North-West face of Corno del Doge in the Marmarole group. For local climbers, the Frenchman's ascent constituted a challenge that was rapidly answered. The venue was the "impressive, daunting big wall" of Cima Scotoni, on the border between Val Badia and Cadore. The climbers were the Cortina Scoiattoli, who had attempted the Su Alto groove just before Livanos and Gabriel.

Luigi "Bibi" Ghedina had identified the problem in 1944 while skiing down the Lagazuoi valley. Awed by the big wall, he returned to the foot of the mountain

for four years, armed with camera and binoculars, looking for a feasible route amid that maze of "overhangs and slabs of yellow and black rock with no cracks," topped by a "huge groove with no exit visible from below."

"Bibi" decided to make the attempt on 15th July 1951 with Lino Lacedelli, the future first ascensionist of K2. Taking turns to lead, the pair climbed to the wide grassy ledge that runs across the wall 200 metres from the scree. After a bivouac enlivened by a thunderstorm, they started climbing again. This time, Lacedelli led. Sixty metres farther up, a slab that was "as smooth and compact as a block of marble" finally barred the way.

Bolts would have provided the only solution, but the two "Scoiattoli" refused to use them. "The mountain is a living thing, and we pit our wits against it, exploiting to the utmost the resources it offers, with its cracks and rugosities, but never profaning it with drills," wrote Ghedina. A hazardous abseil amid continual hails of stones took the two men back to the scree.

176 left The South-West face of Cima Scotoni, attempted in 1951 and conquered the following year, put the technique of the Scoiattoli to the test. In this photo, Luigi Ghedina is climbing the lower part of the wall.

176 right This photo shows brilliant Ampezzo climber Luigi Ghedina (known as "Bibi" to the other Scoiattoli) aid climbing a particularly marked overhang.

177 left The elegance and style of Marino Stenico from Trento are evident in this photo, taken in summer 1953 on the friable walls of Campanile di Val Montanaia in the Oltre Piave Dolomites.

177 right Some of the most difficult routes in the Dolomites were put up after the war on the towering, vertical walls of Cima Terranova and Cima Su Alto in the Civetta massif.

The next June, Lacedelli and Ghedina were back in action with Guido Lorenzi. The only way of conquering that diabolical slab was a three-man human pyramid, with the bottom man standing on the stirrup. The trio performed this acrobatic manoeuvre at 9 a.m. on 11th June, with concerned glances at the webbing of the stirrups, which "narrowed worryingly beneath our weight." Then Lacedelli managed to place a good piton, swung to the right and started climbing again. The great groove was climbed without excessive difficulty, and after a second bivouac, the team finally reached the summit.

Bibi Ghedina's account of the ascent mainly concentrates on the aid pitches. Several years passed before it was discovered that the South-West face of Cima Scotoni was actually one of the masterpieces of free climbing. In his books, Reinhold Messner, who made one of the first repeats of the route, emphasised the outstanding level of the feat achieved by the three Scoiattoli, on a route where it is impossible to place pitons for entire pitches.

In the years that followed, top-level climbers

multiplied, and so did major ascents. Classic ascents included the Great Groove of Brenta Alta, climbed in July 1953 by Andrea Oggioni and Josve Aiazzi from Lombardy, and the North-West face of Punta Civetta, climbed the next summer by Armando Aste and Fausto Susati from Rovereto.

The ascent that marked a turning point in climbing history, however, took place between 6th and 10th August 1958 on the great overhangs of the North face of Cima Grande di Lavaredo, which the Comici-Dimai route of 1933 skirted to the right. The first few pitches

some nasty moments. In the years that followed, Hasse and Brandler opened a route of the same sort on Roda di Vaèl.

Both feats, though noteworthy from the technical standpoint, were to cause great controversy in the subsequent years. It is perhaps helpful to recall the balanced judgement made by Gian Piero Motti in his *Storia dell'alpinismo.* "The ascent aroused endless criticism, but it was unjustified. The feat was exceptional; the four Germans made fantastic use of aid, and it was a very clean climb. Where possible,

178 top *The routes put up on Cima Ovest in the Fifties include some of the largest overhangs in the Dolomites, as demonstrated by this photo, which shows a Scoiattolo climbing in the heart of the great wall.*

178-179 *The North faces of the Tre Cime were the favourite venue of the best climbers of the post-war period. This photo shows (from left to right) Punta di Frida, Cima Piccola, Cima Grande, Cima Ovest and Sasso di Landro.*

were attempted by the Scoiattoli, but the route was finally climbed by Saxons Dietrich Hasse, Lothar Brandler, Jorg Lehne and Sigi Low, who were forced to make four acrobatic bivouacs on the wall.

The result was a classic direct route; an elegant, highly demanding line, where the overhanging wall prevents climbers from abseiling back down. For the first time in the Dolomites, the hardest four pitches on the route were solved by systematic use of bolts. Awesome and difficult, the Hasse-Brandler route was one of the most feared in the Dolomites for 15 years, and gave some of the best climbing teams of the period

taking great risks (as the repeaters realised later), they attempted to free climb. In creating a route of this kind and scaling the overhangs, which cut off all chance of a return, they demonstrated extraordinary courage. Another inhibition had been broken down, and that allowed others to look with different eyes on walls which until then had been considered impossible. How true this was appeared clearly the next summer. This time, the stirrup and bolt experts turned their attention to the great overhangs on the North face of Cima Ovest, which Cassin and Ratti had skirted to the left in 1935.

Piqued by the success of the Saxons the previous

summer, the Scoiattoli prepared to scale the Ovest. On 9th April 1959, however, news came from Misurina which angered half of Cortina; a Swiss team had assaulted the wall right in the middle, and was climbing towards the great overhangs. Hugo Weber and Albin Schelbert, both aid-climbing experts from Basle, managed to climb for a hundred metres or so before being driven back by a raging blizzard.

Highly affronted, Scoiattoli Claudio Zardini, Candido Bellodis, Beniamino Franceschi and Albino "Strobel" Michielli made their own attempt on 22nd

It is not clear whether the Scoiattoli suggested to Schelbert and Weber that they should join forces. However, the two Cortina men completed the route the next day, while the Swiss exited after two more bivouacs along the Cassin route. With Swiss obstinacy, Schelbert and Weber were back after two days' rest to open an independent exit from the route they considered theirs. However, the entire route went down in climbing history, quite fairly, as the Italo-Swiss route.

179 top right An easy footpath allows walkers to admire the North faces of the Tre Cime from below.

179 bottom right The Scoiattoli Candido Bellodis and Beniamino Franceschi were among the first ascensionists of the North face of Cima Ovest in summer 1959.

June, taking no notice of a note left by the Swiss climbers asking for the route they had begun to be left for them.

On 30th June, after a week's exertion, an accident suffered by Zardini forced the team to descend. On 2nd July the Swiss were back again, but after a number of new pitches they stopped, exhausted, on a ledge halfway up the wall. There they were joined on 6th July by Bellodis and Franceschi, who according to contemporary reports were cheered on by something like a "football stadium crowd" gathered under the Tre Cime.

Beyond the vertical

Rivalry has always existed in top-level climbing. In 1786, Paccard and Balmat raced one another to the summit of Mont Blanc, and in 1865, Whymper and Carrel competed to be the first to climb the Matterhorn. In the Thirties came the Eiger, the Grandes Jorasses, and the North faces of the Tre Cime. But never had rivalry between climbers reached the pitch of involving insults, overtaking and fans rooting for the climbers at the foot of the wall, as it did in late 1959. And the hatchet had not been buried yet.

On 21st July, seven Scoiattoli set off on a new route along the overhanging edge that closes the wall to the right. They climbed much of it, and abseiled down the fixed ropes to spend the night in the refuge hut. Under cover of darkness, Schelbert and Weber turned up to get their own back on the Cortina men, but were chased off by a group of Scoiattoli who had stayed behind to guard the start of the route. The next day Lino Lacedelli, "Strobel," Gualtiero Ghedina and Lorenzo Lorenzi completed Spigolo degli Scoiattoli in 21 hours of actual climbing.

Peace was made between the rivals by the brilliant French team that assaulted the wall on 6th July, on the perpendicular of the most fearsome overhangs. René Desmaison and Pierre Mazeaud climbed three pitches on the first day, and Pierre Kohlmann and Bernard Lagesse added two more on the second. Desmaison and Mazeaud were back in action on the 8th, determined to continue to the summit, which they reached after an exhausting four-day battle.

For two days their companions supplied them with food and gear hauled up with a long rope, then started

180 top Lorenzo Lorenzi (second from left) and Albino "Strobel" Michielli (right) are shown in this photo, taken after the ascent of Spigolo degli Scoiattoli (Squirrels' Corner) on Cima Ovest. The third climber from the right is Lino Lacedelli, who had reached the summit of K2 five years earlier.

climbing in their turn. There was no competition between the men this time, only the gruelling battle against a wall that overhangs by more than 80 metres in the first 350 metres of the climb. René Desmaison nearly always led. Pierre Mazeaud belayed him, encouraged him, and hauled up a gigantic rucksack. His book *Montagne pour un homme nu* describes a fight for survival, put up by men at the end of their tether. "Our bodies were covered in sores, and after days on the étriers, we suffered violent cramps in the legs. Our stomachs were racked by hunger, and our nerves were at breaking point."

The crux of the ascent was the scaling of a 5-metre horizontal ceiling, which Desmaison conquered by placing one piton after another in cracks in the crumbling dolomite, then shifting his weight from one stirrup to another with the greatest care. After placing 40 pitons, with ropes that would not slide for the friction, the leader reached the edge of the overhang,

scaled it, and suddenly found himself on a vertical wall. "We shouted for joy… we went crazy… I bet they could hear us in Cortina," wrote Pierre Mazeaud.

Of the three routes opened that amazing July, the French route, named after Jean Couzy, is unanimously considered the toughest, and at least partly attenuated the resentment between the Scoiattoli and the Swiss climbers. While Desmaison was busy on the toughest pitches, Weber and "Strobel" shouted encouragement from the scree. Twice, Gino Soldà climbed up from Demuth Edge, which closes the wall to the left, to cheer on the team. When it was all over, the Swiss team was waiting for the French climbers on the summit, brought them drinks, and went down with them to the Auronzo refuge hut, which was packed with journalists and sightseers.

After the epic ascent on the Cima Ovest, bolted direct routes proliferated on the big dolomite walls. In the summer of 1958, the same summer as the Hasse and

180 bottom left The routes put up on the North face of Cima Ovest are marked on this photo. From left: the Jean Couzy route, the Italo-Swiss route, the Cassin-Ratti route and Spigolo degli Scoiattoli.

180 bottom right René Desmaison leads the overhangs on the North face of Cima Ovest.

181 top left Pierre Mazeaud was one of the best French climbers of the post-war period. However, he climbed as second man on the Jean Couzy route.

181 bottom left Pierre Mazeaud and René Desmaison pose for photographers at the foot of the Tre Cime after the first ascent by the Jean Couzy route.

181 right This photo of the North face of Cima Ovest shows the great overhangs (in shadow in the photo) which form part of the Jean Couzy route.

Brandler ascent, Ignazio Piussi and Giorgio Redaelli put up a direct route on the South face of Torre Trieste in the Civetta massif, using 300 pitons and 150 bolts and free climbing some extreme pitches. In June 1960, Cesare Maestri and Claudio Baldessari from Trento put up an "ultra-direct" route on Roda di Vaèl.

Then Bepi De Francesch came onto the scene. As Gian Piero Motti put it, "he deliberately went in search of walls as smooth as river pebbles" which he managed to climb with his sophisticated bolting technique. His best-known route is Italia '61 on Piz Ciavàzes, which crosses an edge interrupted by huge overhangs. Now, however, the balance between the gear used and the difficulty of the climb was beginning to tip too far one way.

For example, the Saxon (or Kolibris) route, the new "ultra-direct" route on the North face of Cima Grande halfway between the Hasse-Brandler and Comici routes, was rather exaggerated. Its creators, Germans Peter Siegert, Rainer Kauschke and Gert Uhner, took eighteen hard days in freezing cold weather to beat the wall in January 1963. The next summer, Scoiattoli Lorenzo Lorenzi, Albino "Strobel" Michielli, Bruno Menardi, Carlo Gandini and Arturo Zardini put up the Paolo VI route on Pilastro di Rozes with five bivouacs, using 350 bolts to climb a 600-metre wall.

Then things calmed down; rivalry between climbers seemed to have gone out of style, and the fashion for ultra-direct routes and over-generous use of bolts died a natural death.

*182 left Cesare Maestri from
Trento became universally
known in the Fifties as the
"Spider of the Dolomites." He
made numerous outstanding
first ascents, and amazed
climbers and the general
public alike with his fast solo
climbs.*

*182 right This fascinating
photo shows Cesare Maestri
from Trento soloing a
difficult pitch in the Brenta
Dolomites with his rope
slung over his shoulder.*

*182-183 Cesare Maestri
performed many great
ascents on the walls of Cima
Tosa (left) and Crozzon di
Brenta, seen here in a winter
view, including the first
ascent (1953) and the first
solo descent (1956) of the Via
delle Guide on the Crozzon.*

However, at least 10 years were to elapse before
there was a return to free climbing. Its best-known
practitioner, mainly active in the Brenta Dolomites, was
Cesare Maestri, who shot to fame on 6th September 1956.

Born in Trento, Maestri had hoped to be an actor, but
had to earn his living with casual jobs as a bricklayer,
porter for the refuge huts, and even as a boxer. Then he
became a mountain guide, and he wanted to obtain the
CAI (Club Alpino Italiano) national instructor's qualification
too. By this time, he had already made the first solo
ascents of many of the toughest walls in the Dolomites.

In view of his track record, Cesare should have been
given an honorary instructor's qualification. But the
examining commission did not agree. After convening
Maestri as an instructor, they informed him that the usual
procedure must be followed. Like any other candidate, he
had to attend a course and pass an exam. But getting on
the wrong side of Maestri always led to spectacular results.

Highly offended by the decision, he climbed Cima
Tosa by the ordinary route, and continued along the
switchback ridge that leads to Crozzon di Brenta. By
10 a.m. he was looking down into the awesome void of
the North-East face, crossed by the Via delle Guide put
up in 1935 by Bruno Detassis and Enrico Giordani.
Three years earlier, Maestri had made the first solo
ascent of the route. But no one had ever attempted the
solo descent of a sixth-grade route.

The record was established when Cesare began to
free climb rapidly down the broken rocks on the last
section of the route. Under the admiring gaze of none
other than Detassis, who ran the Brentei refuge hut, and
the CAI instructors, Maestri continued down the wall,
which was becoming more and more difficult.

Before downclimbing the vertical section, streaked
with dark rivulets of water, which constitutes the crux of
the route, the "Spider of the Dolomites" made yet
another provocative move. Up to that point he had
climbed with a rope over his shoulders; it was obviously
no use in the event of a fall, but it would have allowed
him to abseil down if he found a pitch too difficult to
free climb, or to belay himself while awaiting help if he
got into real trouble.

*183 right Despite his stiff-
soled boots and the étriers
hanging from his waist,
Cesare Maestri, shown here
again on the walls of the
Brenta, was a totally modern
climber in terms of climbing
speed and style.*

Instead, Maestri untied the rope and threw it down, watching its 600-metre fall to the scree. "It prevented me from seeing the holds" was his sarcastic explanation. As was to be expected, Maestri's arrival at the refuge hut was welcomed with a standing ovation, together with the apologies of the commission. Detassis, a man of few words, opened his mouth for once. "That took guts," he murmured, embracing the "Spider" who had just descended by his own route of 21 years earlier.

The Via delle Guide was not the only provocative move in Maestri's climbing career. In 1954, he reacted angrily to his exclusion from the expedition to K2, and his rage with climbers and the British climbing press who cast doubt on his first ascent of Cerro Torre in the Sixties is also famous. However, nearly all Maestri's major ascents took place in the Dolomites. The only aid climb among them was the ultra-direct route on Roda di Vaèl, as already mentioned. All the others demonstrated that free climbing had never really gone out of style on the great Dolomite walls.

"When I came to grips with rock for the first time, I immediately decided that I wanted to be the best climber in the world." This comment is typical of Maestri, described even by the restrained Gian Piero Motti as "ambitious, narcissistic, argumentative, jealous, envious, touchy, intolerant and hypersensitive, but at the same time unusually generous, pure as a child, and sensitive to the point of being wounded by a pinprick."

After climbing for the first time in 1949, Cesare moved to live in the mountains in 1950, and became a guide two years later. He began his solo ascents of the most difficult routes in the Dolomites in 1953. In four years, he conquered the Via delle Guide on Crozzon di Brenta (which he ascended in 1953 and descended three years later), the Detassis route on Brenta Alta, the Comici route on Salame del Sassolungo, the Solleder route on the North-West face of Civetta, and the Soldà and Micheluzzi routes on the South face of the Marmolada, together with the Micheluzzi route on Piz Ciavàzes, nearly all the routes on Croz

dell'Altissimo, and the Solleder route on Sass Maòr, which Maestri first climbed and then downclimbed. After climbing Roda di Vaèl with Claudio Baldessarri in a week's effort, Cesare returned solo and also downclimbed it, to debunk the legend he had created himself.

Here, a comment is required. If the media are to be believed, Maestri's solo ascents were the only feats in the Dolomites to bear comparison with the proliferating ultra-direct bolted routes. But although the image of climbing in the Dolomites publicised by the media in the Fifties and Sixties was symbolised by an overhanging wall and a climber on stirrups, free climbing continued to be practised.

This is demonstrated, as we have seen, by the Cortina Scoiattoli, known to the general public for their aid routes on Cima Ovest, who gave a lesson in free climbing on the elusive wall of Cima Scotoni. But for nearly 20 years, the distorted view shown by the media not only influenced the man in the street, but also many climbers.

While Cesare Maestri achieved bombproof fame, the other protagonists of the revival of free climbing tended to be cold-shouldered, even by the climbing press, climbing schools and Alpine Clubs. This was the case with Enzo Cozzolino from Trieste, who made numerous outstanding ascents in a casual fashion, wearing sneakers. One of the most brilliant is the very difficult Via dei Fachiri, which Cozzolino put up with Flavio Ghio in the winter of 1972 on Cima Scotoni, to the right of the Lacedelli-Ghedina-Lorenzi route.

Six months later, Cozzolino was killed during a solo ascent of Torre di Babele in the Civetta group. Another star of climbing in the Dolomites was Renato Reali from Trento, who put up a dozen routes of extreme difficulty before falling to his death in a solo attempt on the East face of the Grand Capucin, the most "Dolomite-like" of the walls of Mont Blanc, in summer 1968.

Belgian climber Claudio Barbier, who put up a number of new routes and made solo ascents of the Cassin Route on Cima Ovest (1959) and the Comici route on Civetta (1960), is also practically unknown.

Barbier performed a magnificent *enchaînement* in the summer of 1961, when he scaled the Cassin route on Cima Ovest, the Comici route on Cima Grande, the Preuss route on Cima Piccolissima, the Innerkofler route on Cima Piccola and the Dulfer route on Punta di Frida, one after another.

"He always gave the impression of daydreaming, of being in another world. Yet he climbed effortlessly, like a monkey," wrote Reinhold Messner, who put up a variation on the Piz Ciavàzes route with him. Highly cultured and curious, from a wealthy Belgian family, Barbier climbed confidently on all kinds of terrain. In a short absence from his beloved Dolomites he performed the first solo ascent of the Cassin route on Piz Badile. Like that other great romantic, Emilio Comici, he was killed in a fall from a climbing wall in Belgium.

The performers of other great free climbs, like Walther Philipp and Dieter Flamm from Vienna, who scaled the most attractive groove on the North-West face of Civetta, reached the summit ridge at 2992 metres (Punta Tissi), with two bivouacs in

September 1957, climbed more in the traditional style.

This 900-metre route, put up without using bolts (which were placed by repeaters), runs to the left of the Solleder route, and long remained one of the most difficult in the Alps. Even now that seventh- and eighth-grade pitches are commonly climbed, this 40-pitch route, mainly in cracks and chimneys, remains a fundamental testing ground for young climbers before tackling routes with higher ratings.

"I'd been dreaming for a long time of making an ascent that gave free climbing, which was actually boycotted in certain circles, new glory and a new reputation," wrote Walther Philipp in *Der Bergkamerad Magazine*. Philipp, the inventor and leader of the 1957 ascent, had the class to become one of the best climbers of all time in the Dolomites. However, a terrifying adventure on the North face of Cima Grande, where a 40-metre fall took him to within inches of the scree (totally unscathed!), persuaded him to give up extreme climbing and concentrate on gentler mountain sports.

184 top Aid climbing played an important part in the image of mountaineering in the Dolomites in the Fifties and Sixties. In this 1967 photo, Marino Stenico from Trento tackles the walls of Romagnano.

184 bottom Donato Zeni was another of the best climbers from Trento in the post-war period. This photo shows him scaling an overhang on the South face of the Mugoni in the Catinaccio massif.

185 left This photo, taken in the Nineties, shows a climber scaling the compact slabs of the Ideale route. This route, put up by Armando Aste and Aldo Solina on the South face of

Marmolada d'Ombretta in August 1964, was one of the first in the Dolomites to include seventh-grade pitches. Routes of this kind led to the great revival of free climbing in the Dolomites.

185 right Though not often climbed, the Conturines massif is one of the most impressive in the Dolomites. This photo shows its northern buttresses at sunset, from Cima Scotoni.

186-187 The North face of the Civetta, which is very difficult in summer, becomes extremely severe in winter, when snow and ice cover the gentler slopes and ledges. The first winter ascent of the Solleder route, the most classic route on the wall, was made in 1963 by Italians Ignazio Piussi and Giorgio Redaelli and German Toni Hiebeler.

187 left The awesome walls of the Pale di San Lucano, which dominate the valley of the same name, offered an excellent playground in the Sixties for climbers in search of new and challenging routes. In this photo, Italian Alessandro Gogna leads the West face of the second Pala di San Lucano.

187 top right This photo, taken on the Pale di San Lucano, shows Piero Ravà during the first ascent of the South face of the third Pala di San Lucano, a 1500-metre-high wall.

187 bottom right Italian Alberto Dorigatti climbs the direct route on the South face of Marmolada di Rocca as second man. Alessandro Gogna, Almo Giambisi and Bruno Allemand also took part in the first ascent of this route, which involves an 800-metre climb, in the summer of 1970.

A number of magnificent routes were also put up in those years on the pillars and cracks of the Marmolada (whose great compact flanks provided a new challenge for the next generation). The most frequently repeated was put up by Alessandro Gogna, Bruno Allemand, Almo Giambisi and Alberto Dorigatti in 1970.

The most difficult, which is now rated at lower seventh grade, is Via dell'Ideale on Marmolada d'Ombretta, put up by Armando Aste and Aldo Solina, a team which made many other great climbs. Other major routes were opened in those years on Crozzon di Brenta, Sorapìss, Brenta Alta and Mount Agnèr.

In May 1970, Alessandro Gogna and Leo Cerruti "discovered" the awesome walls of the Pale di San Lucano, and put up a 50-pitch route on the Seconda

Pala. Two years later Gogna, with Piero Ravà and Gianluigi Lanfranchi, scaled the Terza Pala which, at 1500 metres, is the third-highest in the Dolomites. Also in the San Lucano massif, Renato Casarotto and Piero Radin from Vicenza conquered the South-West face of Spiz di Lagunàz, another wall over 1000 metres high, in five days in 1973.

However, at that period, the impassable witnesses of the very toughest adventures were the rocks of Civetta. In July 1964, Domenico Bellenzier from Alleghe put up a magnificent route on the North-West pillar of Torre d'Alleghe. Despite the five bolts used, this is an extraordinary free climb, now rated between the seventh and upper seventh grades. "Those who climb the grey slab and the next one are appalled at Bellenzier's boldness, which was not far short of suicidal," wrote Alessandro Gogna in his book *Sentieri verticali*.

Another route to Punta Tissi was put up from 28th July to 2nd August 1965 by the Italo-French team of Ignazio Piussi, Roberto Sorgato and Pierre Mazeaud. But that ascent nearly turned into tragedy. Thought up

by Piussi, one of the best Italian climbers of the post-war period, the climb took place with no problems until the morning of the third day. Up to then, the ascent, including long aid sections, had been difficult but presented no special problems. Then a cloudburst gave way to a thunderstorm, and lightning struck a pillar resting on the wall, causing stones to rain down on the team, seriously injuring Mazeaud and Piussi.

"A hail of stones struck me on the back like machine

gun fire, and I felt a terrible pain," recounted Piussi. "Then another projectile hit me right on the hand I was covering my head with, and smashed everything – bones, arteries, the lot... there was blood spurting everywhere.... 'OK?' asked Roberto, who'd only taken a few hits here and there. 'The Frenchman's dead', I said. 'He's all white.' But he'd only been knocked unconscious. Just then he came round, yelled '*Merde! Je ne suis pas mort!*' and passed out again."

Somehow the trio managed to reach a hole at the

foot of an overhang, under which they set up their bivouac. But instead of the good weather they had hoped for, the night brought half a metre of snow. Roberto Sorgato, the only one in decent shape, had to lead his two companions down "a chimney with terrifying overhangs," trying not to think about the ropes severed by the stones, which he had knotted as best he could.

Despite a head wound, Mazeaud managed to climb as second man. Piussi, whose hand was "swollen up like a balloon," had to be hauled bodily up the slope. On the summit, the sun finally came out, and a large party of climbers greeted the three survivors of the North face and helped them down the gruelling descent to the Coldai refuge hut.

The winter ascent of the legendary Solleder route, performed by Piussi with Giorgio Redaelli and Toni Hiebeler just over two years earlier, was less dramatic, though still very tough in both mental and physical terms. The ascent was organised by the Bavarian climber, who put to good use the experience he had gained two years earlier on the first winter ascent of the North face of the Eiger.

However, it was Piussi who led the ascent from start to finish. At the third bivouac (of seven!) the stove broke, and the only way of heating anything to drink was to burn the wooden wedges. On the sixth day, while Ignazio was trying to scale an icy overhang, a hard block of snow broke off, and knocked him into an icefield 30 metres below. "I was like a machine; I knew there was nothing for it, that after the third bivouac the only thing to do was to keep going, and I only had one thought in my head – to get to the summit," wrote Piussi. At 11 a.m. on the eighth day the team reached the summit, then descended to the Torrani refuge hut, where they made soup with hot water and bread left over from the previous summer. "Somebody up there must like us!" said Piussi.

The victory over the Solleder route brought the craze for great winter ascents, which was in full swing at the other end of the Alps thanks to Walter Bonatti and René Desmaison, to the Dolomites too. At the beginning of this chapter we mentioned the winter ascents of the Soldà route on the Marmolada (Buhl and Rainer, 1950) and the Cassin route on Cima Ovest (Bonatti and Mauri, 1953).

Some great climbs were also performed by other teams from Lombardy, who scaled the Cassin route on Torre Trieste (Aldo Anghileri, Ermenegildo Arcelli, Andrea Cattaneo and Pino Negri, 1964) and the Via delle Guide on Crozzon di Brenta (Antonio and Giovanni Rusconi, Roberto Chiappa, and Gianluigi Lanfranchi, 1969).

Of all of them, the winter ascents of the Vinatzer route on the South face of the Marmolada, performed in 1967 by Otto Wiedmann and Walter Spitzenstatter, and the Lacedelli route on Cima Scotoni, climbed in 1970 by Bepi Loss, Marco Pilati and Vincenzo Degasperi, stand out for their technical level. In the realm of sunny vertical walls, the battle with cold and ice is also an important part of the game.

The wild challenge

On 20th August 1955, at the first light of dawn, a man was sitting on a narrow ledge in the heart of the South-West Pillar of the Dru, one of the most awesome and difficult rock faces in the Alps. After a four-day struggle with the rock, his hands were swollen and sore. Walter Bonatti's morale was low too.

For days, the best Italian climber of the moment had been totally alone, in an unreal silence interrupted only by the rockfall in the nearby gully. A small plane appeared, and when it had gone, the silence seemed even more oppressive than before.

Beneath his feet were the horrific overhangs that Bonatti had dubbed the "Ramarro" (lizard), and a succession of vertical red slabs.

Just when Bonatti thought that the hardest pitches were behind him, a smooth overhang where it was impossible to drive in pitons presented a last terrible obstacle. But Walter's stamina was legendary. Metre by metre he scaled the wall, which was "smooth all around, receding in the centre and immensely overhanging above."

In the end, he reached a position in which he could go neither up nor down. The 12-metre overhang

188 top In the Fifties and Sixties, Walter Bonatti came to symbolise top-level climbing on Mont Blanc and the other Alpine ranges for the general public as well as for climbers. In this photo, he is preparing his bivouac. Note the hemp ropes, heavy steel krabs and wooden wedges.

188 bottom During his solo ascent of the South-West face of the Dru, Walter Bonatti dragged behind him a huge haul bag, which was torn as a result of the friction against the rock. This photo, taken after the descent of the Dru, shows Bonatti mending the bag.

above him, beyond which the rock seemed to get easier, represented the boundary between life and death. Here, desperation counted for more than class. Bonatti tied "a tentacular system of knots" to the rope, then tried to throw it over some flakes of rock he could see a dozen metres above.

After numerous attempts, the rope seemed to hold. While "a hundred thoughts crossed my mind and remained imprinted on it for the rest of my life," Bonatti let the improvised lasso take his weight, found

because money was tight in the post-war period.

In the Sixties, nylon ropes and Vibram soles, helmets and pitons with a more sophisticated design, warmer and more waterproof clothing enabled Walter and other top climbers like Pierre Mazeaud, Chris Bonington, John Harlin and René Desmaison to tackle new problems like the great winter climbs, solo ascents and the most vertical, difficult granite walls.

However, the new gear had not yet come onto the scene when, on a hot August day in 1949, Bonatti

188-189 The gigantic granite bulk of the Dru, with its smooth and overhanging rock slabs, gave the boldest climbers of the 20th century the chance to tackle one of the most important, difficult walls in the Alpine range.

that it held, and hauled himself up to the easier rocks. twenty-four hours after scaling that overhang, at 4:37 p.m. on 21st August, the best European climber of the day was sitting on the summit of the Petit Dru, next to the small, lightning-damaged statue of the Madonna. Three friends and a last bivouac awaited him on the descent.

Walter Bonatti, born in Bergamo in 1930, was the best-known climber on the Alpine scene in the Fifties and Sixties. His style of climbing, like that of French mountaineers of the same age, required all the courage of the pre-war champions, but also began to benefit from new and better equipment, though only gradually,

climbed the Vallée Blanche to the Torino refuge hut. As he looked up towards the buttresses of Mont Blanc du Tacul, a "great red pillar dominating the complex of pinnacles" appeared before his eyes; a peak which, as he recounted in his memoirs, was "so steeply regular and elegant that the mere thought of reaching the summit made me feel dizzy. Its verticality was too disconcerting for a climber. One of my first thoughts was to wonder whether the man had ever existed who dared to scale that wall."

In fact it was he who, the next summer, attempted the vertical, compact East wall of the Grand Capucin,

the red monolith that watches over the countless outriders of Mont Blanc du Tacul like an older brother. The successful attempt was the third, performed in July 1951. In four days, after a hard struggle "surrounded by total emptiness," Bonatti and his climbing companion Luciano Ghigo reached the narrow rocky ridge of the summit after writing one of the most important pages in climbing history on the granite of Mont Blanc. Their victory was particularly meritorious in view of the poor equipment they still used – hemp ropes and particularly heavy pitons.

190 top The four French climbers who made the July 1952 ascent celebrate their achievement at the historic Hotel du Montenvers. Left to right: Guido Magnone, Lucien Bérardini, Adrien Dagory and Marcel Lainé.

190 bottom John Harlin, one of the best of the American mountaineers, began climbing in the Alps in the Sixties and was founder and director of the International Mountaineering School in Leysin, Switzerland. He

made the first ascent of the Hidden Pillar of Frêney in 1963 with Tom Frost. In 1965 he put up a direct route on the West face of the Dru with Royal Robbins, and took part in the first ascent of the right-hand Brouillard

Pillar with Chris Bonington, Robert Baillie and Brian Robertson. The next winter Harlin was killed when a fixed rope snapped during the opening of a new route on the North face of the Eiger.

190-191 The ice and mixed walls of the Aiguille Verte (on the left in the photo) and the granite walls of the Dru are among the most spectacular and difficult in the Mont Blanc massif. The ascent of the compact West face of the Dru, made in July 1952 by French

climbers Lucien Bérardini, Adrien Dagory, Marcel Lainé and Guido Magnone, constituted a breakthrough in climbing in the massif. Three years later, Walter Bonatti scaled the South-West Pillar of the Dru, which terminates the wall on the right. In the Sixties, more great routes were put up on the West face by American climbers who had developed their skills on the granite of Yosemite.

As often happens, the solution to one problem led climbers to tackle many others. From the Petites Jorasses to the Aiguille du Fou, from the Frêney Pillars to the Aiguille du Midi, Mont Blanc was still full of compact, vertical walls that had been beyond the reach of pre-war climbers. The tallest and most awesome was the West face of the Dru, whose fiery red granite wall, 1000 metres high, dominates the crevasses of the Mer de Glace and the terraces of Montenvers where tens of thousands of hikers, climbers and tourists throng every year.

Between 1947 and 1951 it was attempted by climbers like Gaston Rébuffat, Jean Couzy and Georges Livanos. Victory came in 1952, with a two-stage ascent performed by Lucien Bérardini, Adrien Dagory, Marcel Lainé and Guido Magnone. During the first five days of July the Frenchmen climbed the wall by way of a long series of extreme pitches. Then, before a pendulum which would have cut off their way back, they were forced to descend because their supplies of food and water had run out.

Ten days later, the unstable weather made a new attempt from the bottom unthinkable, so the climbers scaled the less difficult North face, and then traversed to the heart of the West face with a horrifying downward aid climb. This passage, led by Lainé who placed the protection, took half a day. Then Bérardini took the lead, and reached "the two most appalling roofs we'd ever seen." He kept climbing, "suspended over a void where it was best not to look down."

When the leader accidentally dropped a piton, Magnone saw it whistle past, and waited in vain to hear the metallic clang when it hit the rock. "If we'd fallen here," he wrote, "we'd certainly have beaten the free fall record." Then a cleft enabled them to get across the overhangs, and an easier crack brought the team to the exit.

The West face of the Dru, the ideal wall of a perfect mountain, became one of the major venues of world climbing after the 1952 ascent. In 1955, Walter Bonatti

191 right With Walter Bonatti's solo and team ascents, climbing in the Mont Blanc massif made great progress in the Fifties and Sixties. This photo shows him in 1955, returning from the South-West Pillar of the Dru. He is wearing gloves to protect his hands, lacerated by five days of strenuous climbing and bolting.

soloed the South-West Pillar on his third attempt. Then the Americans came along. Royal Robbins, one of the leading climbers from Yosemite Valley, put up a route which rectified the French itinerary with Gary Hemming in 1962.

Three years later, with John Harlin, Robbins put up another outstanding route on "that protogine diamond which has become the symbol of mountaineering." The team set off along the 1962 route, then branched off towards the most impressive roofs on the wall. The climb was one of extreme difficulty, but the team was using Yosemite gear and techniques, which were

making their début in the Alps. Chrome-molybdenum pitons, metal bongs instead of wooden wedges, skyhooks, étriers and seats designed for hanging belays aided their progress, while jumars enabled the second man to climb fast on a rope fixed by the leader.

Robbins led for the first few pitches, then Harlin took over as far as the terrace where the pair made their first bivouac. The next day they embarked on a treacherous sector where great unstable slabs seemed liable to break off any minute. A falling stone suddenly hit Harlin "with the force of a dumdum bullet," causing serious bleeding of the thigh, but descending from there

would have been more dangerous than climbing on.

Robbins continued to lead, aid climbing among roofs and unstable blocks to conquer "the most dangerous pitch of my entire career." Behind him, Harlin pulled himself up painfully with the aid of the jumars. He was tortured by his injured leg at every movement, but kept going. A "prettily curved" crack that cut through some huge overhangs took the two Americans out of the high-grade section. From the top of the Bonatti Pillar, a ledge enabled the pair to reach the ordinary route. After a raging blizzard, a helicopter took Robbins and Harlin back to Chamonix.

After the ascents of the East face of the Grand Capucin and the West face of the Dru, the other great rock walls of Mont Blanc were conquered one after another. In June 1952, French climbers Michel Bastien and André Contamine scaled the South face of the Grand Dru. Two years later, British climbers Joe Brown and Don Whillans climbed the West face of the Aiguille de Blaitière by a route that includes a crack which goes beyond the sixth grade.

In August 1955 Contamine, together with Marcel Bron and Pierre Labrunie, scaled the smooth West face of the Petites Jorasses. A year later, Gaston Rébuffat and Maurice Baquet put up a very elegant route on the short, vertical South face of the Aiguille du Midi, which is now crossed by various modern routes. New routes were also opened on the Grand Capucin by Lucien Bérardini and Robert Paragot (North face, 1955) and by C. Asper, M. Bron, M. Grossi and M. Morel (Swiss Route, 1956).

An extraordinary feat was accomplished in 1955 by Philippe Cornuau and Marcel Davaille, two little-known climbers who scaled the North face of the Droites, the most difficult ice wall in the Argentière basin, with no less than four bivouacs. Their achievement was not to be surpassed until the invention of the ice-axe traction technique nearly 20 years later.

But the outstanding personality on Mont Blanc in the Fifties and Sixties was still Walter Bonatti, who continued to identify and solve the "last great problems" on the massif. The first was the Grand Pilier d'Angle, the impressive rock and ice pillar over 1000 metres tall which closes to the south the side of Mont Blanc overlooking the Brenva serac band.

At the beginning of August 1957 Bonatti, together with Toni Gobbi, performed the first ascent of the Pilier along a mixed route. Five years later, climbing with Cosimo Zappelli, he scaled the North face of the Pilier, which is highly exposed to falls of stones and ice. The next year, again with Zappelli, Bonatti completed his hat trick on the Pilier d'Angle by scaling the rocky (and dangerous) South-East face.

192-193 Between 1950 and 1965, Walter Bonatti devoted a great deal of time to systematic exploration of the south side of Mont Blanc, where he identified and climbed numerous top-class routes. Here, he is at the exit of the direct route he put up on the South face of the highest peak in Europe with Cosimo Zappelli in September 1961.

192 bottom In addition to his new routes on Mont Blanc, Gaston Rébuffat of Marseilles is famous for his books and films devoted to the massif. In this photo he is climbing on the East face of Grand Capucin, following the route inaugurated by Walter Bonatti and Luciano Ghigo in 1951.

193 top left Toni Gobbi, who was born in Veneto but moved to Courmayeur, was known for his activity as a guide and for his ski mountaineering. On Mont Blanc, he made the first winter ascents of the Major route, the Hirondelles ridge and the South ridge of the Aiguille Noire. He made the first ascent of the Grand Pilier d'Angle with Walter Bonatti in 1957.

193 top right Though less severe than the nearby North face of the Grandes Jorasses, the West face of the Petites Jorasses is one of the loveliest granite walls in the Mont Blanc massif. The first ascent, made in 1955 by Marcel Bron, André Contamine and Pierre Labrunie, was one of the most significant of the decade. Here, the three men pose for the photographer on their return from the ascent.

193 bottom left Of all the "major problems" on Mont Blanc, Walter Bonatti was particularly fascinated by the Pilier d'Angle, the rock and ice pillar 900 metres tall that closes the Brenva face on the left. Between 1957 and 1963 Bonatti put up no less than three routes on the Pilier. In this photo, he is scaling the South-East face, which he climbed with Zappelli in 1963.

193 bottom centre Cosimo Zappelli, Walter Bonatti's climbing companion for many years, follows his leader on the exposed snow-covered ridges at the exit of the South face of Mont Blanc.

193 above The wild Frêney Glacier at the foot of Point Gugliermina and the Aiguille Noire de Peuterey witnessed numerous major ascents by Walter Bonatti and his climbing companions.

reach the summit of Mont Blanc and the Vallot hut.

Two years later, another blizzard turned yet another ascent by Bonatti into one of the best-known tragedies in the history of mountaineering. The destination of the team (Bonatti, Oggioni and Roberto Gallieni) was the Central Frêney Pillar, which stands on the south side of Mont Blanc between the Innominata and Peuterey Ridges. The three Italians met the French team of Pierre Mazeaud, Antoine Guillaume, Pierre Kohlman and Antoine Vieille at the Fourche bivouac on the evening of 9th July 1961. The two groups made friends, and decided to join forces.

At dawn on the 10th, the French made the first assault on the rocks. The next day Bonatti took the lead. At midday, when the party had reached the base of the Chandelle, the monolith that crowns the Pillar, the weather broke. After a 60-hour wait in the hope that the weather would improve, the seven climbers were forced to descend. But the mountain had been transformed by

194 top left On 9th July 1961, a strong French-Italian team made the first attempt on the Central Frêney Pillar. This photo shows Walter Bonatti in the central part of the route. The terrible blizzard of 11th July caused the deaths of Antoine Guillaume, Pierre Kohlmann, Andrea Oggioni and Antoine Vieille.

194 bottom left The pillars that crown the Brouillard Glacier offer some magnificent routes, first climbed in the Sixties. In this photo, Robert "Rusty" Baillie abseils across the bergschrund at the foot of the right-hand Brouillard pillar. The bad weather at the exit of the route had forced the climbers to abseil down the ascent route.

The next stage in his methodical conquest brought Bonatti to the granite pillars of the Brouillard basin. In June 1959, accompanied by his friend Andrea Oggioni, the "King of Mont Blanc" climbed to the Gamba hut, tackled the tortured Brouillard Glacier, reached and rapidly climbed the magnificent Red Pillar. But when the two men were at an altitude of 4100 metres, bad weather unexpectedly set in, and they found themselves in trouble. A metre of snow fell, preventing them from continuing the ascent and making it extremely dangerous to abseil down and cross the glacier. However, after a struggle lasting nearly 20 hours, Bonatti and Oggioni returned safe and sound to the Gamba hut.

Less than a month later, history seemed to be repeating itself. This time, the storm broke when the pair had already crossed the summit of the Pillar. But despite snow, wind and lightning, the two men managed to

over a metre of snow, and the descent turned into a nightmare.

Snowslides accompanied the abseils on the Pillar and the Rochers Gruber, and the traverse of the Frêney Glacier was horrific in the deep snow. Vieille was the first to succumb, even before the end of the rocks. Then, one after another, three more climbers died. In the end, only Bonatti, Gallieni and Mazeaud reached the Gamba hut, where they embraced, weeping.

Twenty days later, other climbers tackled the Pillar. This decision upset Bonatti and Mazeaud, who felt that their dreadful experience in July entitled them to make a new attempt. However, the British team of Chris Bonington, Don Whillans and Ian Clough (climbing with Pole Jan Djuglosz) and the French team of René Desmaison, Yves Pollet-Villard and Pierre Julien (climbing with the Italian Ignazio Piussi) decided not to make way for the survivors of the tragic July attempt.

The two teams climbed one after another, without joining forces. While Whillans and Bonington were tackling the Chandelle, the French team refused to lend them any pitons or wedges. Whillans attempted a free climb, but fell. Chris Bonington eventually solved the problem with the "chockstones" technique (stones inserted into cracks), which was commonly used on British walls. After the Chandelle, an easy ridge took the climbers to the summit.

After that dramatic summer on the Pillar, top-level climbing went on. Two months after the drama, Bonatti put up a new route on the Frêney wall with Zappelli. In July 1962, he joined forces with Pierre Mazeaud to climb the East face of the Petites Jorasses. A year later, Americans Tom Frost, Steve Fulton, John Harlin and Gary Hemming put up another route destined to become legendary on the compact South face of the Aiguille du Fou. Between 6th and 10th August 1964, Walter Bonatti and Swiss guide Michel Vaucher put up a direct route on the North face of the Grandes Jorasses which led directly to Point Whymper.

194 centre right This famous photo, taken by a French journalist, shows Chris Bonington and Don Whillans on the summit of Mont Blanc at the end of the first ascent of the Central Pillar. Ian Clough and Jan Djuglosz arrived later. Next came René Desmaison, Yves Pollet-Villard, Pierre Julien and Ignazio Piussi.

194-195 The dramatic events of summer 1961 made the Central Pillar of Mont Blanc famous even among non-climbers. In this photo, Don Whillans leads one of the most difficult sections of the initial part of the route.

196 top left In February 1965, Walter Bonatti concluded his climbing career by soloing a new route on the North face of the Matterhorn. This photo was taken by a reporter to record the Italian climber's achievement.

196 top right This photo shows Walter Bonatti on the afternoon of 22nd February, beside the metal cross on the summit of the Matterhorn.

Between the Fifties and Sixties, two more variations on top-level climbing rapidly became popular throughout the Alpine range. Solo climbing made its début in the western Alps in 1959, when Bonatti soloed Via Major, Carlo Mauri soloed Via della Pera and Dieter Marchart soloed the North face of the Matterhorn.

In 1963, solo ascents of the North ridge of the Peigne and the West face of the Dru made René Desmaison one of the best-known climbers on the Chamonix scene, while Michel Darbellay from Valais became famous in Switzerland and among German-speaking climbers for the first solo ascent of the North face of the Eiger. His climb was certainly not helped by knowing that in the two preceding years, three solo

attempts (by Adi Mayr, Adolf Derungs and Dieter Marchart) had ended with the climber's death.

Winter climbing became increasingly popular, and competition was soon rife between the best climbers. On Mont Blanc, the first feat of this kind was the ascent of the West face of the Dru by Desmaison and Jean Couzy in the winter of 1957. Four years later, between 6th and 12th March 1961, came the first winter ascent of the North face of the Eiger, the most dangerous and inhospitable wall in the Alps. Before that, 17 of the 47 climbers who had scaled the wall had died on the mountain.

The winning team consisted of Toni Hiebeler, Toni Kinshofer and Anderl Mannhardt from Bavaria, and Austrian climber Walter Almberger. Hiebeler, also known as a mountaineering writer, planned the climb and solved the countless organisational problems involved in a week-long ascent.

However, the lead climber was nearly always Kinshofer, a highly skilled mountaineer who fell to his

196 bottom As in a Himalayan expedition, mountaineers use fixed ropes to ascend and descend the wall of the Eiger. John Harlin was killed when one of these ropes snapped, and the five climbers still on the wall (Haston, Lehne, Strobel, Hupfauer and Voetteler) had to force the exit despite the prohibitive weather conditions.

196-197 On the direct route on the North face of the Eiger, vertical or overhanging rock alternates with steep ice slopes. In this photo, Dougal Haston is scaling the second ice slope of the route.

197 right The 1966 direct route on the North face of the Eiger was criticised in some quarters for the use of fixed ropes. However, the size and difficulty of the wall took five weeks' strenuous climbing.

man did alone on that wall is fantastic and incredible."

After a four-day struggle, Bonatti was close to the summit. He was dead tired, his haul bag was unbearably heavy, and light aircraft were coming in close so that TV cameras and photographers could film the lone climber. Then the metal cross on the summit "suddenly shone before me." Bonatti covered the last few metres in silence, and finally, as he recounted in his autobiography, "as if hypnotised, I reached out my arms to the cross and clutched its metal skeleton to my breast. My knees buckled, and I burst into tears." It was 22nd February 1965.

The next winter, there was a very different atmosphere at the foot of the Eiger. In the Kleine Scheidegg hotel at the foot of the wall, journalists and sightseers besieged the two rival teams (one German and the other Anglo-American) who were attempting to put up a direct route on the North face.

The route was one of extreme difficulty, though somewhat looked down on in climbing circles (however, the rather morbid attention of the media is usual on a "killer wall"), and competition between the two groups was as fierce as on the North-West face of

death on the Battert crag near Baden Baden after suffering severe frostbite on Nanga Parbat. After an attempt foiled by bad weather, the four made another assault from the Stollenloch, the Jungfraujoch railway aeration duct that runs through the mountain.

Hiebeler's account is a succession of "prohibitive conditions," "horrifying pitches" and "very few belays." The Difficult Crack and the Hinterstoisser Traverse, the first difficult pitches on the route, were encrusted with ice, but "Kinshofer climbed like a god. Good, great, marvellous Toni!"

On the three great icefields that followed, things went better, but the Ramp was covered with ice, and a blizzard blew up on the Traverse of the Gods. In the icy Spider hollow the weather improved, but a fall by Hiebeler nearly pulled his companions after him into the void. On the morning of the seventh day, Almberger, Mannhardt, Kinshofer and Hiebeler embraced in the icy sunshine of the summit.

The next winter, Swiss climbers Hilti von Allmen

and Paul Etter climbed the steep, icy North face of the Matterhorn in two days, without too many problems. Between 25th and 31st January 1963, in a week-long battle amid blizzards and Arctic temperatures, Walter Bonatti, climbing with Cosimo Zappelli, won the race to make the first winter ascent of the Walker. French climbers René Desmaison and Jacques Batkin, beaten by a short head, repeated the ascent a week later.

After twenty years of extreme climbing Bonatti felt like a change of scene, but the tough climber from Bergamo who had moved to Courmayeur wanted to go out in a blaze of glory. After an attempt with two companions, he soloed a new and very difficult route on the North face of the Matterhorn in the depths of winter.

It was a hard battle, in which the character and class of this outstanding climber proved crucial. A few years later, the equally great Reinhold Messner unsuccessfully attempted to repeat the route, and had the courage to admit, "I couldn't get through. What that

Lavaredo eight years earlier. "The editorial staff of *Quick, Stern, Epoca* and *Paris Match* have gone down with Eigeritis!", commented Toni Hiebeler.

The Germans made their assault on 17th February, followed three days later by their rivals. Thanks to fixed ropes and bivouac caves excavated in the ice, the climbers scaled the wall fast, by turns, but the competition soon became fierce. On 21st March, Jorg Lehne and Karl Golikow came out onto the slopes of the Spider.

The next day, John Harlin was killed when a fixed rope snapped. The tragedy dramatically instilled a more human atmosphere into the ascent. The break in the ropes prevented the climbers at the bottom from continuing upwards. Above them, the weather was rapidly deteriorating, and Dougal Haston roped himself to Lehne, Gunther Strobel, Sigi Hupfauer and Roland Voetteler. A two-day battle in a raging blizzard took the five men to the summit. "It was the most terrible adventure of my entire life," recounted Jorg Lehne.

198 bottom left The North face of the Grandes Jorasses was attempted by the best climbers in the word from the beginning of the 20th century. In this photo, taken from the Leschaux Glacier, the spurs that rise towards Point Walker (on the left) and Point Croz can be seen, together with the ice slope of the Linceul (far left), climbed by René Desmaison and Robert Flematti in 1970, and the gully of Point Whymper, scaled by Walter Bonatti and Michel Vaucher in 1964.

198-199 The best climbers of the Sixties and Seventies did not disdain classic climbing venues and routes of average difficulty. In this photo, Chris Bonington and his team perform a "Tyrolean" rope traverse on the Grépon Ridge.

199 top Their experience of freezing cold weather and hard ice in the Scottish Highlands means that British climbers can tackle the most difficult walls of Mont Blanc in winter. In this photo, Dougal Haston is attempting to put up a new route on the North face of the Grandes Jorasses.

After Bonatti retired from mountaineering, Frenchman René Desmaison remained the most active climber on the great walls of Mont Blanc. In February 1967, climbing with Robert Flematti, he performed the first winter ascent of the Central Pillar. A year later, with no less than seven bivouacs, the same team scaled the Linceul, the "shroud" of ice on the North face of the Grandes Jorasses which was one of the last great logical routes on the Mont Blanc massif.

The steep, elusive Linceul, continually hit by small avalanches, resisted the two men for all it was worth, but Desmaison and Flematti never had any thought of giving up. Halfway through the ascent a blizzard trapped them for three days on a narrow ledge cut in the ice with the ice-axe. Their food ran out on the sixth day. On 25th January 1968, at 1:30 p.m., René and Robert came out onto the summit ridge of Point Walker, the highest point in the Jorasses. But their adventure was not over yet; it took them another day's struggle to abseil down the ascent route.

On the Grandes Jorasses, there was no lack of great winter problems, and René Desmaison was quick to identify and tackle them. In February 1971 Desmaison, who now lived in Chamonix, attempted to put up a direct route on the wall of Point Walker with Serge Gousseault. Like the Linceul, this route is hit by continuous rockfall, and can only be tackled safely in cold weather. Once again, the class and tenacity of the Frenchmen seemed to prevail over all obstacles.

After a four-day climb, the party was 300 metres from the exit. Rockfall had severed a rope, but morale was high, and there were still two days' worth of provisions in their rucksacks. But now the drama began. Weakened by an illness, Serge Gousseault collapsed. He died on the afternoon of 21st February, less than 100 metres from the ridge. Desmaison remained alone on the wall for four more days, until the wind died down and rescue helicopters could land on the summit.

At 10 a.m. on 25th February, pilot Alain Frébault managed to put down his Alouette on the fork between Points Whymper and Walker. By midday the rescuers were on the summit. Then, with the aid of a winch, Gérard Devouassoux was lowered down to Desmaison, who released him from the pitons and hauled him to safety. Half an hour later, Serge Gousseault's body was brought out of the abyss.

At about the same time, an Italian team consisting of Bruno Allemand, Gianni Calcagno, Alessandro Gogna and Guido Machetto attempted the first winter ascent of the Great Peuterey ridge. They scaled the Aiguille Noire and the Aiguille Blanche without difficulty, but the arrival of a front forced the climbers to bivouac for two nights in a crevasse on Col de Peutére. Then another helicopter took advantage of a pause in the blizzard to take them back to Courmayeur. A few weeks later, Polish climbers Dworak, Kurczab, Morz and Piotrowski scaled the Bonatti-Gobbi route to the Pilier d'Angle.

In the following months, during a long period of convalescence, René Desmaison was obsessed by the idea of the Walker. The most famous French climber of

the day attempted it twice more in the winter of 1972, together with Frenchman Michel Claret and Italian Giorgio Bertone. The right occasion came a year later. After a difficult five-day climb the team was on the last ledge reached in 1971, where "memories gushed from the granite as if they had remained encrusted on it." Then a snowstorm turned the wall white, and the thermometer fell lower and lower. But Desmaison and his new companions held out, kept climbing, and reached the summit.

Three months earlier, on Christmas 1972, French climbers Louis Audoubert, Marc Galy, Yannick Seigneur and Michel Feuillarade, together with Italians Arturo and Oreste Squinobal, had made the first

winter ascent of the "great ridge" of Peuterey, the fantastic ride leading from Val Vény to Mont Blanc across the South ridge of the Aiguille Noire, the summits of the Aiguille Blanche, and the Peuterey ridge. Two months later, another skilled French team (Pierre Béghin, Pierre Caubert, Olivier Challéat and Pierre Guillet) made the first winter ascent of the North-West face of the Ailefroide, the most difficult wall of rock and mixed terrain in the Oisans massif, with three bivouacs on the wall.

199 bottom This photo, taken by Chris Bonington, shows Dougal Haston on a steep slope of very hard ice in the heart of the North face. Slopes like this have been climbed more easily since the mid-Seventies thanks to the invention of ice-axes and hammers suitable for use with the ice-axe traction technique.

The wild challenge

200 top Alessandro Gogna from Genoa became known as one of the best active climbers in the Sixties. He can be seen in the centre of this photo, taken in July 1968 on the Planpincieux Glacier, on his return from the first solo ascent of the Walker Spur on the Grandes Jorasses.

200-201 The North face of the Grandes Jorasses, one of the most severe and spectacular walls in the Mont Blanc massif, witnessed numerous outstanding ascents in the Sixties and Seventies. In this photo, the snow-covered slope of the Linceul, the wall of Point Whymper and the spur that climbs to Point Margherita can be seen beyond the Walker Spur (left) and the Croz Spur.

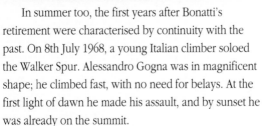

In summer too, the first years after Bonatti's retirement were characterised by continuity with the past. On 8th July 1968, a young Italian climber soloed the Walker Spur. Alessandro Gogna was in magnificent shape; he climbed fast, with no need for belays. At the first light of dawn he made his assault, and by sunset he was already on the summit.

"Here everything's fearful – the emptiness, the loneliness, the terrible couloir on my right. But I don't feel afraid," wrote Alessandro. "My feet aren't trembling and my heart isn't beating – it's as though someone behind me were encouraging me and telling me what to do. I'm progressing at an incredible rate, skipping pitons and pulling myself up by microscopic handholds."

Above the Grey Slabs, fatigue slowed Alessandro's rate of progress; then the ice blocking the last chimneys forced him to engage a fierce battle. He crawled up a narrow passage encrusted with green ice, helped by a number of aid pitches, and came out onto some easier slabs. Finally, "with great delight," Gogna planted his ice-axe in the snow on the summit, climbed over the cornice, and took a rest on the easy Italian side of the mountain. By 8:30 the next morning he was sitting on a bench in Courmayeur reading an account of his climb in the newspaper.

Among the changes of the "Bonatti years" was the coverage given by the media to top-level climbing on the great walls of the Alps. However, only the most perspicacious climbers noticed that another young man destined to become world-famous had made his mark on the walls of Mont Blanc. Reinhold Messner was born at Funes (Villnoss) in the Italian South Tyrol (Alto Adige), and we shall be reading about his adventures in the Dolomites and the Himalaya in later chapters. On 19th July 1969 he scaled the North face of the Droites in nine hours. The first ascensionists had taken five days.

At about the same time Gogna, together with the inseparable Leo Cerruti, was tackling another of the "last great problems" in the Alps. The two climbers conquered the "Nose" of Z'mutt, the awesome overhang that closes the North face of the Matterhorn to the right, after a four-day battle. The third and toughest bivouac took place on two "filthy steps," where they were only able to prepare their supper by holding the primus stove between their knees. Finally, two aid pitches of extreme difficulty, similar to the style of climbing performed on the great walls of the Dolomites, took the two Italians to the gentle slopes of the upper part of the North face.

The list of great solo ascents made in that period lengthened in 1971, when Georges Nominé soloed the Central Pillar of Mont Blanc, and Jean-Claude Droyer emulated his feat on the American Direct Route to the Dru. Between 10th and 12th July 1972, René Desmaison soloed the "great Peuterey ridge," and between 22nd and 28th February 1975, French climber Ivan Ghirardini performed the first solo ascent of the Linceul. This was another dramatic climb, which Ghirardini performed "to lay my life open to question before God."

But the years of heroic climbing were drawing to a close, and the near future was to speak a different language – the language of speed, elegance and sportsmanship, which now reclaimed its rightful place in the mountaineering world.

The wild challenge

On the threshold of the Arctic

The epic ascent of Mount McKinley concluded on a sunny day in 1913, when four exhausted men reached the small snow-covered ledge that forms the highest peak in North America. The expedition was organised by Rev. Hudson Stuck, who brought in another parson, Robert Tatum. However, Harry Karstens, a pioneer with great experience in Alaska, must take much of the credit for the achievement; it was he who transported the material needed by the expedition to the Kantishna River valley, alone, the previous autumn. On the last exhausting day of the ascent, the party was led by Walter Harper, who had worked for Stuck as a sled-dog driver in previous winters.

"At last the crest of the ridge was reached. Walter, who had been in the lead all day, was the first to scramble up. A native Alaskan, he was the first human to set foot upon the top of Alaska's great mountain, and he had well earned the lifelong satisfaction. Karstens and Tatum were hard on his heels, but the last man on the rope, in his enthusiasm somewhat overpassing his narrow wind margin, almost had to be hauled up the last few feet, and fell unconscious for a moment upon the floor of the little snow basin that occupies the top of the mountain. So soon as wind was recovered we shook hands all round, and a brief prayer of thanksgiving to Almighty God was said."

That is how Rev. Stuck, with a glimmering of humour, recounted the final stages of an ascent that had lasted several months, the crux was the methodical climb of the steep snow ridge now known as Karstens Ridge. Outstanding both as an exploratory feat and for the physical stamina required, the ascent by the four climbers to the 6194-metre summit of Mount McKinley dissolved the aura of mystery that had surrounded the mountain in earlier years.

That "stupendous mountain covered with snow" was first sighted in 1794 by British captain George Vancouver. In the Alaska of the day, inhabited only by small communities of Athapaskan Indians, no one was yet capable of tackling the challenge posed by the eternal snows of the mountain that the natives called *Denali* (the High One). In 1867, however, Secretary of State William Seward purchased Alaska from Russia for the astonishing price of two cents an acre. The newspapers called the venture "Seward's folly," but soon, small groups of colonists began to settle in that icy, inhospitable land in search of gold and furs.

As recounted in an earlier chapter, climbing in the wildest mountains of the Americas began in 1897, when the expedition led by Luigi Amedeo of Savoy, Duke of Abruzzi, reached the 5514-metre summit of Mount St. Elias, an impressive mountain that is relatively easy to reach from the coast.

The same year, as reported by the *New York Sun*, a group of gold prospectors identified the highest peak on the continent in Alaska. As in the case of Everest half a century earlier, the local name of the mountain was simply ignored, and the peak was named after William McKinley, who was about to begin his term as President of the USA.

202 top Mount McKinley, known to local native Americans as Denali, attracted the attention of explorers and climbers in the early 20th century. This photo shows Hudson Stuck and Harry Karstens, two members of the victorious 1913 expedition, during the interminable walk-in.

202 centre Another photo of the 1913 expedition, which shows the climbers crossing a crevasse on Muldrow Glacier. Note the large showshoes worn to facilitate progress on snow-covered glaciers.

202 bottom Although the summit is "only" 6194 metres high, climbers heading for Mount McKinley have to tackle the same problems as expeditions heading for the "eight-thousanders" of the Himalaya. This photo shows a long line of climbers carrying loads towards the mountain.

203 The high altitude and deep snow make the mountains of Alaska particularly attractive, as demonstrated by this photo, which shows a detail of the snow ridges and cornices of Mount McKinley.

Five years later, an expedition organised by the United States Geological Survey and led by Alfred Brooks drew the first maps of the area and confirmed that Mount McKinley really was the highest of all. In 1903, two separate expeditions, one led by Judge James Wickersham from Fairbanks and the other by polar explorer Frederick Cook, reached the foot of the great mountain. However, the problems it posed were formidable.

In a land with no roads whatever, where overland travel was complicated by rivers, lakes and marshes (not to speak of grizzly bears!), reaching Mount McKinley was a feat in itself. Now, on fine days, the light aircraft that take off from Talkeetna take less than an hour to fly climbers up to an altitude of 2500 metres and put them down on the Kahiltna Glacier, which flows at the foot of the mountain, but it took the first Cook expedition a full nine weeks to reach Peters Glacier, which seemed to offer the best ascent route to the summit. Later parties also took a similar length of time, despite the fact that they were operating in known territory.

After that, the mountain had to be tackled, and there too, things were far from easy. Claude E. Rusk, the leader of the expedition that attempted the ascent in 1910, wrote as follows about the Alaskan mountains. "… Not that they are the highest in the world, for the great peaks of Himalaya overtop them by thousands of feet. But the Himalayan snow line is sixteen or eighteen thousand feet above sea level, while Mount McKinley, on some sides at least, can be said to have no snow line. The whole region from its base, for miles upon miles, is loaded with a fathomless burden of perpetual ice and snow." And as Bradford Washburn, a climber and photographer from Boston who made some great ascents in the Yukon and Alaska in the years around the Second World War, commented later, "the climate on the summit of Mount McKinley is probably the severest on earth apart from the Polar regions."

The first Cook expedition reached an altitude of 3500 metres, circuited the mountain, then abandoned its horses and returned to the Pacific coast by sailing down swift-flowing rivers on a raft. In the spring of 1906, Frederick Cook again embarked from Seattle, heading for Alaska. He was accompanied by Ed Barrill, Hershel Parker and Belmore Browne.

There was no mistaking the fact that the Gold Rush was in full swing. The ship, which had been almost empty in 1903, was now jam-packed with gold prospectors, and the boomtown of Cordova, where prospectors sold their gold and got their fill of cheap whisky and women before going back into the interior, had sprung up on the banks of Cook Inlet (named not after Frederick but James Cook, the famous British navigator).

This time, Cook was aiming to reach the south side of Mount McKinley, but after two and a half months of unsuccessful attempts, the expedition seemed to be at an end. Browne stayed in Alaska to collect rare plants, Parker set off back to New York, and Cook and Barrill returned to the interior for what they described as a "short exploration." However, a month later, Frederick Cook returned triumphantly to the coast to announce to the world that he had reached the summit.

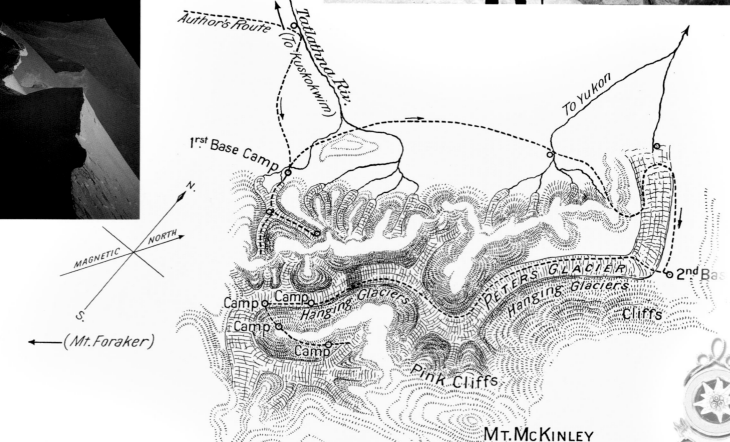

204 left This famous photo, taken by Galen Rowell, shows the snow ridges of Mount McKinley reddened by the last glimmers of twilight.

204 top right This 1900 photo shows that even the topographers of the United States Geological Survey had to tackle glaciers in order to draw the first topographical map of Mount McKinley.

An article published in *Harper's Monthly Magazine* in May 1907, which included a photo of Barrill flying a flag on the summit, made Cook the most famous explorer in America. The book *To the Top of the Continent*, published in 1908, increased his fame. And in September 1909 a telegram received by the Explorers' Club of New York announced that Frederick Cook had just reached the North Pole. However, his fame was short-lived, for a scandal soon broke.

Robert Peary, who also claimed to be the first man to reach the North Pole, cast doubt on Cook's feat in the Arctic. The evidence given by the two Eskimos who had accompanied him was unconvincing. Then the "McKinley bomb" exploded. On the basis of the pictures published in the book, Browne and Parker alleged that the "summit photo" taken by Cook had been faked.

On their return to Alaska in 1910, Frederick Cook's two accusers and former companions identified the modest 2000-metre hill where the famous photo had been taken. "As he sowed so he reaped. If he is mentally unbalanced, he is entitled to the pity of mankind. If he is not, there is no corner of the earth where he can hide from his past," commented Claude E. Rusk ruthlessly.

For the perpetrator of the fraud it was the end. Perhaps, however, the fake photo cost Frederick Cook even more than he deserved. After the Alaskan fraud had been revealed to the world, no one believed his claim to have reached the North Pole. "What irony if the Mount McKinley fiction denied permanent recognition to the first man to reach the North Pole!", wrote Chris Jones in *Climbing in North America* in 1976.

The Mount McKinley enigma had not yet been solved, however. In April 1910, while Frederick Cook's "trial" was still in progress, the *Fairbanks Daily Times* again announced the conquest of the mountain. This time, the ascent was claimed by miners Pete Anderson, Charley McGonagall and Billy Taylor, who went down in history as "the Sourdoughs" (the nickname for gold prospectors).

Though proud of their alleged triumph over the "doctors and expeditions from outside," the trio did not bring any photo back to prove their ascent. A few weeks later, mountain blizzards rebuffed an expedition from Oregon led by Claude E. Rusk and another

attempt by Browne and Parker. In 1912, a new attempt by Frederick Cook's former companions took them to within a few hundred metres of the summit, but a particularly fierce blizzard forced them to give up forever.

The next year, when Stuck and party finally reached the 6194-metre summit of South Peak, the highest in the Mount McKinley range, the next year, they saw the wooden stake left by the Sourdoughs on the slightly lower North Peak. "Of course we climbed that peak; there was more chance of the stake being seen from Fairbanks there," explained Billy Taylor, one of the members of the most adventurous expedition in the history of the great Alaskan peaks in 1937.

When the age of the pioneers was over, the great mountains of Alaska and the Yukon were enshrouded in silence once again. After the ascent by Stuck and party, nearly 20 years passed before another expedition tackled the glaciers of the "Roof of North America." In the meantime, in 1917, the government in distant Washington instituted the Mount McKinley National Park (renamed Denali in 1980) which, with its 2,411,236 hectares, is still the largest national park in the world.

206 top left Mount Logan (5951 metres) is the highest peak in Canada. When the first ascent was performed in 1925 by an expedition of the Alpine Club of Canada led by Albert MacCarthy, the climbers had to cover hundreds of kilometres of virgin terrain to reach the mountain.

206 bottom left The walk-in to the East ridge of Mount Logan forces climbers to cross numerous huge snow-covered crevasses.

206-207 The ordinary ascent route on Mount McKinley offers outstanding views of some of the highest and most spectacular mountains in Alaska. In this photo, Mike Nelson admires the impressive Mount Foraker from near the last camp, pitched at an altitude of 5500 metres.

In the years leading up to the First World War, a style of climbing similar to the European brand spread rapidly in the USA and Canada. For mountain lovers, however, Alaska was too distant and too expensive. It was more convenient to visit the mountain chains closer to home: the Tetons and the Wind River Range in Wyoming, the Sierra in California, Mount Rainier and the Cascades in the State of Washington. North of the border the Canadian Rockies, with the elegant profiles of Mount Assiniboine and Mount Robson, were also rapidly becoming popular.

Albert MacCarthy, who made the first ascent of Mount Robson in 1913, led the expedition organised by the Alpine Club of Canada which attempted the highest peak in the country in 1925. Mount Logan, a magnificent mountain with a height of 5951 metres, stands on the border between the USA and Canada some 30 kilometres farther inland than Mount St. Elias. The nearest town is 250 kilometres from the mountain, and half the walk-in takes place on glaciers.

However, Albert MacCarthy was known for his willpower and stamina. In the summer of 1926, he climbed 101 peaks in the Alps in two months, wearing out a number of famous Swiss guides. In February 1925, with five companions, three sledges pulled by dogs and two by horses, the tireless MacCarthy began to transport material towards Mount Logan. He returned after a two-month struggle in the freezing cold, and set off back to the mountain with the rest of the group a fortnight later.

It took another four weeks' effort to reach King Col, at the start of the most technical part of the climb. After that, the difficulties were never excessive. Apart from the distance, the high altitude and bad weather conditions caused the climbers considerable problems, but at last, on 23rd June, six climbers finally crossed the interminable summit plateau and reached the summit of Mount Logan.

During the descent, Fred Lambart's poor physical condition slowed the group's progress, and another blizzard after a bivouac made the going difficult. On

their return, even the austere *Alpine Journal* conceded that "greater hardships have probably never been experienced in any mountaineering expedition."

In 1930, the first attempts were made on Mount Fairweather (4669 m), another splendid mountain overlooking the Pacific. However, the summit was not reached until the next summer, by Allen Carpé and Terris Moore, who had to scale slopes covered with half a metre of fresh snow.

In 1934, a team composed of Charles Houston (who later led two expeditions to K2), Thomas Graham Brown and C. Waterston reached the 5304-metre summit of Mount Foraker, the highest of the peaks near Mount McKinley.

Though less difficult than the ascent of Mount Logan, all these climbs involved a particularly severe environment. The first to tackle the great technical difficulties of the harsh mountains of the Far North was a climber who had emigrated to the States from Europe – Fritz Wiessner, whom we have already seen in action on the walls of the Odle range

and Pelmo just after the First World War.

With his friend Bill House in the summer of 1935, he was the first to climb the 3994-metre Mount Waddington, a splendid rock and ice mountain that marks the highest point of the Canadian Coast Mountains in the heart of British Columbia. Vertical, difficult and frequently showered with stones, the South face of the mountain bears comparison with the North faces in the Western Alps which were conquered during the same period, one after another. Wiessner, who changed his boots for the light rope-soled climbing shoes used in the Dolomites in the most difficult pitches on rock, proved to be up to the challenge.

After that, the first ascensionists of Mount Waddington turned their attention to K2 in two separate expeditions. In 1938, climbing with Charles Houston's first expedition, Bill House successfully led the crux of the Abruzzi Spur. The next year, Fritz Wiessner came within a hairs breadth of the summit of the second-highest peak on earth.

207 top right Although it is "only" 3994 metres high, Mount Waddington, in the Canadian Coast Mountains, is one of the loveliest mountains in Canada. It was first climbed by American Bill House and Fritz Wiessner, who had already made some great ascents in the Dolomites and had just moved to the USA.

Both men made some excellent ascents on K2 in later years. This photo shows the ascent route.

207 bottom right This photo of the first ascent of Mount Waddington shows a moment during the strenuous walk-in to the South face of the mountain.

208 top left This photo of
Fritz Wiessner on the summit
of Mount Waddington was
taken by his climbing
companion Bill House.
Although the summit is snow-
covered, the difficult parts of
the climb mainly take place
on rock and mixed terrain.

208 top right The North face
of Mount Hunter, which
overlooks the Kahiltna
Glacier, is one of the steepest
and most difficult of the great
mountains of Alaska.

*On the threshold
of the Arctic*

In 1946, Wiessner attempted the ascent of the Devils Thumb, a lower (2736 m) but particularly difficult rocky pyramid on the border between Alaska and the Yukon, with Donald Brown and Fred Beckey. The party was forced to give up the attempt when Wiessner sprained his knee, but a few weeks later, Beckey was back in action with Bob Craig and Cliff Schmidtke.

On 18th August, a lovely sunny day, the team climbed the most difficult sections of the route, wearing tennis shoes. They included "a sheer pinnacle, encrusted in places with verglas and nearly devoid of piton cracks," which Fred "led with a considerable jolt of adrenaline." The next day, a terrible storm pinned down the team for three days and nights in a small cave excavated in a snowfield.

At last, on 24th August, magnificent weather arrived. A delicate climb on rock encrusted in snow after the blizzard brought the three climbers out onto the exposed summit of the Devils Thumb. "The atmosphere was so clear that Mounts Fairweather and Crillon, 230 miles to the north-west, were visible. At the time it was the ultimate satisfaction of my climbing career," recounted Beckey later.

The descent to the Stikine River seemed endless. A long series of abseils down the wall and a traverse of the glacier on skis, followed by an interminable walk on moraines and through forests, took the climbers to the spot where a boat was due to meet them and take them to Wrangel. Before it arrived, Craig and Schmidtke decided to take a dip. While they were doing so, the sudden appearance of a female grizzly and her two cubs risked bringing another great achievement of American climbing to a tragic conclusion.

Mount McKinley was back in the headlines in the Fifties. In 1951, a group led by Bradford Washburn flew to the Kahiltna Glacier and made the first ascent of the West Spur, which has been used as the ordinary ascent route ever since.

Three years later, an expedition organised by the University of Alaska made the first crossing of the mountain. Elton Thayer, George Argus, Les Viereck and Morton Wood reached the base of the mountain via Ruth Glacier, collected food and gear launched earlier from the plane, then climbed the spur that closes the South face to the right. During the descent,

their SOS. Wood and Viereck walked for three days before finding rangers who could send for help, and it was not until two weeks after the accident that George Argus was finally reached by a rescue team.

In the Fifties, some of the best European climbers joined the Americans and Canadians on the icy mountains of the Far North. In 1954 Fred Beckey, who was rapidly making a name for himself as one of the best mountaineers in the States, joined forces with German Henry Meybohm and Austrian Heinrich Harrer, who had just returned from his famous "Seven Years in Tibet," to perform the first ascents of Mount Deborah (3762 m) and Mount Hunter (4372 m), two of the most attractive unclimbed mountains in Alaska.

Five years later, another Austrian, Leo Schleiblehner, organised and led the ascent of the South-East face of Mount La Pérouse, an elegant 3225-metre peak in the Mount Fairweather massif, which he performed with Richard Griesmann.

At the first attempt, in 14 hours, they scaled that steep, avalanche-prone wall of ice and mixed terrain over 2000 metres high, which Schleiblehner compared with the North face of the Courtes. It was "a climb ahead of its time" in the opinion of climbing historian Chris Jones.

the four followed Karstens Ridge, the steep snow ridge used by the 1913 party, which was rendered dangerous by the poor condition of the snow.

Thayer, who was climbing as last man and belaying the other three, slipped, pulling his companions 300 metres down the ridge. Three of the four climbers were saved by a ledge. Viereck had chest pains, and Argus had a broken leg. Elton Thayer was dead. Viereck and Wood left Thayer's body on the glacier, pitched a tent in which they sheltered Argus, traced signals in the snow, and waited six days for a plane to find them. In the end, they had to admit to themselves that no one had seen

208-209 The highest peaks of North America still offer many opportunities to put up new ascent routes. In this photo, Scott Backes is tackling a difficult ice pitch during the opening of the Deprivation route on the North face of Mount Hunter.

209 above This photo, taken during the first ascent of Deprivation, shows Scott Backes scaling a very steep ice-filled gully. The Alpine style normally practised on these walls forces mountaineers to climb weighed down by gigantic backpacks, even when leading.

*210 bottom left Although the climate is totally different, climbers use the same progression techniques on the granite walls of Alaska and Canada as on the sunny walls of Yosemite.
In this 1972 photo, Jim MacCarthy scales the vertical slabs of the Moose's Tooth with the aid of fixed ropes.*

210-211 The awesome East face of the main peak of the Moose's Tooth is one of the most difficult granite walls in Alaska.

As a new decade opened, Mount McKinley was back in the limelight again. In 1961 Riccardo Cassin, who had made numerous great ascents in the Alps in the Thirties, organised an expedition by the "Ragni di Lecco" (Lecco Spiders) to the most evident spur on the South face of the mountain, which Bradford Washburn had described as the major climbing problem on the continent.

When they disembarked in New York and later in Anchorage, the Lecco men seemed like hayseeds. Amazed, they photographed the skyscrapers and relied on Italian immigrants to help them tackle problems that seemed daunting because of their unfamiliarity with the English language. In mid-June, however, pilot

Don Sheldon put Cassin and party down on the Kahiltna Glacier, at the foot of the great mountain. Here, the "Ragni" (Spiders) felt much more at home.

Helped by American Bob Goodwin for the first two weeks, Riccardo Cassin, Jack Canali, Gigi Alippi, Romano Perego, Luigi Airoldi and Annibale Zucchi transported their gear to the start, then began laboriously climbing the lower part of the wall. After scaling a sharp snow ridge and a small hanging glacier, they pitched camp three at 5200 metres in readiness for their assault on the summit.

The six Italians scaled the last section of the difficult rocky spur, then continued along the easier slopes towards the summit. Now, however, the main problem was the weather. "The temperature was very low, 30° or 35° below freezing point, and the fine, icy snow tore at our faces. Rock-hard ice alternated with powder snow and an icy crust that snapped under our feet. Our boots were hard, and seemed to be glued to our feet," recounted Cassin in his book *Cinquant'anni di alpinismo*. At 11 p.m. on 19th July, the six Italian climbers embraced on the 6194-metre summit.

The freezing cold and their fatigue made the descent at least as difficult as the ascent. Canali, whose feet were severely frostbitten, slipped several times on the slope. At camp three, Gigi Alippi gave his friend his own warm reindeer-skin boots, and continued the descent wearing four pairs of socks and overshoes. Dressed like that, he could not use crampons, and had to be lowered down on the rope. The fog caused problems of orientation, and a horrific fall by Romano Perego fortunately ended in a snowdrift. On the afternoon of 23rd July, the climbers were finally safe and sound in the base camp.

Class and stamina had enabled the great Cassin to add another magnificent route to his outstanding curriculum, but the suffering undergone by the climbers, though to some extent inevitable on a mountain like Mount McKinley, had been aggravated by the use of the wrong clothing. The weather on Mount McKinley resembles conditions on Everest

rather than Mont Blanc. "The Italians had made the boldest and most continuously difficult climb in Alaska. Yet they seriously misjudged Alaskan conditions. They came equipped with knickers, knee socks and ordinary Alpine boots. The frostbite was a mild penalty," commented historian Chris Jones.

Three years after Riccardo Cassin's ascent, another great name in European climbing appeared on the Alaskan scene. Together with seven fellow-countrymen, Frenchman Lionel Terray aimed to climb two magnificent virgin peaks, Mount Huntington and the Moose's Tooth, one after another, and then put up a new route on the South face of Mount McKinley. But despite his experience on Annapurna and Makalu, in the Peruvian Andes and on Fitz Roy, the author of *I conquistatori dell'inutile* had underestimated Alaska.

On the North-West ridge of Mount Huntington, the temperature never exceeds -10°C, and the ice is exceptionally compact. On the ninth day, Terray had a nasty fall, and climbing companion Jacques Soubis had great difficulty in holding him. Despite a badly sprained arm, Terray reached the summit ten days later with the others. Worn out by exertion, nervous strain and the cold, the Frenchmen decided to forego the rest of their ambitious plans. The Moose's Tooth, a magnificent rocky pyramid 3150 metres tall, was climbed a few days later by Germans Klaus Bierl, Arnold Hasenkopf, Alfons Reichegger and Walter Welsch.

The Americans soon got their own back. In 1965, Don Jensen, Dave Roberts, Ed Bernd and Matt Hale scaled the severe West face of Mount Huntington, a tougher route than the one climbed by Terray and party. However, during the descent, an ill-placed abseil rope caused Bernd to fall to his death.

That same summer, a California team consisting of Dick Long, Jim Wilson, Allen Steck, Joe Evans, Paul Bacon and Frank Coale scaled the interminable South ridge of Mount Logan, which is over 10 kilometres long, after a month's effort.

211 top The sharp pyramid of Mount Huntington is one of the few great Alaskan peaks first climbed by European mountaineers. The first ascent of the mountain was made in 1964 by Frenchmen Lionel Terray and Jacques Soubis, who scaled the North-West ridge of the mountain despite the prohibitive temperatures.

211 bottom This 1964 photo shows the French climbers in a fairly easy section of the long North-West ridge of Mount Huntington.

In early 1967, winter climbing made its first appearance in the Alaskan mountains. Ascents in the coldest season of the year had been common for some time on the big walls of the Alps, but winter conditions are much worse on Mount McKinley. Apart from the temperature and the bad weather, the very short days of the Arctic winter make life even more difficult for climbers.

In addition to Americans Gregg Blomberg, Dave Johnston, Art Davidson, George Wichman and John Edwards, the expedition's members included Shiro Nishimae from Japan, Frenchman Jacques Batkin and Swiss climber Ray Genet. In mid-January, pilot Don Sheldon put the climbers down as usual on the Kahiltna Glacier. A few days later, Jacques Batkin was killed when he fell into a crevasse concealed by the fresh snow.

After lengthy discussions, the others decided to keep going. Despite the cold, the darkness and the bad weather, they pitched a series of camps along the West Spur of the mountain. Eventually, Davidson, Johnston and Genet reached the summit, but on the descent they were pinned down by a raging blizzard with gales of up to 150 kilometres an hour. Johnston, the only one still in good

ill-prepared groups is causing an increasing number of accidents, as on all the "fashionable" mountains of the world.

Numerous routes have been opened on the steepest walls of Mount McKinley, located not far from the beaten track and the perennially occupied camps along the ordinary route up the mountain. On the South face, where the route put up by Riccardo Cassin and party is now frequently repeated, the route opened in 1976 by British climbers Dougal Haston and Doug Scott, and the one opened solo by Czech Miroslav Smid in 1991, are also worthy of mention.

Another solo climbing specialist, Renato Casarotto from Vicenza, climbed the North-East ridge of Mount McKinley, which he christened "The Ridge of No Return," in 1977. In addition to the many extreme climbing routes he put up in the Dolomites, Casarotto also made some excellent solo ascents in the Andes, in Patagonia, and on Mont Blanc. Two years later, his climbing career ended tragically when he fell to his death in a crevasse at the foot of the Magic Line on K2. In Alaska, Renato had no hesitation in describing the ascent he had just performed as "the most dangerous of my life."

On the threshold of the Arctic

shape, prepared the bivouac and food for his companions.

After they had spent three nights in a snow-hole on the 5460-metre Denali Pass the blizzard abated, but clouds enshrouded the mountain, and the trio were unable to descend until the sixth day. Unfortunately their companions, believing them dead, had dismantled the camps pitched along the spur, forcing them to make a horrific descent without food or shelter. After a last bivouac, the exhausted climbers were finally located by a helicopter, which took them back to Talkeetna.

In the Seventies and Eighties, climbing on the highest mountains of Alaska became much more common. Expeditions following the ordinary route on Mount McKinley are becoming more numerous every year; between May and June, hundreds of climbers set off from the Kahiltna Glacier along the West Spur. This overcrowding has caused serious problems of environmental pollution, while the presence of

In recent decades, new routes have multiplied on the other great Alaskan peaks, as everywhere. Every year, new routes are put up and major existing ones repeated on Mounts Huntington and Logan, the Moose's Tooth and the elegant Mount Deborah. In the Sixties, the best European and American climbers identified two areas offering more unexplored big walls.

The most frequently climbed (relatively speaking) are on Baffin Island, the easternmost sector of the Canadian Arctic. First visited for mountaineering purposes by Tom Longstaff in 1934, and systematically climbed in the Sixties, the extraordinary granite walls of Mounts Asgard, Odin, Breidablik and Overlord dominate the impressive glaciers that flow down to Penny Ice Cap and Pangnirtung fjord, and are now visited by numerous climbing expeditions every year.

214 The extraordinary granite walls of Baffin Island in the Canadian Arctic have been popular with mountaineers looking for new and challenging routes since the Seventies. In this photo, American climber Ryan Shellborn skis towards the west side of Mount Asgard.

215 top left The South face of Mount Proboscis is one of the most difficult and spectacular of all the granite walls in the Cirque of the Unclimbables.

215 top right The best American climbers are forced to summon up all their resources on the walls of the Cirque of the Unclimbables. In this photo, Todd Skinner leads a 5.12a pitch (between the eighth and upper eighth grade on the European scale) during the inauguration of the Great Canadian Knife route on the South face of Mount Proboscis.

215 top centre The new routes put up on the vertical walls of Baffin Island, where the climbing difficulties can reach 8a and the mountains are often hit by violent storms, attract the most fearless lovers of the North American wilderness every summer.

On the threshold of the Arctic

In 1963, another area containing some outstanding walls was discovered at the opposite end of that endless country. The Cirque of the Unclimbables is an amphitheatre of granite walls of outstanding beauty overlooked by elegant, remote peaks like Mount Proboscis, Mount Harrison Smith and Lotus Flower Tower. With the aid of the American Alpine Club, Jim MacCarthy, Royal Robbins, Layton Kor and Dick McCracken climbed the South-East face of Mount Proboscis, a gigantic vertical wall in a particularly remote area, in 1963.

Since then, the big walls on the border between the Yukon and North-West Territories have been visited ever more frequently by the world's top climbers. Seaplanes and helicopters provide relatively quick access to the foot of the walls, and the bad weather and mosquitoes leave climbers in peace for long enough to tackle the rock with the required concentration.

The modern routes opened on Lotus Flower Tower and Mount Proboscis, which include pitches rated at up to 8a (the tenth grade on the Welzembach scale), demonstrate that the two major versions of North American climbing meet on these faces. Here, in order to scale the big walls, lovers of the Arctic wilderness have to use the sophisticated climbing techniques developed on the granite of Yosemite.

215 centre bottom Mount Breidablik is one of the most difficult peaks on Baffin Island. Here, it is seen from the west, in a photo taken from the summit of Mount Tyr.

215 bottom Portaledges (tents with rigid bases that can be hung from the rock face) allow climbers to bivouac comfortably in the heart of the most compact walls. This photo shows Paul Piana and Todd Skinner during the opening of the Great Canadian Knife route on the South face of Mount Proboscis.

On the granite of California

Yosemite National Park, California, one summer's night in 1975. "An alarm sounds at 2 a.m. Three bodies rise quickly and move, not with the usual dragging motions of an early rise, but with precise movements and an economy of action. They dress in costumes for the occasion, à la Jimi Hendrix. All sit down to a breakfast of king-sized omelettes, followed by beans, to get the day moving. Quickly, their gear is checked and found to be in order. They shift to the base of the Nose, and go through the final ritual of putting on E.B.s, swamis and tape."

A hundred years had gone by since the peaceful excursions undertaken by John Muir, and there was no mistaking the fact. Since then, the magnificent Yosemite Valley, which became the heart of the National Park of the same name in 1890, has turned into one of the most popular tourist areas in California. The footpaths and peaks of the "back country," the most remote areas of

the park, are still roamed by bears and small groups of backpackers who followed the Pacific Crest Trail or the John Muir Trail.

Yosemite Valley teems with cars and buses bringing thousands of visitors from all over the world to gaze at the impressive walls of El Capitan, the Royal Arches, Lost Arrow and Half Dome. Hikers and riders throng the trails that climb to waterfalls and crags. In summer, it's no easy task to find accommodation in the campsites and lodges.

Not far from the Valley bottom, the roads and the crowd, Jim Bridwell, John Long and Bill Westbay were

concentrating hard on their objective – the first one-day ascent of the Nose, the most classic route on the biggest and most difficult wall in the valley. eighteen years earlier, it had taken first ascensionist Warren Harding seventeen days of actual climbing and 125 bolts. We'll come back to the climbing history of the Valley in a moment; in the meantime, it's instructive to watch the three climbers at work.

"It's 4 a.m. We take off on the initial pitches, rehearsed a few days before, but this time under the light of headlamps," recounted Bill Westbay. "Darkness still engulfs us as we hit Sickle Ledge, although the false dawn begins to lend a hint of light. John assumes the lead and tackles his section of the route. Our plan is to have each of us lead approximately the third of the climb best suited to our own capabilities." The race had begun.

The first section was led by John Long, "the most powerful climber to have come to the Valley, blasts pitches off before we can smoke a cigarette." Their hands began to ache with the effort, but by 6 a.m. the trio had woken another group who were just finishing their bivouac on Dolt Tower. "The total commitment by each of us seems to bring the energy level to an unbelievable pitch. I perceive this energy flow to be seen and felt equally by the others." At 11 a.m., they threw down their sweaters and other superfluous gear from the ledge of Camp Four.

At 1:30 p.m., with 700 metres of the climb already accomplished, Jim Bridwell, known to Yosemite climbers as "the Bird," finally took over the lead. They were very tired, and there were fewer bolts on the route than they expected. A rope that got caught under a huge flake of rock seemed likely to hamper their progress for a while, but they quickly freed it by shaking it frantically.

"Somehow, energy and luck sustain us in the final pitches. El Cap in a day! 7 p.m. Three weary bodies stand on the summit of El Cap. Beginning an epic descent in E.B.s, they return to the Valley floor seventeen hours after leaving it. Still wired, they adjourn to the bar to share the hospitality of friends," concluded Bill Westbay.

The three climbers' long hair tied with coloured headbands, flowered waistcoats and slang recall the world of the hippies who became famous all over the world in the Sixties and Seventies. However, the record-breaking climb by Bridwell, Long and Westbay on the granite cracks of the Nose was an outstanding achievement, performed on walls whose existence was only just beginning to be discovered by European climbers. Not long afterwards, all the best European climbers would make pilgrimages to the Valley.

216 left The southern ramparts of El Capitan form the highest and most famous wall in Yosemite Valley. This photo clearly shows the gigantic edge known to climbers as the "Nose." The Merced River can be seen in the foreground.

216 right The long, difficult aid-climbing sections present on nearly all routes of El Capitan require climbers to take a large amount of gear with them. The "soft" étriers used by American climbers can be seen in this photo in addition to the pitons, nuts and friends clipped to Kurt Smith's harness and shoulder strap.

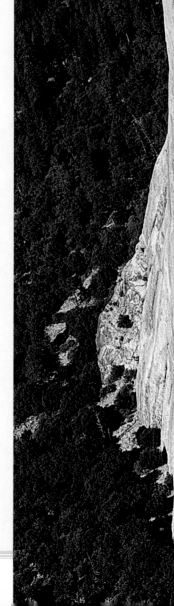

217 left The great routes on El Capitan (a pitch of Zenyatta Mondatta is shown in this photo) force climbers to spend several days on the wall. In addition to outstanding technical expertise, these routes require great physical and psychological stamina.

217 below Cracks are found on all the granite faces in the world, but are particularly long on the walls of Yosemite. To tackle them safely, California climbers have invented gear like nuts, bongs, rurps and friends. In this photo, Swiss climber Conrad Anker is scaling the Nose, the first route put up on El Capitan.

However, climbing in Yosemite had already been going strong for decades. Known since the 19th century by nature lovers and ramblers (a walkers' route protected by handrails, ropes and ladders was installed on Half Dome soon after it was first climbed in 1875), the great granite walls of Yosemite Valley were too vertical and compact to attract the interest of the first American climbers, who came onto the scene shortly after the First World War.

The granite walls of the Sierra were first tackled in the late Twenties by a group of climbers from San Francisco including Robert Underhill, Norman Clyde and Jules Eichorn. At first, however, they concentrated on the higher and more accessible Mount Whitney.

Eichorn arrived in Yosemite Valley for the first time in September 1933, accompanied by Dick Leonard and Bestor Robinson. First of all, they attempted the ascent of the Higher Cathedral Spire, an awesome pinnacle on which the trio only managed to climb a few dozen metres in seven hours, because their home-made pitons and karabiners buckled under their weight. In order to go farther up, they would need to get hold of better gear from Europe, but in the Depression years, imported goods were prohibitively expensive in the States.

Two months later, having obtained pitons and karabiners from Munich, the three young men were back at the Spire. However, halfway up the wall they

had to give up once more. In April 1934 they were back in action again, equipped with "two half-inch ropes (120 feet long, tensile strength 2650 pounds), 200 feet of roping-down line (tensile strength 1000 pounds), 60 feet of extra rope, 55 pitons, 13 karabiners, two piton-hammers, three piton step-slings, extra clothing, first-aid kit, two small cameras, one movie camera, and food."

After scaling the steepest and most compact sections with some difficult roping manoeuvres, Eichorn, Leonard and Robinson finally reached the summit. A few months later, the trio also climbed the Lower Cathedral Spire, described in the Sierra Club's official bulletins as "the most difficult rock climb in America." Then they turned their attention to Lost Arrow, "the most interesting problem to be solved in the States" and even the vertical wall of Half Dome, which dominates the upper Yosemite Valley. After a few brief reconnaissance trips, however, they reluctantly had to leave

both these structures to future generations.

In October 1939, to make up for this disappointment, the Californians (known to other American climbers as "the Sierrans") turned their attention to Shiprock, a forbidding monolith of volcanic rock in the North-Western corner of New Mexico. In preceding years, this tower had rebuffed no less than twelve attempted ascents. During one of them, Robert Ormes, the organiser of the attempt, was saved from a fall by the skin of his teeth when a piton bent, but fortunately did not pull out of the crack into which it had been driven.

The climbers who attempted the ascent were Dave Brower, John Dyer, Raffi Bedayn and Bestor Robinson. On the third day, after a bivouac on the face, Robinson aid climbed a wall by driving pitons into a crack that widened with each blow of the hammer. Then Dyer took the lead, lassoed a spur of rock, pulled himself up along the rope and reached the summit.

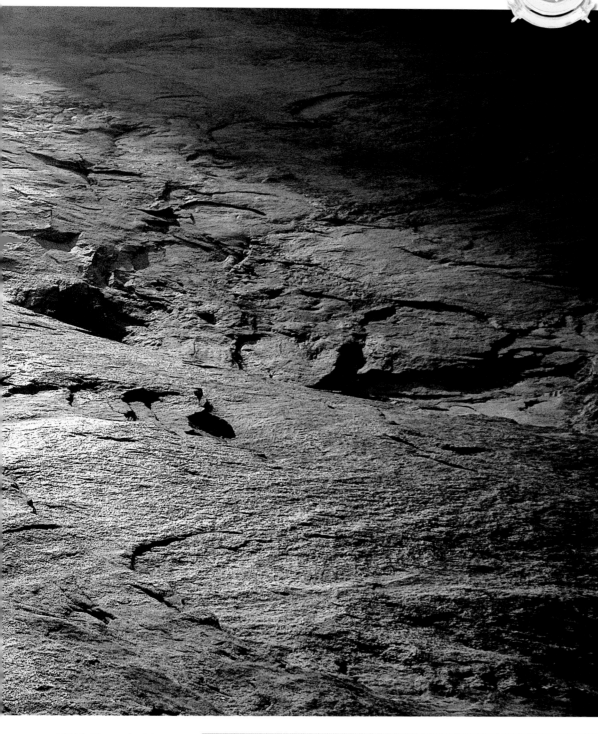

219 top Mount Whitney (4418 metres), situated in the Sequoia National Park, is the highest peak in California and the 48 contiguous States of the USA (ie. with the exception of Alaska and Hawaii). In this photo, the granite of the East Face looks particularly attractive in the light of dawn.

219 bottom Although the attention of climbers from all over the world focuses on the walls of El Capitan and Half Dome, many other rock structures offer some very interesting routes. The Lower (left) and Higher Cathedral Spires, shown in this photo, were the first major formations in Yosemite Valley to be climbed. The two ascents were made in the spring of 1934 by Jules Eichorn, Dick Leonard and Bestor Robinson.

218 left The granite slabs and cracks of the East Face of Mount Whitney are quite the equal of those found in Yosemite in terms of difficulty and solidity. This 1991 photo shows the first ascent of the Left-Wing Extremist route.

218-219 All the granite walls of Yosemite Valley were worn smooth at the bottom during the great Ice Ages, and therefore call for some particularly difficult smearing. In this photo, a climber is scaling the slabs of the Lower Cathedral.

Thanks to their training on the granite of Yosemite Valley, the Californians had proved to be among the best climbers in America. Then, the Second World War dampened the enthusiasm of an entire generation.

When peace returned, a new personality made a breakthrough in climbing in Yosemite Valley. John Salathé, a wrought iron worker by trade, was born in Switzerland, but had become a naturalised American citizen. He was well over 40, and not particularly attracted to the short free-climbing problems on which his younger friends concentrated. He was more interested in the use and development of pitons, because the iron type imported from Europe, designed for the limestone of the Dolomites and the Wilder Kaiser, easily bent on the hard granite of the Sierra.

In his workshop, Salathé used an old Ford axle to make high-tensile steel pitons. He went back to Yosemite to try them out, and found they worked. It was these pitons that enabled him to reach the summit of Lost Arrow, after a number of attempts, in the summer of 1947. His climbing companion in that

220 top left The North-West face of Half Dome, nearly 600 metres high, is the second-highest wall in Yosemite Valley and was the first to be climbed. The first ascent was made in five days in the summer of 1957 by Royal Robbins, Jerry Gallwas and Mike Sherrick.

220 bottom left Sentinel Rock, which overlooks the central and most popular part of Yosemite Valley from the south, dominates the valley bottom with an attractive granite wall, which is fairly well differentiated at the bottom but very compact at the summit section.

ascent, as in the previous ones, was Ax Nelson. A year earlier, again with Nelson, Salathé had scaled the South-West face of Half Dome, the first major rock wall in the Valley to be climbed by man.

John Salathé made his last great ascent in July 1950. This time, his objective was Sentinel Rock, the last great unclimbed monolith in Yosemite Valley. Climbing with Allen Steck, who had made a previous attempt on the summit, 55-year-old Salathé scaled the interminable series of chimneys that now constitute the ordinary route on the mountain in five days, then left California and went back to live in Switzerland.

A new generation of climbers appeared in Yosemite Valley in the mid-Fifties. This time, the young granite climbing enthusiasts were aiming at the most awesome and difficult rock faces in the area – the big walls. Two of these climbers – Warren Harding and Royal Robbins – were destined to become famous.

The pair met in 1955 on the rocks of Tahquitz, a magnificent granite canyon 170 kilometres from Los Angeles, where Robbins risked his life in a fall while aid climbing. Shortly afterwards, Harding and Robbins made a joint attempt on the vertical North-West face of Half Dome, almost 700 metres high, but they were forced to give up after three days. Two years later, in July 1957, Robbins returned to the wall with Jerry Gallwas and Mike Sherrick, and they succeeded in scaling it after a five-day struggle.

In the lower part, a series of particularly difficult cracks were climbed with the aid of specially forged pitons. Then came the crux, a traverse to the right which the leader crossed with a heart-stopping pendulum. Farther up the going got easier, but the hot July sun sapped the energy of the three climbers, and their progress remained slow. At the end of the route, an easy but daunting traverse along a ledge suspended over "the most awesome void in the history of mountaineering" took Robbins, Gallwas and Sherrick to the summit. One of Yosemite's "big walls" had been climbed for the first time.

220 right The big walls of Yosemite Valley are not only compact and smooth but often perfectly vertical, as demonstrated by this photo of American climber Todd Skinner tackling the direct route on the North-West face of Half Dome.

221 bottom left One of the most outstanding protagonists of climbing history in Yosemite Valley was Royal Robbins from California. He made the first ascents of the North-West face of Half Dome, the Salathé Wall and the North America Wall on El Capitan and inaugurated the solo climbing era in Yosemite Valley on the West face of the Leaning Tower in 1963. This photo shows him scaling a typical (awkward) crack.

221 right Nearly all the great routes in Yosemite Valley, that were put up with extensive use of aid climbing, were later free climbed. In this photo, Todd Skinner is scaling a dynamic 5.13 section (between the ninth and tenth grade on the UIAA scale) of the 11th pitch on the West face of Half Dome.

Harding got even a few weeks later. In early July, accompanied by Bill Feuerer and Mike Powell, Warren made a determined assault on the most awesome wall in the Valley, which no other climber had ever dared to attempt. It was the Nose, the southern spur of El Capitan, which offers an obvious but intimidating route in the middle of a particularly smooth, endless wall (over 1000 metres high!). "I'm gonna climb that goddam line!", exclaimed Warren Harding before setting off.

The climbers practically laid siege to the mountain. In the absence of the steel pitons forged by John Salathé and Jerry Gallwas, the trio had difficulty reaching the ledge of Camp One, 100 metres from the base. Then, with a pendulum, they arrived at a crack that was too wide for the pitons and wooden wedges

they had brought with them. To continue climbing, they had to hammer in the metal legs of an old stove they had picked up at a dump in Berkeley. After 7 days and 300 metres of the route, Harding, Feuerer and Powell returned satisfied to the base of the wall.

The head Park Ranger did not look kindly on climbing, and prohibited further attempts during the Yosemite tourist season. In the winter, Powell broke his ankle badly, while Feuerer worked hard to prepare new gear, including a truck for provisions that could be winched up the wall. In the spring they recommenced the ascent, but Powell's ankle prevented him from leading, while Feuerer appeared less and less interested in the climb.

In September 1958, when the ban on climbing in the Park ended, Harding returned to the Nose with new companions. However, their progress was even slower than before. In the end, the rangers presented the climbers with an ultimatum. If they failed to make the summit by Thanksgiving Day, at the end of November, they would not be allowed to make any further attempts. Harding himself was beginning to get heartily sick of the Nose. So at the beginning of the month he made an all-out assault on the wall with Wayne Merry, determined not to be beaten this time.

From the ledge of Camp Five, the highest point reached the previous September, the pair scaled the

great roof that seemed to block the way without too much difficulty, and continued laboriously upwards. On the eleventh day their friends, who believed that Harding and Merry must be too exhausted to continue on their own, let down a rope to help them finish the climb.

However, the leader indignantly refused this help, which would have diminished their achievement, and kept climbing. The weather seemed to be worsening, so he couldn't waste a

minute. After spending a whole night on the stirrups driving the last 26 bolts into the granite, Harding left the stirrups and free climbed to the great summit plateau. The sun was rising from behind Half Dome. The most famous route in Yosemite Valley and the whole of America had been conquered.

Two years later, Harding's friend and rival Royal Robbins made the first repeat of the Nose route in seven days with Chuck Pratt, Tom Frost and Joe Fitschen. The next year, again with Pratt and Frost,

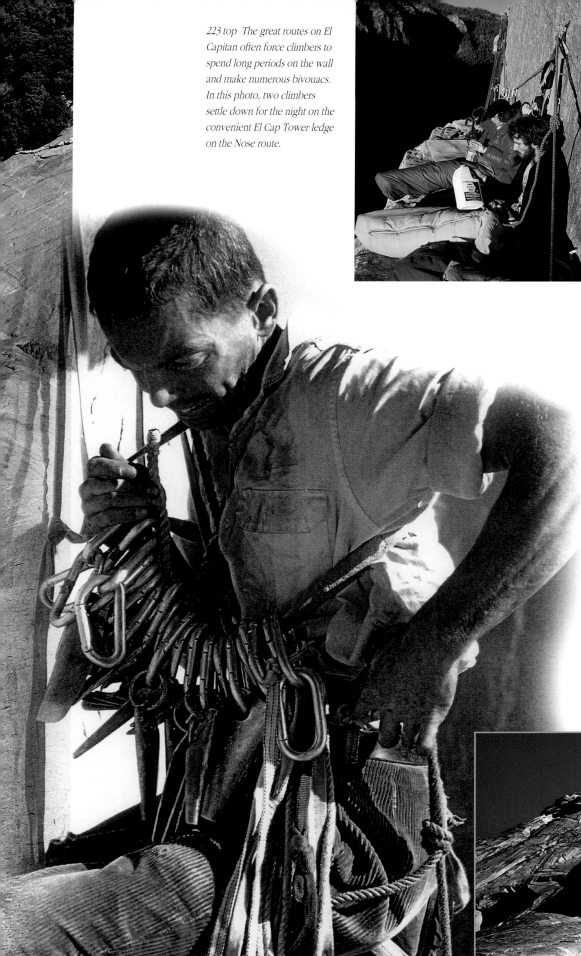

223 top The great routes on El Capitan often force climbers to spend long periods on the wall and make numerous bivouacs. In this photo, two climbers settle down for the night on the convenient El Cap Tower ledge on the Nose route.

commitment was much greater. On the Nose, you climb practically in a straight line, and you can leave fixed ropes or rappel down. Our route, on the other hand, involves long zigzags on the wall, and a rescue in a location of that kind would have been absolutely impossible at that time. When we threw down the fixed ropes a third of the way up, it took all the courage we had."

Taciturn and calm, and famous among his friends for always being in control of the situation, Robbins opened other major new routes on El Capitan. In 1963 he climbed the West Buttress, and three years later, the West face. The most difficult route put up by Robbins on "El Cap" was the North America Wall, a complicated, demanding route interrupted by long pendulums that make it impossible to turn back. When Robbins reached the summit with Yvon Chouinard and the inseparable Frost and Pratt, he was already universally acknowledged to be the best climber in the States.

In 1963, on the West face of the Leaning Tower, Robbins inaugurated the solo climbing era in Yosemite Valley. Despite the storms that slowed his progress, Robbins completed the route in four days, whereas the first ascensionists two years earlier had taken eighteen days. Later, Robbins wrote one of the most interesting definitions of solo climbing.

"The thing about a solo climb is that it's all yours. You are not forced to share it. It's naked. Raw. The fullest expression of the climbing egoist. It's also a way of exploring oneself. A solo climb is like a big mirror. You are looking at yourself all the way up. If it is a way of proving something, it is also a test, a way of finding out what you are made of."

Royal put up a new route on the huge unclimbed wall to the left of the Nose. He climbed this route, which he named the Salathé Wall, in nine days, using only 13 bolts. However, apart from the aid- and free-climbing difficulties involved, this route also posed another problem.

"Harding had the courage and the vision to attempt the Nose. He was exceptional in that way," recounted Robbins in an interview with the author. "But on the Salathé Wall, the psychological

222 left To save time and effort, only the leader actually climbs routes in Yosemite Valley. His companions, who have to haul up the rucksacks and recover the gear, use jumars and étriers to ascend the fixed ropes. This photo shows a section of the Salathé Wall, one of the most famous routes on El Capitan.

222 right When the wall overhangs, it becomes even more difficult to recover bolts, nuts and friends from the cracks, as shown by this photo, taken on the Headwall of the Salathé Wall on El Capitan.

223 bottom left The California climbers of the Fifties and Sixties did not have the benefit of today's gear for their ascents. Tom Frost, shown in this 1961 photo, is using some of the first étriers, but does not yet have a harness.

223 bottom right On the great routes of Yosemite, the members of the team perform set roles. In this photo, taken by the third man as the team ascends the fixed ropes, the leader can be seen climbing while the second man belays him, hanging from the belay pitons.

In the Seventies, a number of widely differing characters climbed in Yosemite Valley. In addition to Robbins, Chouinard, Pratt and the other creators of great routes in the previous decade, Jim Bridwell, a broad-shouldered, incredibly tough Texan, was rapidly becoming the star of the big walls. Having begun his climbing career with great enthusiasm and a hemp rope that was both heavy and dangerous, Bridwell tackled the Nose in 1967, then set off into uncharted terrain.

In 15 years, as well as the first one-day ascent of the Nose recounted earlier, Bridwell put up three new routes on Half Dome and six on El Capitan. Two of the latter, Sea of Dreams and Pacific Ocean Wall, are Yosemite classics of extreme difficulty. On the first, opened in seven days in 1978, no less than five pitches are rated A5, a grade that "guarantees" the leader at least 30 metres of free fall in the event of accident because of the precarious belays.

There are seven A5 pitches on the Pacific Ocean Wall, which Bridwell climbed in 1975 with Bill Westbay and Jay Fiske. In all, the ascent took the three climbers 9 days, and 110 bolts were placed. "All the second ascensionists of my routes on El Capitan have had to drill again," recounted Jim Bridwell to the author in 1978, with legitimate pride.

Two conversations, the first recounted by Bill Westbay and the second by John Cleare, give an insight into the style of personalities like Royal Robbins and Jim Bridwell. "You know," said Bridwell to Westbay as they rested at the base of an A5 pitch, "what makes the Pacific Ocean Wall different from all the other big walls is that there are no cracks where you can hide your ass if you get scared. If sticking your nose in a two-inch wide crack makes you feel safe, that is."

"Back in the States, they say you can tell an aid man by his hands", said Robbins to Tom Patey, who was struggling with a particularly tough pitch on the Old Man of Hoy in Scotland. "Covered in scars?" asked Patey hopefully, his hands dripping with blood. "Not a one," answered Robbins, shaking his head.

Apart from "the Bird," other big-wall specialists like Charlie Porter, Dale Bard and Hugh Burton made a name for themselves in the Seventies and Eighties. These climbers dressed extravagantly, and cannabis and other drugs were common at Camp Four, which served as the climbers' base. The names of the routes, like Mescalito, Excalibur, Cosmos and Tangerine Trip also had a hippy ring to them. However, the difficulties overcome by these climbers were exceptional. "For the first time in climbing history, the Americans are in the lead," commented Chris Jones in *Climbing in North America* as early as 1976.

However, not all climbers in Yosemite concentrated on big walls. In addition to those who specialised in faces that took a week or more (and who were invariably equipped with hammocks, portaledges and gigantic haul bags), there were purists who preferred short but extreme routes on the rock structures closest to the valley bottom or extreme pitches on the boulders which are so plentiful in Yosemite Valley. The most outstanding personalities among them were John Bacher, Ron Kauk and Ray Jardine; and photos of exceptional routes, such as the huge roof of Separate Reality and the smooth slabs of Glacier Point Apron, were published all over the world.

In those years, nearly all the best European climbers put in an appearance in Yosemite Valley. Thanks to them (British climbers Pete Livesey and Ron Fawcett, Frenchman Jean-Claude Droyer, Germans Reinhard Karl and Wolfgang Gullich and Italians Franco Perlotto and Alessandro Gogna), the message of the new style of climbing rapidly spread all over Europe.

225 top One of the most spectacular of the many characteristic pitches on the big walls of Yosemite is Thank God Ledge on the West face of Half Dome. Thanks to this dizzying monolithic ledge, a very compact section of the wall can be climbed around to reach some easier cracks.

225 bottom When there are no ledges, Yosemite's big wall climbers have to bivouac in hammocks or small platforms (portaledges) anchored to pitons, nuts or friends. This 1968 photo shows Warren Harding, who had made the epic first ascent of the Nose a few years earlier.

224 left Among the protagonists of recent climbing history in Yosemite Valley, an important role has been played by Ron Kauk, seen here climbing a 5.11c crack (eighth grade on the UIAA scale) on Astroman.

224-225 Many climbers in Yosemite Valley totally ignore the big walls and concentrate on the short (and often difficult) walls closer to the valley bottom. This 1997 photo shows John Bachar soloing Crack à Go Go.

On the other side of the Atlantic, the long hair and casual look of the California climbers soon caught on, as did the smooth-soled shoes that allowed them to smear the walls, their willingness to undergo continuous technical and gymnastic training, their concentration, and their ability to take free climbing to its very limits.

The gear used by climbers also changed on the granite of Yosemite. After the revolution commenced by John Salathé, special steel pitons were mass-produced by Yvon Chouinard, an excellent climber who soon became a big name in the mountain clothing and equipment business. In addition to the classic spikes and U-shaped pitons used in the Alps, manufacturers developed some slender models like rurps, the size of a razor blade, and bongs, which replaced the old wooden wedges but were much more effective.

In addition to pitons and bolts, American manufacturers developed new shapes and measurements for nuts (blocks of metal that can be inserted into cracks with no need for a hammer, known also as "chocks"), while brilliant climber Ray Jardine invented the first "friends" (spring-loaded camming devices which widen after being inserted into cracks). The gear used by aid climbers came to include copperheads (copper-covered metal cables designed to be hammered into the most insignificant cracks or depressions in the rock) and skyhooks (designed

to hook onto notches or pockets as small as a few millimetres deep), all objects onto which climbers can hook a stirrup to ascend, though with little guarantee that they will hold.

Ever since their sport began, American climbers had been more environment-conscious than their European counterparts, and improvements in nuts and the invention of friends in the early Seventies checked the proliferation of pitons and bolts. The years of bolted routes were followed by the fashion for "clean climbing." Already widely practised on the crags of England, Scotland and Wales, this new ethic, which requires climbers not to deface the rock, reached the big walls of Yosemite in 1973, when Doug Robinson, Dennis Hennek and Galen Rowell repeated the route put up by Royal Robbins on Half Dome

without using a single piton or bolt.

Rowell's account and the photos of this climb, published in the *National Geographic Magazine*, helped spread the clean-climbing message even more quickly. A sentence from that article indicates the new attitude of climbers. "By the end of the Sixties, thousands of climbers had placed and removed tens of thousands of bolts in the Yosemite rocks, turning natural cracks into hideous scars. Of course, it would be possible to prevent damage to cracks by leaving bolts in situ, but this would take much of the adventure out of climbing. Mountaineering is essentially a wilderness activity, and a row of bolts snaking up a rock face takes a lot out of the experience of being part of an unspoilt natural landscape." John Muir, the first to fall in love with Yosemite, would certainly have agreed.

226 top Lost in America has become one of the classic routes on El Capitan, although it was opened more recently than the Nose and the Salathé Wall. This photo shows Randy Leavitt jumaring up a sharply defined crack in the route.

226 bottom left Galen Rowell, one of the best American climbers, became a professional photographer as a result of an article on climbing in Yosemite published by National Geographic in 1973. Here he is shown climbing Half Dome in 1994.

226 bottom right Although climbing on granite is far more tiring than climbing on limestone, many women climb the major routes in Yosemite Valley. This 1994 photo shows Nancy Feagin tackling the direct route on the North-West face of Half Dome.

227 This photo, which has been published all over the world, shows Ron Kauk climbing next to Upper Yosemite Falls. Behind him is a rainbow created by the sun's rays playing on the waterfall.

On the walls of Patagonia

North face of Cerro Torre, 1st February 1959. The loveliest and fiercest mountain in the Patagonian Andes was reluctant to let go of the two men who had reached its summit 24 hours earlier. They were fighting for their lives, with no holds barred. The pair were Cesare Maestri from Trento, the "Spider of the Dolomites" whose ascents on his home mountains we described a few chapters earlier, and Toni Egger, a Tyrolean from Lienz, an equally fast, skilled climber. A few years earlier, just like Maestri, Egger had soloed the Solleder route on Civetta in 4 and a half hours. In 1957, with fellow Austrian Jungmeier, he reached the 6126-metre summit of Jirishanca, the "icy Matterhorn of the Andes," one of the most elegant peaks in the Huayhuash range of the Peruvian Andes.

For the two climbers, the ascent to the summit of the Torre had been a four-day adventure on vertical, compact granite walls often covered with a dangerous layer of unstable snow, whose only advantage was that it enabled them to dig holes where they could bivouac out of the wind. After climbing Colle della Conquista, which separates the Tower from a series of other elegant granite pinnacles, later christened Torre Egger, Punta Herron and Cerro Standhardt, the ascent continued on the north side of the mountain, along snow-covered cracks and slabs that tested the nerve of Maestri and Egger to the limit. This was followed by short vertical walls, an overhang encrusted with scaly ice, and an easier gully.

After one of the many overhangs, Toni found that the summit was close at hand. Cesare took the lead, amid the great ice overhangs that make the silhouette of the Torre so unmistakable. He helped up his companion, and embraced him on the 3128-metre summit. "It wasn't a happy embrace, but fear," he recounted later in his book *Arrampicare è il mio mestiere*. "A hot wind was blowing fiercely from the west, the snow would soon be wet, and avalanches would fall. It was a titanic force, an invincible power, a cataclysm."

It is this wind, which blows directly onto the mountains with incredible force from the perennially rough waters of the Pacific, that makes climbing in Patagonia so demanding and dangerous, and features prominently in all accounts of ascents in those mountains. Despite the storm, however, Egger and Maestri were able to begin their descent. A series of abseils anchored to ice pitons took the two men to the snowhole where they had

made their last bivouac, and they spent the night there again.

The next day they continued abseiling, mainly anchored to bolts placed with difficulty in the granite. They set up their fifth bivouac a little lower than the second. Their food and fuel for their small spirit stove had run out long since. Avalanches thundered continually down the wall, making the long diagonal route that led back to Colle della Conquista interminable and dangerous. Apart from that, the worst seemed to be over at last. Now, the vertical walls of the Torre would protect the two climbers against the strongest gusts of wind.

Evening fell. Maestri wanted to stop and bivouac, and wait for the light of dawn before continuing down the 300 metres of rope they had fixed during the ascent to the glacier where their friend Cesarino Fava was awaiting the return of the victorious team. But Egger insisted on going on. Maestri lowered him for 20-30 metres, but then Egger's luck ran out. "A strange noise, a hissing sound heavier than wind" warned Maestri that an avalanche was coming. Then "a mountain of snow burst out of the fog," and swept Egger down the mountainside.

When it was all over, the end of the severed

rope flapped loose in the wind. At the bottom, the fallen snow had covered much of the surface of the glacier. Cesare Maestri was alone. It took him hours to reach the base of the Torre, and towards the end, bad luck nearly killed him too. The last abseil rope of that nightmare descent came off the anchor, and Cesare fell into a snowdrift which broke his fall and saved his life. Fava only managed to find him, half-buried and suffering from shock, 48 hours later.

So ended one of the most dramatic mountain-eering adventures in Patagonia, where the Andes encounter the icy winds of the South Pacific and the freezing breath of the nearby Antarctic.

Starting in the mid-19th century, small groups of colonists, mainly from Wales, Scandinavia and Scotland, settled in Patagonia and nearby Tierra del Fuego, the lands of pampas and glaciers, fjords and perennially rough seas, grazing sheep and colonies of seals and sea birds.

This was followed by the first geographical surveys, interminable boundary disputes between Argentina and Chile, and finally the arrival of writers like Bruce Chatwin, Luis Sepùlveda and Fernando Coloane, who made this frontier country an irresistible legend for travellers from the rest of the Americas and Europe.

Right from the outset, travellers and climbers realised that the peaks and glaciers of Patagonia could offer the ideal playground for adventure lovers. The first to take up the challenge was Friedrich Reichert (known as Federico to the Argentinians), a chemist from a German-speaking family in Alsace who emigrated to Argentina in 1904 to teach at Buenos Aires University. He had already made some fine ascents in the Alps and the Caucasus, and climbed many peaks in the north Argentinian Andes during his first few years in South America. In 1910 the Argentinian government sent him to Comodoro Rivadavia to study the oil fields,

and he was immediately fascinated by the landscape and solitude of Patagonia.

In the Southern Hemisphere summer of 1913-14, Reichert performed the first of his eight exploratory and climbing expeditions in the mountains and lakes of West Patagonia, with botanist Cristobal Hicken. The pair set off on horseback from the Atlantic coast, took a month to reach Lake Argentino, rowed across it, and continued along the Moreno Glacier to the main divide.

In his later expeditions, Reichert visited the San Martìn Lake region, explored Hielo Patagonico Norte and Hielo Patagonico Sur, and fell in love with two

231 top The expeditions of
Father Alberto Maria De
Agostini, made between 1912
and 1943, made a decisive
contribution to knowledge of
the Patagonian mountains.
This photo, taken by De
Agostini in 1931, shows three
Italians at the foot of the
seracs of Mount Torino. The
snowy waste opposite the
climbers is Altiplano Italia,
which stretches into the heart
of Hielo Patagonico Sur.

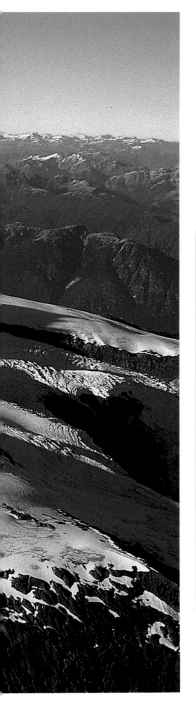

of the most beautiful mountains in the Southern Andes. Despite three expeditions, he failed to reach the summit of one of them, the magnificent ice pyramid of Cerro San Valentìn (which stands at 4058 metres according to the official maps, although its actual height is probably a little lower). His other favourite peak was Mount Tronador (3450 m), situated in the northernmost sector of Patagonia. Reichert's attempts on this summit began in 1919, when he discovered that the first explorers to visit the area had been wrong in considering it a volcano. He eventually reached the summit in 1942, at the age of 66.

A year later, another climber in his sixties brilliantly concluded a long series of ascents and explorations in Patagonia when he reached the 3706-metre summit of Cerro San Lorenzo, another of the most spectacular peaks in the area, with two Argentinian climbers. Alberto Maria De Agostini was a Salesian missionary who had left Italy for Punta Arenas immediately after being ordained in 1909. Right from the start, the Italian priest could only perform his explorations and climbing activities in the spare time left by his missionary work. However, De Agostini's superiors appreciated his observations and travels, and often allowed him to visit the country's mountains and glaciers.

231 centre This photo, taken by Father De Agostini, shows three Italian mountaineers climbing towards camp one on San Lorenzo. The sharp Feruglio Towers, which reach a height of 2140 metres, can be seen in the background.

231 bottom In this photo, taken by Father De Agostini in 1931, Egidio Feruglio and Courmayeur guides Evaristo Croux and Leone Bron can be seen on the Upsala Glacier.

In the summers of 1912/13 and 1913/14, accompanied by geologist Giovanni de Gasperi and Valtournenche guides Abele and Agostino Pession, Father De Agostini visited Tierra del Fuego, where he climbed Mount Olivia and attempted the ascent of Mount Sarmiento. This achievement was followed by 15 years of intensive work in the Salesian missions. Then, in 1928, De Agostini recommenced his expeditions to the Patagonian mountains. In one of them, performed in 1935/36, De Agostini and his guides, Giuseppe Pellissier and Luigi Carrel, visited the Rio Eléctrico Valley and climbed to the summit of Loma Blanca. They camped for a long time at the foot of the boulder which now serves as a stopover for many climbing expeditions heading for Fitz Roy, Aguja Guillaumet and Hielo Continental, and has been known in his honour as Piedra del Fraile (the Friar's Stone) ever since.

For many years, the peaks of Patagonia were too far away and too low to be considered interesting destinations by European climbers. British climber Martin Conway and Valtournenche guides Antoine Maquignaz and Louis Pellissier were the first climbers to visit the southernmost corner of the continent, after summiting Mount Illimani in 1898. From Bolivia they travelled down to Chile and embarked in Valparaiso for Tierra del Fuego, where they made an unsuccessful attempt to climb Mount Sarmiento, a magnificent peak overlooking the fjords, which Conway nicknamed "the Chilean Weisshorn."

The Fitz Roy chain, which includes the loveliest and most difficult granite peaks in Patagonia, was first tackled in 1936/37 by an Italian expedition, whose members were Aldo Bonacossa, Ettore Castiglioni, Leo Dubosc and Titta Gilberti. From Laguna de los Tres, Castiglioni and Gilberti set off along the Piedras Blancas Glacier towards the granite walls of Fitz Roy, which at 3441 metres is the highest and most spectacular peak in the group.

The Tehuelche Indians, who have lived in the area for centuries, have always called the mountain Chaltén, but Charles Darwin, who saw it from far off in 1834, named it after Robert Fitz Roy, Captain of the Beagle, the ship on which he was making his famous voyage round the world.

However, the mountain immediately proved too much for the small Italian expedition. The East face of Fitz Roy, which dominates the Piedras Blancas Glacier, was too high (1200 metres!) and too compact to be climbed with the equipment of the Thirties. The South spur of Fitz Roy was more feasible and shorter, and Gilberti and Castiglioni scaled it by climbing a steep mixed wall, a saddle and a snow-covered ridge. However, although it is

shorter and less steep than the wall, this route also proved impossible. After descending from the saddle, which has been called "Brecha de los Italianos" ever since, the climbers consoled themselves with the less difficult ascent of Cerro Nato, a peak of ice and mixed terrain that stands to the south of Cerro Torre.

It was not until the Fifties, when the compact walls of the Grand Capucin and the Dru were conquered in the Alps, that the big walls of Patagonia were successfully climbed, and it was the protagonists of the best ascents on the walls of Mont Blanc who came onto the Patagonian scene one after another.

In January 1952, René Ferlét led a French expedition to Fitz Roy. Its members were received with full honours by President Juan Domingo Peròn in Buenos Aires, but the expedition was marred by the tragic death of Jacques Poincenot, who drowned while fording Rio Fitz Roy at the point where the bridge that now gives access to the town of El Chaltèn was later built.

While geographer Louis Liboutry drew a topographical map of the area and named the sharp rocky pinnacles surrounding Fitz Roy after French pilots Antoine Saint-Exupéry, Henry Guillaumet and Jean Mermoz who had made the first adventurous flights across the South Atlantic, the others continued towards the highest summit.

Twenty days of continuous bad weather made them wonder whether they should give up the attempt, but then, conditions suddenly improved. On 31st January, Lionel Terray and Guido Magnone made their assault on Fitz Roy. However, the wall soon proved to be a tough nut to crack, even with pitons and ropes far superior to those used by Castiglioni and Gilberti. It took them a whole day to protect the first 120 metres of the route with fixed ropes. The next day the weather was fine, and the two Frenchmen set off confidently towards the summit.

A gruelling climb on slabs, grooves and cracks took up much of the day. At 4 p.m., an awesome overhang seemed to bar the way. Inside a "deep cave," with "a colossal heart-shaped block for its ceiling," Guido and Lionel tasted defeat for a

moment. Magnone, an aid-climbing expert, led the overhang, placing their very few remaining pitons one after another, with great care. When they were just a couple of metres from the end of the difficult section, an over-enthusiastic blow of the hammer sent their next to last piton plunging down the mountainside, and the last one was too wide for the single narrow crack within the leader's reach.

For a moment, all seemed to be lost. Then Terray had an inspiration. Two days earlier, he had used a tiny piton known as the "ace of hearts" to open a can of sardines, and left it at the bottom of his haulbag. A frantic search brought it to light, and Magnone climbed back up with the precious metal spike dangling from a krab. He managed to drive it into the cleft and finally,

232-233 Cerro Fitz Roy (3441 metres) is one of the loveliest and most difficult peaks in South Patagonia. This photo shows the west side of the mountain, first climbed in

1965 by Argentinians José Luis Fonrouge and Carlos Comesana. On the right of Fitz Roy stand the granite towers of Aguja Poincenot and Aguja Saint-Exupéry.

233 bottom The west side of Fitz Roy, seen here from Laguna de Los Tres, is the most spectacular and popular on the mountain. Cloud hides much of the route followed by the first

ascensionists, the 1952 French expedition. The East Pillar, North-East Dihedral and North-North-East Pillar, soloed in 1979 by Renato Casarotto from Vicenza, can be seen clearly farther to the right.

standing on the stirrup, he reached a good hold and hauled himself up onto the summit ridge of Fitz Roy. They'd made it.

Although the westerly wind was becoming stronger every minute, Terray, the only one of the pair who had brought crampons, kept leading along a 40-degree snow slope. Magnone, following, did the best he could with the aid of a hammer, the few outcrops of rock, and the rope which Terray held taut. At the end of the slope, a "very wide, very safe" ridge took the pair to the 3441-metre summit. After a long, emotional embrace, the two men left a small krab in a cleft between two boulders, and began the difficult descent back to *Brecha de los Italianos*, the glacier, the Rio Blanco valley and home.

neighbouring Cerro Adela Nord, which they named Colle della Speranza. Argentinians Folco Doro Altan and René Eggmann waited for the two Italians at the end of the fixed ropes. However, an unpleasant surprise awaited Mauri and Bonatti on the exposed snow ridge of the pass. A tall vertical wall, invisible from below, barred the way to the summit.

"We immediately realised that however hard we tried, we would never reach the summit in our present condition," recounted Walter Bonatti in *Le mie montagne*, one of the most frequently read climbing books of all time. Toughness, anger and determination led the pair to climb for another hundred metres or so on vertical and overhanging ice. Then, after fixing their last rope to a piton, Bonatti and Mauri rapidly abseiled down to the saddle and the companions who had been waiting for them since before dawn.

They had been defeated, but expected to return the next year. In the meantime, so as not to leave empty-handed, the four decided to attempt the ascent of Cerro

234 top left The 1958 expedition from Trento was the first to attempt the east side of Cerro Torre. This photo shows Catullo Detassis, Marino Stenico and Cesare Maestri on the flattish surface of the Torre glacier, in sight of the summit and its main outriders.

234 top right Maestri at the foot of Cerro Torre in 1958. The battle with the "stone scream" played an important part in the Italian climber's life for 12 years.

234 bottom In addition to rock and ice peaks, the beauty of the Patagonian mountains is associated with the glacial wastes of Hielo Patagonico, which offer some crossings that are not technically difficult but are demanding because of the climate and the distances to be covered.

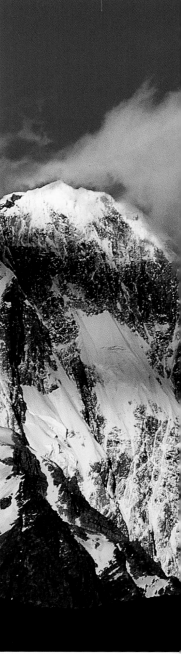

After the conquest of Fitz Roy, Cerro Torre still remained to be climbed. In early 1958, all the best Italian climbers of the day seemed to have made a rendezvous at its foot. Walter Bonatti, the hero of Mont Blanc, arrived with the inseparable Carlo Mauri and a group of Argentinian climbers. Cesare Maestri, the "Spider of the Dolomites", was a member of the expedition from Trento led by Bruno Detassis, which also included Cesarino Fava, Catullo Detassis, Luciano Eccher and Marino Stenico.

However, the two groups were soon at loggerheads. Maestri and party climbed Cerro Grande, but gave up the idea of attempting the Torre. Bonatti and Mauri crossed Paso del Viento, continued onto Hielo Continental and made their assault on the remote West face of the mountain after a two-week struggle.

Their surroundings were exceptionally severe and the rock wall was totally exposed to the elements, but the skills of the two Italian climbers enabled them to climb to the snow-covered saddle that separates the Torre from the

Mariano Moreno, the attractive 3554-metre ice peak separated from the slopes of Cerro Torre by Hielo Continental. Though not difficult from the technical standpoint, the ascent proved to be an extraordinary feat in terms of the stamina required. The crossing of the glacier took the climbers the whole night of 3rd February, and the ascent to the summit, 2000 metres above the Hielo, took Bonatti, Mauri, Altan and Eggmann another seven hours. Then another interminable night's walk (described by Bonatti as "nightmarish," "gruelling" and "painful") took the climbers back to their tents after a 70-kilometre hike lasting 30 hours.

Before setting off back home, the two Italians also made the first ascent of Cerro Adela, a magnificent 2960-metre ice peak. The crossing by ridge of the entire Cordón Adela, which includes Cerro Doblado, Cerro Nato and Cerro Grande, completed a very successful day.

234-235 There is no longer any need to be a trekker or mountaineer to watch the amazing sight of dawn breaking on the walls of Cerro Torre and the nearby peaks. Photos like this one can be taken nowadays from the entrance to the El Chaltèn tourist centre, built in the late Seventies at the confluence of Rio Fitz Roy and Rio de Las Vueltas. In the Fifties and Sixties, climbers could only reach the area on horseback, crossing some difficult, dangerous fords.

235 top When crossing Hielo Patagonico, climbers have to use a system of progression similar to that employed by expeditions to the Poles. They normally use skis (or sometimes snowshoes), while their loads are pulled on sledges.

Despite his promise, Walter Bonatti never went back to Colle della Speranza, and the wild west side of the Torre was left to the climbers from Lombardy. In 1970, Carlo Mauro took part in an expedition that halted just 250 metres from the summit. Four years later, four more "Spiders" from Lecco (Casimiro Ferrari, Mario Conti, Pino Negri and Daniele Chiappa) managed to complete this ascent, which comprises no less than 57 pitches. In the meantime, the 3128-metre summit had been reached from the pampas side by the team of Maestri and Egger. However, bitter controversy soon surrounded that ascent.

the Torre. Then, as mentioned earlier, Carlo Mauri's second expedition was forced to turn back too. Doubts gradually began to be aired. How could Egger and Maestri possibly have made it to the summit with their meagre resources? Had they really climbed the Torre?

Such doubts have rarely been expressed in climbing history. Of course, the team's camera had been buried with the unfortunate Toni Egger, and Maestri, used to fast solo climbs, was not forthcoming with much technical detail about the route they followed. However, if lack of photos and details are sufficient to cast doubt on an ascent, many other

In the Southern Hemisphere summer of 1967/68, a small British expedition consisting of Mick Burke, Pete Crew, Martin Boysen and Dougal Haston tried to repeat the ascent of Cerro Torre. Accompanied by Argentinian José Luis Fonrouge, the four reached Colle della Conquista, left the ice overhangs of the North face on their right, and climbed towards the summit along the compact, vertical East face of the Torre, with long aid sections of extreme difficulty. After 35 days' continuous bad weather, a colossal avalanche buried much of their gear, forcing them to give up the ascent.

The next year, a Japanese expedition and a Spanish team were also defeated by the east side of

mountaineering achievements could easily be challenged. What made the Torre different was the fact that it had defeated the best British climbers of the day, and the national pride of the British, who in many respects were leading the international climbing field at the time, caused them to stir up trouble.

After the doubts expressed by the team from Lombardy, Ken Wilson, editor of the magazine *Mountain*, also challenged the 1959 ascent. His example was followed by Leo Dickinson, one of the most famous mountain film directors, who devoted an entire film, *The Cerro Torre Enigma*, to the question of whether the magnificent obelisk had

really been climbed. However, the British had overlooked one detail.

The man whose achievement and honour had been publicly called into question was famous not only for his exceptional ascents, but also for his angry outbursts.

"Signor Maestri, may I ask whether you really did climb the Torre?", enquired a journalist from an Italian weekly in the spring of 1970. His question triggered a chain reaction. Maestri was first upset, then furious, and eventually decided to return to the Torre to prove that "there are no impossible mountains, only men incapable of climbing them."

236-237 The granite massif of Cuernos del Paine, well known to visitors to the Paine Towers National Park in Chile, culminates at a height of 2100 metres, concealing from the view of those looking at it from the south the higher and more spectacular Paine Towers, on which the first difficult climbing routes in Chilean Patagonia were inaugurated.

236 bottom In January 1963, 18 months after the first ascent of the Central Freney Pillar, the British team formed by Chris Bonington and Don Whillans made the first ascent of the Central Paine Tower, covering a route involving difficulties rated at sixth grade and A3. This photo shows the two climbers at the base of the wall after the ascent (Whillans is on the left, wearing a hat).

For his return to Patagonia, Cesare Maestri chose the most difficult route and the hardest season, aiming to be as provocative as possible. Instead of the North face he had climbed with Egger ("one of the least demanding ascents in my climbing career – any climber who doesn't give a damn about his life could have done it"), he attempted the vertical East face, which had rebuffed the British, in the depths of the harsh winter of the Southern Hemisphere. Above all, he hauled an Atlas Copco compressor up the wall to place the inevitable bolts.

In a month and a half, Maestri, Carlo Claus, Ezio Alimonta, Renato Valentini and Pietro Vidi climbed to within 600 metres of the summit in a battle which, despite the equipment used, was rendered epic by frostbite, storms and lack of food. On 9th July, fuel for the stoves ran out, forcing the climbers to turn back. However, in mid-November, Maestri was back in action on the Torre with Claus and Alimonta and two different team members, Claudio Baldessari and Daniele Angeli. The days were long, the weather was pretty good, and Maestri

was fiercely determined to succeed. In less than a week, the first rope arrived at the highest point reached in the July expedition. At dawn on 2nd December, the leader left the rock and began to climb the tongues of ice at the foot of the unmistakable mushroom-shaped summit. In the early afternoon, Maestri, Alimonta and Claus embraced on the small ice shelf of the summit. During the descent, Maestri gave way to uncontrollable anger, cut the fixed ropes and smashed the bolts with his hammer. Only the compressor, deprived of fuel and starter, still hangs from the face, bearing witness to the victory of the men from Trento. But the controversy was still not over. After the doubts expressed about the 1959 ascent, the editorial staff of *Mountain* considered the 1970 ascent "invalid" because of the equipment used. After the ascent by the Lecco team led by Casimiro Ferrari in 1974, the magazine's headline read "Cerro Torre Climbed." Five years later, Jim Bridwell, one of the stars of American mountaineering, repeated the "compressor" route with Steve Brewer. The distance between the last

237 top left This photo of Jim Bridwell on Cerro Torre demonstrates one of the most serious problems facing climbers in Patagonia: the continual alternation of rock and ice pitches forces them to tackle even some difficult granite climbing pitches while wearing crampons.

237 top right Renato Casarotto from Vicenza, known for his numerous solo ascents in the Alps, the Cordillera Blanca and the Karakorum, put up his most elegant route on the North-North-East Pillar of Fitz

Roy in eight days in 1979. In this photo, Casarotto is in the ice cave used as base camp, preparing to tackle the mountain.

237 bottom American climber Jim Bridwell, known for the great routes he put up on the walls of Yosemite Valley, made the first repeat of the Cerro Torre "compressor route," opened nine years earlier by Cesare Maestri and party, with fellow-American Steve Brewer. This photo shows Jim Bridwell in the Sixties, climbing an aid pitch on the Torre.

bolts and the ice led him to express further doubts, although it changes every year. But now, climbing in Patagonia could make a fresh start. As so often happens, the future had already begun.

In 1962, well away from controversy and the limelight, Irishman Frank Cochrane and Englishman Don Whillans climbed Aguja Poincenot, the most elegant of the peaks surrounding Fitz Roy. The next year, Chris Bonington and Don Whillans climbed the Central Torre of Mount Paine, while an Italian expedition consisting of Armando Aste, Vasco Taldo, Josve Aiazzi, Carlo Casati and Nando Nusdeo scaled the less difficult but higher South Torre.

In 1965, Argentinians Carlos Comesana and José Luis Fonrouge conquered the *Supercanaleta*, an ice gully 1700 metres long that cuts through the north-western side of Fitz Roy. Three years later, Californians Yvon Chouinard, Dick Dorworth, Chris Jones, Lito Tejada-Flores and Douglas Tompkins put up a magnificent route on rock to the summit, to the left of the cracks climbed by Guido Magnone and Lionel Terray.

In the Seventies, more and more climbers visited Patagonia, new routes multiplied, and the wild, elegant pinnacles surrounding the Torre and Fitz Roy were climbed one after another. Of the many ascents performed in those years, the solo climb of the sharp North-North-East pillar of Fitz Roy which took Italian Renato Casarotto eight days in January 1979 stands out for difficulty, elegance and commitment.

However, mountaineers and mountaineering enthusiasts should not overlook the ascent of the most elegant outrider of Cerro Torre, which was climbed on 22nd February 1976 by John Bragg, John Donini and Jay Wilson. Although it was climbed by an American team, the peak was named Torre Egger in honour of the climber from Lienz killed on Cerro Torre in 1961. That day, comradeship between climbers finally put an end to the controversy. In the Eighties and Nineties, the towers of Patagonia emerged from the mists of legend to become a mandatory destination for climbers from all over the world. Roads and bridges enabled them to reach the trails leading to Cerro Torre, the Paine Towers and Fitz Roy without the dangerous adventures and river crossings of the past. The town of El Chaltén appears out of nowhere in the Rio de las Vueltas plain, forming an excellent base for climbers just back from the mountain blizzards. Many of the "last problems" in Patagonia have been solved in the past 20 years. Swiss climber Marco Pedrini soloed Cerro Torre and an Italian team made the first winter ascent in 1985. Two difficult routes were opened on the South face of the mountain in 1988 and 1995. The first was put up by Slovenians Janez Jeglic and Silvo Karo in summer, and the second by Italians Ermanno Salvaterra, Piergiorgio Vidi and Roberto Manni in winter.

The first winter ascent of Fitz Roy, made in 1986 by Sebastiàn de la Cruz, Gabriel Ruiz and Eduardo Brenner,

238 top The west sides of Mount Fitz Roy (on the left in the photo), Aguja Poincenot and Aguja Saint-Exupéry act as the backdrop to a climber on the snow slopes leading to the rocks of Cerro Torre. The Torre Glacier can be seen on the left.

238 centre The East Face of the Central Paine Tower is one of the most vertical and difficult in Chilean Patagonia. It was first climbed in 1974 by South Africans Michael Scott and Richard Smithers, and a direct route was put up 12 years later by Maurizio Giarolli, Elio Orlandi and Ermanno Salvaterra from Trento.

marked the revival of climbing in Argentina. Five years later, the East Pillar was climbed by Swiss mountaineer Kaspar Ochsner and Czech Michal Pitelka. Some excellent routes were also put up in the same period on the Paine Towers (the ascent of the South face of the Central Tower by Americans Alan Kearney and Bobby Knight in 1982) and hitherto unknown peaks like Cerro Piergiorgio, whose vertical North-West face dominates the Marconi glacier between Fitz Roy and the Hielo Continental. However climbers are still attracted by the Torre. After the epic feat performed by Maestri, another climber from Trento was bewitched by the "Stone Scream." Between 1985 and 1999, Ermanno Salvaterra summited the most famous peak in Patagonia 15 times, and he hasn't stopped yet.

238 bottom The South Spur of
Fitz Roy, partly used by the
1952 French expedition, was
climbed in 1984 by
Argentinians Alberto
Bendinger, Eduardo Brenner,
Marcos Coach and Pedro
Friedrich. This photo shows
American climber Mike Graber
approaching the spur in 1985.
Graber made the first repeat of
the Argentinians' route with
Galen Rowell and David
Wilson.

238-239 In this photo, taken
by Swiss climber Robert
Bösch on the ordinary route
on Fitz Roy, the silhouette
of his climbing companion
can be seen against the wide
snow-covered saddle that
leads to the base of the
perpendicular granite
rocks of the Patagonian
giant. The arrival of a front,
a fairly common event in
this area, threatened the
expedition.

239 bottom Slovenian
climber Frances Knez is
a frequent visitor to
Patagonia, where he
made the first ascents
of the North-East Dihedral
of Fitz Roy and the
dangerous East face of Cerro
Torre, among others. Here,
he is shown jumaring in a
typical Patagonian blizzard.

The frozen mountains of the North

North side of Ben Nevis, a freezing cold morning in February 1957. As the bright winter sunshine illuminated the hollow of Allt'a Mhuillin, three men opened a passage through a metre of fresh snow towards the menacing North face of the highest mountain in the British Isles. They had spent the night in the Charles Inglis Clark Hut, a small refuge hut in the wildest part of the range.

Their goal was a vertical ice gully which had been attempted by top climbers for years. In climbing circles, the route already had a name: Zero Gully. "Whoever christened it a gully was an optimist," wrote Tom Patey, one of the members of the team, in the *Scottish Mountaineering Club Journal.* "For 400

feet it is no more than a vertical groove bulging with overhangs." Patey, who shot to fame in international climbing circles in 1956 with the Alpine-style ascent of Muztagh Tower, a magnificent peak in the Pakistani Karakorum, led the first pitch on Zero Gully, "a shallow trough in the centre of the 85-degree wall." He stemmed the pitch, where there was no chance of a belay: "the rope hung absolutely free from my waist to the two at the bottom."

In the second pitch, the vertical wall gave way to an awesome overhang, which Patey scaled with a delicate aid climb on ice pitons. This was followed by a diagonal traverse to the right along

"a narrow strip of high-angled snow between two overhangs," which offered the three climbers "some quite superb exposure" and led to an easier slope.

Then "a gigantic ice-patch soaring up vertically for 100 feet seemed to seal off all access to the upper gully." Graeme Nicol, Patey's regular climbing companion, caught up with his friend at the base of the step, where the pair fixed up a sound belay using two ice-axes and three ice pitons.

Next, Hamish MacInnes, the best known Scottish climber of all time, came into action. Although he was only 26, this top-class adventurer, born and bred in the Highlands, had already made

an illicit attempt on Everest with John Cunningham a few weeks after the ascent by Hillary and Tenzing, and numerous first ascents on the rock walls and ice gullies of the Highlands.

MacInnes had also made numerous attempts on Zero Gully. The highest point he had reached was the base of the huge ice-patch. After a few metres of rapid climbing, the difficulty of the wall forced him to slow down, while Patey and Nicol at the belay station sang in his honour "Oh, didn't he ramble," the classic New Orleans funeral march.

But the climber from Glencoe was not to be intimidated by the macabre humour of his companions or the difficulty of the route. With the aid of the "Message," the heavy hammer he had invented himself, MacInnes slowly climbed on, cutting steps in the ice which Patey described as "worthy of a Yeti." After a two-hour battle, he called down to the others to climb when ready.

Then the gradient eased off, and the route became much easier. Hamish announced that he would rather climb as last man from then on. "It's the interesting stuff that gets me, I'm afraid. I'm not much of a hand at step bashing," he commented laconically. A simul-climb, interrupted here and there by short rocky steps where a belay was required, took the three men to the summit plateau of Ben Nevis, which was bathed in warm sunlight.

"It was one of those rare days on Ben Nevis. Everyone satisfied, perfect climbing conditions and an unlimited vista as far as Sutherland and the Western Isles," concluded Tom Patey's account. Despite his understatement, the first ascent of Zero Gully was one of the most important achievements in the history of Scottish mountaineering.

Scotland, the land of moors and castles, Celtic sagas and bagpipes, windswept rocks and fjords, had long fascinated travellers from central and southern Europe. Described by Sir Walter Scott as the "land of mountains and tides," it attracts hordes of tourists from all over the world every summer.

For visiting climbers, however, the peak season in Scotland is winter, when the Atlantic fronts that bring copious amounts of rain and

snow to the Highlands alternate with brief thaws and with the icy wind that blows straight in from the Arctic, covering the mountains with a shiny shield of ice.

In summer, the rock faces of Scotland offer some attractive, difficult climbs, but Ben Nevis, which is only 1343 metres high, is little more than a hill to those used to the Alps. Despite the frequency and force of the wind and storms, all the major peaks can be reached by following footpaths that present no particular difficulty.

In winter, however, all 543 "Munros," the Scottish peaks over 3000 feet (roughly 900 metres), offer some spectacular, wild scenery in which mountaineers feel perfectly at home. On the highest and steepest ranges (Ben Nevis and the Cairngorms, the peaks of Lochnagar and the Cuillins of Skye, Creagh Meaghaidh and the peaks that overlook the famous Glencoe Valley) the routes are usually very serious, and the most difficult are a tough testing ground for ice climbing.

Continental climbers manifested a curious lack of interest in British mountains for over a century. Although the exploits of the British on the Matterhorn, the Brenva Spur and the Grépon were universally acclaimed, their home mountains were long snubbed by mountaineers from the rest of Europe.

Yet the damp, dark rocks of Cornwall and Wales have served as a training ground for generations of top-class climbers, and the ice of the Highlands, as well as training mountaineers who climb all over the world, has made an important contribution to the development of gear and progression techniques which are now used worldwide.

"Icemanship can only be acquired through a long apprenticeship, by tramping many a weary mile helplessly tied to the tail of a guide. But one principal charm of hill-climbing lies in the fact that it may be picked up by self-directed practice and does not demand the same preliminary subjection," as Walter P. Haskett-Smith wrote in the introduction to his guide Climbing in the British Isles, published in 1894.

Known for his brilliant ascents on rock (including the first ascent of Napes' Needle in 1886), Haskett-Smith published the volume devoted to England, Wales and Ireland, but never completed the second part of the work devoted to Scotland. However, his lighthearted, sportsmanlike tone is perfectly in tune with the first winter ascents in the Highlands, performed by Norman Collie and party starting in 1890.

Easter day 1892, when the team composed of Collie, Joseph Collier and Godfrey Solly climbed Buachaille Etive Mor in Glencoe followed by the long, spectacular Tower Ridge of Ben Nevis, is considered by historians as the date when winter climbing in Scotland was born.

Norman Collie, who climbed with Albert F. Mummery on Mont Blanc and in the tragic expedition to Nanga Parbat, was a leading personality in exploratory mountaineering, and also made his mark in the Lofoten Islands and the Caucasus. He shared this

latter interest with Harold Raeburn, the other great climber in the early years of ice climbing in the Highlands.

Raeburn, famous for the first guideless ascents of the East face of Monte Rosa, the Viereselgrat, Dent Blanche and the Z'mutt ridge leading to the Matterhorn (while Collie made the first guideless ascent of the Brenva Spur), opened a dozen new routes on Ben Nevis in winter and summer. He made the first ascent of the difficult Observatory Ridge in the summer of 1901, and the first winter ascent of that route 19 years later.

On the gullies and icy ridges of the Highlands, Raeburn, a climber who deserves to be better known, often tackled almost vertical pitches, much tougher than those being climbed in the Alps at the same period. In 1898 he scaled the gully now named after him on the walls of Lochnagar, which form the backdrop to the Royal residence of Balmoral, scaling

some vertical pitches by hauling himself up with his long ice-axe placed in a way not unlike the present-day ice-axe traction technique.

In his book *Mountaineering Art*, published before he set off for Tibet with the first exploratory expedition to Mount Everest, he actually suggested using "a light tomahawk-like hatchet" in the most difficult pitches on ice instead of the cumbersome ice-axes of the period. However, this brilliant intuition was only put into practice half a century later.

In the years between the two World Wars, Bill Murray, Graham MacPhee, Bill MacKenzie and other climbers continued the systematic exploration of the Scottish mountains in winter, putting up some demanding routes like Glovers' Chimney on Ben Nevis, Deep Cut Chimney on Stob Coire nam Beith, Crowberry Gully (now a top-level classic) and Garrick Shelf on Buachaille Etive Mor, the most attractive peak overlooking Glencoe Valley.

243 bottom left This picture shows a climber of the past tacking Crowberry Ridge on Buachaille Etive Mor. This rock climb, one of the classic routes in Glencoe and the whole of the Highlands, was first performed in 1900 by a team consisting of A.P. Abraham, G.D. Abraham, E.A. Baker and J.W. Puttrell.

243 bottom right The impressive Liathach chain, which overlooks Loch Torridon, is widely considered to be the most spectacular mountain range in the Scottish Highlands. The slender, exposed summit ridge provides a route suitable for sure-footed hikers in summer, and becomes a spectacular snow climbing route in winter.

242 left The unmistakable pointed silhouette of Buachaille Etive Mor surveys the central part of the Glencoe Valley. The mountain was first climbed from this side in 1898, when G. Gibbs scaled Curved Ridge. However, the classic winter route is the deep Crowberry Gully, clearly visible in this photo, which was first climbed in 1936.

242-243 Bidean nam Bian (1148 metres), on the south side of the Glencoe Valley, is one of the Scottish peaks most popular with mountaineers. The most interesting routes on rock, snow and mixed terrain have been put up on the walls of Stob Coire nan Lochan, Stob Coire nan Beth and Aonach Dubh.

245 bottom left *Climbers who do not need to call back at the Charles Inglis Clark Hut on their way down can follow the easy slopes of the ordinary summer route, climbed by thousands of hikers in good weather. The two climbers shown in this photo are in sight of Lochan Meall an t'Suidhe, the largest mountain lake in the range.*

244 left Climbers began to tackle vertical walls of ice and mixed terrain in the Scottish Highlands as early as the Sixties, well before the introduction of the Terrordactyl and other ice-axe traction gear among British climbers.

244 bottom right The Cairngorms range is one of the most popular with climbers in the Highlands, and offers some very interesting winter routes. This 1964 photo shows Tom Patey scaling the Y Gully on Coire an Lochan.

244-245 Cloud, storms and blizzards can cause serious complications even on the easy route (a mere footpath in summer) which leads from Fort William to the Charles Inglis Clark Hut, a small but cosy refuge hut at the foot of the North Buttress of Ben Nevis.

The most important and difficult routes on Ben Nevis and in the Cairngorms were climbed in the Fifties, thanks to the class and courage of a new generation of mountaineers. The leading names among the Scottish climbers of the period (who were divided by the fierce rivalry between Aberdeen, Edinburgh and Glasgow) were Hamish MacInnes, John Cunningham, Tom Patey, Robin Smith and Dougal Haston. The best Sassenach climbers, such as Chris Bonington, Ian Clough and Don Whillans, often climbed those ice-encrusted walls too.

As we recounted at the beginning of this chapter, Hamish MacInnes, Tom Patey and Graeme Nicol conquered Zero Gully in 1957. The best

crossing of the Cuillins on the Isle of Skye, which he finally completed in February 1965 with Hamish MacInnes, Davie Crabb and Brian Robertson.

"There are many harder and more exacting routes, and many more still to be explored, yet I feel confident that the Winter Traverse of the Main Ridge will always retain its place as the greatest single adventure in British mountaineering," commented Patey.

The ascents mentioned so far are made all the more impressive by the fact that they were performed with traditional equipment: the ice-axes used were around a metre long, and had a straight pick unable to gain any purchase on the ice, while the crampons were the 12-point type made in

Courmayeur and Chamonix, commonly used on ice routes in the Alps.

The first to invent gear better suited to Scottish conditions was Hamish MacInnes, who produced one prototype ice-axe after another at the well-equipped workshop in his Glencoe home. Climbers in the Highlands operate on particularly steep ground, which makes shorter gear more useful.

A disaster on Ben Nevis, when three climbers were found dead, still grasping the broken-off wooden handles of their ice-axes, persuaded MacInnes to make all-metal gear. The idea of hammers and ice-axes with an inclined, serrated pick, which could be used to aid progression not only on ice but also on the frozen turf and soil so often found on Scottish walls, gradually gained ground.

The "Message," the first hammer designed and made by MacInnes, was used in Zero Gully in February 1957. American Yvon Chouinard, who had made some great ascents in Yosemite and invented specific gear for the big walls of America, visited the Highlands several times in the Sixties. His collaboration with MacInnes led to the design of modern ice climbing gear. In California, Chouinard made the first rigid crampons, which supported the foot better when climbing on vertical ice.

In his Glencoe workshop, Hamish MacInnes designed the *Terrordactyl*, a very short hammer-cum-ice-axe with the pick inclined at a 45-degree angle. Though difficult to use without bruising the knuckles, this fearful-looking gadget allowed frontal progression on almost vertical ice and mixed slopes, thus enabling the Scottish climbers of the Seventies to climb open walls and scale even the most difficult summer routes under winter conditions.

climbers then turned their attention to the nearby Point Five Gully, on which attempts were made by Cunningham, MacInnes and famous Welsh climber Joe Brown, who fell from the second pitch of the route and landed on the snowfield at the start, practically unscathed.

In January 1959, Point Five was finally scaled by an English team consisting of Ian Clough, Alexander, Pipes and Shaw after a siege lasting several days. The flag of Scottish mountaineering was flown the next weekend by Robin Smith and R.K. Holt, who climbed the awesome Orion Face of Ben Nevis, soon nicknamed "the Scottish Nordwand."

A year later, together with Jimmy Marshall, Smith put up half a dozen difficult routes on the walls of Ben Nevis in a single winter. The most difficult of all is the Direct Route on the open wall, which starts not far from Zero Gully. Their campaign involved "cleaning up all the outstanding problems on the Ben," as Jimmy Marshall somewhat immodestly wrote. "We included Point Five as a gesture – it's a fine climb, but a wee bit old-fashioned now."

Tom Patey, a particularly creative climber (by profession a GP in Ullapool), performed girdle traverses on the walls of Ben Nevis and Creagh Meaghaidh. He also organised the first winter

245 bottom right This photo, taken from the Charles Inglis Clark Hut, shows a classic winter view of the north-east side of Ben Nevis. This side of the mountain, now

crossed by dozens of routes, was first climbed in winter in 1892, when Norman Collie, Joseph Collier and Godfrey Solly made the first ascent of Tower Ridge.

The frozen mountains of the North

246-247 Of the nearly 200 routes put up on Ben Nevis, the North-East Buttress and the other great ridges (Tower Ridge and Observatory Ridge) are the only ones to offer an elegant, exposed climb on a snow and ice ridge that recalls the great summer routes on Mont Blanc and in the Pennine Alps because of the atmosphere and the difficulty involved. The North-East Buttress is one of the most spectacular and panoramic winter routes on Ben Nevis. Climbed for the first time in summer 1892 (the date of the first winter ascent is unknown), this 400-metre-long ridge offers an outstanding view of Orion Face, Zero Gully and the rest of the north-east side of the mountain.

On routes put up by earlier generations, the new equipment allowed climbers to proceed faster and much more safely than before. This was demonstrated by Ian Nicholson, a young instructor from the Glencoe climbing school, who climbed Zero and Point Five Gullies in a single morning in winter 1972/73. Neither of the two routes took him more than an hour.

In the same period, as a result of the outstanding ascents made by British teams in the Alps, the best continental climbers finally began to discover and visit the Highlands. Just like the great granite walls of Yosemite Valley, the ice-encrusted faces of Ben Nevis and Glencoe began to be visited by many of the best teams from the Western Alps, as if on a pilgrimage.

As a result of their experience amid the blizzards and frozen turf slabs of Ben Nevis, climbers like Jean-Marc Boivin, Patrick Gabarrou, Walter Cecchinel and Giancarlo Grassi revolutionised the ice climbing

247 top One of the most important characteristics of winter climbing in the Highlands is the precarious nature of the belays. In places where there are no cracks for driving in anchors, climbers have to use ice pitons, an ice-axe driven into the snow, or deadmen, a type of "snow anchor" invented in the Scottish mountains.

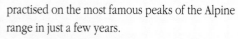

practised on the most famous peaks of the Alpine range in just a few years.

Then, as always happens, the newcomers' interest in the Highlands abated somewhat. Once accepted in the Alps, frontal progression was adapted to a different terrain (especially icefalls), and became routine practice all over the world.

Overseas visitors continue to crowd the streets of Fort William and the winter routes of Buachaille Etive Mor, Creagh Meaghaidh and Ben Nevis, but from the technical standpoint, the breakthrough has now been made. For the new generation of Scottish climbers, the challenges are speed, elegance and direct progression on increasingly dangerous ground, while the blizzards that blow in from the Arctic are as sudden and fierce as ever.

247 bottom This photo, taken on one of the steepest pitches on the North-East Buttress of Ben Nevis, shows the position used in modern ice climbing. The ice axes are driven into the slope one at a time. The legs are spread fairly wide apart so that climbers can keep their balance without difficulty.

Beyond the sixth grade

In 1968, an article in the *Rivista Mensile* published by Club Alpino Italiano caused a sensation in Italian climbing circles. It was called *L'assassinio dell'impossibile* (The Murder of the Impossible), and it was written by Reinhold Messner, a young climber from the Italian South Tyrol who had performed numerous great ascents all over the Dolomites.

"Once, climbing history was written on rock with the symbolic pen of boldness; today it's written with bolts. Times change, and ideas and values change with them. Secure belays have taken the place of inner security, and the skills of a team are evaluated on the basis of the number of bivouacs, while those who still free climb are dismissed as reckless," wrote Messner.

"Climbers are doing more and more drilling and less and less climbing. The impossible has been routed; the dragon has been poisoned, and the hero Siegfried is unemployed. Everyone works on the wall, bending it with iron to match their skills. Get smart, cheat the mountain by all possible means if you want to be a success. But I care about the dead dragon; we've got to do something before the impossible is buried entirely. Let's save the dragon. And in the future, let's continue along the route indicated by the men of the past; I'm convinced it's still the right one!"

Messner's ideas, now shared by thousands of climbers, were received with biting criticism at the time of their publication. Among the few to understand their value was Claudio Barbier, who called a fifth-grade route that he put up the next summer on Lagazuoi Nord *Via del Drago* (Dragon Route). Now, however, the free-climbing dragon was about to rise from its own ashes. This was clearly demonstrated by the achievements of Messner himself.

In 1965, this young man from Val di Funes, who was destined to become more famous than any other climber in history, scaled the North-West Pillar of Odla di Funes with his brother Gunther, Paul Kantioler and Heindl Messner. This ascent was followed by other new routes. In addition, the methodical Reinhold climbed the greatest routes put up by earlier climbers, one after another.

Among the destinations reached on this historical pilgrimage were the South face of Cima Scotoni, the North face of Pelmo, Via dell'Ideale on Marmolada d'Ombretta, the Aste route on Punta Civetta and the South-East face of Burèl. Between February and March 1967, Messner made the first winter ascents of the Solleder route on Furchetta and the North edge of Agnèr.

Messner's greatest free-climbing achievement came in July 1968 when, again with the inseparable Gunther,

he scaled Pilastro di Mezzo on Sass dla Crusc in the Conturìnes group. On the morning of the second day, Reinhold tackled "a smooth slab with no cracks and very few holds," suspended over a great overhang. After half an hour of fruitless attempts, he was seriously considering giving up. Then he made a last desperate attempt, clawed at a microscopic notch with his fingernails, and found himself safe and sound on the slab, unable to remember the moves he had made. Ten years later, the first repeaters of the route described that pitch as upper seventh, possibly eighth grade.

In 1969, Messner made a number of solo ascents, including the Vinatzer route on the Marmolada (where he created a variation that was almost a new route in its own right), the Philipp-Flamm groove on Punta Tissi of Civetta, and the direct route on the North edge of Sassolungo. In 1970, the expedition to Nanga Parbat which we shall be recounting in detail in the next chapter took the life of Gunther Messner, and made a dramatic impact on Reinhold's life and mountaineering activities.

Before any other ascents are recounted, a brief digression is required. Those who have read so far will be well aware that the seventh grade did not begin with Messner or the ascents performed by Manolo, Mariacher and party. Only seven years after the Solleder and Lettenbauer route was opened on Civetta, the great Hans Vinatzer climbed the most difficult pitches of the

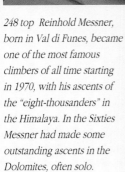

248 top Reinhold Messner, born in Val di Funes, became one of the most famous climbers of all time starting in 1970, with his ascents of the "eight-thousanders" in the Himalaya. In the Sixties Messner had made some outstanding ascents in the Dolomites, often solo.

248 bottom The compact slabs of Pilastro di Mezzo on Sass dla Crusc, in the Conturìnes massif, witnessed a great ascent by the Messner brothers in the summer of 1968. Reinhold (wearing rigid boots) led the "smooth slab, with no cracks and few handholds" which constitutes the crux of the route. Repeaters were to rate this pitch at between the seventh and eighth grade.

248-249 Although it is less well known than the major routes put up by Messner on Marmolada, the Aste route on the North-West face of Civetta is a top-class route on one of the largest and most severe walls in the Dolomites.

249 right The wall of the Conturìnes that faces the upper Val Badia is one of the most compact in the Dolomites. The top photo shows a pitch on the Gran Muro route. The bottom photo shows a climber making one of the first repeats of the route put up by the Messner brothers on the Gran Pilastro of Sass dla Crusc.

"old" sixth grade on the overhanging North face of Furchetta (barefoot, and with hardly any pitons!), and repeated his feat on Stevia in 1935.

Other pitches "beyond the sixth grade" were climbed by Bruno Detassis on the Piccolo Dain of Pietramurata in 1938, by Mariano De Toni and Cesare Pollazzòn on Torre di Valgrande in 1941, and by Domenico Bellenzier on Torre d'Alleghe in 1964. From the mid-Sixties, with the routes put up by Reinhold Messner and Armando Aste, pitches now rated at seventh grade became relatively numerous.

However, all these ascents remained isolated feats, performed by individual champions on the best days of their careers. But in the mid-Seventies, the entire climbing world made a great leap forward in terms of the difficulty of the pitches climbed. This was partly an "internal" phenomenon caused by the reaction of skilled young climbers to the excesses of aid climbing, and partly due to examples from distant countries.

The ascents of British and American climbers, who had been taking free climbing to extremes for years, were little known in the Dolomites. The highly skilled climbers of the sandstone towers of Bohemia and East Germany, who had been mainly responsible for the progress made in climbing in the Dolomites in the early years of the century, were prevented from returning by the Iron Curtain, which was only lifted in 1989, while the *bleausards* (the French climbers who flocked to the sandstone boulders of Fontainebleau, just outside Paris), who had been climbing well beyond the classic sixth grade for some time, rarely visited the Eastern Alps.

It was one of them, Jean-Claude Droyer from Paris, who astonished the Dolomite climbing world in the late Seventies with the first all-free ascents of great classics like the Cassin route on Cima Ovest and the Carlesso route on Torre di Valgrande. On both routes, the French champion scaled seventh-grade pitches, with some eighth-grade moves. The achievements that followed were performed by a new generation of local climbers.

250 top left In the Seventies, the wall of Mount Totoga became something of a "private crag" for Manolo, who put up some very difficult routes there. This photo shows him scaling an 8a+ slab on the Borderline route.

250 top right Parisian Jean-Claude Droyer, known for his ascents on the sandstone of Fontainebleau and the limestone walls of the south of France, made the first free climbs of some of the most difficult routes in the Dolomites in the late Seventies. In this photo he is tackling the famous traverse of the Cassin route on the North face of Cima Ovest di Lavaredo.

250-251 Maurizio Zanolla, who was born at Fiera di Primiero at the foot of the Pale di San Marino and became famous among climbers and the general public with the nickname "Manolo," made numerous major climbs in the Dolomites starting in the early Seventies.

They went into action on the Pale di San Martino on 14th November 1978. On the South face of Cima della Madonna, a piton placed by Alessandro Gogna and Piero Ravà in 1973 had been awaiting a new generation of climbers for five years in the middle of an exceptionally compact yellow slab, impossible even for one of the best Italian teams of the day. The ascent was tackled on that sunny November day by a climber from Fiera di Primiero; his name was Maurizio Zanolla, but his friends knew him by the nickname "Manolo," which was to stick for the next 20 years.

In many of his best ascents, this outstanding climber worked alone. This time, however, Manolo was leader of a four-man rope, followed by Aurelio De Pellegrini, Daniele Ruggero and Marco Simone. When he reached Gogna's last piton he hesitated for a moment, then started climbing confidently again, exploiting his great class as a pure climber, his extraordinary agility and his intuition, developed in many other ascents of extreme difficulty.

In previous years, Manolo had put up some top-class routes, such as those on the South face of Cima di Val Scura in the Vette Feltrine, the South-West face of Dente del Rifugio, and the North-East face of Cima Immink in the Pale chain. In subsequent years, his routes on the vertical wall of Totoga, overlooking the Schenèr ravine, reached the eighth and ninth grades.

But it was his route on Cima della Madonna that officially revealed Manolo's class to the world of climbing in the Dolomites. "In ridiculous positions, barbarously protected, Manolo placed a few pitons, which he clutched at like a drowning man in that vertical yellow ocean of absurd stone," wrote Alessandro Gogna a few years later in his book *Sentieri Verticali*. "That was real progress. Via dei Piazaroi is an essential chapter in the history of recent years."

Five days went by, and another outstanding ascent was made, this time on the South face of the Marmolada. The ascensionists, Reinhard Schiestl and Ludwig Rieser from the other side of the Brenner

Pass, had already free climbed many of the great classics of the Dolomites in exceptional times. Here too, they were by no means liberal with pitons. Despite the short autumn days, the pair managed to avoid a bivouac. They set off in the morning, climbed fast along the huge grey slabs to the right of the Conforto route, were on the summit eight hours later, and returned to the valley in the last cable car of the day.

The result of their efforts was *Schwalbenschwanz* (Swallowtail), a 750-metre-long route rated overall at lower seventh grade, with some much tougher pitches. "Ludwig spontaneously called it his most difficult route, but that's not important. However, it is definitely the finest," wrote Reinhard Schiestl in *Alpinismus*. The Austrian team only used five pitons in the whole route, excluding stances. *L'assassinio dell'impossibile* had been written 10 years earlier, but the dragon bewailed by Reinhold Messner seemed finally to have woken up, and was roaming around the Dolomites, alive and kicking.

Faced with the evidence of the Piazaroi route and the *Schwalbenschwanz*, European Alpine clubs

realised that the sixth-grade taboo had been demolished. These were the first two routes to receive an official seventh-grade rating in the Dolomites. The previous year, a similar rating had been accepted for the Precipizio degli Asteroidi (Asteroid Precipice) in Val di Mello and the *Pumprisse* in the Wilder Kaiser. The achievements of Manolo and the Austrians, together with the example of British climbers, were destined to have a sensational effect on the closed, conservative Veneto climbing circles.

251 top This photo, taken on the walls of Mount Totoga, shows Manolo scaling an overhanging wall with few handholds. This is an 8b pitch, equivalent to the 10th grade on the UIAA scale.

251 bottom Although many of his best-known ascents were made solo, Manolo also put up some major routes with other climbers. This photo shows him cragging on a 7c+ route, equivalent to the 9th grade on the UIAA scale.

One of the first to visit the British crags was Renato Casarotto, the brilliant climber from Vicenza who was to perform some great climbs in the Julian Alps and on Mont Blanc, and met a tragic death on the Magic Line of K2. After a few days on the Welsh crags with a group of the best British and Italian climbers, he kept saying disconsolately, "Those guys are the best!", as Gianni Battimelli reported in *Rivista della Montagna*.

But Casarotto himself was a real champion, and the encounter with personalities like Pete Livesey, Ron Fawcett and Joe Brown was highly stimulating. Even before that trip, Renato, like many of the best Italian climbers in the Dolomites in the early Seventies (Franco Miotto and Riccardo Bee from Belluno, Enzo Cozzolino from Trieste and Alessandro Gogna from Genoa), had turned his attention to the gigantic walls of the Belluno Dolomites and the Pale di San Lucano on the southern edge of the Dolomites.

There with Piero Radin he scaled the West face of Spiz di Lagunàz, a daunting wall over 1000 metres high which Gogna later described as "imperiously superior to Burèl, Civetta and Marmolada" in five days

in June 1975. Then, after assimilating the lesson learned in Wales, Casarotto further refined his free-climbing technique, and put up numerous spectacular routes with pitches "beyond the sixth grade" on Busazza and Antelao.

On Spiz di Lagunàz, to which he returned in 1977 with Bruno De Donà to open a second magnificent new route, Casarotto took free climbing to its extreme limit when he scaled a seven-metre groove rated at seventh grade. However, the editorial staff of *Le Alpi Venete*, the respected journal of the Veneto section of the Club Alpino Italiano, censored his report "so as not to generate scandal and controversy in Veneto climbing circles." However, this was one of the last victories for the bigots. Four years later, when the seventh grade had been accepted by European Alpine Clubs, the same journal gave wide coverage to reports on the difficult routes opened by Renato Casarotto and party.

The outstanding solo ascents performed by Messner also appealed to young people. With his example in mind, a generation of new talent set off on the routes of the past, first wearing ancient sneakers and then the new rubber-soled climbing shoes designed for smearing, and demolished all previous records.

They included Pierluigi Bini from Rome, who soloed the Gogna route on Marmolada and Via dei Fachiri on Cima Scotoni at a breakneck pace, Manolo, who made some magnificent solo ascents on the Pale, Franco Perlotto from Vicenza, later famous for his explorations and writing, who mainly climbed in the Tofane area during that period, young German climber H. Grill, who performed the first solo ascents of the Don Quixote and Ezio Polo routes on the South face of the Marmolada in 1980, and Heinz Mariacher, a Tyrolean from Worgl, who soloed the Vinatzer and Conforto routes on the South face of the Marmolada, and then put up new routes of extreme difficulty on the same wall.

Of the previous generation, Riccardo Bee from Belluno was still climbing, and soloed three magnificent new sixth-grade and aid routes in 1982. The first was located in the right-hand sector of the South face of Piz Seràuta (Marmolada), and the other two on the North-West face of Agnèr, one of the highest and most awesome rock walls in the Alps. Bee was killed on Christmas Day 1982, when he fell from the north side of Agnèr.

The achievements of Lorenzo Massarotto from

Beyond the sixth grade

252 left Tyrolean Heinz Mariacher, born in Worgl, rivalled Manolo for the title of best climber in the Dolomites in the Seventies and Eighties. The great compact slabs of the South face of Marmolada were his favourite venue. This photo shows him climbing on the crags of Valle di San Nicolò.

252-253 Roman climber Pierluigi Bini, who was very active throughout the Dolomites in the Seventies, performed numerous ascents in record time. The first solo ascents of the Gogna route on the South face of Marmolada and Via dei Fachiri on Cima Scotoni were particularly impressive.

253 top right This photo shows famous Tyrolean climber Heinz Mariacher tackling a demanding pitch on a difficult section of a crag consisting of "droplet" limestone similar to that found on the walls of Marmolada.

253 bottom right The Vinatzer route, put up on the South face of Marmolada di Rocca by the famous climber from Val Gardena with Ettore Castiglione in 1936, was one of the most important routes inaugurated in the golden years of the sixth grade, and is often repeated even now.

Padua were even more outstanding in terms of both quality and quantity. This taciturn, methodical climber, little-known outside his home region, made dozens of top-level ascents, and was eventually described by Gogna as "the most accredited climber of big walls in the Dolomites, in summer, in winter and solo, who uses as few pitons as possible, and no bolts whatever."

The list of his new routes includes the North face of Spiz d'Agnèr Nord, 700 metres of sixth- and seventh-grade pitches climbed in 1980 with Ilio De Biasio without using any pitons except at the stances. The next year, Massarotto put up a new route on the Terza Pala di San Lucano, then a direct route on Spiz de la Lastia, and finally a new route on the North-East face of Agnèr, to the right of the route opened in 1967 by the Messner brothers and Heini Holzer.

The eighth pitch on Spiz de la Lastia was probably the toughest in Lorenzo Massarotto's entire climbing career. It's a compact slab 45 metres high, rated at between the seventh and eighth grades, where he placed six of the eleven pitons he used in the whole ascent. "At the exposed stance at the end of that pitch we wondered why there was now so much more interest in the California mountains and so much less in these star-spangled slabs, which still offer so many possibilities," wrote Leopoldo Roman, Massarotto's climbing companion and spokesman, in the Club Alpino Italiano's *Rivista Mensile.*

"On Agnèr, you can still isolate yourself from the rest of the world. If what you're interested in is solving major problems, there's no need to invent them on these mountains," added the ever caustic Massarotto in a 1987 interview. Used to climbing with very few pitons, Lorenzo also enjoyed solo climbs. In his best year, 1980, he soloed the Mayerl Groove on Sass dla Crusc, the Navasa route on Rocchetta Alta di Bosconero, and the routes pioneered by Armando Aste and Enzo Cozzolino on Spiz d'Agnèr Nord, in record times.

254-255 *The West face of the Conturines, which is little known to the general public, overlooks the upper Val Badia with one of the most vertical walls in the Dolomites. Some of the first routes exceeding the sixth grade were put up on these walls in the Sixties.*

254 bottom *The slabs of Marmolada d'Ombretta, crossed by the Conforto, Ideale, Abrakadabra and Ali Baba routes among others, are among the most compact sectors of the South face of the "Queen of the Dolomites." The top cable* car station, clearly visible from the summit, makes the descent more convenient, but has caused serious environmental problems since the Seventies. Scrap metal, refuse and sewage had been thrown down the wall for years.

These climbs were followed by two adventurous ascents of Via dell'Ideale, the magnificent route opened by Armando Aste on the South face of Marmolada d'Ombretta. Massarotto climbed it for the first time in the summer with his friend Cesare De Nardin. However, 50 metres from the exit, that magnificent ascent suddenly turned into a nightmare. The exit gully had been turned into a vertical dump by the "plastic, iron piping, wedged metal drums, wooden planks and corrugated iron" thrown over the edge of the precipice from the cable-car station above.

Worse still, sewage from the toilets and jets of used oil were discharged from the building at regular intervals, after which they were nebulised by the wind and stuck to the rock. Climbing under those conditions would have been pointlessly dangerous. The pair shouted to the tourists on the terrace of the cable-car station to throw them a rope. Instead, the visitors called the mountain rescue service, which brought the two men out of the midden with the winch used for injured climbers. For the brilliant, touchy Massarotto, that inglorious rescue was a very sore point, which he aimed to remedy as soon as possible.

To do so, he returned at the end of October, when the wall was encrusted with snow and ice. After phoning the management of the cable-car station and asking them "not to throw down blunt instruments," he set off to solo the route. He climbed fast to the upper chimneys, which this time had a veritable river running down them.

Massarotto decided to bivouac, but the next day he found that the pitch had been reduced to a single sheet of ice, which he climbed by hammering out small notches for his hands and feet. Under those conditions, no protection was possible. "I watched the rope dangling down diagonally for 40 metres towards the belay piton. Clinging to a fifth-grade slab covered with ice, I lived through some crazy, unique moments." The stinking final stream was also frozen, but a detour round the outside enabled Massarotto to complete the dangerous first solo ascent of the route.

Massarotto's attempt at the first winter solo ascent of the *Via della Canna d'Organo* (Organ Pipe), another magnificent route put up by Armando Aste in 1965, concluded in an equally unexpected way in March 1982. Just 200 metres from the exit after a two-day climb, Massarotto encountered a raging blizzard, then avalanches falling from the upper part of the wall. He abseiled down to a small cave, where he spent three days. He signalled to a helicopter that flew in close to take a look that all was well, then the weather improved and he started climbing again. Not long afterwards, however, he was brought out by the mountain rescue service once again.

An expert in this type of ascent, carrying sufficient food and equipped with excellent gear, he could easily have continued. But in his absence, he had been reported missing, then dead. *Il Gazzettino*, the newspaper with the largest circulation in Veneto, announced "With the death of Lorenzo Massarotto, Italy has lost one of its best climbers." The parish priest broke the news of Massarotto's "tragic death" to his mother. The steel cable that hauled him up to the summit and the uproar that broke out on his return upset Massarotto once again. The interviews clearly demonstrate that he believed his ascent had been deliberately sabotaged. The next year, he returned to the Via della Canna d'Organo without publicising his intentions, and completed the first winter solo of the route in two and a half days.

Six years later, in the winter of 1988, Massarotto made his greatest climb, the first winter solo ascent of the Philipp-Flamm groove on Punta Tissi, in the wild setting of the north side of Civetta.

255 left Climber Lorenzo Massarotto from Padua, who is little known to the general public, was one of the most active climbers on the great walls of the Dolomites from the Seventies onwards. His best climbs include the solo ascents of the Mayerl Groove on Sass dla Crusc, the Navasa route on Rochetta Alta di Bosconero, and Via dell'Ideale on the South face of Marmolada d'Ombretta.

255 right Via dell'Ideale, put up by Armando Aste and Aldo Solina from Rovereto on the South face of Marmolada d'Ombretta in summer, was one of the first routes in the Dolomites to include numerous seventh grade pitches.

However, as demonstrated by his own solo ascents, the "wall of walls" in the Dolomites was now the South face of the Marmolada.

In the Eighties and Nineties, the best climbers in Europe tackled its diabolically smooth slabs, awesome overhangs and superficial cracks in which it was hard to place pitons. The contest was opened in the late Seventies by the team of Heinz Mariacher, Ludwig Rieser and Reinhard Schiestl, soon joined by Luisa Jovane from Venice, Mariacher's girlfriend and an excellent climber.

In 1979, less than a year after the creation of the *Schwalbenschwanz*, Schiestl and Mariacher opened the Don Quixote Pillar, a long and demanding sixth-grade route. Ludwig Rieser and Heinz Zak scaled Via degli Elfi, the second seventh-grade route on the wall. A year later, Heinz Mariacher and Luisa Jovane wrote another important page in the history of the Marmolada when they put up Abrakadabra, a seventh- and upper seventh-grade route over 850 metres long, which they climbed in less than 11 hours.

With its pitches on crumbling rock and streams of water that continue flowing for much of the summer, this route has seldom been repeated, but remains an outstanding feat. However, it was superseded only a year later, when young Czech climbers Igor Koller and Indrich Sustr put up *Weg durch den Fisch* (Route through the Fish) on the magnificent compact slabs of Marmolada d'Ombretta.

Identified and attempted by Mariacher, Manolo and Luisa Jovane, who were forced to make an adventurous descent in the darkness, the route required the Czech team to scale some 20 aid pitches using pitons or "skyhooks," which climbers can hook

over the tiny "drops" in the rock. Mariacher's first reaction was annoyance.

"There's an exceptionally difficult free climbing pitch (upper seventh grade) with a very bad piton as the only protection 7 metres away. It makes me think that Sustr, only 17 years old, must have been out of his mind when he took the lead," he wrote in the Club Alpino Italiano's *Rivista Mensile*. However, it was Mariacher himself who finally gave the "Fish" its place in history, when he performed the first all-free climb of the route with Bruno Pederiva a few years later, rating the most difficult pitches at eighth grade.

In 1982, Heinz Mariacher and Luisa Jovane made another excellent ascent of a big wall. *Moderne Zeiten* (Modern Times) is an extraordinary route on the slabs of Marmolada di Rocca, with pitches of up to lower eighth grade, which the team free climbed. Relatively well protected and on fantastic rock, the route soon became "the greatest object of desire on the Marmolada" according to Alessandro Gogna.

That year, another outstanding climber appeared on the South face for the first time. Maurizio Giordani, born in Rovereto, had undergone a silent apprenticeship on the great routes of the Dolomites, and gained vital experience on the

great slabs of the Verdon canyons in Provence.

In winter 1982/83, Maurizio performed the first winter ascents of Don Quixote and Hatschi Bratschi, two of Mariacher's great routes, with Fausto Zenatti. The next July, he opened the Sandro Pertini route on the slabs of Piz Seràuta, his first seventh-grade route, with Paolo Cipriani. At the end of the month he climbed Pilastro Agnese, a "great rock prairie" which gave the team (Rosanna Manfrini, Maurizio's girlfriend, was climbing with him and Cipriani) a "dream of a climb." The summer ended with Via dell'Irreale, 33 pitches of up to the seventh grade, thus concluding an outstanding season.

The next winter, again with Cipriani, Maurizio tackled the daunting "Fish," which had never been repeated, even in summer. But after two days, a raging blizzard forced the climbers to abseil down hazardously. Giordani, Cipriani and Zenatti succeeded in making the winter ascent of the Koller and Sustr route in March 1986 with 35 hours' actual climbing, despite the fact that another blizzard complicated matters during the final section of the route.

256 left The wall is so vertical and compact that snow is almost absent from the slabs of the Abrakadabra route in winter. In this photo, Maurizio Giordani leads the first winter ascent of the route.

256 right The Don Quixote Pillar, first climbed by Reinhard Schiestl and Heinz Mariacher in 1979, was one of the first modern routes put up on the great slabs of Marmolada. This photo shows Heinz Mariacher leading the route.

256-257 The best climbers of the Seventies and Eighties were by no means overawed by the most vertical, compact walls in the Dolomites. This photo shows Heinz Mariacher climbing Via Maestri on the Rotwand on Rosengarten.

257 top right Weg durch den Fisch (Route through the Fish), put up on the South face of Marmolada in 1981 by Czechs Igor Koller and Indrich Sustr, includes some long seventh grade sections, and is still one of the most difficult routes in the Dolomites. In this photo, Heinz Mariacher leads the first repeat of the route.

257 bottom right In the winter of 1986, Maurizio Giordani, Paolo Cipriani and Franco Zenatti took 35 hours of actual climbing to make the first winter ascent of Weg durch den Fisch on the South face of Marmolada. A raging blizzard hit the wall, complicating the last part of the climb.

258 left The East face of Sass Maòr in the Pale di San Martino, where one of the first sixth-grade routes in the Dolomites was inaugurated in 1926, was back in the news in 1979 when Manolo and Piero Valmassoi climbed Supermatita, a 1200-metre route with seventh grade pitches.

258 bottom right This photo, taken on the South face of Marmolada, shows Maurizio Giordani opening Andromeda, one of his many routes on this spectacular wall.

259 left The soil and tufts of grass on the ledges and in the cracks demonstrates the low altitude of the peak, but does not reduce the difficulty of the South-West face of Croz dell'Altissimo in the Brenta Dolomites. This photo shows the first ascent of Via degli Accademici, an 850-metre route put up by Maurizio Giordani and Marco Furlani in 1983.

259 top right This photo, taken during the first ascent of Athena, shows the typical scenario of the South face of Marmolada, with its compact slabs and great pillars slashed by narrow cracks.

259 bottom right This photo, taken on the East face of Sass Maòr, shows Maurizio Giordani from Rovereto making one of the first repeats of the Supermatita route. In 1989, Giordani made the first winter and first solo ascent of this spectacular route.

Between 1984 and 1985, the list of major routes opened by Giordani lengthened with the addition of Futura, Estasi, Fortuna and Athena, all with pitches rated at up to the upper seventh grade. Summer 1985 brought another brilliant ascent by Maurizio who, after a lightning-fast solo repeat of Via dell'Ideale, made the first solo ascent of Modern Times, the masterpiece by Heinz Mariacher and Luisa Jovane.

"I started climbing rather doubtfully, then continued faster and more confidently. The climb never proved dangerous, even in the most difficult sections, though I often felt the strain due to concentration. I didn't relax until I was on the summit

of Punta Rocca," wrote Giordani in *Rivista della Montagna*. As was to be expected, there were a few clashes between the two stars, Giordani and Mariacher, in the months that followed.

In the second half of the Eighties, Maurizio continued chalking up new routes on the South face, reaching the eighth grade with Specchio di Sara (1988) and Andromeda (1989). Giordani was very fond of the granite towers of Pakistan, and also made some great solo and team ascents of other great Dolomite walls, ranging from the South face of Croz dell'Altissimo to the East face of Sass Maòr. Then, back on the Marmolada, he performed another outstanding feat, the first solo ascent of the "Fish" (1990).

Heinz and Luisa preferred to "retire" for a few years to the rocks of Valle di San Nicolò in Val di Fassa. Then, they put up a 300-metre route called *Tempi Modernissimi* (Ultramodern Times) on Sasso delle Undici that caused a big row. They bolted the route from the bottom using a drill, with a few belays anchored to bolts, then repeated it with an all-free climb that included pitches of up to the lower 10th grade, corresponding to 7c+ on the French scale used on crags all over Europe. This style of climbing is accepted in other parts of the Alps, but caused bitter controversy among climbers mainly associated with the Dolomites. Mariacher deliberately chose an almost

unknown wall for his provocative feat. If he had bolted the Marmolada, it would have meant war.

Many other leading climbers visited the Dolomites in the Eighties, when some top-level routes were put up by Marco Furlani, Ermanno Salvaterra and Rolando Larcher from Trento, Tomo Cesen, Slavko Sveticic and Francek Knez from Slovenia, and the new generation of climbers from Alto Adige (South Tyrol), including Ivo Rabanser, Christoph Hainz and Roland Mittersteiner.

Thomas Bubendorfer, an Austrian climber to whom the media gave a great deal of coverage, performed an *enchaînement* in 1988 in which he was airlifted by helicopter between ascents including the Cassin route on Cima Ovest, the Comici route on Cima Grande, *Schwalbenschwanz* on the Marmolada, and the Niagara route on Sass Pordoi. The more ecology-minded Manrico Dell'Agnola from Veneto soloed the five major routes on Torre Venezia (the Tissi, Ratti, Andrich, Livanos and Cassin routes) in a single day (1989), and then concatenated the Solleder route and the Philipp-Flamm groove on Civetta with Alcide Prati (1990). In 1993, the same team climbed the West edge of Busazza and the North edge of Agnèr on the same day, covering the long distance between them by mountain bike.

Maurizio ("Icio") Dell'Omo and Gigi Dal Pozzo, who have put up dozens of new routes on Antelao and Sorapìss and the other Cortina massifs, climb in the valleys of Cadore, while Mauro Corona, a brilliant climber from Erto and an outstanding wood carver, prefers the Oltre Piave Dolomites.

City-dwellers who have performed great ascents include Piero Dal Pra from Vicenza, who has opened new routes and performed first winter ascents on the Marmolada and the Tofane, and Ivo Ferrari from Bergamo, who specialises in high-level solo ascents.

However, the greatest climber of all is still Manolo. Shy and retiring despite the fact that he is one of the few top-level climbers to appear fairly often on television and in the non-specialist press, he devotes his time to his family and his beloved Totoga, where he continues to pioneer routes at the top end of the rating scale.

In the Dolomites proper, his favourite massif is still the Pale di San Martino, where he created Via dei Piazaroi on Cima della Madonna and Supermatita on the East face of Sass Maòr in the Seventies. In the summer of 1993, Manolo returned to Sass Maòr to open the outstanding Nureyev route, a 600-metre line with pitches rated as high as the upper ninth grade.

The elegant route created by Emil Solleder in the early years of the sixth grade is on the same wall, not far from Manolo's new route. During the descent, Manolo downclimbed the ordinary route opened in 1875 by a local guide and one from faraway Chamonix. From the summit, the passes beloved of Douglas Freshfield and the walls climbed by Gunther Langes and Hermann Buhl could be glimpsed beyond the deep Val Canali and the minor towers surrounding Sass Maòr. That day, the past and future of climbing in the Dolomites seemed to shake hands on the solid limestone of the Pale di San Martino.

Beyond the sixth grade

Revolution on ice

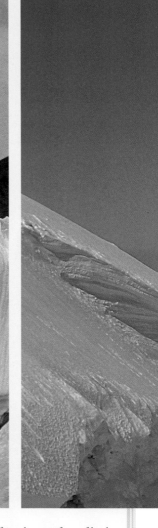

First light of dawn, 28th December 1973. Bowed under the weight of their gigantic rucksacks, two climbers made their way through deep snow towards one of the steepest and most awesome ice gullies in the Alps. "Overloaded, we tried to clutch at the powder snow that refused to stick to the soles of our boots," recounted Claude Jäger. What was waiting for Jäger and Walter Cecchinel (both guides from Chamonix) was the North-East couloir of the Drus, the "75-degree bob-sleigh run" that rises from the Nant Blanc glacier to the saddle that separates the Petit Dru from the Grand Dru. Too dangerous in summer because of the frequent hails of stones, the couloir becomes safer in winter, when a shield of ice holds in place the precariously balanced rocks. However, the unusual feature of this climb was not the choice of the coldest time of year.

Using the classic climbing technique, cutting foot- and hand-holds, and using aid where the slope exceeded 60-65 degrees, it could take climbers a week or more on the wall to complete this kind of route. Five years earlier, René Desmaison and Robert Flematti

had taken eight days to climb the Linceul.

However, a revolution that began in Scotland had finally reached the Alpine range, starting in 1970. Rigid crampons and "banana" ice-axes allowed frontal progression even on the steepest ice slopes. Walter Cecchinel had been teaching the new "piolet-traction" technique for two years at the courses run by ENSA (École Nationale de Ski et Alpinisme) in Chamonix.

On reaching the bergschrund, the two climbers were able to shrug off their heavy rucksacks and fill their haulbag, which they would pull up with them to the summit, pitch by pitch. On the schrund, the fresh snow gave way to ice. Cecchinel set off confidently to lead the tough slope that starts with a 60-degree gradient, and then becomes even more vertical.

After four pitches, a step excavated in the ice allowed the two climbers to rest their aching calf muscles. Claude and Walter bivouacked in hammocks suspended from ice pitons. Lengthy contortions were needed to get into their sleeping bags, melt a few flakes of ice over the stove and make a hot drink. Despite their awesome position, the

only thing that bothered the two friends was "fear of bad weather, which could trap us in this forbidding avalanche funnel." Cecchinel was particularly worried about this risk, having had to abseil down the first part of the couloir at the end of an unsuccessful attempt in the spring of 1971.

On the morning of 29th December, a delicate traverse on "hump-backed rocks encrusted in ice," with "risky belays and pitons of doubtful safety" took the two climbers to the foot of a overhanging crack. After scaling this pitch without difficulty, they used a great slab of rock resting on the slope for their second bivouac. On the third day, while the leader was busy on a new, almost vertical route, a helicopter flew past. Then, step by step, the two climbers approached the great unknown of the wall: a sinuous bottleneck, invisible from the Grands Montets. However, after three diagonal pitches, the mystery was solved. It was possible to continue entirely on ice, along the uninterrupted couloir. "Walter's technique was perfect, no time wasted," commented Claude. Cecchinel placed two ice pitons per pitch for protection, and fixed up safe belays on the solid granite of the sides. During the third bivouac, a light snowfall covered the climbers' hammocks, but the next day, the weather was glorious again.

The first pitch on the last day's climb offered more extreme difficulties, then the going got rapidly easier. At 1 p.m., while Cecchinel and Jäger were resting in the sun, the helicopter returned, and dropped the two friends their New Year's Eve dinner. They ate it later, after descending much of the difficult ordinary route on the Petit Dru.

The conquest of the North-East couloir of the Drus, an outstandingly evident line on one of the loveliest and most celebrated mountains in the Alps, made it quite clear that a turning point in climbing history had been reached. In

(which had taken eight days' effort by Desmaison and Flematti) in just 2.45 hours. To a journalist who asked how he managed to go so fast, Boivin replied with a dazzling smile, "The fact is that at night, I'd rather sleep with Françoise than in a cold bivouac in an icehole!"

Practitioners of the "piolet-traction" technique have become increasingly numerous since the mid-Seventies. Patrick Gabarrou has undertaken a systematic exploration of the steepest goulottes on Mont Blanc and in the Pennine Alps. Gabarrou's favourite destinations include the south-east side of Mont Maudit, the North face of the Grandes Jorasses, the Aiguille Noire de Peuterey and the Aiguille Sans Nom.

261 top right In the coldest weeks of winter, fascinating icefalls form in every part of the Alpine chain and the other mountain ranges of the world. In this photo, a climber is scaling Gin Tonic, a difficult frozen waterfall in the Somprade gorge in the Dolomites.

261 bottom Frenchman Patrick Gabarrou is one of the most outstanding modern ice climbers. The new routes he has put up include the Supercouloir on Mont Blanc du Tacul (1975), the Hypercouloir on the Brouillard (1982), Freneysie Pascale next to the Central Frêney Pillar, Divine Providence on the Pilier d'Angle and the Notre Dame icefall on the Brouillard (all in 1984).

reality, however, the revolution on ice had started a couple of years earlier, in September 1971, a few months after the first attempt on the Dru couloir, when Cecchinel put up a direct route on the menacing North face of Pilier d'Angle with Georges Nominé, directly scaling various goulottes with a gradient of around 70 degrees.

It was the performers of these ascents who invented the first gear for the "piolet-traction" technique in their makeshift workshops, and when specialist companies from the Alpine countries put the new models into production, the word spread like lightning. In May 1975, again in the Mont Blanc massif, Jean-Marc Boivin and Patrick Gabarrou scaled the Supercouloir, a very steep icy gully 800 metres high, that reaches a gradient of 80 degrees, with three bivouacs. Two months later, with extreme skier Patrick Vallençant, Boivin climbed another ice gully on the North face of Pilier d'Angle. The next year, Jean-Marc identified and climbed the Raye des Fesses, a gully that reaches the summit of the Pic Sans Nom, which Boivin scaled with Diaféria, Vionet and Fuasset.

In 1977, Boivin climbed the ice slope of the Linceul

260 The use of the ice-axe traction technique requires climbers to be thoroughly familiar with the structure of ice (far more than before) because ice, unlike rock, is a continually transforming material. This photo shows a climber tackling an ice wall on Shisha Pangma.

261 top left The ice-axe traction technique, used for great ascents on many of the highest mountains in the world (from the Alps to Alaska, from Patagonia to the Himalaya), enables climbers to scale even seracs and ephemeral towers of ice.

No less than 20 routes inaugurated by Patrick lead directly to the highest summit in Europe. They include the Divine Providence route to Pilier d'Angle (climbed with François Marsigny in 1984) and the seven icefall-couloirs that Gabarrou identified between the Frêney and Brouillard Pillars. As a result of routes like Freneysie Pascale (with Marsigny, 1984) and the Hypercouloir (with Pierre-Alain Steiner, 1982), Patrick rapidly became one of the most respected climbers on the Alpine scene. Gabarrou has also climbed in the Pennine Alps, putting up some great routes like the "Shroud" on the East face of Nordend (with Christophe Viard, 1984), a 2300-metre

climb which includes pitches on vertical ice. Patrick also has some great rock climbs to his credit, such as the Direct Route to the Red Pillar of the Brouillard, which he scaled in 1983 with Alexis Long.

In the late Seventies, climbers of different nationalities began to challenge the French dominance. The British put up some excellent routes, starting with the now classic MacIntyre Goulotte on the North face of the Grandes Jorasses. However, the Italian team from Piedmont formed by Giancarlo Grassi and Gianni Comino was particularly outstanding.

Grassi put up hundreds of new routes on the ice of

Valle d'Aosta and Piedmont, and around 50 routes in the Mont Blanc massif alone. Comino was the creative, decisive member of the team. He entered the world of top-class mountaineering in 1978 when he performed the first solo ascent of the Supercouloir of the Tacul. A few days later, Grassi and Comino were roped together on the south side of the Grandes Jorasses, where they climbed the Hypercouloir, an interminable goulotte which includes some vertical sections and various overhang pitches. This was followed by a direct route along the serac on the north side of the Aiguille Verte (with Renato Casarotto), and a number of routes on the goulottes of Cirque Maudit. But

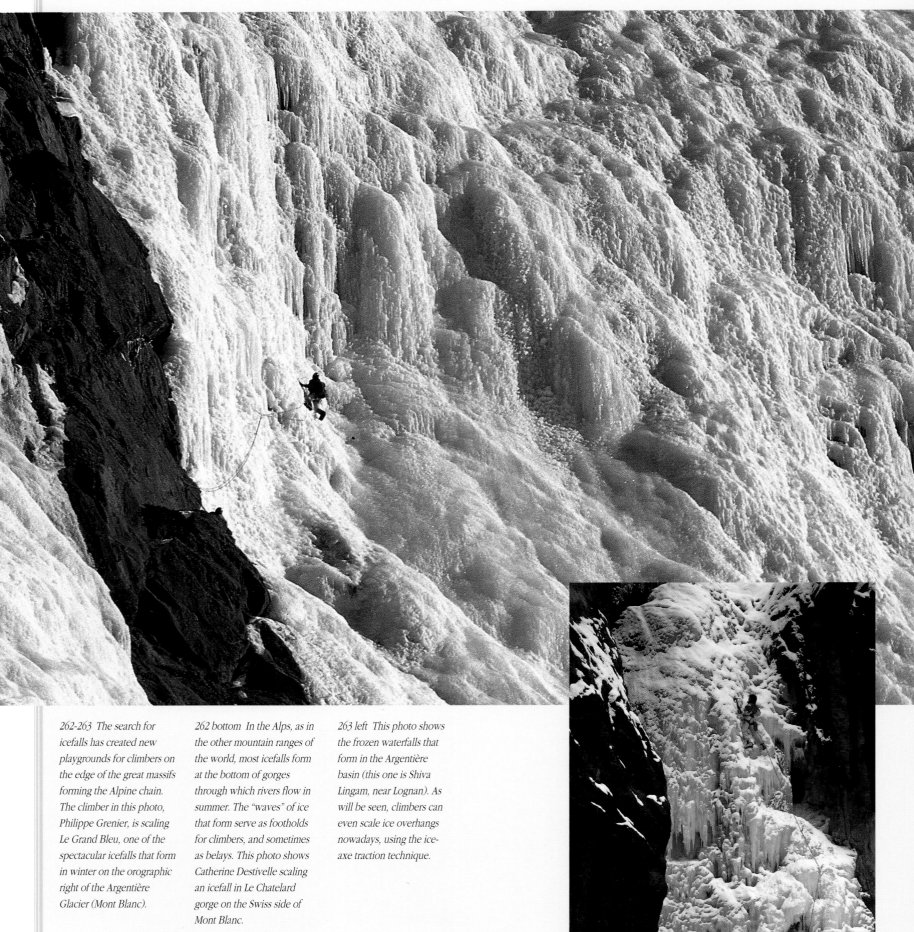

262-263 The search for icefalls has created new playgrounds for climbers on the edge of the great massifs forming the Alpine chain. The climber in this photo, Philippe Grenier, is scaling Le Grand Bleu, one of the spectacular icefalls that form in winter on the orographic right of the Argentière Glacier (Mont Blanc).

262 bottom In the Alps, as in the other mountain ranges of the world, most icefalls form at the bottom of gorges through which rivers flow in summer. The "waves" of ice that form serve as footholds for climbers, and sometimes as belays. This photo shows Catherine Destivelle scaling an icefall in Le Chatelard gorge on the Swiss side of Mont Blanc.

263 left This photo shows the frozen waterfalls that form in the Argentière basin (this one is Shiva Lingam, near Lognan). As will be seen, climbers can even scale ice overhangs nowadays, using the ice-axe traction technique.

Revolution
on ice

their real love was the great Brenva wall, where the huge, dangerous seracs separating the spurs and ridges used by the classic routes were still unclimbed. In August 1979, the pair climbed the awesome ice wall to the left of Via della Pera. The next February, Gianni Comino attempted a solo ascent of the couloir that separates the rocks of the Pera route from the snow-covered ridge of the Major route. But he was killed by falling blocks of ice almost at the end of the route. Giancarlo still continued his systematic ascents. Among the numerous routes he put up, one of his most impressive was the direct route on the South face of the Grandes Jorasses, a "ghost couloir" that involves a climb of up to 1500 metres, then the North Groove of Roccia Nera and the Ice Fresser gully on the same mountain.

On Easter Sunday 1991, a cornice broke off, bringing his mountaineering adventures to an end.

In the Eighties and Nineties, while the great ice routes

are only seldom climbed, climbing on low- and medium-height icefalls has become enormously popular. This new climbing sport, attracts thousands of climbers because of the short walk-in, the beauty of the settings crossed by the routes, and the possibility of abseiling down most routes and returning to the starting point. However, climbing icefalls is quite a different kettle of fish from climbing crags protected by bombproof bolts.

Icefalls are always prone to collapses and shattering, while ice screws, which are hard to place, are not particularly reliable in the event of a fall. Despite this problem, however, the icefall craze has greatly increased the popularity of the ice of the Mer de Glace, Val Varaita, and the ravines of Sottoguda at the foot of Marmolada. Outside the Alpine range, there are some exceptionally beautiful icefalls among the Norwegian mountains and in the Pyrenean amphitheatre of Gavarnie.

The real mecca of icefall climbers, however, is British Columbia in Canada. Here, thanks to the Arctic temperatures, huge ice structures, often of exceptional difficulty, form on the slopes of the Rockies every winter. The great Canadian icefalls, explored by climbers of Scottish descent like Bugs McKeith, Dick Howe and Rob Wood as from the early Seventies, include some outstanding routes like Takkakaw Falls, the Weeping Wall and the particularly difficult Nemesis at the foot of the north side of Mount Stanley. What a wonderful playground!

263 top right The climate of British Columbia (Canada) is directly influenced by the icy winds of the Arctic, which makes it one of the most interesting venues for modern ice climbing. The climber in the photo is tackling an "inner" pitch on the Pilsner Pillar icefall near Field.

263 bottom right When the cold is particularly intense, the icefalls of the Alps, Norway, North America and the Pyrenees include vertical columns of ice detached from the rock face. Anyone climbing these structures not only requires outstanding technical skill, but must also pay great attention to the solidity of the ice.

The Himalayas, alpine-style

In July 1975, an expedition unlike any other crossed the desolate moraines of the Baltoro Glacier in the heart of the Pakistani Karakorum.

Twenty years had gone by since the conquest of the 8000-metre peaks, and the groups tackling the highest mountains in the world were getting bigger and bigger. A few months later, the great British expedition led by Chris Bonington finally conquered the South-West face of Mount Everest; three years later, the Japanese arrived at the base of the Abruzzi Spur on K2 with no less than 42 climbers, and a procession of over 1200 porters. Two months earlier, in the pre-Monsoon season of 1975, a great Italian expedition led by the legendary Riccardo Cassin had to withdraw from the South face of Lhotse after colossal avalanches destroyed the base camp twice, miraculously leaving the climbers and sherpas unscathed. Now, one of those other men was about to tackle an 8000-metre peak again.

The style of the expedition could not have been more different, however. Instead of rigid organisation, fixed ropes and exhausting transport of the provisions required by the leading ropes to the upper camps, the two climbers heading for the 8068-metre Hidden Peak, the highest in the Gasherbrum range, were aiming for speed and total self-sufficiency, and travelled light. This called for first-class climbers, which Peter Habeler and Reinhold Messner certainly were.

Habeler, born in Austria 33 years earlier, was on his first visit to the Himalaya, but he had climbed some of the most difficult routes in the Alps at an extraordinary speed. He and Messner had despatched the North face of the Eiger in six hours. Though known by climbers, Reinhold Messner was not yet the star he was to become a few years later, when the ascent of all fourteen 8000-metre peaks was to make him as famous as a rock singer or soccer player.

At the age of 31, Reinhold had already performed a series of outstanding ascents in the Dolomites (described in another chapter) and achieved two hard-won victories over 8000-metre peaks in the Himalaya. In 1970, Messner had climbed the Rupal wall, the tallest and most difficult on Nanga Parbat, but lost his beloved brother Gunther, who had been his favourite climbing companion for many years, during the descent.

Two years later, he reached the 8163-metre summit of Manaslu alone. A few hours later, a raging blizzard caused the death of Franz Jäger and Andreas Schlick. "For the second time I experienced frostbite of the limbs and the loss of companions. I didn't think I would be able to

stand the desperation I felt in climbing up there and getting down again alive for a third time," wrote Messner after completing his collection of 8000-metre peaks.

As always, however, time healed the suffering experienced in the "death zone." Three years after Manaslu, Reinhold was back in the Himalaya to attempt another 8000-metre peak. The high valleys had been closed for years because of perennial conflict with India, but now, the Pakistan government reopened the Baltoro Glacier to foreigners and granted permission for an attempt on Hidden Peak.

First, however, there was another big wall to be climbed. It was the South face of Lhotse, to which Messner (who comes from South Tyrol and is therefore German-speaking, though he carries an Italian passport) had been invited as a member of the Club Alpino Italiano's expedition, in which many of the top names in Italian climbing participated. However, the difficulties of the wall, one of the highest and most dangerous in the Himalaya, halted the progress of the climbers at an altitude of 7500 metres.

For Reinhold, however, this adventure marked a major turning point. Used to climbing alone or with a few trusted companions (just like Riccardo Cassin in the Alps 30 or 40 years earlier), Messner had no patience with the organisation and down times of a large-scale expedition.

Mountaineering

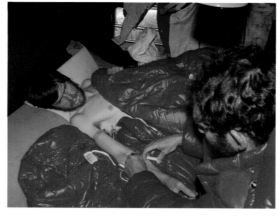

264 top left The South face of Hidden Peak (8068 metres), the eleventh-highest mountain on earth, was first climbed in the summer of 1975 by Reinhold Messner and Peter Habeler. This was the first new route to be put up in Alpine style on an "eight-thousander."

264-265 The awesome South face of Lhotse, which dominates the pastures of Chukhung, is one of the highest and most dangerous walls in the Himalaya. Reinhold Messner's participation in

the 1975 Italian expedition, which was forced off the mountain by great avalanches, persuaded him that the Alpine style was ideal for this kind of wall.

264 bottom Reinhold Messner, born in Val di Funes in 1944, amazed climbers with his ascents in the Dolomites in the Sixties. He climbed in the Himalaya for the first time in 1970, with the dramatic expedition to the Rupal face of Nanga Parbat.

265 top With his ascent of Manaslu, performed in 1972 with the Tyrolean expedition led by Wolfgang Nairz, Reinhold Messner became the third man in the world to climb two "eight-thousanders." The expedition concluded tragically with the deaths of Franz Jäger and Andreas Schlick, who disappeared in the blizzard on the huge summit plateau.

From then on, he intended to travel fast and light, even on the world's greatest mountains. He and Habeler set off for Hidden Peak with 200 kilos of luggage, and only needed a dozen porters. "If we had not been forced to take the liaison officer with us, half as much would have done," commented Messner on his return home.

After a visit to the base camp at the foot of the mountain devoted to acclimatisation and a detailed study of the ascent route, Messner and Habeler returned on 8th August to sleep at the foot of the steep slopes of Hidden Peak. At dawn the next day they set off

confidently, unroped, and scaled the central part of the North-West face, which Messner compared to "two North faces of the Matterhorn stacked on top of one another," with a difficult climb on mixed terrain.

The pair spent the night at an altitude of 7100 metres. The next day they climbed fast towards the summit, which they reached in the early afternoon with no particular problems. Next came the descent, which is nearly always the most delicate part of a climb on the world's highest mountains. After an unpleasant night in a raging blizzard, the two men left their tent, now in shreds, at dawn, returned to the

edge of the wall and started downclimbing the ascent route, which was demanding but finally sheltered from the wind.

"Extremely tense, like wild animals ready to pounce," they retraced the difficult rock pitches they had scaled on the ascent with the greatest concentration. On the final slope, exhausted, they threw down their rucksacks, which they would recover on reaching the glacier. Then, unburdened and happy, they returned to the Gasherbrum Valley and the Baltoro Glacier after an achievement that changed the face of mountaineering.

Three years later, the best team of the day tackled the highest mountain on earth. As Messner and Habeler admitted before setting off, their expedition was not wholly independent. Officially, as far as the Nepalese authorities were concerned, the two men were part of a Tyrolean group led by Wolfgang Nairz, heading for the summit of Mount Everest in the traditional style.

The group fixed the ropes, pitched the tents for the high altitude camps, and supplied them with food and fuel. However, on Everest, Reinhold and Peter had to tackle a problem that was much more serious than the technical difficulties of the route. While Hidden Peak is only just over 8000 metres high, Everest reaches nearly 9000, and lack of oxygen presents a serious risk to man. "A number of voices criticised my plan. They said that even if we reached the summit of Everest, we'd never come back alive – at best, we'd go mad," recounted Messner in *All Fourteen Eight-thousanders*, the 1986

book in which he recounts his ascents of the fourteen 8000-metre peaks.

On 23rd April, while Habeler was lying sick in the tent, Messner attempted to reach the summit with two sherpas, but a blizzard that raged for 48 hours postponed his date with the summit for two weeks. On 3rd May, equipped with breathing apparatus, Wolfgang Nairz, Robert Schauer, Horst Bergmann and sherpa Ang Phu reached the summit. Messner and Habeler set off five days later.

They left the tent they had pitched on the freezing, inhospitable South Col in pitch darkness, and climbed slowly towards the summit along the route followed by Hillary and Tenzing. Violent gusts of wind blew onto the mountain from the south-west. "We suddenly realised that we were through the clouds, and closer to our destination," wrote Peter Habeler. Just before the fore-summit, Habeler abandoned his rucksack, then Messner took the lead and filmed his companion tackling the Hillary Step, which interrupts the ridge just before the summit.

Their arrival on the summit was an extraordinarily intense moment. "I'd been gripped by an incredible feeling of euphoria. I felt free and relaxed, and I was convinced that nothing bad could ever happen to me again," continues Habeler's account. Once again, however, the greatest problems awaited Peter and Reinhold during the descent.

Before their ascent, the doctors had clearly explained to the two climbers that every minute spent without breathing apparatus in the "death zone" above 8000 metres increases the risk of permanent brain damage. Obsessed by this threat, Habeler rapidly outstripped his companion, who was having serious problems with snow-blindness, crossed the fore-summit, then, taking a great risk, slid down fast on his buttocks towards the South Col, using his ice-axe as a brake. Messner followed more slowly, tormented by the

266 top left Tyrolean Wolfgang Nairz, one of the most expert climbers in the Himalaya, led the 1978 expedition where Reinhold Messner and Peter Habeler joined forces. Nairz and six more climbers reached the summit with the aid of oxygen. Messner and Habeler were the first to do without it.

266-267 Even with the aid of fixed ropes and oxygen, the ascent of the ice-covered wall of Lhotse is the most monotonous and strenuous part of the ordinary Nepalese route on Mount Everest. This photo again shows the Austro-German expedition of 1978.

266 bottom left With his long hair and headband, Reinhold Messner, shown here at the Everest base camp, looks like a climbing hippy. As he himself writes, however, Messner is meticulous in his training and the logistical preparation of his expeditions.

266 bottom right The tripod left by the Chinese in 1975 acts as the background for photos of climbers who pose on the summit of Mount Everest. In this photo, a member of the Nairz expedition smiles after reaching the 8848-metre summit.

267 The Khumbu Icefall presented the 1978 expedition, like all those which follow the ordinary Nepalese route, with a difficult, dangerous task.

pain in his eyes which forced him to rest more and more often.

When Reinhold reached the Col, Peter Habeler, cameraman Eric Jones and the sherpas took him into the relative safety of the tent. During the night the pain in his eyes worsened, but Messner firmly refused the oxygen offered by his companions. The descent along the steep wall of Lhotse was gruelling, but the fixed ropes and rapidly diminishing altitude helped the climbers continue. At the foot of the steepest section, Messner and Habeler were welcomed by Oswald Oelz, the expedition's doctor, who reached the 8848-metre summit himself a few days later. By the time they reached the base camp, the two climbers were world-famous.

At the foot of Mount Everest, the partnership between Messner and Habeler split up forever. Peter returned to the Tyrol and his job as a mountain guide, while Reinhold stayed in the heart of Asia to perform another amazing ascent. He was at the peak of his Himalayan career, and he knew it. For his next feat, he had long since chosen the mountain that reminded him of the greatest sorrow of his life. To make "the greatest leap in my climbing career" he returned alone to Nanga Parbat, to the ice wall that had killed his brother eight years earlier.

On 7th August 1978, Messner left the moraines of the Diamir valley at 5 a.m., and set off up the steep sides of the mountain that had rebuffed attempts by the best Austrian and German climbers in the Thirties. In a few hours he reached 6400 metres, where an ice shelf allowed him to pitch his tent and prepare for the night. He devoted the whole of the next day to acclimatisation and rest. On 9th August, at 5 a.m., an earthquake caused a gigantic avalanche, but Reinhold and his tent were miraculously unscathed.

However, the first part of the ascent route was now too dangerous to be used for the descent. The only way out was upwards. Overwhelmed by "a kind of over-confidence" which soon turned into "a state of euphoria," Reinhold continued through the deep snow with greater and greater effort, scaled some steep rock pitches, and finally reached the 8125-metre summit, where he took several photos with an automatic shutter-release camera, and left a piton as evidence of the ascent.

"I imagined I was a shadow… only action puts an end to the essential questions of life… I myself was the answer, the questions made no sense any more," wrote Messner on his return. During the descent, he was pinned down in his tent at 7400 metres by a raging blizzard for two nights. When the weather improved, Messner's extraordinary instinct guided him along a steep new route which took him back safe and sound to the glacier and the base camp. "In my first expedition to Nanga Parbat I knew hell. In my second, alone, I experienced paradise." That, in Messner's concise words, effectively sums up this new and amazing expedition.

In 1979, again without oxygen, Messner headed for K2, the second-highest mountain on earth, which posed much greater difficulties than Everest. Leading a small expedition that included German climber Michl

Dacher, Austrian Robert Schauer, Friedl Mutschlechner from South Tyrol and Italians Alessandro Gogna and Renato Casarotto, Messner was intending to climb the Magic Line, an elegant pillar of snow and rock in the heart of the steep south-west side.

However, delays in the walk-in and the death of a porter in a crevasse forced the expedition to give up the new route and fall back on the ordinary ascent route along the Abruzzi Spur, identified in 1909 by the Duke of Abruzzi's expedition. The route, which had been attempted by Wiessner and Houston, was first climbed by Compagnoni and Lacedelli in 1954. Messner and Dacher summited on 12th July 1979.

The ascent route was difficult and the weather was glorious. "Not a cloud as far as the eye could see. The mountains and valleys lay at our feet like a black-and-white photo. No green, no red, no yellow. Just the blue

of the sky. The farther we climbed, the darker it got." The next day, the rapidly worsening weather put an end to the attempt by Schauer, Mutschlechner and Gogna, but Messner had now climbed five 8000-metre peaks.

Messner's last great feat in the Himalaya was again performed on Everest, when he climbed it from the Tibetan side, which had finally been reopened to foreign travellers and climbers by the Chinese authorities. The expedition was heading for the ordinary route from the north to the summit, attempted by British teams in the Twenties and Thirties and completed by a Chinese expedition in 1960.

Once again, Reinhold climbed without oxygen. The new step forward in his confrontation with the mountain lay in the fact that this time, he was climbing the highest mountain on earth alone. Only his

268 left After deciding not to attempt the Magic Line on the south side, the 1979 expedition made a rapid ascent of K2 by the 1954 ordinary route. In this photo, Reinhold Messner and Michl Dacher are resting on the snow slopes of the Shoulder after the strenuous effort required to reach the 8616-metre summit.

268-269 With the ascent of K2, his fifth "eight-thousander," Reinhold Messner became the unchallenged leader of Himalayan climbing. The Godwin Austen Glacier, the upper Baltoro glacier and the unmistakable snow-covered pyramid of Chogolisa can clearly be seen in this photo, taken from the Shoulder of K2.

Canadian girlfriend Nena Holguin was waiting for him at the base camp on the moraines of the Rongbuk Glacier. "I wanted that expedition like no other before or since," wrote Messner in *Everest – the First Solo Ascent*, the book devoted to the feat.

A few days after his arrival in Rongbuk Valley, Messner climbed to 7800 metres, alone and travelling light. After a short rest at the base camp, he set off for the summit on 18th August. Above the North Col, however, great masses of unstable snow prevented him from following the ridge identified by the British 60 years earlier, where Mallory and Irvine had disappeared. Like the last British pre-war expeditions, Reinhold climbed diagonally along the steep north side of the mountain, bivouacked at 8200 metres, then continued towards the summit, which he believed to be very near, carrying only his camera and ice-axe. But the last day's ascent was to test the world's best climber to his limit.

After crossing the dangerous Norton Gully, he climbed to the last part of the North-East ridge, skirted the Second Step, then continued towards the summit. He covered the last few metres on all fours, summoning up all his extraordinary willpower. "I have never felt as tired as I did that time on the summit of Everest. I knew I had reached the utmost limit of my physical strength," he commented on his return.

During the descent, partly due to exhaustion, Messner fell some 10 metres into a crevasse just below the North Col, managed to get out alone, and somehow got back to the camp. The gruelling ascent left its mark on him, but also suggested his next destination. "I was halfway through my life, and I felt strong. Above all, the solo ascent of Everest had shown me that using the same tactic, I could climb lower mountains in a jiffy."

269 top On the summit of the Abruzzi Spur, the tent of camp three offers a short break for climbers before tackling the last 1000 metres of K2, where climbers face the problems caused by high altitude as well as the actual climbing difficulties.

269 bottom left The steep, often dangerous Abruzzi Spur is protected by all expeditions with a line of fixed ropes, allowing them to climb the first 2000 metres of the ordinary route on K2.

269 bottom right German climber Michl Dacher, seen in this photo on the snow-covered ridge of the Shoulder, proved a fast and reliable companion for an inspired Reinhold Messner during the 1979 expedition.

The Himalayas, alpine-style

In the next six years, Reinhold Messner concentrated on the systematic ascent of all fourteen 8000-metre peaks. After climbing Shisha Pangma (1981), Kangchenjunga, Gasherbrum II and Broad Peak (1982), Cho Oyu (1983), Annapurna and Dhaulagiri (1985) and Makalu (1986), he concluded his epic on 16th October 1986 on the 8516-metre summit of Lhotse, the fifth-highest mountain on earth, which he climbed with South Tyrolean friend Hans Kammerlander. To describe that moment, Messner used the word that Tibetan merchants and pilgrims utter when they cross a particularly difficult pass: *Lhagyelo* (the gods have won).

Four years later, in 1962, Germans Toni Kinshofer, Anderl Mannhardt and Sigi Low, who had performed some great ascents in the Alps, put up a new and difficult route on the Diamir wall of Nanga Parbat.

But things were really changed in 1970 by a British expedition led by Chris Bonington, which conquered the awesome South face of Annapurna, a steep wall almost 3000 metres high. The summit was reached on 27th May by Don Whillans and Dougal Haston, who embraced on the snowcap after a nonstop two-month battle with the mountain. After their victory, the climbers rapidly left the mountain, but the 8000-metre peaks are liable to be treacherous. A

The great years of Reinhold Messner revolutionised climbing in the Himalaya, which in those years completed its transformation from geographical exploration to sporting adventure – the same process undergone by mountaineering in Europe a century earlier.

The opening of new routes by teams with no outside support, considered impossible until the ascent of Hidden Peak in 1975, became routine practice in just a few years. The same happened to ascents of the 8000-metre peaks without oxygen, and solo ascents of the highest peaks on earth, after Messner's two ascents of Everest.

Top-level climbing in these mountains began long before Messner's ascents, however. As early as 1958, an American expedition led by Norman Dyrenfurth made the third ascent to the summit along the British route, and added the first crossing of Everest, which Tom Hornbein and Willy Unsoeld accomplished by climbing the West Ridge and descending by the ordinary route from the south.

stone's throw from safety, Ian Clough was killed by an unforeseeable avalanche. However, his tragic death does not detract from the technical significance of the feat.

A month later, at the opposite end of the Himalayan chain, a Tyrolean expedition led by Karl Herrigkofler conquered the Rupal wall of Nanga Parbat. The first to reach the summit were brothers Reinhold and Gunther Messner, whose ascent, as we have seen, turned into a tragedy.

Then, ascents of the biggest walls became increasingly numerous in the Himalayas and the Karakorum. In 1971, a French expedition led by Robert Paragot scaled the West Pillar of Makalu. The next year, two international teams unsuccessfully attempted the threatening South-West face of Everest, which dominates the Valley of Silence and the ordinary ascent route to the summit. In 1975, a Yugoslav expedition led by Alex Kunaver conquered the steep South face of Makalu.

The Himalayas, alpine-style

*271 bottom right
Ian Clough, seen here
jumaring on an overhang
pitch on ice, was killed by
an avalanche at the foot of
the wall during the descent.*

272 top left Like all expeditions that follow the ordinary Nepalese route, the 1975 British expedition had to tackle the steep, dangerous pitches of the Khumbu Icefall, protected by the sherpas with fixed ropes and ladders.

272-273 Britons Nick Kekus (in the foreground) and Rick Allen (a little higher up) are recognisable in this photo, taken by Doug Scott during the 1987 attempt along the North-East ridge of Everest.

272 bottom Blizzards can create serious problems for climbers even on the ordinary Nepalese route on Everest. This photo shows one of the tents of the 1975 British expedition blown down by the wind in the Western Cwm.

But the same year, the attention of the media was galvanised once again by Everest, and a team led by Chris Bonington. Carrying excellent equipment and composed of some of the best climbers of the day, the expedition avoided the band of rocks that had hampered previous attempts by making a detour to the left and scaling a difficult couloir that reminded Nick Estcourt and Paul "Tut" Braithwaite of classic winter ascents in Scotland.

On 22nd September, Dougal Haston and Doug Scott pitched the last camp above the rock band. The next day they fixed ropes along another 500 metres of the wall. On the 24th, they set off confidently towards the summit, scaling the steep, dangerous icefields interrupted by treacherous low rock walls.

At 3 p.m., the pair finally came out onto the South Summit of Everest, where their route met that of Hillary and Tenzing. "In the Alps, it's OK to climb a route without reaching the summit, but it's different in the Himalaya. We knew we hadn't made it yet," wrote Dougal Haston. It took the two exhausted climbers another three hours to reach the 8848-metre summit, where a Chinese expedition had left a metal tripod a few weeks earlier. During the descent, Haston and Scott made the highest bivouac in history a few metres from the South Summit.

The next day, during the descent, the pair met up with three climbers heading for the summit. Mick Burke and Pertemba, the *sirdar* of the expedition, reached the summit of Everest as the weather was rapidly deteriorating. Mick Burke, alone and without ropes, was last sighted on the ridge as he climbed slowly towards the summit. He was never seen again.

The race to the great walls continued in the Eighties with the ascent of the South face of Dhaulagiri (a 4000-metre-high wall!), which was climbed in 1981 by Yugoslavs Stane Belak, Cene Bercic, Rok Kokar, Emil Tratnik and Joze Zupan. Two years later, Poles Jerzy Kukuczka and Woytek Kurtyka opened two new routes on Hidden Peak and Gasherbrum II, one after another. This feat was surpassed in 1984 by Catalans Eric Lucas and Nil Bohigas, who put up another difficult route on the South face of Annapurna, also as a two-man rope.

Of course, the race to climb the most difficult walls did not exclude those mountains that fail to reach the magic height of 8000 metres. This new trend was demonstrated in 1976 in two ascents by the best British climbers of the day. In the Indian Garwhal, Joe Tasker and Pete Boardman scaled the awesome West face of Changabang, an elegant 6782-metre peak, and in the Karakorum, Mo Anthoine, Martin Boysen, Joe Brown and Malcolm Howells conquered Nameless Tower (6239 m), the most spectacular peak in the Trango massif. The next year, the Great Trango Tower (6286 m) was summited by an American expedition.

274 left In the early months of 1985, Polish climbers made the first winter ascent of Cho Oyu, attempted in vain two years earlier by an expedition led by Reinhold Messner. In this photo, expedition leader Andrzej Zawada uses fixed ropes to scale a difficult pitch on mixed terrain.

274 centre right Pole Jerzy Kukuczka (left), shown in this 1980 photo with fellow-countryman Andrzej Czok, was the second man to climb all fourteen "eight-thousanders" in the Himalaya and the Karakorum. Shortly afterwards, Kukuczka was killed on the South face of Lhotse.

274 bottom right Pole Andrzej Zawada is not only an excellent climber but also organised expeditions which attempted the first winter ascents of the "eight-thousanders" in the Seventies and Eighties (and in many cases succeeded).

274 top right Winter expeditions to the "eight-thousanders" force climbers to tackle exceptionally hostile, difficult weather conditions. In this photo, Pole Andrzej Zawada rests in the blizzard next to the tents of the K2 base camp.

275 left Exceptionally difficult Himalayan climbing is not restricted to the "eight-thousanders." In this photo, Joe Tasker takes a breather on the summit of Changabang in the Indian Garwhal range after climbing the difficult vertical West face of the mountain with Pete Boardman.

275 right In the winter of 1987/88, a Polish team led by Andrzej Zawada attempted to climb K2, but had to turn back at an altitude of 7350 metres. In this photo, the climbers are about to reach the base camp.

The Himalayas, alpine-style

276 top While the general public was most interested in ascents of the "eight-thousanders," many of the best climbers in the world were concentrating on the great granite towers of the Karakorum and Garwhal. This photo shows the 1977 American expedition, which was the first to reach the summit of the Great Trango Tower.

276-277 After some extremely difficult pitches on rock and ice, an easy snow-covered ridge leads Americans Dennis Hennek, Jim Morrisey, Galen Rowell and John Roskelley to the summit of the Great Trango Tower.

277 top As in the major ascents in the Alps, Patagonia and North America, those climbing the Trango Towers have to change technique rapidly from very steep ice and snow slopes to equally difficult rock climbing pitches.

277 bottom When seen from Liligo, on the route leading to the foot of K2, the Great Trango Tower looks like a gigantic, awesome granite castle. The shadow of the nearby (equally difficult) Nameless Tower falls on its walls.

278 The route put up by
the British climbers on the
Ogre comprises a series of
difficult traverses on the
steep snow and ice slopes.
Doug Scott's descent of
these pitches, with broken
legs, is one of the most
amazing feats in climbing
history.

279 top Chris Bonington,
who made some major
ascents in the Alps and
Patagonia in the Sixties,
tackled some of the most
difficult walls in the
Himalaya and Karakorum
in the subsequent decades.
This 1977 photo shows him
on the summit of the Ogre.

279 centre left The steep
slopes of the Ogre force
climbers to set up their
camps in particularly
exposed positions. To pitch
their tents, they have to dig
out clearings or snowholes
in the ice.

 The Himalayas,
alpine-style

A year later, Chris Bonington and Doug Scott
reached the summit of the Ogre (7285 m), another of the
most elegant pinnacles in the Karakorum range. During
the descent, Scott slipped while abseiling and broke
both legs, and Bonington was forced to lower him
bodily down the entire wall. On reaching the glacier, the
exhausted Bonington set off in search of help, but before
the rescuers arrived, Doug Scott kept going, crawling on
all fours over the interminable débris-covered glacier to
the relative safety of the base camp.

The ascent performed in the Karakorum in 1985 by
Austrian Robert Schauer and Pole Woytek Kurtyka, who
climbed the awesome South-West face of Gasherbrum
IV which overlooks the Concordia amphitheatre, was
less dramatic, but even more impressive from the
technical standpoint. It was a top-level ascent,
performed on a mountain that fails to reach the magic
8000-metre level by just 20 metres. The descent, along
the 1958 Italian route, was also particularly difficult.

279 centre right This photo,
taken during the 1977
expedition, shows Doug
Scott on the summit of the
Ogre, one of the most
spectacular and difficult
"seven-thousanders" in the
Pakistani Karakorum.

279 bottom left Despite
the high technical level
achieved during the
climb, the first ascent of
the Ogre went down in
the annals of
mountaineering history
because of the terrible

accident suffered by Doug
Scott, who broke both legs
at the beginning of the
descent. In this dramatic
photo, the British climber
can be seen crawling down
the glacier at the base of the
"seven-thousander."

279 bottom right
This photo, taken during the
descent of the Ogre, shows
Doug Scott crawling
towards Clive Rowlands,
using the great steps dug for
him by his climbing
companions.

Light expeditions to the toughest walls of the 8000-metre peaks have continued up to the present day, with outstanding results. The most important ascents include those of the East face of Everest by an American expedition (1983), the Magic Line on K2 by Poles Jerzy Kukuczka and Tadeusz Piotrowski (1986), the North-West ridge of K2 by Frenchmen Christophe Profit and Pierre Béghin (1991), and the South-West ridge of Kangchenjunga South (7476 m) by Slovenians Andrej Stremfelj and Marko Prezelzj (1994).

In the meantime, different kinds of challenge between man and the mountains were becoming popular on the highest summits on earth. The toughest of all are first winter ascents. This is a gruelling form of

climbing which exposes its practitioners to temperatures as low as 60° below zero. Among the best in this field are Polish expeditions, which climbed Everest in the winter of 1980, Cho Oyu in 1985 (by a new route!) and Kangchenjunga in 1986.

Another increasingly popular sport is speed climbing, in which some truly impressive feats have been performed. In 1984, Pole Krzystof Wielicki was the first to ascend and descend an 8000-metre peak (Broad Peak) in a single day. In 1986, French climber Benoit Chamoux emulated his feat on K2, while in 1988, fellow Frenchman Marc Batard became the first man to ascend and descend Everest in a day.

Though amazing from the athletic standpoint, these feats are performed on routes prepared and equipped by other climbers, and their technical content is therefore relatively small. The feat performed on Everest in 1986 by Swiss climbers Erhard Loretan and Jean Troillet, who ascended and descended the steep Norton Couloir which cuts through the north side of the mountain in just 43 hours, was far more demanding in climbing terms.

The solo ascent by Messner on the north side of Everest inaugurated another major type of climbing, namely solo ascents of the highest peaks on Earth. Nanga Parbat had already been soloed by Hermann Buhl in 1951, but the Austrian climber had merely completed the team work performed on the sides of the mountain.

280 left The elegant snow-covered pyramid of Jannu (called Kumbakharna by the Nepalis) is 7710 metres tall, and was first climbed in 1962 by a French expedition led by Lionel Terray.

280 top right The ascent of Jannu, performed with extensive use of fixed ropes by the Terray expedition, was repeated in Alpine style in 1982 by another French team, led by Pierre Béghin.

280 bottom right This photo of the 1982 expedition to Jannu shows some of the climbers scaling a steep snow-covered wall.

281 As demonstrated by the difficult ice pitch being tackled in this photo by members of the 1982 Béghin expedition, many Himalayan "seven-thousanders" involve far more difficult ascents than the majority of "eight-thousanders," even if climbed by the ordinary routes.

*The Himalayas,
alpine-style*

Genuine solo ascents were made by Pierre Béghin on Kangchenjunga (1983) and Marc Batard on the West Pillar of Makalu (1989), while Italian Renato Casarotto made the first ascent of Broad Peak North (7550 m) in seven days in 1982. In 1986, the blackest year for K2, Casarotto soloed much of the Magic Line before falling tragically to his death in a crevasse at the foot of the mountain.

Another great solo climber in the Himalaya is Tomo Cesen, a Slovenian from Kranj, who soloed the North face of Yalung Kang (the 8443-metre northern fore-summit of Kangchenjunga), a new route on K2, and a very difficult route on the North face of Jannu (7710 m) during the Eighties. Cesen's masterpiece, in 1990, was

the first ever and first solo ascent of the South face of Lhotse, the most dangerous wall in the Himalaya, which had rebuffed the 1975 Italian expedition and killed great climbers like Frenchman Nicolas Jaeger and Pole Jerzy Kukuczka.

Initially acclaimed worldwide, the ascent of the South face was later doubted by some French climbers and by Reinhold Messner. Who was right? There were no photos to prove that Cesen had reached the summit of Lhotse, but this also applies to many other major ascents that no one has ever dreamed of challenging. Tomo's track record proves that he was perfectly capable of climbing that terrible wall. No more than that can be said for certain.

283 top This photo, taken in 1988 on the north side of K2, shows the typical high-altitude camp of a modern Himalayan expedition. The outcrop of rock that protects the tent against avalanches also serves to keep the gear tidy, battened down with nails and a tangle of ropes.

283 bottom Despite the intense cold, twilight is a magical moment for expeditions to the highest mountains on Earth. This 1991 photo shows the tents of an expedition at the base camp of K2.

282-283 Although it was sighted by Francis Younghusband in 1887, the north side of K2 remained unknown to climbers until 1982, when a Japanese expedition obtained permission from the Chinese government to climb the North face. Seven climbers reached the summit. This photo shows the French expedition of 1988.

282 bottom The upper part of the North face of K2 features a series of steep snow and ice slopes that rise towards the summit between the rocky contours of the North edge and the North-East ridge. This 1988 photo shows a French climber.

284 top The magical, delicate light of the full moon makes the North face of K2, easily recognisable in this photo, particularly lovely. This face was first climbed by a Japanese expedition in 1982.

284-285 In the summer of 1991, Frenchmen Pierre Béghin and Christophe Profit put up a complicated, difficult route on K2. After setting off from the Savoia Glacier, they scaled the North-West ridge, the North-West face and the last section of the 1982 Japanese route. This photo shows Profit on the upper part of the route.

285 top This photo of the 1991 French expedition shows Christophe Profit during the steep, exposed traverse of the North-West face of K2. The tent pitched by the two men on an outcrop of rock can be seen on the far left of the photo.

285 bottom Among the still unsolved problems of K2, an important one is the North Spur of the mountain, which was attempted several times during the Eighties and Nineties. This photo, taken at the base of the Spur, shows the 1988 French expedition.

The Himalayas, alpine-style

286-287 Despite the opening of numerous very difficult routes on the flanks of Everest, the North Col route, identified and attempted by the seven British expeditions between the wars, remains one of the most popular in the Himalaya. This photo, taken by Canadian Patrick Morrow, shows the trail beaten in the snow with great effort on the ridge above the North Col.

287 top One of the most important ascents made by Italian Renato Casarotto outside Europe was the inauguration of a new route on Broad Peak North. This photo shows Casarotto among the seracs at the foot of the mountain.

287 centre As a result of its height, difficulty and remote position, Kangchenjunga, situated on the border between Nepal and Indian Sikkim, is one of the least often climbed "eight-thousanders." This photo was taken from the summit ridge of Jannu.

287 bottom left French climber Benoit Chamoux was known in the Eighties for his fast ascents of the ordinary routes on the "eight-thousanders." His dream of becoming the world's third climber to scale the fourteen highest peaks on earth led to his death in 1995, not far from the summit of Kangchenjunga.

287 bottom right Another photo of Benoit Chamoux shows the Frenchman, with his skis on his rucksack, resting on the north side of Mount Everest.

The last of the new trends in Himalayan mountaineering is what was once disparagingly called the "rat race," but is now taken seriously by all the world's top climbers. The race to climb all fourteen "eight-thousanders" was won by Messner in 1986, emulated later by Jerzy Kukuczka, Erhard Loretan, Krzystof Wielicki, Carlos Carsolio, Fausto De Stefani and Sergio Martini. However, Pat Morrow, a Canadian climber and mountain photographer, beat Messner and American millionaire Dick Bass in the race to climb all of the Seven Summits – the highest peak on each of the seven continents.

Before ending this chapter, it is worth considering the other face of Himalayan climbing, which often causes Everest, K2 and their neighbours to hit the headlines all over the world. This is the face of death, still an ever-present threat for climbers at high altitude in Asia. The

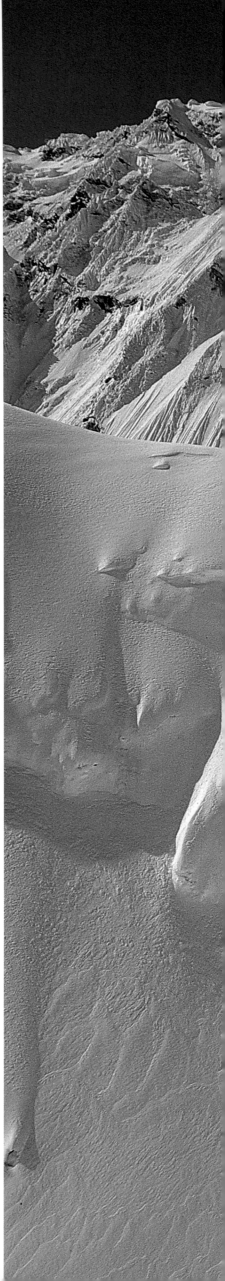

288 top Although a thousand climbers have already made the ascent, the summit of Everest remains a major aspiration for every climber in the world. In this photo, two sherpas who accompanied the 1982 Canadian expedition celebrate on the summit.

288 bottom Many of the numerous mortal accidents that take place on Everest have occurred on the exposed snow ridge that connects the South Peak to the Hillary Step and the summit. A slip at this point nearly always results in a fatality.

deaths of Mummery, Welzembach and Merkl on Nanga Parbat, Mallory and Irvine on Everest, Art Gilkey and Mario Puchoz on K2 stand as a reminder that survival at high altitude has been difficult ever since the very first expeditions to the Himalaya.

In the Eighties and Nineties, however, the increasing difficulty of the routes climbed and the large number of very small expeditions made the sport increasingly hazardous, even for the best climbers in the world. Until the Second World War, many of the best climbers in the Alps died in climbing accidents, but nowadays, thanks to scientific training and increasingly sophisticated gear, climbers who specialise in the Dolomites and Mont Blanc are only rarely exposed to mortal danger.

In the Himalaya, however, the rarefied atmosphere and objective dangers mean that the boundary between life and death is still easily crossed. Sadly, this is demonstrated by the death in the mountains of many of

the best climbers of the past few decades. The tragic fate of Alan Rouse and Pierre Béghin, Benoit Chamoux and Wanda Rutkiewicz, Renato Casarotto and Jerzy Kukuczka demonstrates the aptness of the Italian title of Reinhold Messner's book: *Sopravvissuto* (Survivor) (called *All Fourteen Eight-thousanders* in the English version).

However, it is not only the best climbers who get killed. Everest and the "easy" 8000-metre peaks like Hidden Peak, Cho Oyu, Gasherbrum II and Broad Peak in particular are visited not only by well-prepared expeditions but also by expeditions from countries with little or no climbing tradition, and paying groups organised by mountain guides.

Tragic seasons like summer 1986 on K2 (13 deaths) and spring 1996 on Everest (12 deaths) stand as a dire warning. Even now that all the records have been demolished, the "eight-thousanders" still remain the harshest and most dangerous mountains on Earth.

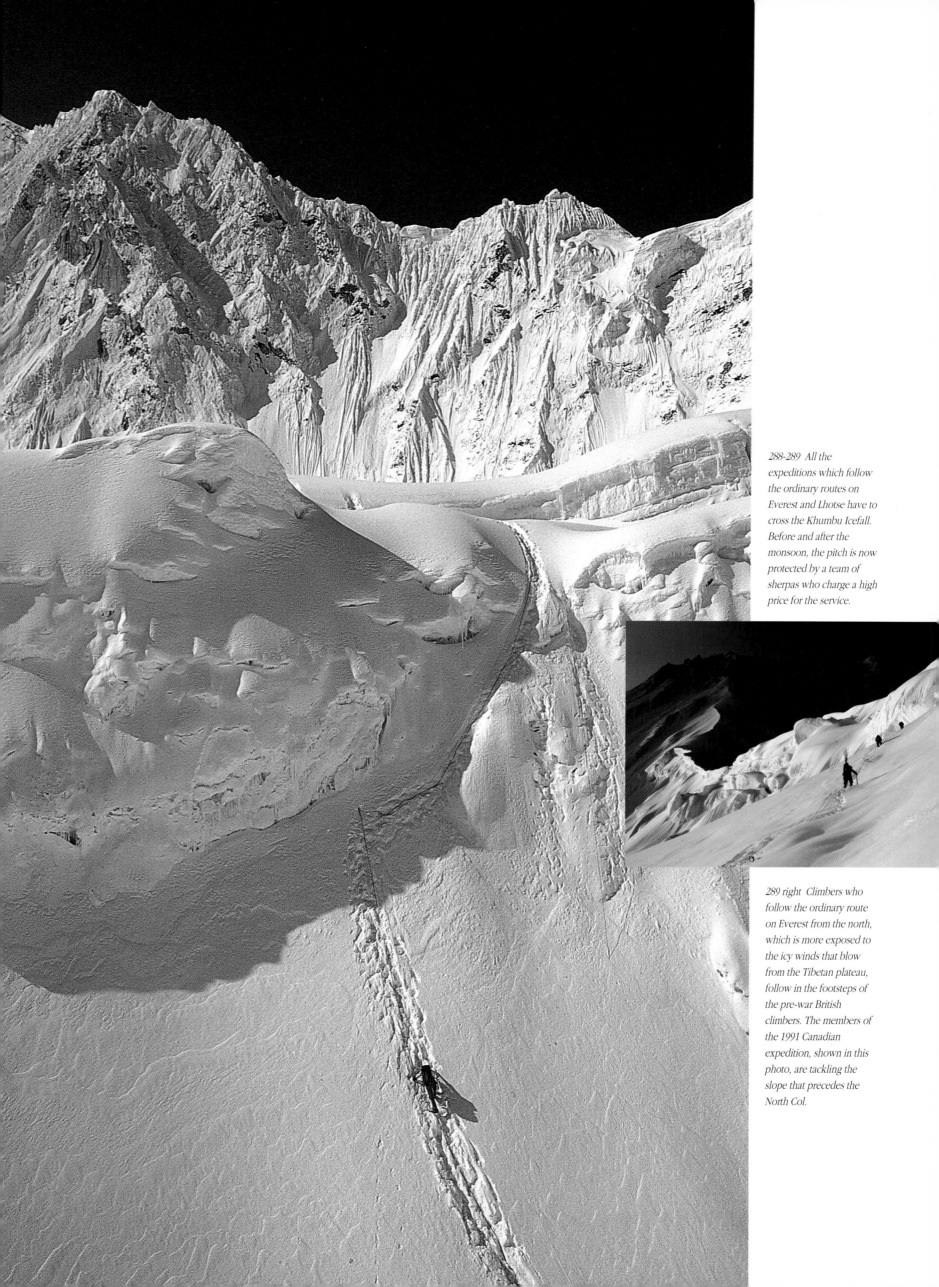

288-289 All the expeditions which follow the ordinary routes on Everest and Lhotse have to cross the Khumbu Icefall. Before and after the monsoon, the pitch is now protected by a team of sherpas who charge a high price for the service.

289 right Climbers who follow the ordinary route on Everest from the north, which is more exposed to the icy winds that blow from the Tibetan plateau, follow in the footsteps of the pre-war British climbers. The members of the 1991 Canadian expedition, shown in this photo, are tackling the slope that precedes the North Col.

290 top Three American climbers, roped together, are slowly scaling the Abruzzi Spur along a narrow snow-covered passage. Behind them, photographer Greg Child has immortalised among the clouds the impressive glaciers at the base of K2: the Godwin Austen and Baltoro Glaciers.

290 bottom American Phil Ershlel, a member of the 1990 American expedition to K2, descends one of the steepest walls of the Abruzzi Spur in a blizzard. The poor visibility increases the difficulty of the pitch, and a tight hold on the rope provides the only link with safety in this hostile environment.

290-291 It is not unusual for violent weather conditions to hit the summit of K2. In this photo of the Pakistani side, the horizontal light of the sun and the snow blown up by the strong wind create an icy maelstrom of colour and movement.

291 bottom left Two American climbers photographed by Scott Darsney at camp one during the 1992 expedition to the west side of K2.

291 bottom right In this photo, American Scott Darsney begins the ascent along the West ridge of K2, leaving the tents of camp two behind him.

292-293 The strenuous effort needed to climb the summit ridge of Mount Everest is rewarded by the amazing view. In the foreground, French climber Christine Janin, close to the summit, is following the tracks left by climber Pascal Tournaire, who took the photo.

293 top In the warm atmosphere of twilight a member of the autumn 1990 French expedition led by Marc Batard climbs towards camp three, pitched on the ordinary Nepalese route on Mount Everest.

293 centre French climbers cross the labyrinth of seracs, great blocks of unstable ice and precarious snow bridges that form the Icefall, one of the most dangerous sections on the ordinary Nepalese route on Mount Everest.

293 bottom The huge terminal pyramid of Everest, lashed by a gale, looms up before these two mountaineers, immortalised by Swiss climber Robert Bösch during the interminable ascent of the west side.

The Himalayas, alpine-style

294

294 top *294 top Two American climbers, members of the 1997 expedition to Kangchenjunga, caught in a blizzard, prepare to batten down the tents of camp three on the north side of the mountain.*

294 bottom Some members of the 1997 American expedition to Kangchenjunga put up a route on the north side of the mountain. Their progress was slowed by the fresh snow.

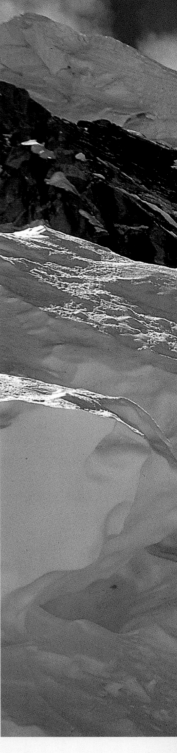

294-295 This eloquent
picture taken by Scott
Darsney gives an insight into
the determination, stamina
and technical skill required
to scale the precipitous sheet
of ice on the north side of
Kangchenjunga.

295 bottom
Kangchenjunga, the third-
highest mountain on earth,
situated on the border
between Sikkim and
Nepal, was first climbed
by a British expedition
in 1955.

Smooth slabs and speed climbing

On the last day of June, 1982, a real breakthrough in mountaineering history took place on Mont Blanc. twenty-four-year-old Frenchman Christophe Profit left Chamonix by helicopter, and by 1 p.m. was ready to tackle the West face of the Dru, which had witnessed the epic feats of Lucien Bérardini, Walter Bonatti, Royal Robbins and René Desmaison, in the previous 30 years.

His predecessors had been equipped with rucksacks full of ropes, pitons, food and bivouac gear. But Christophe attacked the American Direct Route, the most difficult and elegant on the wall, wearing light trousers and a T-shirt. He carried neither rucksack nor ropes, not even a krab to belay himself. He was a little tense during the first part of the route.

Then, Profit's training and class took over. One after another he scaled the 45-metre groove, the *Bloc Coincé*, the 90-metre groove and the other very difficult pitches which have made this route famous among climbers from all over the world. In 3 hours 10 minutes Christophe reached the exit of the American Direct Route, where a group of friends were waiting for him with the climbing boots, ice-axe and crampons he needed to scale the steep pitches of mixed terrain that lay between him and the summit.

Christophe's speed and style attracted great admiration from climbers, although there was some criticism from purists. "I made this ascent for myself," said Profit in an interview with the author in 1984. "Those who accuse me of cheating don't understand. I succeeded in soloing that route because I knew the pitches, I didn't carry a rucksack, and I didn't waste any energy on the walk-in. If anyone repeats the climb on-site, doing the walk-in and carrying their boots and gear with them, I'll be the first to applaud."

The American Direct Route was by no means an isolated feat. In the late Seventies, an entire generation of French climbers had embarked on high-speed climbing on the most difficult routes of Mont Blanc. Apart from Christophe Profit and Jean-Marc Boivin, the group included Eric Escoffier, Patrick Bérhault, Thierry Renault and Catherine Destivelle. Later came Alain Ghersen, Fred Vimal and François Marsigny.

In the early Eighties, however, Profit was the man of the moment. In 1980 he scaled the North-East couloir of the Dru (where Cecchinel and Jäger had required three bivouacs) in 4 and an half hours. In winter 1983 he scaled the North face of the Droites, the North face of the Aiguille de Talèfre and the Linceul on the Grandes Jorasses in succession, in just 22 hours.

In 1984 Profit put up a new route on the Grandes Jorasses with Dominique Radigue, and made a solo repeat of the Hypercouloir in 6 hours. The next winter

he soloed the "Great Peuterey Ridge" in 32 hours. Five years later he repeated the climb, again in winter, this time taking only 19 hours. The spectacular photos published in *Paris Match* turned Christophe Profit into a big star.

In July 1984, climbing with Thierry Renault, Profit scaled the North face of Pilier d'Angle, the Bardill Direct Route and the classic route on the Central Pillar, followed by the easier Innominata Ridge, all in one day. Not long afterwards, with Dominique Radigue, he climbed the four Frêney Pillars on the same day.

However, Profit's most remarkable feat was accomplished in the summer of 1985, when he scaled the three most famous North faces of the Alps, one after another, on the same day, air-lifted from one to another by helicopter. He took 6.45 hours to climb the North face of the Eiger, the longest and most dangerous of the three, then polished off the rocks and ice slopes of the North face of the Matterhorn in 4 hours. At the end of the day, he took just 4 hours to climb the ice slope of the Linceul, where the great René Desmaison had needed seven bivouacs 16 years earlier.

In those years, Christophe Profit found that he had nowhere near reached the limit of his abilities. In early 1987, this astonishing climber repeated the enchaînement of the three North faces in mid-winter, taking 42 hours of actual climbing. This time, the open competition between Profit and his friend and rival Eric

296 bottom right Frenchman Christophe Profit is the best known speed climber on the walls of Mont Blanc and the other great mountains in the Western Alps. This photo shows him soloing the North face of the Matterhorn in winter 1987.

296-297 The solo ascent of the American Direct Route on the West face of the Dru, performed at the beginning of summer 1982, was one of Christophe Profit's most famous climbs. For this ascent, many climbers need one or more bivouacs on the wall, but Profit completed it in just over 3 hours.

297 top right In Christophe Profit's enchaînements, which receive a great deal of media coverage, the use of the helicopter to travel from one peak to the next is often of crucial importance. This photo was taken on the summit of the Grandes Jorasses.

297 bottom right The first ascensionists of the severe North face of the Eiger (1938) and the first winter ascensionists (1961) required numerous bivouacs, but it was scaled in record time by the best climbers of the Eighties.

Escoffier made the venture even more exciting for the general public.

Christophe set off first, and always retained his lead over Eric, who kept close on his heels on the Grandes Jorasses and the Matterhorn. However, on the North face of the Eiger, Profit's lead proved decisive when the arrival in the Oberland of a violent front from the west prevented Eric from attempting the last wall of the three.

Profit was already on the wall when the weather began to break. He decided to stay there, increased his rate of progress, and managed to reach the summit and the helicopter waiting to take him back down to Grindelwald before the storm shrouded the dark walls of the "Ogre."

Fast climbs up the most difficult walls of the Alps were not invented by Christophe Profit, however. French climber Nicolas Jaeger had climbed the Pilier d'Angle and the Central Pillar of Mont Blanc one after another in one and a half days in 1975, and Jean-Marc Boivin had scaled the Linceul in 2.45 hours in 1977.

Next, Boivin climbed the South face of the Aiguille du Fou and the American Direct Route on the Dru one after another with Patrick Bérhault, flying from one to the other in a two-man hang-glider. In the summer of 1983, Boivin climbed the "Great Peuterey Ridge" in 10 hours and a half. Three years later, in the depths of winter, he climbed the North faces of the Verte, the Droites, the Courtes and the Grandes Jorasses one after another.

The supremacy of the French was challenged by Tomo Cesen, a young Slovenian climber who was to become famous in 1989 and 1990 for his solo ascents of the Jannu and Lhotse walls. He also climbed the North faces of the Eiger, the Grandes Jorasses and the Matterhorn, one after another, in summer 1987. Though he was just as fast as the two French champions on the mountain face, Tomo took longer to get from one peak to another because he crossed the Alps in his battered old Yugoslavian runabout instead of using a helicopter.

When Christophe Profit decided to take up less nerve-racking forms of climbing and become a guide in around 1990, the media lost interest in solo speed climbs on the walls of the Western Alps. However, French climbers Fred Vimal, Alain Ghersen, Jean-Christophe Lafaille and Catherine Destivelle continued to perform their remarkable *enchaînements* on the walls of the Mont Blanc massif.

In 1990, Vimal combined the Walker Spur with the Great Peuterey Ridge in a total of 48 hours. Then Ghersen repeated his feat, adding the American Direct route on the Dru at the beginning; he took a total of 66 hours. After that, Catherine Destivelle, the French women's climbing ace, scaled the Bonatti Pillar on the Dru in 5 hours.

The next year, Lafaille put up two new routes in succession on the Pilier d'Angle and the Central Pillar.

However, the most imaginative feat was performed by Alain Ghersen, who raced from Paris to the summit of Mont Blanc in 49 hours via a 7b pitch on the boulders of Fontainebleau, an 8a+ route on the walls of the Saussois, and the Great Peuterey Ridge.

Not all the best mountaineers were interested in speed climbing, however. French climber Louis Audoubert, who was especially at home in the Pyrenees, made first winter ascents of the three great ridges on the Italian side of Mont Blanc – the Peuterey, Innominata and Brouillard Ridges --– between 1972 and 1982, climbing as part of a team, with numerous bivouacs. In the early Nineties, Catherine Destivelle and Marc Batard put up various new winter solo routes on the Grandes Jorasses and the Dru, also with numerous bivouacs.

However, the greatest representative of the blood, sweat and tears style of climbing was Italian Renato Casarotto, who made some great solo ascents in the Dolomites and the Andes as well as Mont Blanc, and was killed in 1986 while climbing the Magic Line on K2.

His most famous ascent on Mont Blanc took place in February 1982. Bowed under the weight of a 40 kg rucksack, which he only dragged behind him on the most difficult pitches, Casarotto climbed the Ratti-Vitali route on the West face of the Aiguille Noire, the Gervasutti-Boccalatte route on Pic Gugliermina and the Central Pillar on Mont Blanc, one after another.

298-299 The best-known climber active in the Western Alps at the end of the 20th century was Frenchwoman Catherine Destivelle. This photo shows her free-climbing a difficult crack on Mont Blanc.

299 bottom This photo shows Tomo Cesen, the outstanding climber from Kranj, scaling the limestone crag of Osp in the Slovenian Carso. The pitch is rated at 7c+.

298 left Slovenian climber Tomo Cesen became famous in the late Eighties for his solo ascents on the Himalayan walls of Jannu and Lhotse. This photo shows him climbing in the Mont Blanc massif.

298 right French climber Jean-Christophe Lafaille switches nonchalantly between the Alps and the Himalaya. In this photo, he is aid-climbing a crack on the granite of Mont Blanc.

Fast or slow, the climbers we have named so far occupied the front pages of the newspapers and appeared on the television news in the Eighties and Nineties. However, for most climbers, the major development of the period was something quite different. The new style of rock climbing developed in Yosemite Valley and on the sunny crags of Verdon began to appear on the walls of the Western Alps too.

As a result of new gear and more specific training, a new generation of explorer-climbers identified and conquered hundreds of "new problems," thus changing the climbing geography of Mont Blanc and the Pennine Alps for the umpteenth time in two centuries.

The "new climbers" can climb fast and light up the most difficult slabs and cracks, as abseiling down bolted routes means that they can quickly return for the gear (climbing boots, ice-axes and crampons) they need to go back down to the valley.

The key personality in the rediscovery of rock climbing on Mont Blanc was Swiss mountaineer Michel Piola. This taciturn mountain guide from Geneva, who had also written climbing guide books, identified and put up hundreds of new routes on the slabs of the Peigne, the Aiguille de Blaitière, the Aiguilles Dorées and the Petites Jorasses.

However, the favourite venues of Michel and his climbing companions Pierre-Alain Steiner, Daniel Anker, Gérard Hopfgartner and Romain Vogler are the magnificent slabs on the east side of the Grépon, the Aiguille du Plan and their complicated buttresses.

Thanks to their new routes, the lonely refuge hut of Envers des Aiguilles, patronised only by imitators of Young, Knubel, the Lochmatters and Ryan until the Seventies, has become the most popular meeting point for climbers in the whole Mont Blanc massif.

Michel Piola and his climbing companions also put up many routes of outstanding difficulty and elegance on the South face of the Aiguille du Midi and the East face of the Grand Capucin, where the great routes pioneered by Gaston Rébuffat and Walter Bonatti were rapidly abandoned in favour of the new Ma Dalton, Monsieur de Mesmaeker, Super Dupont, O Sole Mio and Voyage selon Gulliver, severe high-altitude routes with numerous pitches exceeding the sixth grade.

However, it would be a mistake to dismiss Michel Piola as a specialist in sunny crags. He and his friends have also made their mark on the Frêney and Brouillard Pillars on Mont Blanc and the pillars of Mont Blanc du Tacul, and in 1979, climbing with Gérard Hopfgartner, Piola scaled the rocky pillar that closes the North face of the Eiger to the right.

Four years later, with René Ghilini, Piola returned to the Eiger to tackle the compact, vertical wall on the right of the John Harlin Direct route. This route, which includes some long 6a sections and numerous difficult aid pitches, took the two climbers five days' struggle.

In 1988, climbing with Daniel Anker, Michel Piola completed his hat trick by scaling the grey wall to the left of the 1979 route. Here, the free-climbing rating goes as high as 6c, but the team took "only" three days on the wall. Piola completed his impressive feats in the Alps with a new route on the overhanging Z'mutt Nose on the Matterhorn.

In 1983 and 1984, in two expeditions to Greenland, Piola made the first ascents of granite walls like the South face of the 1000-metre tall Ulamertoksuak and the West face of the 1400-metre Ketil Pingasut. And in 1988, he climbed the West Pillar of the Central Tower of Mount Trango in the Karakorum, a 27-pitch route with pitches of up to 6c and A4, with Stéphane Schafter, Michel Fauquet and Patrick Delale.

Others who made their mark on the rock walls of Mont Blanc in the Eighties and Nineties apart from Michel Piola were French climbers Jean-Marc Boivin, René Ghilini, Jean-Marc Troussier and Bruno Cormier, Swiss brothers Claude and Yves Rémy, and Italians Manlio Motto and Giovanni Bassanini from Rome, a Courmayeur-based guide who specialises in all-free repeats of the toughest routes, and regularly leads his clients on the most difficult walls of the Mont Blanc massif.

While the "roof of Europe" provides the ideal venue for climbing on granite, top-class new routes continue to be put up on ice and mixed terrain in the Bernese Oberland and the massifs of the Pennine Alps. Here too, some brilliant enchaînements have been performed, far from the limelight of Chamonix.

In winter 1986 Swiss mountaineers Erhard Loretan (who became the third climber to scale all fourteen of the world's 8000-metre peaks in 1996) and André Georges took eighteen days to climb the "Imperial Crown," the arc of peaks including Monte Rosa, the Matterhorn, the Dent Blanche and the Weisshorn which surrounds Zermatt and the Mattertal.

Three years later, in winter 1988-89, the same climbers performed another outstanding *enchaînement*, climbing thirteen North faces in the Bernese Oberland, including the North face of the Eiger, one after another, in thirteen days.

Even the "little" old Alps evidently offer adventures that bear comparison with the Himalaya if their possibilities are exploited intelligently.

300 left Despite the exceptionally difficult pitches they climb, the best modern climbers still play around with the rock. This photo shows Swiss climber Romain Vogler "embracing" an overhang on the Rêve de Singe route (Mont Blanc).

300-301 From the late Seventies onwards, Michel Piola from Geneva revolutionised climbing on Mont Blanc, where he put up hundreds of extremely difficult routes. His favourite venues in the massif were the Aiguille du Midi, the Grand Capucin and the buttresses of the Grands Charmoz. However, Piola also inaugurated some important routes in the Karakorum, Baffin Island and Madagascar. This photo shows him climbing the Trango Towers.

301 top right Pierre-Alain Steiner, one of Michel Piola's favourite climbing companions, is shown here climbing the Passage Cardiaque route on the Dru in fog.

301 bottom right Swiss climber Michel Piola is shown here at the start of a bivouac on the North face of the Eiger. Piola put up three very difficult routes on this wall.

Free climbing comes into its own

In the early Eighties, some sensational climbing pictures received widespread coverage all over Europe. Readers of *Epoca*, *Paris Match* and *Stern*, and television viewers all over the continent, who were used to seeing pictures of Reinhold Messner in action in the snows of the Himalaya and old-fashioned climbing in the Dolomites that revolved around aiders and overhangs, were suddenly confronted with a totally different image of climbing.

In photos and films, a young French climber was shown on a compact vertical wall that looked totally impossible to the layman. The general public in Europe knew nothing of Yosemite and the hippy style of its regular climbers. The climber's long hair and brightly-coloured trousers and T-shirt made the scene all the more surprising.

However, the young French climber was not a hippy at all. Patrick Edlinger was just over 20 years old, and was devoting all his energy to cragging after years of top-level climbing in the mountains of the Dauphiné. The location of the photos and films in which he starred were the walls of the Verdon Grand Canyon in Provence.

There, 30 kilometres as the crow flies from the coast of Esterel and St. Tropez, the gentle Côte d'Azur and the pastel shades beloved of Van Gogh seem like pale memories. This is the Provence of stone, the sharp lines of limestone, and the hard, uncompromising contours of rock. There, millennium after millennium, the cold, rushing waters of the River Verdon excavated the most spectacular canyon in France.

Ever since the early days of tourism, French and foreign tourists had described this valley as the "Grand Canyon of Europe." Edouard-Alfred Martel, the inventor of potholing, was the first to tackle the Verdon rapids with three friends and two canvas dinghies in 1905. The complete crossing of the gorge took them four hard days.

In the years between the two World Wars, the Touring Club de France equipped the spectacular trail that crosses the ravine, and is now named after Martel, with tunnels and metal ladders. The roads along the edges of the canyon were also widened, and viewpoints were constructed. The road that follows the southern edge of the gorge from the Artuby Bridge at Aiguines was to become famous with the well-deserved name *Corniche Sublime*.

Its distance from big cities and the Alps, and the exceptionally compact rock, meant that climbing came fairly late to Verdon. It was only in 1968 that Joel Coqueugniot and François Guillot from Marseilles scaled the Escalès wall, the tallest and most compact in the canyon, along the 320 metre *Voie de la Demande*. This is a sixth-grade route, mostly along cracks, which soon became famous.

In the years that followed, many of the best French climbers put up increasingly steep and difficult routes along the cracks and slabs that slope sheer down to the waters of the River Verdon. The ratings of the pitchs climbed went higher and higher, and the exceptionally compact rock soon forced climbers to protect themselves with bolts, which later came into common use on the crags of continental Europe.

The exposure (*gaz* in French climbers' slang) was total. Some long, demanding aid routes were put up in the most overhanging areas in the early Seventies which recall the most famous routes in Yosemite Valley, though on a more limited scale. However, the routes destined to become world-famous were the free-climbing routes, given fanciful names like Necronomicon, Dingomaniaque, La Mangoustine Scatophage, Luna-Bong, Caca-boudin, L'Eperon Sublime and Le Triomphe d'Eros.

Above all, a breakthrough in the exposure and difficulties overcome was made by the Pichenibule route, which totally abandons the cracks and climbs directly along the most compact slabs on the wall. "Pichenibule marked the beginning of a new era in rock climbing in Verdon," said Patrick Cordier before describing the pitch in his book *Les Préalpes du Sud*. "The setting of these pitches is extraordinary, the void is total, and the quality of the rock verges on perfection." Cordier also explained the origin of the route's name. "Pichenibule was a sheep owned by Jean-Patrick Moron, one of the first ascensionists. So this sheep got to be famous among climbers, and not only in France, because that route's now famous all over the world!"

Competition between the top names in the new-style French climbing to open major routes at Verdon, already intense at the time of *Voie de la Demande*, became even fiercer. In the Seventies, the years of exploration, the climbers in action on those crags apart from Coqueugniot and Guillot included Jacques Perrier, known as "Pschitt," Jean-Claude Droyer, Christian Guyomar, Patrick Cordier, Guy Abert, Bernard Gorgeon and Stéphane Troussier.

By the end of the Eighties, all-free ascents of the old routes were the order of the day. Now, the top climbers were Patrick Bérhault and Patrick Edlinger. Edlinger, who frequently appeared in TV commercials and press advertisements, made the compact limestone walls of Provence famous all over the world.

Although Verdon became exceptionally famous in just a few years, low-altitude climbing has always played an important part in the training of city climbers. In the early 20th century, for example, the best German climbers like Rudolf Fehrmann and Fritz Wiessner scaled sixth-grade pitches on the sandstone towers of the Elbsandsteingebirge and nearby Bohemia.

Between the wars, Pierre Allain and other climbers from Paris refined their technique on the boulders of Fontainebleau forest just outside the capital, while climbers from Geneva practised on the limestone walls

302 top Frenchwoman
Catherine Destivelle, an
outstanding cragger, became
known in the mid-Eighties for
her ascents on Mont Blanc
and in the Himalaya. Here,
she is climbing in Verdon.

302 bottom Cragging
is one of the most
spectacular forms of free
climbing. In this photo,
Wolfgang Gullich is tackling
a rather awkward diagonal
crack.

of Mont Salève, located across the French border just
south of the southern shore of Lake Geneva. On the
Italian side of the Alps, Riccardo Cassin and his
climbing companions from Lecco tackled the soaring
limestone pinnacles of the Grigna in the Lombardy
Pre-Alps.

Much farther east, Emilio Comici and other climbers
from Trieste systematically scaled the walls of Val
Rosandra in the Carso. In Great Britain, where the lack
of mountains means that cragging has a much older
tradition, the walls and cliffs of Cornwall, the Lake
District, northern England and Wales have been
popular with climbers ever since the sport began.

However, the loveliest and most spectacular crags
in Europe are undoubtedly the Calanques, an
outstandingly beautiful microcosm of towers, fjords and
limestone walls overlooking the blue waters of the
Mediterranean not far from Marseilles. Popular with
local climbers from the early 20th century, the walls of
Morgiou, Sormiou, Sugiton and En Vau became classics
in the years leading up to the Second World War. When
peace finally returned to Europe, the best climbers from
Marseilles, like Gaston Rébuffat and Georges Livanos,
made these walls famous among European climbers.

In the Seventies, the search for new walls and the
invention of new equipment and new techniques
revolutionised the geography of European climbing,
but this time, along with their shoes, their ropes, and
gear they used to protect themselves, climbers'
attitudes, mindset and values changed too.

Until then, European climbers, with the sole
exception of the British, had considered crags on a par
with mere climbing walls, to be used for practice,
especially in the coldest months of the year, until "real"
climbs on authentic mountains were possible. During
the years of the "invention" of Verdon, however, a new

303 left Hundreds of very
difficult routes have been
put up on the limestone
walls of Verdon in northern
Provence since the
Seventies.

303 right Patrick Edlinger,
famous for his ascents on the
limestone walls of Provence, is
one of the few sports climbers
well known to the general
public. Here, he is scaling an
overhang on the walls of Cimai.

303

attitude gained ground. Crags located far away from the Alps were no longer considered training grounds, but destinations of great interest and appeal in their own right. Cragging became an independent sport, with its own rules and values.

Traditionally, the important thing in mountaineering is to climb higher and higher and get off the wall as quickly as possible, partly to shelter from objective dangers like falling stones and deteriorating weather. If a climber comes across a pitch equipped with pitons, there is consequently little point in free climbing; it makes more sense to clip onto the bolts and keep

going. On crags, where climbers can quickly abseil down to the base, this attitude is no longer acceptable. In fact, scaling the pitch stylishly is the whole point of the exercise.

All-free climbing (known as *Rotpunkt* by the Germans and *en jaune* by the French), already practised for years by the British and East Europeans, became popular all over Western Europe towards the end of the Seventies. As a result of climbers' new attitudes, their increasingly craggly intensive and specific training, and safer protection which meant that falls had no particularly drastic consequences, the ratings of the pitchs climbed

rose with exceptional speed for a few years.

Although the existence of the seventh grade (6b on the French scale used nearly everywhere for sport climbing), was still challenged by Alpine Clubs in the mid-Seventies, by the end of the decade, top climbers were scaling pitchs between the eighth and ninth grades (between 7a and 7c on the French scale). In the Eighties progress continued, albeit more slowly, towards the tenth grade (8b) and above. At the time of writing, the most difficult climbing pitchs in the world are rated at 9a, roughly equivalent to eleventh grade on the classic UIAA scale.

The popularity of free climbing totally redesigned the geography of Europe (and the rest of the world) for climbers. In spring and autumn, and sometimes in the depths of winter, climbers from all over the continent migrate towards the walls of Provence, like Verdon and the Calanques, and to Buoux, Ceuse, Sainte-Victoire and Presles.

Italian cragging venues like Finale Ligure, Arco, Sperlonga, Muzzerone and Gaeta are equally popular. The limestone walls of Sardinia, the boulders and granite towers of Corsica and the numerous limestone structures of Catalonia, Andalusia and the Balearics are a little less crowded. After a pause due to the war in ex-Yugoslavia, climbers have now begun to return to the walls of Paklenica and Tulove Grede in Croatia.

In summer, when the milder climate allows climbers to return to the Alps, they can tackle the granite slabs of Grimsel in the Bernese Oberland, Arnad in Valle d'Aosta and the wild Val di Mello in Valtellina, or the magnificent limestone walls of the Briançonnais district in the heart of the French Alps, which offers climbers hundreds of very well protected routes.

In the heart of the Dolomites, which has been the realm of traditional climbing for 100 years, modern-style

climbing is performed on the Cinque Torri of Cortina and the crags of Crepe d'Oucera and Mèsules de las Bièsces, which overlook some of the loveliest landscapes in the Alps. However, only a few climbers feel confident on the awesome conglomerate walls of Mallos de Riglos (Aragon), the Montserrat massif (Catalonia) and the famous Meteore, on the summits of which stand some of the best-known and most frequently visited monasteries and hermitages in Greece.

Nowadays, tens of thousands of young people all over Europe are climbers. New crags are being bolted all over the place, and indoor climbing walls are also proliferating, especially in colder areas, so that climbers can train even on cold winter evenings.

Modern climbing is now quite distinct from traditional mountaineering, but has had a considerable influence on it. Thanks to their training on low-altitude crags, the average level of rock climbers has risen considerably, while many city kids who find the idea of plodding up a mountainside carrying a heavy rucksack boring are introduced to traditional mountaineering by sport climbing.

The extraordinary popularity of the new sport means that it is very difficult to draw up a comprehensive list of the most important routes. Some of the best climbers (though our list is by no means complete) include Germans Wolfgang Gullich (who put up some of the first 8c pitches and has performed some major ascents in the Himalaya) and Alexander Huber, and Swiss climbers Claude and Yves Rémy, who have made their mark on Grimsel and many other Swiss crags.

The list is completed by French climbers Didier Raboutou, François Petit, Isabelle Patissier and

François Legrand, Americans Ron Kauk and Lynn Hill, who are as happy on the well-protected European walls as those in the States, Italians Maurizio Zanolla (Manolo), Rolando Larcher, Cristian Brenna and Piero Dal Prà, Ben Moon from the UK, Austrian Beat Kammerlander, Spaniard Bernabé Fernandez, Slovenian Tadej Slabe and Yuji Hirayama from Japan.

One of the most interesting developments has been the collapse of one of the most long-standing taboos in the history of climbing — full-scale competitions. It happened in the first weekend of July 1985, when for the first time, many of the best climbers in Europe competed against one another.

Climbing competitions had, in fact, been held in the USSR and other East European countries in the Seventies, but these were speed trials on pitchs with classic ratings. This competition, on the limestone of Parete dei Militi on the border between Italy's Val di Susa and France, focused on the difficulty of the pitch climbed. Many famous climbers openly criticised the venture, and a number of famous personalities like Italian climber Manolo and Jerry Moffat from the UK watched the competitors from below, but chose not to join the fray.

In the end, on two lovely sunny days, an audience of nearly 2000 spectators, mainly climbers themselves, applauded the victories of German Stefan Glowacz in the men's competition and Frenchwoman Catherine Destivelle in the women's, followed by Jacky Godoffe

and Thierry Renault in the men's section and Luisa Jovane and Martine Rolland in the women's.

Though hailed by the organisers as a historic event, climbing competitions have attracted limited interest. After the success of the first event, competitions have continued to be held at regular intervals, with a World Championship circuit similar to those of cycling and skiing. Held on artificial climbing walls to ensure that all competitors climb under the same conditions, they attract the interest of a small in-crowd, but not the general public. Most mountaineers and craggers would rather spend their Sundays climbing than watching others climb, and you can hardly blame them.

304 top left Frenchwoman Catherine Destivelle, the French climbing champion, is shown here stemming a difficult chimney on Mont Blanc.

304 bottom left The walls of Lumignano, not far from Vicenza, are among the best known in Veneto. In this photo, Pietro Dal Prà is climbing Passo Falso, a 7c+ route.

304-305 The crags of Sperlonga, overlooking the Tyrrhenian Sea halfway between Rome and Naples, are popular with climbers from all over Europe for much of the year. In this photo, Cristiano Delisi is scaling the overhang of "Il Tempio" (the Temple).

305 top left Although modern climbing mainly developed on limestone, the granite walls of Yosemite are still a favourite destination for climbers from all over the world.

305 centre left Frenchwoman Isabelle Patissier is one of the best women climbers of the present day. In this photo she is tackling a difficult pitch on the rocks of Verdon.

305 bottom left This photo shows Patrick Edlinger on the cliffs of Calanques, near Marseilles.

305 right This photo, taken on the walls of Mont Blanc, immortalises Catherine Destivelle as she scales the cracks of the Aiguille du Midi.

WESTERN ALPS

1492. Frenchman Antoine de Ville and his companions climb Mount Aiguille (Vercors).
1828. Frenchmen A. Durand, A. Liotard and J.E. Matheoud climb Mount Pelvoux (Oisans).
1861. Britons J.J. Cowell and W. Dundas, with guides J. Payot and J. Tairraz, climb Gran Paradiso. Britons William Mathews and William Jacob, with guides Michel and Jean-Baptiste Croz, reach the summit of Monviso.
1864. Englishmen Edward Whymper, Adolphus W. Moore and Horace Walker, with guides Christian Almer and Michel Croz, make the first ascent of Barre des Écrins (Oisans).
1877. Frenchman Henri Emmanuel Boileau de Castelnau, with guides Pierre Gaspard senior and junior, climbs Mount Meije (Oisans).
1878. American William B. Coolidge, with guides Christian and Ulrich Almer, climbs the Lourousa Couloir of Mount Argentera (Maritime Alps). Italian Leopoldo Barale, with guides Antonio and Giuseppe Castagneri and Antonio Bugiatto, makes the first winter ascent of Monviso.
1881. American William B. Coolidge, with guides Christian Almer senior and junior, climbs the North-East Face of Monviso (Cottian Alps).
1903. Frenchman Victor de Cessole, with guides Jean-Baptiste Plent and A. Ghigo, climbs Corno Stella (Maritime Alps).
1912. Austrians Max and Guido Mayer, with guides Angelo Dibona and Luigi Rizzi, climb the South Face of Mont Meije (Oisans).
1925. Frenchmen Pierre Dalloz, Henri de Ségogne, Jacques Lagarde and Jean Vernet climb the North-West Couloir of Pic Sans Nom (Oisans).
1926. Amilcare Crétier and Lino Binel from Valle d'Aosta climb the North-East Face of Mount Grivola (Gran Paradiso).
1930. Amilcare Crétier, L. Bon and Renato Chabod from Valle d'Aosta climb the North-West Face of Gran Paradiso.
1934. Italian Giusto Gervasutti and Frenchman Lucien Devies climb the North Face of Mount Olan (Oisans). Frenchmen Pierre Allain, Raymond Leininger and Vernet put up a direct route on the South Face of Mount Meije (Oisans).
1936. Italian Giusto Gervasutti and Frenchman Lucien Devies climb the North-West Face of Mount Ailefroide (Oisans). Italians Vitale Bramani and Ettore Castiglioni climb the East Face of Torre Castello (Val Maira).
1956. Frenchmen Jean Couzy and René Desmaison put up a direct route on the North Face of Mount Olan (Oisans).
1961. Frenchmen René Desmaison, Bertrand and Yves Pollet-Villard climb the East Pillar of Pic de Bure (Dévoluy).
1964. The French-Swiss team of E. Stagni, C. Dalphiun, M. Ebneter, S. Martin and R. Wohlschlag put up the Voie du Bouclier on the East Face of Mount Gerbier (Vercors).
1967. Italians Paolo Armando and Alessandro Gogna climb the North-East Face of Mount Scarason (Maritime Alps).
1969. Frenchman P. Renaud puts up a direct route on the North Face of Mount Meije (Oisans).
1970. Giancarlo Grassi and Mike Kosterlitz put up the Anglo-Italian route on the South Face of Corno Stella (Maritime Alps), and the "Tetti a Zeta" Route on Rocca Provenzale (Val Maira). Frenchmen M. Charles and G. Héran climb Éperon Sublime in the Grand Canyon of Verdon.
1973. Frenchmen Jean-Marc Boivin and Jean-Michel Cambon put up the Voie des Dijonnais on Tête d'Aval de Montbrison (Briançonnais).
1974. Frenchmen A. Bultel, J. Ginat, P. Grenier, P. Martinez, J.-P. Moron, J. Perrier, S. Troussier and G. Thomas climb Pichenibule in the Grand Canyon of Verdon.
1975. Frenchmen Pierre Béghin, Pierre Caubet, Olivier Challeat and Pierre Guillet make the first winter ascent of the North Face of Mount Ailefroide (Oisans).
1976. Frenchman Michel Berrueux makes the first solo ascent of the Couzy-Desmaison route on the North Face of Mount Olan (Oisans).
1978. Frenchmen Jean-Marc Boivin, Diaféria and Vionet-Fuasset climb La Raie des Fesses on the North Face of Pic Sans Nom (Oisans).
1979. Italians Giancarlo Grassi, Gianni Comino and Marco Bernardi climb the Great Icefall on the east side of Dôme du Moulinet (Graian Alps).
1981. Italian Marco Bernardi soloes the Armando-Gogna route on Scarason Peak (Maritime Alps).
1983. Frenchmen Christian Ferrera and Jean-Michel Cambon put up the Ranxerox route on Tête d'Aval de Montbrison (Briançonnais).
1992. Frenchman Christophe Moulin performs the solo concatenation of the Renaud direct route on the North Face of Mount Meije and the Gervasutti-Devies route on the North Face of Mount Ailefroide (Oisans). Frenchman Bruno Ravanat climbs Raie des Fesses on Pic Sans Nom (Oisans) in two hours in winter.
1998. Frenchmen Patrick Bérhault and Bruno Sourzac concatenate the Pinard-Ginel route on Mount Pelvoux, the George-Russenberger route on Pic Sans Nom, the Chapoutot route on Pic du Coup de Sabre and the Gervasutti-Devies route on Mount Ailefroide (Oisans) in six days, in winter.

MONT BLANC

1775. Chamonix guides Jean-Nicolas Couteran, François Paccard, Michel-Gabriel Paccard and Victor Tissai make the first attempted ascent of Mont Blanc and reach an altitude of 4000 metres.
1786. Jacques Balmat and Michel-Gabriel Paccard of Chamonix make the first ascent of Mont Blanc by way of the Bossons glacier, the Grand Plateau and the Ancien Passage.
1808. Marie Paradis of Chamonix is the first woman to reach the summit of Mont Blanc.
1821. The Chamonix Compagnie des Guides is founded.
1853. Chamonix Town Council builds the Grands Mulets refuge hut.
1855. Courmayeur guides Gratien Bareux, J.M. "Turin" Chabod, J.M. "Turisa" Chabod, Alexis Clusaz, Alexandre Fenoillet, J.M. Perrod and Alexis Proment explore the ascent route to Mont Blanc by way of Col du Midi and Mont Blanc du Tacul.
1865. Edward Whymper conquers the Grandes Jorasses and the Aiguille Verte. Guides Christian Almer and Franz Biner accompany him on both ascents, and Michel Croz only on the second. Britons G.S. Mathews, A.W. Moore, F. and H. Walker, guided by Jakob and Melchior Anderegg, climb Mont Blanc by way of the Brenva Spur.
1879. Frenchmen Jean Charlet-Straton, Frédéric Folliguet and Prosper Payot climb the Petit Dru.
1881. Englishman Albert F. Mummery, with guides Alexander Burgener and Benedikt Venetz, makes the first ascent of the Grépon.
1882. Italians Alessandro, Alfonso, Corradino and Gaudenzio Sella, guided by Baptiste, Daniel and Jean-Jacques Maquignaz, climb the Dent du Géant.
1888. Italians Corradino, Erminio, Gaudenzio and Vittorio Sella, guided by Émile Rey, Jean-Joseph and Daniel Maquignaz, make the first winter crossing of Mont Blanc.
1892. French astronomer Jules-César Janssen has an observatory built on the summit of Mont Blanc. It was to be swallowed up by the glacier in 1909.
1893. German Paul Gussfeldt, with guides Émile Rey, Christian Klucker and César Ollier, climbs the Peutérey Ridge on Mont Blanc.
1911. Englishmen G.W. Young, H.O. Jones and Ralph Todhunter, with guides Josef Knubel and Henri Brocherel, conquer the East Face (Mer de Glace) of the Grépon.
1928. French guide Armand Charlet makes the first attempt on the Walker Spur of the Grandes Jorasses. Britons Frank Smythe and Thomas Graham Brown put up the Major route on the Brenva wall of Mont Blanc.
1930. Germans Karl Brendel and Hermann Schaller conquer the South Ridge of the Aiguille Noire de Peutérey.
1934. Germans Martin Meier and Rudolf Peters conquer the Croz Spur on the North Face of the Grandes Jorasses.
1938. Italians Riccardo Cassin, Luigi Esposito and Ugo Tizzoni climb the Walker Spur on the North Face of the Grandes Jorasses.
1942. Italians Giusto Gervasutti and Giuseppe Gagliardone climb the East Face of the Grandes Jorasses.
1951. Italians Walter Bonatti and Luciano Ghigo scale the East Face of the Grand Capucin.
1952. Frenchmen Lucien Bérardini, Adrien Dagory, Marcel Lainé and Guido Magnone conquer the West Face of the Dru.
1955. Italian Walter Bonatti soloes the South-West Pillar of the Dru.
1961. The attempted ascent of the Central Pillar of Mont Blanc by Italians Walter Bonatti, Roberto Gallieni and Andrea Oggioni and Frenchmen Antoine Guillaume, Pierre Kohlman, Pierre Mazeaud and Antoine Vieille ends in the death of four climbers. The ascent is completed by Britons Chris Bonington, Don Whillans and Ian Clough and Pole Jan Djuglosz, followed by an Italian-French party.
1962. Italians Walter Bonatti and Cosimo Zappelli conquer the North Face of the Pilier d'Angle. Americans Gary Hemming and Royal Robbins put up the American Direct Route on the West Face of the Dru.
1963. Americans Tom Frost, Steve Fulton, John Harlin and Gary Hemming conquer the South Face of the Aiguille du Fou.
1967. Frenchmen René Desmaison and Robert Flematti make the first winter ascent of the Central Pillar of Mont Blanc.
1972. Frenchman René Desmaison makes the first solo ascent of the Great Peutérey Ridge. His fellow-countrymen Louis Audoubert, Marc Galy, Yannick Seigneur and Michel Feuillarade and Italians Arturo and Oreste Squinobal make the first winter ascent of the same route.
1973. Heini Holzer from Alto Adige (Italian South Tyrol) skis down the Brenva Spur. Frenchmen Walter Cecchinel and Claude Jager climb the North-East Couloir of the Drus.
1975. Frenchmen Jean-Marc Boivin and Patrick Gabarrou scale the Supercouloir on Mont Blanc du Tacul.
1977. Frenchman Jean-Marc Boivin climbs the Linceul on the Grandes Jorasses in 2 hours 45 minutes.
1979. Italians Gianni Comino and Giancarlo Grassi scale the serac on the left of the Pear Route. Stefano De Benedetti skis down Mont Blanc by way of the Major Route.
1981. Frenchmen Jean-Marc Boivin and Patrick Bérhault climb the American Route on the Aiguille du Fou, descend by hang-glider and climb the American Direct Route on the Dru.
1982. Frenchman Christophe Profit soloes the American Direct Route on the Dru in 3 hours 10 minutes.
1984. Swiss climbers Michel Piola and Pierre-Alain Steiner put up the O Sole Mio route on the East Face of the Grand Capucin. Piola, together with Gérard Hopfgartner, inaugurates Ma Dalton on the South Face of the Aiguille du Midi. Frenchmen Christophe Profit and Dominique Radigue scale the four Freney pillars on the same day.
1986. Italian Stefano De Benedetti skis down the Innominata side of Mont Blanc.
1988. Frenchman Bruno Gouvy parachutes from a helicopter onto the summit of the Petit Dru, then abseils down the North Face and snowboards down the 50-degree slope of the Niche.
1990. Frenchman Patrick Gabarrou crosses the massif from north to south, climbing (among others) the North Face of the Courtes, the Walker Spur of the Jorasses and the Pilier d'Angle.
1991. Frenchwoman Catherine Destivelle soloes a new route on the West Face of the Dru.
1993. Italian Giovanni Bassanini climbs an 8a pitch on the Gendarmes des Cosmiques (Aiguille du Midi).
1995. Frenchmen Jerome Ruby and Samuel Bogey ski and snowboard respectively down the Linceul on the Grandes Jorasses.

PENNINE ALPS

1778. Valentin and Josef Beck, Étienne Lisgie, Josef Zumstein, François Castel de Perlatol, Niklaus Vincent and Sebastiano Linty, all from Gressoney, reach the Entdeckungfels ("Discovery Rock"), not far from Col de Lys.
1779. Canon Laurent-Joseph Murit of Grand S. Bernard, with hunters Genoud and Moret, climbs Mount Vélan.
1819. Johann Niklaus Vincent and German Friedrich Parrot climb Pyramide Vincent.
1820. Johann Niklaus Vincent and Josef Zumstein from Valle d'Aosta climb Point Zumstein on Monte Rosa with four companions.
1842. Italians Giovanni Gnifetti, Cristoforo Grober, Giovanni Giordani, Giacomo Giordani, Cristoforo Ferraris and Giuseppe Farinetti, with two porters, reach Point Gnifetti (or Signalkuppe) on Monte Rosa.
1855. Englishmen Charles Hudson, John Birkbeck, E.J. Stephenson, J.G. and C. Smythe, with guides J. and M. Zumtaugwald and Ulrich Lauener, climb Point Dufour on Monte Rosa.
1858. Briton J.L. Davies, with guides Johann Zumtaugwald, Johann Kronig and Hieronymus Brantschen, makes the first ascent of the Dom.
1861. Briton John Tyndall, with guides J.J. Bennen and U. Wenger, makes the first ascent of the Weisshorn.
1862. Britons Thomas S. Kennedy and William Wigram, with guides Jean-Baptiste Croz and Johann Kronig, make the first ascent of the Dent Blanche.
1864. Britons Leslie Stephen and Edward Buxton, with guides Jakob Anderegg and Franz Biner, make the first crossing of the Lyskamm. Later, Stephen and Anderegg, together with Francis Crawford Grove and Melchior Anderegg, climb the Zinalrothorn.
1865. Britons Edward Whymper, Charles Hudson, Francis Douglas and D. R. Hadow, with guides Michel Croz and Peter Taugwalder senior and junior, make the first ascent of the Matterhorn along the Hornli Ridge. Four of the seven climbers fall to their deaths during the descent. Three days later, guides Jean-Baptiste Bich and Jean-Antoine Carrel reach the summit by way of the Italian (Lion) Ridge.
1872. Englishmen Richard and William Pendlebury and Charles Taylor, with guides Gabriel Spechtenhauser, Ferdinand Imseng and Giovanni Oberto, climb the East Face of Point Dufour on Monte Rosa.
1879. Englishman Albert F. Mummery, with guides Alexander Burgener, Johann Petrus and A. Gentinetta, climbs the Z'mutt Ridge on the Matterhorn.
1881. Italian Damiano Marinelli, with guides Ferdinand Imseng and Battista Pedranzini, is killed by an avalanche on the East Face of Monte Rosa.
1882. Italian Vittorio Sella, with guides Jean-Antoine, Jean-Baptiste and Louis Carrel, makes the first winter ascent of the Matterhorn, climbing by way of the Italian Ridge and descending by the Hornli Ridge.
1887. Briton Harold W. Topham, with guide Alois Supersaxo and a porter, climbs Signal Ridge on Point Gnifetti (Monte Rosa).
1890. Swede Ludwig Norman-Neruda, with guides Christian Klucker and Josef Reinstadler, climbs the North-East Face of the Lyskamm.
1893. The Margherita refuge hut is inaugurated at an altitude of 4554 metres on Point Gnifetti, on Monte Rosa.
1906. Briton Valentine J. E. Ryan, with guides Franz and Josef Lochmatter, climbs the North-East (or Santa Caterina) Ridge of Nordend (Monte Rosa). The same team, with Geoffrey W. Young, climbs the South Face of the Taschhorn. Young, with fellow-countrymen R.Y. Mayor (R.J. Major?) and C.D. Robertson and guides Josef Knubel and Moritz Ruppen, climbs the North Ridge of the east Breithorn.
1909. Briton Geoffrey W. Young and American Oliver Perry-Smith, with guide Josef Knubel, climb the South Face of the Weisshorn.
1911. Italian Mario Piacenza, with guides J. Gaspard and J. Carrel, climbs the Furggen Ridge on the Matterhorn. German climber Dietrich von Bethmann-Hollweg, with guides Oskar and Othmar Supersaxo, scales the North Face of the Lensspitze.
1925. German Willo Welzembach conquers the North Face of Dent d'Hérens.
1928. Swiss climber E. R. Blanchet, with guide Kaspar Mooser, climbs the South-East (or

Kanzelgrat) Ridge of the Zinalrothorn.

1930. Austrians Hans Kiener and Rudolf Schwarzgruber make the first ascent of the North-East Face of the Obergabelhorn.

1931. Germans Franz and Toni Schmid climb the North Face of the Matterhorn. Frenchmen Lucien Devies and Jacques Lagarde climb the East Face of Point Gnifetti on Monte Rosa.

1932. Germans Willo Welzembach and Eugen Allwein climb the North Face of the Gletscherhorn. German Karl Schneider and Austrian Franz Singer climb the North Face of the Dent Blanche.

1945. Swiss climbers André Roch, Robert Gréloz and Ruedi Schmidt climb the East Face of the Zinalrothorn.

1953. Italians Emilio Amosso and Oliviero Elli make the first winter ascent of the East Face of Monte Rosa.

1956. Austrians Kurt Diemberger and Wolfgang Stefan put up a direct route on the North Face of the Lyskamm.

1962. Swiss climbers Hilti von Allmen and Paul Etter make the first winter ascent of the North Face of the Matterhorn.

1965. Italian Walter Bonatti puts up a direct route on the North Face of the Matterhorn alone, in winter.

1966. Swiss climbers Michel and Yvette Vaucher put up a direct route on the North Face of the Dent Blanche.

1969. Italians Alessandro Gogna and Leo Cerruti climb the Z'mutt Nose on the North Face of the Matterhorn.

1974. Heini Holzer from Alto Adige (Italian South Tyrol) is the first to ski down the North-East Face of the Lyskamm.

1979. Italian Stefano de Benedetti is the first to ski down the East Face of Monte Rosa (via the French Route).

1981. Swiss climbers Michel Piola and Pierre-Allain Steiner put up a new route on the Z'mutt Nose on the Matterhorn.

1984. Italian Giancarlo Grassi and Canadian Bernard Mailhot put up the "Immaginando l'inimmaginabile" route on the North-East Face of the east Breithorn.

1985. Italian Marco Barmasse climbs the four Matterhorn ridges on the same day.

1986. Swiss climbers Erhard Loretan and André Georges cross the "Imperial Crown", the arc of peaks (including 30 "four-thousanders") that encircle Zermatt and the Mattertal, in 18 days, in winter.

1993. Scotsmen Simon Jenkins and Martin Mora climb all the "four-thousanders" in the Alps in 50 days, cycling from one to another.

1994. Frenchwoman Catherine Destivelle makes a solo winter repeat of the Bonatti route on the Matterhorn. Slovenians Matjaz Jamnik and Bojan Pockar put up the Slovenian route on the East Face of Point Gnifetti (Monte Rosa).

BERNESE OBERLAND

1811. Swiss climbers Hieronymus Meyer and Johann Rudolf Meyer, with guides Alois Volker and Josef Bortis, make the first ascent of the Jungfrau.

1829. Guides Jakob Leuthold and Hans Wahren climb the Finsteraarhorn. Geologist Franz Josef Hugi has a refuge hut built on the Aar glacier.

1859. Briton Francis F. Tuckett, with guides Johann Josef Bennen, Victor Tairraz and Peter Bohren, climbs the Aletschhorn.

1861. Briton Leslie Stephen, with guides Christian Michel, Peter Michel and Ulrich Kaufmann, makes the first ascent of the Schreckhorn.

1866. Edmund von Fellenberg, with guides Christian Michel and Peter Egger, climbs the Nollen (Nose) of the Mönch.

1904. Swiss climbers Gustav Hasler and Fritz Amatter climb the North-West Spur of the Finsteraarhorn.

1907. Britons J.H. Wicks, E.H.F. Bradby and C. Wilson climb the South-West Ridge of the Schreckhorn.

1912. The rack railway that climbs to the Jungfraujoch by way of the rocks of the Eiger and the Mönch is inaugurated.

1921. Japanese climber Yukio Maki, with guides Samuel Brawand, Fritz Amatter and Fritz Steuri, scales the Mittellegi Ridge on the Eiger.

1930. Germans Willo Welzembach and Heinz Tillmann climb the North Face (or Fiescherwand) of the Gross-Fiescherhorn.

1932. German Willo Welzembach climbs the North Face of the Gletscherhorn. Swiss climbers Hans Lauper and Alfred Zurcher, with guides Alexander Graven and Josef Knubel, climb the North-West Face of the Eiger.

1935. Germans Karl Mehringer and Max Sedlmayr make the first attempted ascent of the North Face of the Eiger; they die at an altitude of 3300 metres, on the ledge now known as "death bivouac".

1937. Germans Andreas Hinterstoisser and Toni Kurz and Austrians Willi Angerer and Edi Rainer make a new attempt on the North Face of the Eiger; they die while abseiling down the mountain.

1938. Germans Anderl Heckmair and Ludwig Vorg and Austrians Fritz Kasparek and Heinrich Harrer climb the North Face of the Eiger.

1961. Austrian Walther Almberger and Germans Toni Kinshofer, Anderl Mannhardt and Toni Hiebeler make the first winter ascent of the North Face of the Eiger.

1963. Swiss climber Michel Darbellay makes the first solo ascent of the North Face of the Eiger.

1966. Briton Dougal Haston and Germans Jorg Lehne, Gunther Strobel, Roland Votter and Siegfried Hupfauer put up a direct route (the John Harlin route) on the North Face of the Eiger in winter.

1970. Swiss climber Sylvain Saudan skis down the west side of the Eiger.

1979. Swiss climbers Michel Piola and Gérard Hopfgartner climb the Geneva Pillar on the North Face of the Eiger.

1983. Swiss climber Michel Piola and Frenchman René Ghilini put up a new route on the North Face of the Eiger. Austrian Thomas Bubendorfer climbs the classic route on the North Face of the Eiger in 4 hours 50 minutes.

1985. Frenchman Christophe Profit climbs the North Faces of the Matterhorn, the Grandes Jorasses and the Eiger in 22 hours, travelling from one to another by helicopter.

1987. Christophe Profit repeats his hat-trick in winter taking 42 hours, 16 of them spent on the North Face of the Eiger.

1989. Swiss climbers Erhard Loretan and André Georges climb 13 north faces in the Bernese Oberland in 13 days.

1990. Slovenian Slavko Sveticic makes the first solo winter ascent of the John Harlin route on the North Face of the Eiger.

1991. American Jeff Lowe, climbing alone, puts up a new direct route on the North Face of the Eiger in 13 days.

CENTRAL ALPS

1804. Josef Pirchler from Alto Adige (Italian South Tyrol), with two companions, reaches the summit of Mount Ortles.

1850. Swiss climbers J. Coaz and J. and L. Ragut Tscharner climb Piz Bernina.

1862. Britons Leslie Stephen, E.S. Kennedy and M. Cox, with guide Melchior Anderegg, climb Monte Disgrazia.

1863. Britons A.W. Moore and H. Walther, with guide Jakob Anderegg, climb Piz Roseg.

1864. Britons F.F. Tuckett, E.H. Buxton and E.N. Buxton, with guides F. Biener and C. Michel, climb the Gran Zebrù.

1867. American William A.B. Coolidge, with guides Henri and François Devouassoud, makes the first ascent of Piz Badile.

1878. German Paul Gussfeldt, with guides Hans Grass and Johann Gross, climbs the North Ridge (Biancograt) of Piz Bernina.

1887. Swiss climber Hans Bumiller, with guides Martin Schocher, Johann Gross and Hans Zippert, climbs the North Spur of the central Pizzo Palù.

1890. Swede Ludwig Normann-Neruda, with guide Christian Klucker, climbs the North-East Face of Piz Bernina.

1895. Italian Scipione Borghese, with guides Martin Schocher and Christian Schnitzler, climbs the North-West Face of Pizzo Cengalo.

1910. Britons Harold Raeburn and W. H. Ling climb the North Face of Monte Disgrazia.

1912. Italians B. de Ferrari and I. dell'Andrino

climb the North-North-East Ridge (or Corda Molla) of Monte Disgrazia.

1923. Swiss climbers W. Risch and A. Zurcher climb the North Corner of Piz Badile.

1930. Germans Hans Ertl and Hans Brehm climb the North Face of the Gran Zebrù.

1931. Germans Hans Ertl and Franz Schmid climb the North Face of Mount Ortles.

1937. Italians Riccardo Cassin, Luigi Esposito, Vittorio Ratti, Mario Molteni and Giuseppe Valsecchi climb the North-East Face of Piz Badile.

1947. Swiss climbers B. and E. Favre and L. Henchoz climb the West Ridge of the Salbitschijen (central Switzerland).

1956. Austrian Kurt Diemberger soloes the "meringue" on the North Face of the Gran Zebrù.

1958. Austrians Kurt Diemberger and Karl Schontaler put up a direct route on the North-East Face of Piz Roseg.

1959. Italians Nando Nusdeo and Vasco Taldo climb the South-East Face of Pizzo Luigi Amedeo.

1963. Dieter Drescher from Alto Adige (Italian South Tyrol) makes the first solo ascent of the North Face of Mount Ortles.

1968. Britons Richard Isherwood and Mike Kosterlitz put up a new route on the North-East Face of Piz Badile. Swiss climbers Michel Darbellay, Camille Bournissen and Daniel Troillet and Italians Paolo Armando, Gianni Calczagno and Alessandro Gogna make the first winter ascent of the same face.

1972. Italians Ermanno and Franco Gugiatti make the first winter ascent of the North-West Face of Pizzo Cengalo.

1976. Swiss climbers M. Bellini, Marco Grandi and Romolo Nottaris put up a direct route on the North Spur of the central Pizzo Palù.

1977. Italians Ivan Guerini and Mario Villa put up the Oceano Irrazionale route on Precipizio degli Asteroidi (Val di Mello). Heini Holzer from Alto Adige (Italian South Tyrol) skis down the North-East Face of Mount Zebrù, but is killed falling from the North Face of Piz Roseg.

1981. Reinhard Patscheider from Alto Adige (Italian South Tyrol) concatenates the North Faces of the Ortles, Mount Zebrù and the Gran Zebrù in 10 hours.

1985. Italians Tarcisio Fazzini, Ottavio Fazzini and Tita Gianola put up the Ringo Starr route on the North-East Face of Piz Badile.

1988. Italians Tarcisio Fazzini, Ottavio Fazzini and Norberto Riva put up the Spada nella Roccia route on Pizzo Qualido (Val di Mello). Czech women climbers Zuzana Hofmannova and Alena Stehlikova make the first winter ascent of the British route on the North-East Face of Piz Badile.

1991. Austrian Beat Kammerlander free-climbs the South Face of the seventh Kirchlispitze (Ratikon).

1992. German Tobias Heymann concatenates the North-East and North-West Faces of Mount Scerscen, the North-West and West Faces of Piz Bernina and the Diemberger direct route on Piz Roseg in 11 hours. Italian Guido Lisignoli concatenates the North-West Pillar of Pizzo Cengalo, the Pinardi route on Punta Sertori and the Cassin route on the North-East Face of Piz Badile in 7 hours.

EASTERN ALPS

1778. L. Willonitzer makes the first ascent of Mount Triglav (Julian Alps) with three companions.

1800. Three mountain men from Heiligenblut climb the Grossglockner (Upper Taurus mountains).

1801. V. Stakig makes the first ascent of Mount Watzmann (Berchtesgaden Alps).

1820. Germans D. Deutschl, Maier and K. Naus climb the Zugspitze (Wetterstein).

1848. Austrian L. Klotz makes the first ascent of the Wildspitze (Otztal Alps) with a companion.

1865. Austrian Paul Grohmann, with guide Napoleone Sottocorona, climbs Mount Coglians (Carnian Alps).

1876. Count A. Pallavicini, with G. Bauerle, J. Kromser and V. Tribusser, climbs the North Couloir of the Grossglockner (Upper Taurus Mountains).

1881. J. Kederbacher and O. Schuck climb the East Face of Mount Watzmann (Berchtesgaden Alps).

1886. German Georg Winkler puts up a new route on the East Face of the Totenkirchl (Kaisergebirge).

1895. Austrian Hans Kofler soloes the North Face

of Creta da Cjanevate (Carnian Alps).

1905. Julius Kugy, with G. Bolaffio, A. Oitzinger and G. Pesamosca, climbs the north side of Jof Fuart (Julian Alps).

1908. Julius Kugy, with G. Bolaffio, A. Oitzinger and G. Pesamosca, climbs the South-West Pillar of Jof di Montasio (Julian Alps). H. Matejak climbs the North Ridge of the Predigstuhl (Wilder Kaiser). Tita Piaz, J. Klammer, R. Schietzold, F. Egger and Schroffen climb the West Face of the Totenkirchl (Wilder Kaiser).

1911. Austrians Guido and Max Mayer, with guides Angelo Dibona and Luigi Rizzi, climb the North Face of the Lalidererspitze (Karwendel). Austrian Paul Preuss soloes the West Face of the Totenkirchl (Wilder Kaiser).

1913. Germans Hans Dulfer and W. von Redwtiz put up a direct route on the West Face of the Totenkirchl (Wilder Kaiser). Germans Hans Fiechtl and Otto Herzog climb the South Face of the Schusselkarspitze (Wetterstein).

1924. Germans Willo Welzembach and F. Rigele climb the North-West Face of the Grosses Wiesbachhorn (Upper Taurus Mountains).

1925. Germans Fritz Wiessner and Roland Rossi climb the South-East Face of the Fleischbank (Wilder Kaiser).

1926. Germans Willo Welzembach and Karl Wien put up a direct route on the North Face of the Grossglockner (Upper Taurus Mountains).

1928. Italians Celso Gilberti and G. Granzotto put up a direct route on the North Face of Mount Triglav (Julian Alps).

1929. Germans Ernest Krebs and Toni Schmid put up a new route on the North Face of the Lalidererspitze (Karwendel).

1930. Austrians Peter Aschenbrenner and Karl Lucke climb the South-East Face of the Fleischbank (Wilder Kaiser).

1946. Austrians Mathias Rebitsch and S. Spiegl put up a direct route on the North Face of the Lalidererspitze (Karwendel).

1943. Austrians Hermann Buhl, Hans Reischl and Wastl Weiss climb the West Face of the Maukspitze (Wilder Kaiser).

1947. Austrian Hermann Buhl makes the first solo ascent of the Fiechtl-Herzog route on the Schusselkarspitze (Wetterstein).

1949. Italians Cirillo Floreanini and M. Kravanja climb the North Face of Piccolo Mangart di Coritenza (Julian Alps).

1955. Slovenians Ales Kunaver and Ante Mahkota make the first winter ascent of the direct route on the North Face of Mount Triglav (Julian Alps).

1957. Austrian Hermann Buhl makes the first solo ascent of the North Face of Mount Watzmann (Berchtesgaden Alps).

1970. Italians Enzo Cozzolino and A. Bernardini climb the great dihedral on Piccolo Mangart di Coritenza (Julian Alps). Germans Helmut Kiene and Reinhald Karl climb the Pumprisse route on Mount Fleischbank (Wilder Kaiser).

1977. Austrians Heinz Mariacher and Peter Brandstaetter put up the Charlie Chaplin route on the North Face of the Lalidererspitze (Karwendel).

1981. Germans Kurt Albert and Wolfgang Gullich put up the Locker vom Hocker route on the South Face of the Schusselkarspitze (Wetterstein).

1983. Italian Renato Casarotto makes the first solo winter ascent of the great dihedral on Piccolo Mangart di Coritenza (Julian Alps).

1987. Austrian Heinz Zak and Germans Peter Gschwendtner and Georg Walch put up the Maerchenprinz route on the Schnitlwaende (Karwendel).

1990. Austrian Heinz Zak and German Peter Gschwendtner concatenate the north dihedral, the Schmid-Krebs route and the Charlie Chaplin route on the North Face of the Lalidererspitze (Karwendel) in 16_ hours.

1991. Slovenians Marko Lukic and Miha Praprotnik make the first winter ascent of the Tuhinjska Smer route on Mount Travnik (Julian Alps).

DOLOMITES

1726. Venetian botanists Pietro Stefanelli and Giovanni Zanichelli reach the summit of Cimon del Cavallo (Oltre Piave Dolomites).

1802. Don Giuseppe Terza makes the first attempted ascent of Mount Marmolada with six companions, but is killed on the mountain.

1857. Irishman John Ball, with a guide from Val di Zoldo (perhaps Giovan Battista "Sgrinfa" Giacin), makes the first ascent of Mount Pelmo.
1863. Austrian Paul Grohmann, with guides Francesco Lacedelli, Alessandro Lacedelli and Matteo Ossi, climbs Mount Antelao.
1864. Austrian Paul Grohmann climbs Marmolada di Penìa, the highest peak in the Dolomites, with Angelo and Fulgenzio Dimai, and Mount Sorapìss with Francesco Lacedelli and Angelo Dimai. While descending Mount Sorapìss he performs the first abseil in history.
1867. Englishman Francis Fox Tuckett, with guides Melchior and Jakob Anderegg, makes the first ascent of Mount Civetta.
1869. Austrian Paul Grohmann, with guides Franz Innerkofler and Peter Salcher from Sesto, climbs Cima Grande di Lavaredo.
1876. On the initiative of the Agordo section of Club Alpino Italiano (CAI), an artificial cave is excavated near the summit of Marmolada di Rocca. This was the first "refuge" in the Dolomites.
1877. Guide Luigi Cesaletti from Cadore climbs Torre dei Sabbioni, a difficult secondary pinnacle between the Marmarole and Mount Sorapiss.
1887. Bavarian Georg Winkler climbs the tower now named after him in the Torri del Vajolet.
1892. German Theodor von Wundt, with guides Michele Bettega and Johann Watschinger, makes the first winter ascents of Cima Grande and Cima Piccola di Lavaredo.
1897. Nino Pooli, Carlo Garbari and Antonio Tavernaro from Trento attempt Campanile Basso di Brenta, and get to within 25 metres of the summit.
1898. Guide Tita Piaz climbs seven peaks in the Catinaccio group in eight hours.
1899. Tyroleans Otto Ampferer and Karl Berger reach the summit of Campanile Basso di Brenta.
1900. Guide Tita Piaz climbs the crack now named after him on Punta Emma (Torri del Vajolet).
1901. Englishwoman Beatrice Thomasson, with guides Michele Bettega and Bortolo Zagonel, climbs the South Face of Mount Marmolada.
1902. Austrians Viktor von Glanvell and Gunther von Saar climb Campanile di Val Montanaia (Oltre Piave Dolomites).
1903. The Nuremberg section of DOAV inaugurates the first klettersteig (climbing path) in the Dolomites on the West Ridge of Mount Marmolada.
1908. German Rudolf Fehrmann and American Oliver Perry-Smith climb the great dihedral of Campanile Basso di Brenta.
1910. Austrians Max and Guido Mayer, with guides Angelo Dibona and Luigi Rizzi, climb the South-West Face of Croz del Altissimo (Brenta Dolomites).
1911. Austrian Paul Preuss soloes the East Face of Campanile Basso di Brenta: a few days later he descends by the same route with Paul Relly. The same climbers scale the North-East Face of Crozzon di Brenta and the North-East Face of Cima Piccolissima di Lavaredo.
1913. Germans Hans Dulfer and Willy von Bernuth climb the West Face of Cima Grande di Lavaredo.
1924. Germans Roland Rossi and Felix Simon scale the North Face of Mount Pelmo.
1925. Germans Emil Solleder and Gustav Lettenbauer climb the North-West Face of Mount Civetta, the first sixth-grade route in the Alps.
1929. Italians Renzo Videsott and Domenico Rudatis and Austrian Leo Rittler climb the West Edge of Mount Busazza, in the Civetta group. Luigi Micheluzzi, Demetrio Christomannos and Robert Perathoner climb the South-West Pillar of Marmolada di Rocca.
1932. Hans Vinatzer and Hans Riefesser from Alto Adige put up a direct route on the North Face of Mount Furchetta (Odle).
1933. Italians Emilio Comici, Angelo and Giuseppe Dimai climb the North Face of Cima Grande di Lavaredo. Then Comici, with Renato Zanutti and Mary Varale, conquers the Yellow Edge of Cima Piccola di Lavaredo.
1934. Bruno Detassis and Enrico Giordani from Trento put up the Guides' Route on the East-North-East Face of Crozzon di Brenta. The same climbers, with Ulisse Battistata, scale the North-East Face of Brenta Alta.
1935. Italians Riccardo Cassin and Vittorio Ratti climb the North Face of Cima Ovest di Lavaredo.
1936. Italians Gino Soldà and Umberto Conforto put up a direct route on the South Face of Marmolada di Penìa. Later, Hans Vinatzer and Ettore Castiglioni put up a new route on the South Face of Marmolada di Rocca.
1938. Austrians Fritz Kasparek and Sepp Brunhuber make the first winter ascent of the Comici-Dimai route on the North Face of Cima Grande di Lavaredo.
1946. Italians Ettore Costantini and Luigi Ghedina climb the South-West Edge of Pilastro di Rozes (Tofane).
1950. Austrians Hermann Buhl and Kuno Rainer make the first winter ascent of the Soldà route on the South Face of Mount Marmolada.
1951. Frenchmen Georges Livanos and Robert Gabriel climb the Great Dihedral on Cima Su Alto (Mount Civetta).
1952. Squirrels Lino Lacedelli, Luigi Ghedina and Guido Lorenzi scale the South-West Face of Cima Scotoni (Fanes). Cesare Maestri from Trento soloes the Solleder route on Mount Civetta.
1956. Cesare Maestri soloes the descent of the Guides' Route on Crozzon di Brenta.
1957. Viennese climbers Walter Philipp and Dieter Flamm climb the dihedral that cuts through the North-West Face of Punta Tissi (Mount Civetta).
1958. Germans Dietrich Hasse, Lothar Brandler, Jorg Lehne and Sigi Low put up a direct route on the North Face of Cima Grande di Lavaredo.
1959. Frenchmen René Desmaison, Pierre Mazeaud, Pierre Kohlmann and Bernard Lagesse put up the Jean Couzy route on the North Face of Cima Ovest di Lavaredo.
1961. Belgian Claudio Barbier concatenates the Cassin route on the North Face of Cima Ovest, the Comici route on the North Face of Cima Grande, the Preuss route on Cima Piccolissima, the Innerkofler route on Cima Piccola and the Dulfer route on Punta di Frida.
1963. Italians Ignazio Piussi and Giorgio Redaelli and Bavarian Toni Hiebeler make the first winter ascent of the Solleder route on Mount Civetta.
1964. Italians Armando Aste and Aldo Solina put up Via dell'Ideale on the South Face of Marmolada d'Ombretta.
1967. Reinhold Messner, Gunther Messner and Heini Holzer from Alto Adige put up a new route on the North-East Face of Mount Agner. Italians Giorgio Garna and Gianni Gianeselli and Poles Roman Bebak, Janusz Ferenski and Ryszard Zawadski climb the South-West Face of Mount Burèl (Belluno Dolomites).
1968. Reinhold and Gunther Messner scale Pilastro di Mezzo on Sass dla Crusc (Conturines).
1969. Reinhold Messner makes the first solo ascent of the Philipp-Flamm dihedral on Mount Civetta and the Soldà route on the North Face of Mount Sassolungo.
1974. Italian Renato Casarotto soloes the Simon-Rossi route on the North Face of Mount Pelmo in winter.
1978. Frenchman Jean-Claude Droyer free-climbs the Cassin-Ratti route on Cima Ovest di Lavaredo. Italians Maurizio "Manolo" Zanolla, Aurelio De Pellegrini, Daniele Ruggero and Marco Simoni put up Via dei Piazaroi on the South Face of Cima della Madonna (Pale di San Martino). Austrians Reinhard Schiestl and Ludwig Rieser put up the Schwalbenschwanz (Swallowtail) route on the South Face of Mount Marmolada.
1980. Italian Lorenzo Massarotto soloes the Mayerl dihedral on Sass dla Crusc (Conturines) and Via dell'Ideale on the South Face of Marmolada d'Ombretta. Manolo and Piero Valmassoi put up the Supermatita route on the East Face of Sass Maor (Pale di San Martino). Tyrolean Heinz Mariacher and Italian Luisa Jovane put up Abrakadabra on the South Face of Mount Marmolada.
1981. Czechs Igor Koller and Indrich Sustr put up Weg durch den Fisch (Route through the Fish) on the South Face of Mount Marmolada.
1982. Heinz Mariacher and Luisa Jovane climb Moderne Zeiten (Modern Times) on the South Face of Mount Marmolada.
1984. Italians Maurizio Giordani and Rosanna Manfrini put up the Futura route on the South Face of Marmolada di Rocca.
1985. Maurizio Giordani makes the first solo ascent of Modern Times and puts up the Olimpo and Fortuna routes on the South Face of Mount Marmolada, accompanied by Rosanna Manfrini on the first route and Fabio Zenatti on the second.
1986. Maurizio Giordani, Paolo Cipriani and Franco Zenatti make the first winter ascent of Weg durch den Fisch on Mount Marmolada. Heinz Mariacher and Bruno Pederiva free-climb the same route. Heinz Mariacher and Luisa Jovane climb Tempi Modernissimi (Ultra-modern Times) on the East Face of Sasso delle Undici (Mount Marmolada).
1988. Lorenzo Massarotto soloes the Philipp-Flamm route on Punta Tissi (Mont Civetta) in winter. Austrian Thomas Bubendorfer concatenates the Cassin route on Cima Ovest di Lavaredo, the Comici route on Cima Grande di Lavaredo, the Helversen route on Cima Piccola di Lavaredo, the Schwalbenschwanz route on Mount Marmolada and the Niagara route on Sass Pordoi (Sella), travelling by helicopter from one to another.
1989. Maurizio Giordani makes the first solo and first winter ascent of the Supermatita route on Sass Maòr. Slovenian Tomo Cesen makes the first solo winter ascent of Tempi Moderni. Ermanno Salvaterra from Trento concatenates Pilastro dei Francesi on Crozzon di Brenta, the Detassis-Graffer route on Pilastro della Tosa, the Graffer route on Campanile Basso, the Detassis route on Brenta Alta and the Oggioni dihedral on Campanile Alto di Brenta. Venetian Manrico dell'Agnola concatenates the Tissi, Ratti, Andrich, Livanos and Castiglioni routes on Torre Venezia (Mount Civetta).
1990. Christoph Hainz and Valentin Pardeller from Alto Adige put up the Elefantenohr (Elephant's Ear) route on Torre del Murfreid (Sella). Maurizio Giordani makes the first solo ascent of Weg durch den Fisch on the South Face of Mount Marmolada.
1991. Christoph Hainz and Oswald Celva from Alto Adige put up the Zauberlehring route on the South Face of Cima Scotoni (Fanes).
1992. Slovenians Slavko Sveticic and Francek Knez put up five routes ranging from the 7th to upper 8th grade on the South Face of Piz Seràuta (Mount Marmolada).
1993. Manolo protects and then free-climbs the Nureyev route on the South-East Face of Sass Maòr, in the Pale di San Martino.
1999. Italian Mauro Bole makes the first all free-climbing ascent of the Jean Couzy route on Cima Ovest di Lavaredo.

OTHER EUROPEAN MASSIFS

1573. Italian Francesco de Marchi climbs Corno Grande (Gran Sasso) with guide Francesco di Domenico and two more companions.
1799. German Alexander von Humboldt, Frenchman Aimé Bompland and some local guides climb Pico de Teide (Canaries).
1802. Frenchman Louis Ramond de Carbonnières reaches the summit of Mont Perdu or Monte Perdido (Pyrenees).
1827. Norwegians C. Hoel and H. Bjermeland make the first ascent of Mount Romsdalhorn (Norway).
1842. Frenchmen A. de Franqueville and P. de Tchihatcheff, with guides B. Arrazau, P. Redonnet, P. Saniau and G. Sors, climb Pico de Aneto or Néthou (Pyrenees).
1850. Norwegians L. Arnesen, S. Flotten and S. Sulheim climb Mount Goldhoppigen (Jotunheimen).
1855. Poles Bozniachi and W. Grzegorszek make the first ascent of Gerlachowski Stit (Upper Tatra Mountains).
1877. Poles L. Chalubinski, M. Sieczka and W. Roj climb the Wieliki Mieguszowiecki (Upper Tatra Mountains).
1886. Englishman W. P. Haskett-Smith makes the first ascent of Napes' Needle (Lake District).
1889. Frenchmen H. Brulle, J. Bazillac, R. de Monts, C. Passet and F. Salle climb Couloir de Gaube on Pique Longue du Vignemale (Pyrenees). Norwegians Martin Ekroll and Angel Johansson climb Vagakallen (Lofoten Islands).
1894. Britons Norman Collie, Joseph Collier and Godfrey Solly climb Buachaille Etive Mor and Tower Ridge on Ben Nevis (Highlands).
1904. Spaniards Pedro Pidal and Gregorio Pérez make the first ascent of Naranjo de Bulnes (Picos de Europa).
1906. Poles S. Krygowski, J. Marusarsz-Startsky and J. Stopka-Ceberniak climb the North Face of Wieliki Mieguszowiecki (Upper Tatra Mountains).
1913. Swiss climbers D. Baud-Bovy and F. Boissonnas and Greek climber K. Kakalòs make the first ascent of Mount Mytikàs (Olympus).
1920. Briton Harold Raeburn makes the first winter ascent of Observatory Ridge on Ben Nevis (Highlands).
1922. Italians Enrico Jannetta, Michele Busiri Vici, Giulio Tavella, Mario Giaquinto, Raffaele Rossi and Raffaello Mattiangeli climb the Paretone (Big Wall) of Corno Grande (Gran Sasso).
1924. Spaniards V. Martinez Campillo and V. Carriòn Roca climb the South Face of Naranjo de Bulnes (Picos de Europa).
1930. Italians Emilio Comici and Anna Escher climb the North Faces of Mounts Mytikàs and Stefani (Olympus).
1933. Frenchmen H. Barrio and R. Bellocq climb the North Face of Pique Longue du Vignemale (Pyrenees).
1936. A Bulgarian team climbs the North Face of Mount Vihren (Pirin Mountains). Poles Z. Korosadowicz and J. Staszel make the first winter ascent of the North Face of Wieliki Mieguszowiecki (Upper Tatra Mountains).
1938. Bulgarians Konstantin Savadjev and Georgi Stoyanov climb the North Face of Mount Maljovitsa (Rila Mountains).
1940. Italians Nino Oppio and S. Colnaghi climb the North Face of Pizzo d'Uccello (Apuan Alps).
1946. Spaniards Jordi Panyella and Jordi Casasayas climb Mallo Pisòn (Mallos de Riglos).
1949. Frenchmen B. Clos and M. Jolly climb the North Face of Mount Vignemale (Pyrenees) in winter.
1956. Spaniards J. Alvarez, J. Ayats and M. Navarro climb the North Face of Cavall Bernat (Montserrat).
1957. Britons Tom Patey, Graeme Nicol and Hamish MacInnes climb Zero Gully on Ben Nevis (Highlands).
1958. Norwegians R. Hoibakk and A. Randers Heen make the first ascent of the East Pillar of the Trollryggen (Norway).
1959. Britons Ian Clough, John Alexander, Don Pipes and Robin Shaw climb Point Five Gully on Ben Nevis (Highlands) in winter. Robin Smith and R.K. Holt climb the nearby Orion Face.
1960. Frenchmen P. de Bellefon and S. Sarthou and Spaniards J.M. Anglada and F. Guillamon climb the South Face of Tozal de Mallo (Pyrenees).
1961. Spaniards A. Rabada and E. Navarro climb Mallo Firé (Mallos de Riglos, Spain).
1962. Spaniards A. Rabada and E. Navarro climb the West Face of Naranjo de Bulnes (Picos de Europa). Poles C. Momatjuk, K. Jurkowski, A. Nowacki, A. Szurek and A. Wojnarowicz put up the Monatiukowka route on Mount Kazalnica (Upper Tatra Mountains).
1965. Britons Tom Patey, Hamish MacInnes, Davie Crabb and Brian Robertson make the first winter crossing of the Cuillins of Skye (Scotland). Norwegians L. Pettersen, J. Tiegland, O.D. Enersen and O. Eliassen make the first ascent of the Trollveggen (Troll Wall) (Norway).
1967. Frenchmen Patrice de Bellefon and Raymond Despiau climb the South Edge of Petite Aiguille d'Ansabère (Pyrenees).
1972. Britons E. and H. Drummond put up the Arch Wall route on the Trollryggen (Norway) .
1974. Britons Ken Crocket and Colin Stead climb Minus One Gully on Ben Nevis (Highlands). Doug Lang and Neil Quinn put up the Slav route on the same mountain.
1975. A British team led by S. Chadwick puts up a new difficult, direct route on the South Face of Mount Ingolsfield (Norway).
1978. Frenchmen Dominique Julien, M. Boulang and F. Tomas climb the Grande Cascade of Cirque de Gavarnie (Pyrenees). Norwegians Arild Meyer and Brynjar Tollefsen climb the West Pillar of Mount Presten (Lofoten Islands).
1974. Britons Mick Fowler and Victor Saunders climb Shield Direct on the Carn Dearg Buttress of Ben Nevis (Highlands).

1980. Italian Giampiero Di Federico makes the first winter ascent of the Third Pillar on the Paretone (Big Wall) of Corno Grande (Gran Sasso).

1983. Spaniards José Luis and Miguel Angel Gallego totally free-climb the West Face of Naranjo de Bulnes (Picos de Europa).

1986. Britons Kenny Spence and Spider McKenzie climb Centurion on the Carn Dearg Buttress of Ben Nevis (Highlands).

1992. Poles W. Derda and A. Marciaz free-climb the Monatiukowka route on Mount Kazalnica (Upper Tatra Mountains).

1994. Frenchman R. Thivel concatenates the three couloirs (Arlaud-Souriac, Y and Gaube) on the North Face of Mount Vignemale (Pyrenees) in one day.

THE KARAKORUM AND THE HINDU KUSH

1887. Briton Francis Younghusband is the first European to see K2 at close range.

1895. Albert Frederick Mummery, accompanied by two gurkhas, attempts Nanga Parbat but disappears on the mountain.

1899. Britons Martin Conway and Charles Bruce, Anglo-German Oskar Eckenstein and guide Mathias Zurbriggen climb the Golden Throne.

1909. An expedition led by the Duke of Abruzzi identifies the ascent route of K2 (the Abruzzi Spur).

1933. Germans Peter Aschenbrenner and Erwin Schneider reach an altitude of 7850 metres on Nanga Parbat. Four climbers and six sherpas are killed during the descent.

1934. An international expedition led by Gunther O. Dyrenfurth attempts to climb Hidden Peak and Gasherbrum II.

1937. An Austro-German expedition makes a further attempt on Nanga Parbat. A huge avalanche kills the seven climbers and nine sherpas.

1939. German Fritz Wiessner (a naturalised American) and sherpa Pasang Dawa Lama reach an altitude of 8300 metres on K2. A climber and three sherpas are killed during the descent.

1950. Norwegians Arne Naess, P. Kvenberg and H. Berg and Briton Tony Streather make the first ascent of Tirich Mir (Hindu Kush).

1953. An Austrian expedition conquers Nanga Parbat. Hermann Buhl reaches the summit alone.

1954. An Italian expedition climbs K2: Achille Compagnoni and Lino Lacedelli reach the summit.

1956. Austrians Fritz Moravec, Hans Willenpart and Sepp Larch climb Gasherbrum II.

1957. Austrians Kurt Diemberger, Fritz Wintersteller, Markus Schmuck and Hermann Buhl climb Broad Peak. A few days later, Buhl is killed on Chogolisa.

1958. Americans Nick Clinch, Pete Schoening and Andy Kauffman climb Hidden Peak. An Italian expedition makes the first ascent of Gasherbrum IV: Walter Bonatti and Carlo Mauri reach the summit.

1960. An American expedition makes the first ascent of Masherbrum: G. Bell and W. Unsoeld reach the summit.

1962. Austrians Toni Kinshofer, Anderl Mannhardt and Sigi Low put up a new route on Nanga Parbat. Low falls to his death during the descent.

1970. Reinhold and Gunther Messner from Alto Adige make the first ascent of the Rupal wall of Nanga Parbat. Gunther is killed by an avalanche during the descent by the west side.

1975. Reinhold Messner and Austrian Peter Habeler put up a new route on the North Face of Hidden Peak.

1976. Britons Joe Brown, Mo Anthoine, Martin Boysen and Malcolm Howells climb Nameless Tower (Trango Towers). Americans Dennis Hennek, Jim Morrissey, Galen Rowell and John Roskelley climb the Great Trango Tower.

1977. Britons Chris Bonington and Doug Scott make the first ascent of the Ogre (or Baintha Brakk). Scott breaks his legs at the start of the descent, but manages to return to the base.

1978. Reinhold Messner soloes the Diamir wall of Nanga Parbat, following a partially new route.

1980. A Japanese expedition climbs the West Ridge of K2.

1982. A Japanese expedition climbs the North Edge of K2. Swiss climber Sylvain Saudan skis down Hidden Peak, becoming the first man to ski

down an "eight-thousander".

1984. Reinhold Messner and Hans Kammerlander from Alto Adige climb Gasherbrum I and then Hidden Peak without returning to base camp.

1985. Austrian Robert Schauer and Pole Woytek Kurtyka climb the South-West Face of Gasherbrum IV.

1986. Poles Tadeusz Piotrowski and Jerzy Kukuczka climb the "magic line" on the South-West Face of K2. Thirteen climbers are killed on the mountain as a result of bad weather conditions.

1987. Slovenians Francek Knez, Slavko Cantarm and Bojan Srot put up a route on Nameless Tower (Trango Towers). Swiss climbers Michel Piola, Stéphane Schafter, Michel Fauquet and Patrick Delale climb the West Pillar of the Great Trango Tower.

1988. Italians Maurizio Giordani, Rosanna Manfrini, Kurt Walde and Maurizio Venzo climb the South Pillar of the Tower of Uli Biaho.

1991. Frenchmen Pierre Béghin and Christophe Profit climb the North-West Ridge of K2.

1992. Australian Greg Child and American M. Wilford put up a new route on the South Face of the Great Trango Tower. Italian Alberto Soncini and Spaniards Oscar Cadiach, Luis Rafols and Enrico Dalmao climb Broad Peak from the Chinese side.

1997. Alexander and Thomas Huber from Alto Adige and Swiss climber Conrad Anker climb the South-West Face of Latok II.

THE INDIAN HIMALAYAS

1828. Briton J. G. Gerard climbs an unnamed 6220-metre peak in the Garhwal Himalayas.

1907. Briton Tom Longstaff, with Courmayeur guides A. and H. Brocherel, climbs Mount Trisul.

1931. Britons Frank Smythe, Eric Shipton and Holdsworth, with sherpa Lewa, reach the summit of Mount Kamet.

1936. Britons Harold Tilman and Noel Odell climb Nanda Devi.

1939. A Swiss expedition led by André Roch makes the first ascent of Dunagiri and two more peaks in the Garhwal Himalayas.

1947. A Swiss expedition led by André Roch makes the first ascent of Mount Satopanth and three more peaks in the Garhwal Himalayas.

1974. An Indian expedition led by H. Singh makes the first ascent of Mount Shivling (Garhwal). An Anglo-Indian expedition climbs Mount Changabang (Garhwal): Chris Bonington, Martin Boysen, Doug Scott, Dougal Haston, Balwant Sandhu and Tashi Chewang reach the summit.

1976. Britons Pete Boardman and Joe Tasker climb the West Face of Mount Changabang (Garhwal). Japanese climbers Y. Hasegawa and K. Tagami cross the summit ridge of Nanda Devi (Garhwal).

1977. An Indian expedition led by N. Kumar climbs the North-East side of Kangchenjunga.

1978. An international expedition consisting of A. McIntyre, J. Porter, V. Kurtyka and K. Zurek conquers the formidable South Face of Mount Changabang (Garhwal).

1979. Americans R. Kliegfield, J. Trackeray and P. Thexton make the first ascent of Thalay Sagar (Garhwal).

1981. Britons Doug Scott and R. White, Frenchman Georges Bettembourg and Australian Greg Child climb the East Ridge of Mount Shivling (Garhwal). A Czechoslovakian expedition led by V. Smida puts up a very difficult route on the gigantic North-East Face of Nanda Devi. An international team consisting of G. Bettembourg, D. Scott, G. Child and R. White makes the first ascent of the East Ridge of Mount Shivling (Garhwal).

1982. Scotsmen R. Barton and A. Fyffe conquer the West Pillar of Bhagirathi III (Garhwal).

1984. Spaniards J. O. Aldeguer, S. Martinez, J.L. Moreno and J. Tomas climb the West Pillar of Bhagirathi III (Garhwal).

1986. Italians P. Bernascone, F. Manoni and E. Rosso put up a difficult new route on the North-East Face of Mount Shivling (Garhwal).

1990. Slovenians Silvo Karo and Janez Jeglic climb the East Face of Bhagirathi III (Garhwal).

1993. Hans Kammerlander and Christoph Hainz from Alto Adige put up a direct route on the North Pillar of Mount Shivling (Garhwal). Czechs Z. Michalec and Z. Slachta put up a difficult route

on the Central Pillar of the West Face of Bhagirathi III (Garhwal).

1994. Italians E. Rosso, G. Ruffino and E. Vanetti put up a new route on the North-East Pillar of Thalay Sagar (Garhwal).

1997. Australians A. Lindblade and A. Whimp put up a very difficult route on the North Face of Thalay Sagar. Australians A. Cave, B. Murphy, M. Fowler and S. Sustad climb the North Face of Changabang (Garhwal).

1998. American Carlos Buhler and Russians Pavel Shabalin, Ivan Dusharin, Andrei Mariev and Andrei Volkov put up a direct route on the North Face of Mount Changabang (Garhwal). Russians I. Potankin, V. Kachkov, A. Lukin and Y. Koshlenko put up a very difficult new route on the West Face of Baghirati III (Garhwal).

THE HIMALAYAS OF NEPAL AND TIBET

1899. Britons Douglas Freshfield and Edmund J. Garwood, Italian Vittorio Sella and Nepali Rinzin Namgyal make the circuit of Kangchenjunga.

1921. The first British expedition explores Rongbuk valley and attempts the North Ridge of Mount Everest, reaching the North Col.

1922. During the second British expedition, George Finch and Geoffrey Bruce reach an altitude of 8320 metres. Seven sherpas are killed by an avalanche.

1924. During the third British expedition, E.F. Norton reaches an altitude of 8580 metres. George Mallory and Andrew Irvine attempt to reach the summit, are seen at 8450 metres, then disappear.

1929. A German expedition attempts Kangchenjunga for the first time: an altitude of 7400 metres is reached.

1933. During the fourth British expedition, Percy Wyn Harris, Lawrence Wager and Frank Smythe reach an altitude of 8580 metres.

1934. Briton Maurice Wilson attempts the ascent of Everest alone, without permission. His body is found the next year at an altitude of 6400 metres.

1938. During the seventh British expedition, Frank Smythe and Eric Shipton reach an altitude of 8320 metres.

1950. Frenchmen Maurice Herzog and Louis Lachenal make the first ascent of Annapurna, the first "eight-thousander" to be climbed.

1951. After the frontiers of Nepal are opened to foreigners, Eric Shipton leads an exploratory expedition in the Khumbu Valley. What is now the ordinary route on the mountain is identified and climbed up to an altitude of 6400 metres.

1952. Two Swiss expeditions attempt the mountain from the south. In May, Raymond Lambert and sherpa Tenzing Norgay reach an altitude of 8595 metres. During the post-monsoon attempt, the climbers fail to get past the South Col.

1953. A British expedition makes the first ascent of Mount Everest. New Zealander Edmund Hillary and sherpa Tenzing Norgay reach the summit.

1954. An Austrian expedition makes the first ascent of Cho Oyu: Herbert Tichy and sherpa Pasang Dawa Lama reach the summit.

1955. A British expedition makes the first ascent of Kangchenjunga: George Band, Joe Brown, Norman Hardie and T. Streather reach the summit. A French expedition conquers Mount Makalu: the first team to reach the summit is formed by Jean Couzy and Lionel Terray, followed by the rest of the climbers and sherpa Gyalzen Norbu.

1956. A Swiss expedition makes the second ascent of Everest (Jurg Marmet, Ernst Schmied, Adolf Reist and Hans Rudolf von Gunten reach the summit) and the first ascent of Lhotse (summited by F. Luchsinger and E. Reiss). A Japanese expedition climbs Mount Manaslu: T. Imanishi, K. Kato, M. Higeta and sherpa Gyaltsen Norbu reach the summit.

1959. Britons Mike Ward and Mike Gill, American Barry Bishop and New Zealander Wally Romanes climb Ama Dablam.

1960. A Chinese expedition makes the first ascent of Everest from the Tibetan side: Wang Fu-chou, Chu Yin-hua and Tibetan Kombu reach the summit. An international expedition makes the first ascent of Dhaulagiri: Swiss climbers E.E. Forrer, A. Schelbert, M. Vaucher and H. Weber, German P. Diener, Austrian Kurt Diemberger and

sherpas Nyima Dorje and Nawang Dorje reach the summit.

1963. During an American expedition, Tom Hornbein and Willy Unsoeld make the first ascent of the West Ridge and the first crossing of Everest.

1964. Ten members of a Sino-Tibetan expedition climb Shisha Pangma.

1970. Japanese climber Yuichiro Miura skis down the South Col of Everest. A British expedition climbs the South Face of Annapurna: Dougal Haston and Don Whillans reach the summit.

1971. A French expedition climbs the West Pillar of Makalu: Bernard Mellet and Yannick Seigneur reach the summit.

1975. Japanese climber Junko Tabei is the first woman to reach the summit of Mount Everest. The Yugoslav expedition led by Alex Kunaver conquers the steep South Face of Makalu. A British expedition climbs the South-West Face of Everest: the summit is reached by Dougal Haston, Doug Scott, Pete Boardman, sherpa Pertemba and perhaps Mick Burke, who disappears on the mountain.

1978. Reinhold Messner from Alto Adige and Austrian Peter Habeler make the first oxygenless ascent of Everest by the ordinary route from Nepal.

1979. Britons Doug Scott, Pete Boardman and Joe Tasker and Frenchman Georges Bettembourg climb the North Face of Kangchenjunga Alpine style, without oxygen.

1980. A Polish expedition makes the first winter ascent of Everest by the ordinary Nepalese route: Leszek Cichy and Krzystof Wielicki reach the summit. Reinhold Messner soloes Everest from the Tibetan side without using oxygen.

1981. Yugoslav climbers Stane Belak, Cene Bercic, Rok Kokar, Emil Tratnik and Joze Zupan scale the South Face of Dhaulagiri.

1982. Britons Doug Scott, Alex McIntyre, Baxter-Jones and Prescott climb the South Face of Shisha Pangma.

1983. An American expedition climbs the East (Kangshung) Face of Mount Everest. Carlos Buhler, Kim Momb, Louis Reichardt, Jay Cassell, George Lowe and Dan Reid reach the summit.

1984. A Nepali expedition makes the first attempt to clean up the rubbish left on Everest by previous expeditions. An Australian team climbs the Great Couloir on the North Face of Everest: Tim McCartney-Snape and Greg Mortimer reach the summit.

1986. Reinhold Messner reaches the summit of Lhotse, becoming the first mountaineer to climb all 14 "eight-thousanders".

1988. A Chinese-Japanese-Nepali expedition makes the first crossing of Everest from north to south and back. The first live TV broadcast is made from the summit. An expedition organised by French and Swiss guides is the first to lead clients on Everest. Frenchman Marc Batard makes the return trip from the base camp to the summit of Everest by the ordinary Nepali route in 22 hours.

1989. American Tom Whittaker is the first disabled climber to reach the summit of Everest. Slovenian Tomo Cesen soloes the North Face of Jannu.

1990. Slovenian Tomo Cesen makes the first ascent of the South Face of Lhotse, alone.

1992. A Japanese expedition climbs Namche Barwa (7782 metres), the highest unclimbed peak on earth.

1995. Reinhard Patscheider from Alto Adige makes the return trip from the base camp to the summit of Everest by the ordinary Tibetan route in 21 hours.

1996. A violent blizzard on Everest causes the death of nine climbers. Hans Kammerlander from Alto Adige is the first man to ski down from the summit of Everest. Swede Goran Kropp climbs Everest by the ordinary route from the south after cycling to Nepal from Europe.

1997. Sherpa Ang Rita reaches the summit of Everest for the tenth time.

1999. An American expedition finds the body of George Leigh Mallory not far from the North Ridge.

OTHER MOUNTAINS OF ASIA

1788. Russian Denil Gauss climbs the Kliuchevskaya volcano (Kamchatka).

1828. Japanese monk Bannryu climbs Yarigadake

(Japanese Alps).
1829. Swiss climber Friedrich Parrot makes the first ascent of Mount Ararat (Turkey).
1836. Sir W. Taylor Thompson's expedition climbs Mount Demavend (Iran).
1888. Briton Albert F. Mummery, with Swiss guide Hans Zurfluh, makes the first ascent of Dych Tau (Caucasus). Briton J. Cockin and Swiss guides Ulrich Almer and C. Roth climb Mount Shkhara (Caucasus).
1903. Britons Tom Longstaff and R.W. Rolleston climb the West Peak of Mount Shkhara (Caucasus). An Austrian team led by Hans Pfann makes the first crossing of Mount Ushba (Caucasus).
1921. Japanese climber K. Kobayashi scales the North-East Ridge of Mount Yarigadake (Japanese Alps).
1928. Germans Kurt Wien, Eugen Allwein and Erwin Schneider climb Pik Lenin (Pamir).
1931. A Soviet expedition led by P. Pogrebetsky makes the first ascents of Pik Pobedy and Khan Tengri (Tien Shan).
1932. Americans Richard Burdsall, Arthur Emmons, Terris Moore and Jack Young climb Minya Konka (Szechuan, China).
1933. A Soviet expedition led by E. Abalakov makes the first ascent of Pik Kommunizma (Pamir).
1936. Germans Frauenberger, Raditschnig and Peringer cross the ten peaks between Dykh Tau and Koshtan Tau (Caucasus).
1953. A Soviet expedition led by A. Ugatov climbs Pik Evgenia Korzhenevskaya (Pamir).
1956. A Sino-Soviet expedition climbs Muztagh Ata (Kun Lun). A Russian-Mongolian expedition climbs Mount Huithen (Mongolia).
1962. An Anglo-Soviet expedition led by John Hunt and A. Ovchinnikov climbs the South Face of Pik Kommunizma (Pamir).
1964. A Czechoslovakian team led by P. Baudish climbs the North Face of Mount Shkhara (Caucasus).
1971. A small group of Russian climbers, led by J. Arzischwski, puts up a magnificent new route on the West Face of Mount Ushba, which exits on the South Peak. Four Russian climbers led by L. Kensizki put up a difficult new route on the South Face of Mount Shkhara. Britons P. Nunn, H. MacInnes and C. Wood put up a new route on the North Face of Pik Schurovsky. Four Russians inaugurate a difficult new route on the North Face of Mount Tschantschachi (Caucasus). Two Soviet teams make the first ascent of Pik Kirow, climbing by way of the West Face.
1974. A Kazakhi expedition led by B. Studenin climbs the North Face of Khan Tengri (Tien Shan).
1981. A Japanese expedition led by Y. Tada reaches the highest peak of Amne Machin. A few days later, Americans G. Rowell, H. Knutsen and K. Schmitz also reach the summit of the mountain by a more direct, difficult route. A British expedition led by Michael Ward, consisting of Peter Boardman, Chris Bonington, Alan Rouse and Joe Tasher, climbs Mount Kongur (Sinkiang, China).
1982. A Soviet expedition climbs Mount Aksu (Pamir-Alai) by two different routes.
1983. A Soviet team led by Kaluzy climbs the South-East Face of Mount Kamen (Kamchatka).
1988. A Soviet expedition climbs the West Face of Pik 4810 (Pamir-Alai) by four different routes.
1990. A Russian expedition led by V. Khrishchaty makes the first winter crossing from Pik Pobedy to Khan Tengri (Tien Shan).

AFRICA

1503. Portuguese explorer Antonio de Saldanha climbs Table Mountain.
1848. Johann Rebmann from Switzerland sights Kilimanjaro and Mount Kenya.
1886. Hungarian Samuel Teleki de Szek attempts the ascent of Mount Kilimanjaro and Mount Kenya.
1888. Anglo-American Henry Morton Stanley sights Ruwenzori. South Africans A.H. and F.R. Stocker climb Champagne Castle (Drakensberg).
1889. German Hans Meyer and Austrian Ludwig Purtscheller make the first ascent of Kibo (Kilimanjaro).
1899. Scotsman Halford Mackinder and Courmayeur guides César Ollier and Joseph Brocherel climb Batian, the highest peak of Mount Kenya.
1905. Britons Douglas Freshfield and Arnold L. Mumm, with guide Moritz Inderblatten, attempt Ruwenzori.
1906. An Italian expedition climbs all the highest peaks of Ruwenzori: Luigi Amedeo di Savoia, Duke of Abruzzi, and guides Joseph Pétigax, Cesar Ollier and Joseph Brocherel, reach Margherita Peak.
1912. Germans Eduard Oehler and Fritz Klute reach the summit of Mawenzi (Kilimanjaro).
1927. Frenchmen Jacques de Lépiney and A. Stofer climb the South-East Ridge of Jebel Toubkal (Upper Atlas Mountains).
1929. Britons Eric Shipton and Percy Wyn Harris climb Nelion (Mount Kenya).
1932. Belgians X. de Grunne, W.J. Ganshof van der Merck, P. Solvay, J. Georges and H. de Schriver climb the West Face of Margherita Peak (Ruwenzori).
1935. Frenchmen Roger Frison-Roche and Raymond Coche climb Garet el Djenoun (Tefedest), Iharen and Saouinan (Hoggar).
1938. Germans Eugen Eisenmann and Theo Schnakig climb the Decken glacier on Kibo (Kilimanjaro).
1944. Britons A. H. Firmin and P. Hicks climb the north side of Batian (Mount Kenya). South Africans H. and E. Wongtschowski climb the Bell (Drakensberg).
1951. Frenchmen André Contamine, M. Mora and R. Thomas climb the West Face of Aiguille de Tigrite (Upper Atlas Mountains).
1957. Frenchmen M.R. Roussaire, S. Valentini, P. Cauderlier and G. Vidal climb the South Face of South Tehoulag (Hoggar).
1966. Frenchmen Pierre Mazeaud and Lucien Bérardini make the first ascent of Mount Takouba (Hoggar).
1967. Spaniards J-M Anglada, F. Abella, D. Alegre, F. Plana and J. Pons climb the North Spur of Garet el Djenoun (Tefedest).
1968. Frenchmen Bernard Amy and Bernard Domenech climb the North Face of Mount Aroudane (Upper Atlas Mountains).
1973. Englishman Phil Snyder and Kenyan Thumbi Mathenge climb the Diamond Couloir on Mount Kenya, exiting to the left.
1975. American Yvon Chouinard and Briton Mike Covington climb the Diamond Couloir of Mount Kenya, with a direct exit.
1978. Britons I. Allen and I.F. Howell climb the great dihedral on the East Face of Nelion (Mount Kenya). Reinhold Messner from Alto Adige climbs Breach Wall on Kilimanjaro.
1981. Frenchmen Patrick Edlinger, G. Merlin and M. Ricard put up the Tin'Hinan route on the West Face of Mount Daouda (Hoggar).
1983. Britons A. Wielochowski and R. Corkhill make the first ascent of Mount Poi (northern Kenya).
1995. Germans Kurt Albert and Berndt Arnold climb the South Face of Mount Karambony (Madagascar).
1998. Swiss climber Michel Piola, Frenchman Benoit Robert and Italians Manlio Motto and Emanuele Pellizzari climb 11 new routes on the walls of Mounts Karambony, Tsaranoro, Vatovarindry and Dondy (Madagascar).

NORTH AMERICA

1520. A group of Spanish soldiers led by Diego de Ordaz climbs Popocatèpetl (Mexico).
1847. An American military team commanded by William Reynolds climbs Pico de Orizaba (Mexico).
1853. American Thomas Dryer reaches the summit of Mount St. Helens.
1870. Americans Hazard Stevens and Philemon Van Trump make the first ascent of Mount Rainier (Washington State).
1872. Americans Nathaniel Langford and James Stevenson claim to have climbed Grand Teton (Wyoming).
1893. Americans W. Ripley and W. Rogers climb Devil's Tower (Wyoming) with extensive use of artificial aids.
1896. Americans William O. Owen and Franklin Spaulding make the first proven ascent of Grand Teton (Wyoming).
1897. Luigi Amedeo di Savoia, Duke of Abruzzi, makes the first ascent of Mount Saint Elias with Vittorio Sella, Erminio Botta, Francesco Gonella and guides Joseph Pétigax, Laurent Croux, Antoine Maquignaz and André Pellissier.
1906. Americans Frederick Cook, Ed Barrill, Hershel Parker and Belmore Brown claim to have climbed Mount MacKinley (Alaska): the falsehood is unmasked four years later.
1913. Americans Harry Karstens, Walter Harper, Hudson Stuck and Robert Tatum climb Mount MacKinley (Alaska). Austrian Conrad Kain, American Albert H. MacCarthy and Canadian W.W. Forster climb Mount Robson (Rocky Mountains).
1916. Americans Conrad Kain, Albert H. MacCarthy and J. Vincent climb Bugaboo Spire (Purcell Range).
1925. Americans Albert H. MacCarthy, H. Lambart, W. Foster, L. Lindsay, N. Reade and A. Carpe make the first ascent of Mount Logan (Yukon).
1931. Americans Allen Carpé and Terris Moore climb Mount Fairweather (Alaska).
1934. Americans Charles Houston and C. Waterston and Englishman Thomas Graham climb Mount Foraker (Alaska). Americans Jules Eichorn, Dick Leonard and Bestor Robinson climb Higher Cathedral Spire and Lower Cathedral Spire (Yosemite Valley).
1936. Americans Fritz Wiessner and Bill House climb Mount Waddington (Canadian Coast Mountains). Americans Jack Durrance, P. and E. Petzoldt climb the North Face of Grand Teton (Wyoming).
1937. Americans Fritz Wiessner, William House and L. Cloveney free-climb Devil's Tower (Wyoming).
1939. Americans Dave Brower, John Dyer, Raffi Bedayn and Bestor Robinson make the first ascent of the Shiprock (New Mexico).
1946. Americans Fred Beckey, R. Craid and C. Schmidtke climb the Devil's Thumb (Canada).
1950. Americans John Salathé and Allen Steck climb Sentinel Rock (Yosemite).
1954. Americans Fred Beckey and H. Meybohm and Austrian Heinrich Harrer climb Mount Deborah (Yukon). Americans Elton Thayer, George Argus, Les Viereck and Morton Wood make the first crossing of Mount MacKinley (Alaska); Thayer is killed during the descent.
1957. Americans Royal Robbins, Jerry Gallwas and Mike Sherrick climb the South-West Face of the Half Dome (Yosemite).
1958. Americans Warren Harding and Wayne Merry climb the Nose of El Capitan (Yosemite).
1959. Austrians Leo Schleiblehner and Richard Griesmann climb the South-East Face of Mount La Pérouse (Alaska).
1960. Americans Dave Rearick and Bob Kamps climb the East Face (the Diamond) of Long's Peak (Colorado).
1961. Americans Royal Robbins, Chuck Pratt and Tom Frost climb the Salathé Wall of El Capitan (Yosemite). Italians Riccardo Cassin, Jack Canali, Gigi Alippi, Annibale Zucchi, Romano Perego and Natale Airoldi climb the South Face of Mount McKinley (Alaska). Americans H. Swedlund and R. Jacquot climb Black Ice Couloir on Grand Teton (Wyoming).
1963. Americans Jim MacCarthy, Royal Robbins, Layton Kor and Dick McCracken climb the South-East Face of Mount Proboscis, in the Cirque of the Unclimbables (Yukon).
1964. Americans Royal Robbins, Yvon Chouinard, Chuck Pratt and Tom Frost climb the North America Wall of El Capitan (Yosemite Valley). Germans Klaus Bierl, Arnold Hasenkopf, Alfons Reichegger and Walter Welsch climb the Moose's Tooth.
1965. Americans Don Jensen, Dave Roberts, Ed Bernd and Matt Hale climb the West Face of Mount Huntington (Alaska). Dick Long, Jim Wilson, Allen Steck, Joe Evans, Paul Bacon and Frank Coale conquer the South Ridge of Mount Logan (Yukon).
1967. An international expedition makes the first winter ascent of Mount McKinley (Alaska). Americans Dave Johnston and Art Davidson and Swiss climber Ray Genet reach the summit. Frenchman Jacques Batkin is killed.
1972. Americans Bill Forrest and Kris Walker climb the Painted Wall in the Black Canyon of the Gunnison (Colorado).
1973. Americans Doug Robinson, Dennis Hennek and Galen Rowell free-climb the repeat of the South-West Face of the Half Dome (Yosemite Valley).
1975. Americans Jim Bridwell, Bill Westbay and Jay Fiske climb the Pacific Ocean Wall of El Capitan (Yosemite). On the same wall Bridwell and Westbay, with John Long, make the first one-day ascent of the Nose.
1976. Britons Doug Scott and Dougal Haston put up a new route on the South Face of Mount McKinley (Alaska).
1977. American Henry Barber puts up the Mr. Clean route on the Devil's Tower (Wyoming).
1978. Americans "Mugs" Stump and J. Logan climb the Emperor Face of Mount Robson (Rocky Mountains). Americans Jim Bridwell, Dale Bard and D. Diegelman put up Sea of Dreams on El Capitan (Yosemite). Americans S. McCartney and J. Roberts make the first ascent of the North Face of Mount Huntington (Alaska).
1984. Italian Renato Casarotto soloes the North-East Ridge (or Ridge of No Return) of Mount McKinley.
1986. A group of Alaskan climbers make the first ascent of Mount Logan (Alaska).
1988. Swiss climber Xavier Bongard makes the first solo ascent of Sea of Dreams on El Capitan (Yosemite). On the same face, Americans Paul Piana and Todd Skinner perform the first free-climb of the Salathé Wall.
1991. Czech Miroslav Smid soloes a new route on the South Face of Mount McKinley.
1992. Americans Paul Piana, Galen Rowell and Todd Skinner put up the Great Canadian Knife route on the South-East Face of Mount Proboscis in the Cirque of the Unclimbables (Yukon). Spaniards Carlos, Javier, José Garcia and Miguel Angel Gallego climb West Temple (Utah).
1993. Americans Lynn Hill and B. Sandahl make the first free-climb of the Nose on El Capitan (Yosemite).
1994. Americans Marc Twight and Scott Backes put up the Deprivation route on the North Spur of Mount Hunter (Alaska).
1995. Canadians J. Elzinga and D. Serl climb the South Face of Mount Waddington (Canadian Coast Mountains).
1997. Austrian Thomas Bubendorfer makes the first ascent of Mount Laurens (Alaska).

ARCTIC AND GREENLAND

1921. Britons James M. Wordie, Mercanton and Lethbridge climb Mount Beerenberg (Jan Mayen Island).
1935. A British expedition led by L. Wager climbs Gunnbjorns Fjeld (Greenland).
1938. A Swiss expedition led by André Roch climbs Mount Forel (Greenland).
1953. Swiss climbers Hans Weber, J. Marmet-Rothlisberger and F. Schwarzenbach climb Mount Asgard (Baffin Island).
1960. An Italian expedition led by Piero Ghiglione climbs Punta Italia (Greenland).
1972. Britons Doug Scott, Paul Nunn and Paul Braithwaite and American Dennis Hennek climb the South-West Spur of Mount Asgard (Baffin Island).
1975. American Charlie Porter soloes the Asgard Tower (Baffin Island).
1976. Briton Doug Scott and American Dennis Hennek climb the West Pillar of Mount Overlord (Baffin Island)
1984. Swiss climbers Michel Piola, Christian Dalphin and Nicolas Schenkel climb the South Face of Ketil Pingasut (Greenland).
1985. An American team led by Earl Redfern puts up a direct route on the West Face of Mount Thor (Baffin Island).
1994. H. Gargitter and W. Obergolser from Alto Adige, Englishman B. Masterson and Germans H.M. Gotz, K. Albert, S. Glowacz and D. Lang climb the West Face of Ulametorssuaq (Greenland).
1995. Americans Paul Gagner and Rick Lovelace put up the Superunknown route on the South Face of Walker Citadel (Baffin Island). Swiss climber Michel Piola and Italians Paolo Cavagnetto, Manlio Motto and Vincenzo Ravaschietto put up a direct route on the South-

West Face of Mount Suikarsuak (Greenland).
1998. American Jason Smith soloes the West Face of Mount Thor (Baffin Island).

SOUTH AMERICA

1802. German Alexander von Humboldt, Frenchman Aimé Bonpland and Ecuadorian Carlos Montùfar attempt the ascent of Chimborazo (Ecuador).
1834. Briton Robert Schomburg makes the first ascent of Roraima (Venezuela).
1872. German Wilhelm Reiss and Colombian Angel M. Escobar make the first ascent of Cotopaxi (Ecuador).
1879-1880. Briton Edward Whymper, with guides Jean-Antoine and Louis Carrel, makes the first ascents of Chimborazo, Cayambe, Antisana, Carihuairazo, Sincholagua, Cotacachi and Sara Urco in Ecuador. The Carrels make the first ascent of Illiniza Sur alone.
1897. Guide Mathias Zurbriggen makes the first ascents of Aconcagua and Tupungato (Cordillera Central, Argentina).
1898. Briton Martin Conway, with guides Antoine Maquignaz and Louis Pellissier, reaches the summit of Mount Illimani (Cordillera Oriental, Bolivia).
1908. Americana A. Peck, with guides G. Zumtaugwald and P. Taugwalder, makes the first ascent of the North Peak of Mount Huascaràn (Cordillera Blanca, Peru).
1919. German R. Dienst climbs Huayna Potosì (Cordillera Oriental, Bolivia).
1932. Germans H. Bernard, E. Hein, H. Hoerlin and E. Schneider climb South Huascaràn, Huandoy, Artesonraju, East Huasrcaràn and Nevado de Copoa (Cordillera Blanca, Peru).
1934. Poles S. Osiewski, V. Ostrowski, A. Karipnski, J. Dorawski and S. Dassinsky climb Cerro Mercedario (Argentina).
1936. F. Weiss climbs Pico Bolivar (Sierra Nevada de Merida, Venezuela).
1939. A. Bakewell, A. Praolini and W.A. Wood make the first ascent of Pico Colòn (Sierra de Santa Marta, Colombia).
1953. Britons G. Bell, F. Auyres, D. Michael and W. Graham climb Nevado Salcantay (Cordillera de Vilcabamba, Peru).
1954. A French expedition climbs the South Face of Aconcagua: Lucien Bérardini, Adrien Dagory, E. Denis, Pierre Lesueur and G. Poulet reach the summit.
1956. Frenchmen Lionel Terray, M. Martin, R. Davaille and R. Sennelier climb Mounts Chacraraju and Taulliraju (Cordillera Blanca, Peru).
1957. Austrians Toni Egger and Stefan Jungmeier climb Jirishanca (Cordillera de Huayhuash, Peru).
1961. Italians Riccardo Cassin, Gigi Alippi, Casimiro Ferrari, Giuseppe Lafranconi, Annibale Zucchi, Sandro Liati and Natale Airoldi climb the West Edge of Jirishanca (Cordillera de Huayhuash, Peru).
1962. A French expedition led by Lionel Terray climbs the East Face of Mount Chacraraju (Cordillera Blanca, Peru).
1968. Britons Chris Jones and Paul Dix climb the North-East Face of Mount Yerupaja (Cordillera de Huayhuash, Peru).
1973. Britons Joe Brown, Mo Anthoine, Don Whillans and Hamish MacInnes climb the North Spur of Roraima (Venezuela).
1974. Reinhold Messner from Alto Adige makes the first solo ascent of the South Face of Aconcagua.
1975. Italians Casimiro Ferrari, Pino Negri, Antonio Zoia, Danilo Borgonuovo, Sandro Liati and Piero Castelnuovo climb the South-West Face of Mount Alpamayo (Cordillera Blanca, Peru). Frenchman Nicolas Jaeger climbs the South Face of Mount Chacraraju (Cordillera Blanca, Peru).
1977. Britons Rab Carrington and Alan Rouse climb the West Face of Mount Rondoy (Cordillera de Huayhuash, Peru). Italian Renato Casarotto soloes the North Face of Huascaràn Norte (Cordillera Blanca, Peru).
1983. Italians Franco Perlotto and Gianni Bisson climb the wall to the left of Angel Leap (Venezuela).
1988. Frenchman Patrick Gabarrou soloes a route on the South Face of Mount Illimani (Cordillera Oriental, Bolivia).
1991. Slovenian Slavko Sveticic puts up a route on the South-West Face of Mount Huascaràn (Cordillera Blanca, Peru).
1992. Slovenians Dusan Debelak and Tomas Zerovnik climb the Central Pillar on the North Face of Mount Illampu (Cordillera Real, Bolivia).
1996. Slovenians Viktor Milnar, Dusan Debelak and Tomas Zerovnik climb the West Face of Mount Chacraraju (Cordillera Blanca, Peru). American S. House scales a series of difficult ice-filled gullies on the West Face of Chimborazo (Ecuador).

PATAGONIA AND TIERRA DEL FUEGO

1942. Friedrich (Federico) Reichert climbs Mount Tronador.
1943. Italian Alberto Maria De Agostini and Argentinians Alex Hemmi and Heriberto Schmoll climb Cerro San Lorenzo.
1947. An Italian expedition consisting of Aldo Bonacossa, Ettore Castiglioni, Leo Dubosc and Titta Gilberti makes the first attempted ascent of Fitz Roy.
1952. Frenchmen Lionel Terray and Guido Magnone make the first ascent of Fitz Roy. Argentinians Dinko Bertoncelij, Birger Lantschner, Toncek Pangerc, Gregorio Ezquerra, Carlos Sonntag, Otto Meiling and Juan Neumayer climb Cerro San Valentìn. An Argentinian expedition from the Club Andino de Bariloche climbs Mount San Valentìn, the highest peak in Patagonia.
1956. Italians Carlo Mauri and Clemente Maffei, members of a mountaineering expedition led by Padre Alberto Maria De Agostini, make the first ascent of Mount Sarmiento (East Peak).
1957. Italians Jean Bich, Leonardo Carrel, Toni Gobbi, Camillo Pellissier and Pierino Pession climb Paine Grande.
1958. Two Italian expeditions attempt Cerro Torre. Italians Walter Bonatti and Carlo Mauri and Argentinians Folco Doro Altan and René Eggmann climb Cerro Mariano Moreno. Bonatti and Mauri cross Cordòn Adela.
1959. Italian Cesare Maestri and Austrian Toni Egger make the first ascent of Cerro Torre. Egger is killed by an avalanche during the descent.
1962. Irishman Frank Cochrane and Englishman Don Whillans climb Aguja Poincenot.
1963. Britons Chris Bonington and Don Whillans conquer the Central Paine Tower. Italians Armando Aste, Vasco Taldo, Josve Aiazzi, Carlo Casati and Nando Nusdeo climb the South Paine Tower.
1965. Argentinians Carlos Comesana and Josè Luis Fonrouge conquer the Supercanaleta on Fitz Roy.
1966. Italians Casimiro Ferrari, Cesare Giudici, Gigi Alippi, Guido Machetto, Carlo Mauri and Giuseppe Pirovano make the first ascent of Mount Buckland (Tierra del Fuego).
1968. Americans Yvon Chouinard, Dick Dorworth, Chris Jones, Lito Tejada-Flores and Douglas Tompkins climb the South-West Pillar of Fitz Roy.
1970. Italians Cesare Maestri, Daniele Alimonta and Carlo Claus climb the East Ridge of Cerro Torre (using a compressor).
1974. Italians Casimiro Ferrari, Mario Conti, Pino Negri and Daniele Chiappa climb the West Face of Cerro Torre.
1976. Americans John Bragg, John Donini and Jay Wilson climb Torre Egger.
1979. Italian Renato Casarotto soloes the North-North-East Pillar of Fitz Roy. Americans Jim Bridwell and Steve Brewer free-climb the repeat of the East Ridge of Cerro Torre.
1982. Americans Alan Kearney and Bobby Knight climb the South Face of the Central Paine Tower.
1985. Swiss climber Marco Pedrini makes the first solo ascent of Cerro Torre. Italians Paolo Caruso, Maurizio Giarolli, Ermanno Salvaterra and Andrea Sarchi make the first winter ascent of Cerro Torre. Italians Mario Manica and Renzo Vettori climb the North-West Face of Cerro Piergiorgio.
1986. Argentinians Sebastian de la Cruz, Gabriel Ruiz and Eduardo Brenner make the first winter ascent of Fitz Roy. Italians D. Bosisio, M. della Santa, M. Panzeri and P. Vitali climb the West Peak of Mount Sarmiento.
1988. Slovenians Janez Jeglic and Silvo Karo climb the South Face of Cerro Torre.
1991. Swiss climber Kaspar Ochsner and Czech Michal Pitelka climb the East Pillar of Fitz Roy.
1995. Italians Ermanno Salvaterra, Piergiorgio Vidi and Roberto Manni put up a new route on the South Face of Cerro Torre in winter, climbing Alpine style.

AUSTRALASIA AND THE ANTARCTIC

1882. Rev. W.S. Green makes the first attempted ascent of Mount Cook (New Zealand Alps).
1888. An expedition led by W. MacGregor climbs Mount Victoria (Irian Jaya, New Guinea). Briton J. Whitehead climbs Low's Peak on Mount Kinabalu (Borneo).
1894. New Zealanders George Graham, Tom Fyfe and Jack Clark make the first ascent of Mount Cook (New Zealand Alps).
1895. E. A. Fitzgerald and Jack Clarke, with guide Mathias Zurbeiggen, make the first ascent of Mount Tasman (New Zealand Alps).
1908. Britons J. Adams, T. David, A. Mackay, E. Marshall and Australian D. Mawson, starting from E. Shackleton's ship the Nimrod, climb Mount Erebus from the west side (Ross Island, Antarctic).
1922. Briton A. F. Wollaston makes the first attempted ascent of the Carstenz Pyramid (New Guinea).
1934. Americans Q. Blackburn, S. Paine and R. Russel, members of the second Byrd expedition, climb Mount Weaver (Queen Maud Mountains, Antarctic).
1936. A Dutch expedition led by A.H. Colijn climbs Ngga Poloe but fails to conquer the Carstenz Pyramid (New Guinea).
1940. Americans H. Gilmour, C. Passel, L. Warner and L. Wells reach the summit of Mount Berlin (Hal Flood Range, Marie Byrd Land, Antarctic).
1951. New Zealanders George Lowe, Edmund Hillary, Earle Roddiford and Ed Cotter climb the Maximilian Ridge on Elie de Beaumont (New Zealand Alps).
1955. Britons W. Hindson, A. Rennie and A. Shewry climb Mount Français from the west side (Antarctic Peninsula).
1956. Britons J. Cunningham, S. Paterson, T. Price and K. Warburton climb Mount Paterson (South Georgia).
1958. New Zealanders G. Marsh and R. Miller climb Claydon Peak (Queen Elizabeth Range, Antarctic); their fellow-countrymen F. Brooke and B. Gunn reach the summit of Mount Huggins (Royal Society Range, Victoria Land, Antarctic).
1959. Briton J. Pirrit soloes the first ascent of Mount Sidley (Marie Byrd Land, Antarctic), and New Zealanders B. Alexander, M. White and J. Wilson climb Mount Terror (Ross Island, Antarctic).
1961. An Australian team climbs the North-West Face of Federation Peak (Tasmania). Australians D. Keyser, J. Seavers and D. Traill reach the summit of Mount Menzies (Prince Charles Mountains, Antarctic).
1962. Austrian Heinrich Harrer, New Zealander Philip Temple and Dutchmen Kippax and Huizinga climb the Carstenz Pyramid (New Guinea). New Zealanders R. Hewson, G. Grindley and J. Montgomery make the first ascent of Mount Falla (Queen Alexandra Range, Antarctic). Briton W. Herbert and New Zealanders V. McGregor, P. Otway and K. Pain climb Mount Fridtjof Nansen (the southernmost "four-thousander" in the Antarctic). Finally, New Zealanders B. Gunn and J. Wilson make the first ascent of Mount Lister (Royal Society Range, Antarctic).
1964. An expedition led by M.K. Burkley makes the first ascent of Mount Paget (South Georgia).
1965. An Australian team makes the first ascent of Ball's Pyramid.
1966. Americans B. Corbet, J. Evans, W. Long and P. Schoening make the first ascent of Mount Vinson (Antarctic). Americans B. Corbet, C. Hollister, S. Silverstein and R. Wahlstrom make the first ascent of Mount Shinn (Sentinel Range, Ellsworth Mountains, Antarctic); in the same area, Americans J. Evans and B. Marts climb Mount Gardner.
1967. Americans B. Corbet and J. Evans make the first ascent of Mount Tyree, the second-highest peak in the Antarctic (Sentinel Range, Ellsworth Mountains, Antarctic); in the same area, Evans, C. Hollister, S. Silverstein and R. Wahlstrom climb Mount Ostenso. At the same time, also in the Sentinel Range, Americans E. Fukushima, W. Long, B. Martis and P. Schoening conquer Mount Long Gables.
1968. Ignazio Piussi makes various first ascents in the Royal Society Range (Victoria Land, Antarctic): Mount Hercules (with G. Wilson), St. Paul's Mountain (with M. Manzoni), Round Mountain (alone) and Mount Fleming (with M. Manzoni). In the same area, Carlo Mauri and Attilio Ollier make the first ascent of Mount Warren (now Warren Range HP).
1969. New Zealanders George Harris and Murray Jones climb the South Face of Douglas Peak (New Zealand Alps). Carlo Mauri and Attilio Ollier climb Mount Portal (Victoria Land, Antarctic). In the same area, I. Piussi and three New Zealanders make the first ascent of Mount Odin.
1970. New Zealanders Pete Gough and John Glasgow climb the South-East (Caroline) Face of Mount Cook (New Zealand Alps).
1972. New Zealanders Bill Denz and Brian Pooley climb the Nalfour face of Mount Tasman (New Zealand Alps). Britons Richard Isherwood, Leo Murray and Jack Baines climb a direct route on the North Face of the Carstenz Pyramid (New Guinea).
1976. Walter Bonatti and New Zealander Gary Ball make numerous first ascents in the Royal Society Range (Victoria Land, Antarctic): Mount Hooker, Mount Giulia, Mount Rucker and the Twins.
1978. Britons Peter and Hillary Boardman climb the South Face of the Carstenz Pyramid (New Guinea).
1980. Frenchman P. Cardis climbs the North-East Spur of Mount Paget (South Georgia).
1981. New Zealanders W. Atkinson and W. Fowlie make the first ascents of Mount Adam and Mount Black Prince (Admiralty Mountains, Antarctic).
1985. Canadians P. Morrow and M. Williams are the first to ski down Mount Vinson, the highest peak in the Antarctic (Sentinel Range, Ellsworth Mountains). Americans D. Egerton and E. Stumps and Australian R. Korsch climb Mount Korsch and Mount Markham (Queen Elizabeth Range, Antarctic).
1986. Canadian Pat Morrow scales the Carstenz Pyramid to become the first mountaineer to climb the highest peaks on all six continents.
1994. A Norwegian expedition climbs Mount Ulvetanna in Queen Maud Land (Antarctic).
1989. New Zealanders P. Fitzgerald and R. Hall and Americans E. and T. Stump make the first ascent of Mount Vinson in Alpine style (Sentinel Range, Ellsworth Mountains, Antarctic). In the same area, T. Stump makes the first solo ascents of Mount Gardner and Mount Tyree, and R. Hall makes the first solo ascent of Mount Shinn.
1991. Americans D. Elliot, T. Fleming and C. Miller climb Mount Kirkpatrick (Queen Alexandra Range, Antarctic). Austrian R. Lang makes the first solo ascent of Mount Vinson, following a new route on the west side. Americans C. Anker, C. Duval, J. Smith and P. Teten climb Mount Craddock by way of the West Spur (Sentinel Range, Ellsworth Range, Antarctic).
1994. Swiss mountaineer Erhard Loretan, climbing solo, makes the first ascent of Mount Epperly (Sentinel Range, Ellsworth Range, Antarctic).
1996. French climbers Eric Decamp and Catherine Destivelle make the first ascents of Mount Viets and a difficult unnamed peak (4111 m) on the West Face (Sentinel Range, Ellsworth Range, Antarctic).

Pierre Allain *Alpinisme et Compétition*, Paris, 1949
Lain Allan, Gordon Boy, Clive Ward *Snowcaps at the Equator*, London, 1988
Stefano Ardito, *Monte Bianco*, Vercelli, 1995
Yves Ballu, *Les alpinistes*, Grenoble, 1984
Edwin Bernbaum *Sacred Mountains of the World*, 1990
Karl Blodig-Helmut Dumler *Die Viertausander der Alpen*, 1989
Walter Bonatti, *I giorni grandi*, Milan, 1971
Walter Bonatti, *Le mie montagne*, Bologna, 1962
Walter Bonatti, *Montagne di una vita*, Milan, 1997
Chris Bonington, *Annapurna South Face*, London, 1973
Chris Bonington *Everest the Hard Way*, London, 1976
Chris Bonington, *I chose to climb*, London, 1966
Chris Bonington, *The Next Horizon*, London, 1973
Chris Bonington, Alessandro Gogna *La grande montagna*, Novara, 1995
Joe Brown *The Hard Years*, London, 1967
Thomas Graham Brown, *Brenva*, London, 1955
Thomas Graham Brown, Gavin de Beer *The First Ascent of Mont Blanc*, Oxford, 1957
Hermann Buhl *Achttausander druber und dunter*, 1960
Gino Buscaini, Silvia Metzeltin *Patagonia*, Milan, 1999
Riccardo Cassin *Cinquant'anni di alpinismo*, Milan, 1977
Antonio Cembran, Maurizio Giordani *Marmolada*

sogno di pietra, Trento, 1986
Giovanni Cenacchi *Gli Scoiattoli di Cortina*, Cortina, 1989
Tomo Cesen *Solo*, Milan, 1991
Christine de Colombel *Les grands de la montagne*, Paris, 1979
Emilio Comici, *Alpinismo eroico*, Bologna, 1961
William A. B. Coolidge *Josias Simler et les origines de l'alpinisme*, Grenoble, 1904
Filippo De Filippi *Himalaia, Caracorum e Turchestan Cinese*, Bologna, 1924
Ardito Desio *Italia K2*, 1955
René Desmaison, *La montagne à mains nues*, Paris, 1971
Kurt Diemberger *K2, il nodo infinito*
Kurt Diemberger *Tra Zero e Ottomila*, Bologna, 1970
Horace-Bénédict de Saussure, *Voyages dans les Alpes*, Neuchatel, 1779-1796
Claude-Eliane Engel, *Histoire de l'alpinisme des origines à nos jours*, Paris, 1950
Roger Frison-Roche, Sylvain Jouty *Storia dell'alpinismo*, Milan, 1996
Giusto Gervasutti, *Il Fortissimo–Scalate nelle Alpi*, Milan, 1985
Paul Grohmann *Wanderungen im den Dolomiten*, Wien, 1877
Heinrich Harrer, *Das Buch vom Eiger*, Innsbruck, 1988
Dougal Haston *In High Places*

Maurice Herzog *Annapurna Premier 8000*, Paris, 1962
Toni Hiebeler, *Eiger, parete Nord*, Bologna 1966
Edmund Hillary *Nothing Venture Nothing Won*, London, 1975
Edmund Hillary *High Adventure*,
Thomas F. Hornbein *Everest: the West Ridge*, San Francisco, 1966
John Hunt *The Ascent of Everest*
Chris Jones *Climbing in North America*, Berkeley-Los Angeles, 1979
Pierre Joutard *L'invention du Mont Blanc*, Paris, 1986
Jon Krakauer *Into Thin Air*, New York, 1997
Julius Kugy, *Aus dem Leben eines Bergsteigers*, München, 1925
Jerzy Kukuczka, *Na szczytach swiata*, Warsaw, 1990
Georges Livanos *Au delà de la verticale*, Paris, 1958
Cesare Maestri *Il Ragno delle Dolomiti*, Milan, 1981
Roberto Mantovani *Everest, storia del gigante himalayano*, Vercelli, 1997
Roberto Mantovani *K2, sfida ai confini del cielo*, Vercelli, 1998
Fosco Maraini *Gasherbrum IV*, Bari, 1960
Reinhold Messner, *Die Herausforderung*, 1976
Reinhold Messner, *Der 7 Grad*, Munich, 1976
Reinhold Messner, *Der Freiheit, auzubrechen, wohin ich will*, 1989

Reinhold Messner *Der Glaserne Horizont*, Munich, 1982
Reinhold Messner *Uberlebt – Alle 14 Achttausender*, Munich, 1987
Gian Piero Motti, Enrico Camanni *La storia dell'alpinismo*, Torino, 1995
John Muir, Galen Rowell *The Yosemite*, San Francisco, 1989
Albert F. Mummery, *My Climbs in the Alps and Caucasus*, London, 1895
Jim Perrin *Mirrors in The Cliffs*, London, 1983
Tita Piaz *A tu per tu con le Alpi*, Bologna, 1966
Gaston Rébuffat, *Etoiles et Tempetes*, Paris, 1954
Galen Rowell *Mountains of the Middle Kingdom*, San Francisco, 1983
Galen Rowell *Montani Light*, San Francisco, 1986
Doug Scott *Himalayan Climber*, London, 1992
Eric Shipton *The Six Mountain-Travel Books*, London and Seattle, 1995
Lionel Terray *Les conquérants de l'inutile*, Paris, 1961
Walt Unsworh, *Encyclopaedia of Mountaineering*, London, 1992
Edward Whymper *Scrambles amongst the Alps in The Year 1860-69*, London, 1871
Edward Whymper *Travels Amongst the Great Andes of the Equator*, London, 1891-1892
Ken Wilson, *The Games Climbers Play*, London
William Windham, Pierre Martel, *An Account of The Glaciers or Ice Alps in Savoy*, London, 1744

316

PHOTOGRAPHIC CREDITS

Fèdèration française de la montagne et de l'escalade: pages 162 left, 162 right, 163 bottom left, 170 top, 170-171,171 bottom left, 180 bottom left, 180 bottom right.
Ferrero-Labat/ Ardea London: page 104 bottom left .
Fondazione Sella Archive: pages 9 bottom, 70 top, 70 centre, 70-71, 71 centre, 71 bottom left and right, 94 right, 95 bottom left, 97 centre, 97 bottom, 101 top and bottom, 98 top, 98 centre, 99 bottom, 115 right, 114-115 bottom.
Fontanive Archive: pages 60 top left, 126 bottom, 127 right.
A. Gandini: pages 52-53, 54 top, 54 bottom, 56 top, 58 top, 58 bottom, 58-59, 59 top right, 59 centre right, 60 bottom right, 82 top right, 83 bottom, 84 bottom, 91 top left, 91 top centre, 91 top right, 91 bottom right.
Maurizio Giordani: pages 249 bottom, 253 bottom, 25 bottom, 255 right, 256 left, 257 bottom, 258 left, 258 right, 259 top left, 259 top right, 259 bottom right.
Brian Hall / Stock Shot: pages 66 left, 218-219, 280 bottom right.
Harrer: pages 131 bottom, 134 top, 134 centre left, 134 centre right, 134 bottom, 134-135.
David Harris: pages 214, 215 bottom centre.
A. Heinrich: page 274 left.
Toni Hiebeler / Bavaria Bildagentur: pages 172-173.
J. Huber / SIME: pages 20-21, 50-51, 65 top, 78-79.
Sigi Hupfauer / Chris Bonington Picture Library: pages 116-117.
Marco Milani / K 3: pages 53 bottom, 80-81, 83 top, 120-121, 122-123, 130-131, 136-137, 177 right, 178-179, 178-179, 179 top right, 182-183, 248 top, 268-269.
Alessandro Gogna / K 3: pages 88 top, 142-143, 168-169, 185 left, 187 left, 187 top right, 187 bottom right, 200 top, 201 top left, 201 top right, 201 bottom right, 249 top, 252 left, 253

top, 254-255, 264 bottom, 268 bottom left, 269 top, 269 bottom left .
Reinhold Mesner / K 3: page 269 bottom right.
Knez Archive: page 239 bottom.
Gerard Kosicki: pag
Nazima Kowall: pages 114-115 top .
D.Lafond / Ag.Freestyle: pages 18-19, 22-23, 26-27.
Library of Congress: pages 106 top, 106 bottom, 108 top left and right.
J.C. Ligeon / Foc Photo: page 26 top .
Manuel Lugli: page 235 top .
Marco Mairani: pages 104-105, 150 top, 158-159, 230 top, 234 bottom.
Eugenio Manghi: pages 36-37.
Heinz Mariacher: pages 256 right, 257 top
James Martin: pages 108-109.
Mary Evans Picture Library: pages 44 bottom, 161 top left.
Colin Monteath / Hedgehog House: page 155 centre.
Colin Monteath / Mountain Camera: pages 103 bottom right.
Patrick Morrow / Mountain Camera: pages 4-5, 95 top .
Patrick Morrow: pages 163 bottom right, 213, 288 top and bottom, 288-289, 289 right.
J.C. Munoz / Panda Photo: pages 236-237.
Museo Nazionale della Montagna,Turin: pages 7, 72 bottom, 76 right, 77 left, 77 centre, 82 bottom, 141 bottom, 144 top left, 146, 166 top, 166 bottom, 167 bottom, 168 bottom, 169 top left, 169 top right, 169 centre, 169 bottom left, 169 bottom right, 170 bottom right, 172 top left, 172 top right, 172 bottom, 230 top, 230 centre, 230 bottom.
Wolfgang Nairz: pages 265 top, 266 top, 266 bottom left, 266 bottom right, 266-267, 267.
Peter Noebel: pages 206-207.
Michel Piola: pages 300-301, 301 top, 301 bottom.
Jean Marc Porte: page 159 bottom.
Christophe Profit: pages 284-285, 285 top, 296

right, 296-297, 297 top, 297 bottom.
Ruaridh Pringle / Stock Shot: pages 100 top, 240-241, 245 bottom right.
Provincia Autonoma di Trento: pages 128 bottom left, 182 left, 182 right.
Mauro Raffini / Agenzia Franca Speranza: page 67 centre.
René Robert / Ag. Freestyle: pages 2-3, 12 centre, 12-13, 13 bottom, 20 bottom, 23 centre, 150-151, 241 centre, 244-245, 245 bottom, 246-247, 247 bottom, 247 top, 260-261, 262-263, 262 bottom, 263 left, 270, 298-299, 304 top left, 305 right.
Leopold Roman: page 255 left.
Royal Geographical Society: pages 28 bottom, 28-29 bottom, 112 bottom, 113 bottom, 148-149 bottom, 149 top right and bottom, 150 bottom left, 150 bottom right, 152 left, 152 top right, 152 bottom right, 153 top, 154 top, 154 bottom, 155 top, 155 bottom, 158 top, 158 bottom, 159 left, 159 top right, 160-161, 160 bottom, 161 top left.
Royal Geographical Society / The Bridgeman Art Library London: page 161 bottom left.
Galen Rowell/ Mountain Light: pages 106-107, 108 bottom, 109 right, 114 top, 157 bottom right, 162-163, 165 bottom left, 166-167, 204 left, 210 bottom left, 215 top left, 215 top right, 215 bottom, 216 right, 217 right, 218 left, 219 top, 219 bottom, 220 top left , 220 bottom left, 220 right, 221 bottom left, 221 right, 224 left, 224-225, 225 top, 225 bottom, 226 bottom left, 226 bottom right, 227, 228-229, 233 bottom, 238 bottom, 264 top left, 276 top, 276-277, 277 top, 277 bottom
SAT Trieste: pages 62 top, 62 bottom.
Archiv Schmitt: page 133 top left and right.
Doug Scott: pages 6-7, 11, 212 top, 272 top, 272 bottom, 272-273, 273 top, 273 bottom, 278, 279 top, 279 centre left, 279 centre right, 279 bottom left, 279 bottom right.
Andy Selters: pages 216 right, 217 left.

Mark Shapiro: pages 148-149 top
Janez Skok: page 299 bottom
Sean M.Smith / Tibet Images: pages 116 top, 116 bottom, 238 centre.
Società Alpina delle Giulie: pages 122 top left, 122 bottom left, 122 top right.
Società Scoiattoli di Cortina: pages 174 bottom left, 175 left, 176 left, 176 right, 180 top .
Stenico Archive: pages 123 bottom left, 125 top right and bottom, 126-127, 129 bottom, 177 left, 178 top left, 179 bottom right, 180 bottom left, 184 top, 184 bottom.
Tadashi Kajiyama / Mountain Camera: page 164.
The Science Museum: pages 112 top, 113 top .
Adriano Tomba: pages 127 bottom, 128 right.
Pascal Tournaire: pages 10-11, 79 top right, 86 bottom left and right, 89 left, 105 centre, 105 bottom, 136 bottom left, 137 bottom left, 138 bottom, 190 top, 202 bottom, 270-271, 287 bottom left, 287 bottom right, 292-293, 293 top.
Tutino Archive: page 128 top left.
Mark Twight: pages 12 top left, 208 top right, 208-209, 209 bottom.
Sandro Vannini / Agenzia Franca Speranza: page 35 right.
Mario Verin: pages 34 top, 82-83, 126 top
Ed Webster: pages 207 top right, 207 bottom right, 208 top left, 222 left, 222 right, 223 bottom left.
Gordon Wiltsie / Alpen Image: page 215 centre top.
Brad Wroblesky: pages 95 centre; 95 bottom right, 97 top, 206 top left, 206 bottom left, 212 centre, 263 top right.
Heinz Zak: pages 256-257, 264-265, 302 bottom, 305 top left.
Maurizio Zanolla: pages 250 top left, 250-251, 251 top, 251 bottom.
Zappelli Archive: pages 102, 192-193, 192 bottom, 193 bottom left, 193 bottom centre, 193 bottom right, 223 bottom right.
Andrej Zawada: pages 274 top right, 274 centre right, 274 bottom right.

ACKNOWLEDGMENTS

The publisher would like to thank:
Annetta Stenico, Dr. Floriano Menapace of the Autonomous Province of Trento, the SAT of Trento, Manrico Dell'Agnola, Mario Colonel, Pascal Tournaire, the Agordo branch of the CAI, the Cortina branch of the CAI, Walter Bonatti, the Varallo Alpine Club, the Mountain Museum in Turin, the CAI National Library in Turin, Fabrizio De Francesco, Luciano Eccher, the French Climbing Federation, the Sella Foundation of Biella, Salvatore Tutino, the Associazione Scoiattoli of Cortina, Ed Webster of the Alpine American Journal, the SAT of Trieste, Adriano Tomba, Giovanni Cavulli, Angelo Gandini, Studio Donati of Vercelli.